ROSCOE TURNER

SMITHSONIAN HISTORY OF AVIATION SERIES

Von Hardesty, Series Editor

On December 17, 1903, on a windy beach in North Carolina, aviation became a reality. The development of aviation over the course of a little less than a century stands as an awe-inspiring accomplishment in both a civilian and military context. The airplane has brought whole continents closer together, at the same time it has been a lethal instrument of war.

This series of books is intended to contribute to the overall understanding of the history of aviation—its science and technology as well as the social, cultural, and political environment in which it developed and matured. Some publications help fill the many gaps that still exist in the literature of flight; others add new information and interpretation to current knowledge. While the series appeals to a broad audience of general readers and specialists in the field, its hallmark is strong scholarly content.

The series is international in scope and includes works in three major categories:

Smithsonian Studies in Aviation History: works that provide new and original knowledge.

Smithsonian Classics of Aviation History: carefully selected out-of-print works that are considered essential scholarship.

Smithsonian Contributions to Aviation History: previously unpublished documents, reports, symposia, and other materials.

ROSCOE TURNER

AVIATION'S MASTER SHOWMAN

CARROLL V. GLINES

SMITHSONIAN INSTITUTION PRESS
WASHINGTON AND LONDON

TO MADONNA M. TURNER

Editor: Jack Kirshbaum
Designer: Alan Carter

Library of Congress Cataloging-in-Publication Data

Glines, Carroll V., 1920–
  Roscoe Turner: aviation's master showman/Carroll V. Glines.
    p.   cm.
  Includes bibliographical references and index.
  ISBN   1–56098–456–2 (alk. paper)
  1. Turner, Roscoe, 1895–1970.   2. Air pilots—United States—
Biography.   I. Title.
  TL540. T9G58   1995
  629. 13'092—dc20
  [B]   94–24956

British Library Cataloging-in-Publication data available

Manufactured in the United States of America
00 99 98 97 96 95 5 4 3 2 1

∞ The paper used in this publication meets the minimum requirements of the American
National Standard for Permanence of Paper for Printed Library Materials Z39.48-1984.

Jacket illustrations: (front) Roscoe Turner and Gilmore, photo by B. F. Parish; (back) at the
Lockheed factory in 1935. Both photos courtesy Madonna M. Turner

For permission to reproduce any of the illustrations, please correspond directly with the sources.
The Smithsonian Institution Press does not retain reproduction rights for these illustrations
individually or maintain a file of addresses for photo sources.

CONTENTS

ACKNOWLEDGMENTS

The Golden Age of Aviation is generally considered to be the 1920s and early 1930s, when men and women risked their lives for profit and glory by wing walking, racing, setting records, and pushing aircraft performance and their individual abilities to the limits. No one represented this era more memorably than Roscoe Turner. As he often said, "I could never see any other reason for an airplane than to go fast."

Flamboyant, colorful, unabashedly unrestrained in thought and deed, he was the one freelance pilot who not only survived a number of accidents and mishaps but managed to continue in the uncertain and dynamic business of aviation for his entire adult lifetime.

Fortunately, Roscoe retained most of his correspondence through the years, as well as several large scrapbooks containing hundreds of news clippings and magazine articles covering his life from World War I. Most of these materials were deposited in the American Heritage Center at the University of Wyoming, Laramie. Three-dimensional memorabilia such as his uniform, flying equipment, trophies, his famous

Turner Special racer, and Gilmore, his faithful lion companion, can be seen at the National Air & Space Museum, Washington, D.C.

Some of Roscoe's files are still possessed by Mrs. Madonna M. Turner, who graciously permitted me access, granted interviews, loaned photographs, and provided assistance in contacting friends and relatives who could contribute details of his early life. In 1975 she interviewed Don Young, Roscoe's long-time mechanic, and this interview provided a priceless insight and a behind-the-scenes view of Roscoe's racing years. This biography would not have been complete without her unqualified cooperation.

I am also indebted to the late General Jimmy Doolittle for volunteering to write the foreward and thus honor a dear friend. They had known each other since the 1920s, and it was Jimmy who was the presenter when Roscoe was enshrined in the National Aviation Hall of Fame in 1975.

One of the two remaining of Roscoe's siblings is Mrs. Mary Emma Whitaker, his only sister, who still lives on Turner's Hill, the family farm, in Corinth, Mississippi, the hometown of all of Roscoe's immediate family. She not only provided information about her famous brother in an extensive interview but recommended others in Corinth who recalled incidents about Roscoe before she was born. Her brother William granted an excellent interview via video.

Three Corinthians who sent exceptionally valuable and extensive background information, not only on Roscoe's early life but on Corinth's history, were Milton L. Sandy, Jr.; his wife, Stephanie; and their son, David. They are enthusiastic local historians who voluntarily researched newspaper files in Corinth, Memphis, and other cities and interviewed local residents seeking nearly forgotten facts about Roscoe. They readily furnished photographs and answers to the author's many questions and remained undaunted in their search for information about Corinth's famous former resident.

Other Corinthians who helped fill in pieces of the puzzle include Mrs. E. F. Waits; Mrs. Margaret Rodgers; Roscoe's nephew, the late Cecil M. "Mack" Whitaker, Jr.; Gene Greene; Clifford Worsham; William McMullin; and Eddie LaFavour, the founder and director of the annual Roscoe Turner Balloon Race. Also very helpful was Thomas A. Bowman, a former Corinthian who now resides in Atlanta. Ann Wright, special collections librarian of the Asheville-Buncombe Library System, North Carolina, deserves special thanks for reading through the microfilm of many early newspaper files.

After a visit to Corinth, I wrote to Mayor Edward S. Bishop, Sr., and pointed out that there were no signs of any kind showing that Corinth's small but efficient airport is officially named Roscoe Turner Airport. He immediately had large signs erected directing the public to it. The airport is a continuing reminder of the city's aviation heritage and its one citizen whose name is nationally synonymous with speed in the air.

The staff members of the American Heritage Center at the University of Wyoming in Laramie were especially cordial and cooperative during the many days of my research through Roscoe's voluminous files and scrapbooks. My special thanks go to Rick Ewig, Manager/Reference Service, and Loreley Moore, for their efficiency in locating and providing the requisite files and for their personal interest in the Roscoe Turner story. John Hanks of the research staff also responded quickly to requests for photographs.

Others who provided information were Tony LeVier, famous racing and Lockheed test pilot; William A. "Bill" Schoenberger and George E. Haddaway, master aviation writers and historians; the late Ed Rice, who was devoted to preserving the heritage of flight at the University of Texas at Dallas; and the director for special collections there, Dr. Larry D. Sall. Special thanks are reserved for James R. Greenwood, author of *Stunt Flying in the Movies,* who provided photos, background information, and much encouragement. Thanks are also reserved for the assistance of James and Valerie Stephens for details on Roscoe's life with his first wife, who later became Mrs. Carline Stephens. Appreciation is also extended to the American Legion headquarters for providing copies of speeches Roscoe gave in his crusade for a strong national defense. And much gratitude is extended to the many dedicated librarians around the country who responded courteously to requests for information.

Sincere appreciation is extended to Jack Kirshbaum, for his excellent editing suggestions, and to Felix Lowe, director of the Smithsonian Institution Press, for his leadership in developing the Smithsonian History of Aviation Series, of which this book is a part.

FOREWORD

You always knew when Roscoe was around. His broad smile topped with an even broader waxed mustache was the first thing you noticed when he arrived on the scene. Then you saw his uniform—highly polished boots, riding breeches, powder blue military jacket with diamond-studded wings, sometimes a Sam Browne belt or a silver belt buckle, gold-and-crimson helmet and goggles. Then you heard him, joshing with everyone, anxious to meet anybody he hadn't known before.

Although the rest of us in the racing business in the '20s and '30s wore comfortable but often oil-stained clothing when we flew, Roscoe thought we all looked like tramps. We thought he was a little ostentatious in his self-designed get-up and razzed him more than a little, but he thought of his flamboyant dress as "advertising" and was "suitable for all occasions." He said, "If you look like a tramp or a grease monkey, people won't have any confidence in you. A uniform commands respect. Aviation needs it." He was right.

You couldn't help but like Roscoe, and although we were keen rivals in the air, we became close friends on the ground. I had great respect for his flying ability and marveled at how he could bounce back so quickly after some personal adversity and more than a few aircraft mishaps. His life story is characteristic of the ups and downs of most of us in those days when we raced each other or the clock for money and glory. It was an era of individualism in aviation that historians now call the Golden Age of Aviation. No one dominated and popularized it more than Roscoe. He was a colorful survivor who kept the public interested in advancing the science of aeronautics by personally exploring the limits of airplane performance.

The list of Roscoe's speed records and race trophies is outstanding. He is the only pilot ever to win the Thompson Trophy three times. He won the Bendix Trophy once, was awarded the Harmon Trophy twice, the Henderson Trophy three times and set a number of coast-to-coast and point-to-point speed records. As if to prove that he not only could compete in high-speed racing planes, he flew a relatively slow twin-engine transport in the grueling 11,000-mile London-to-Melbourne, Australia, race in 1934. Never having flown the route before, he and his crew placed second in the handicap category and were the only Americans to finish.

Besides his many racing victories, perhaps the public best remembers Roscoe because he flew with Gilmore, a pet lion named for the oil company that hired him to publicize the company's name and products. But Roscoe did more than race airplanes. Having learned to fly following World War I, he was one of the few pilots in the early '20s who dared to enter the airline business. After he declared his racing days were over in 1939, he operated a flying school during World War II and was a highly vocal advocate for a strong, independent air force during his long-time service with the American Legion.

It is unfortunate that Roscoe didn't write his memoirs before his death in 1970. However, the flavor of his life and times has now been captured in the following pages. This biography provides a valuable chapter in the history of manned flight that has long been missing.

James H. "Jimmy" Doolittle
July 1992

1

THE BOY FROM CORINTH

It had been the most grueling air race of Roscoe Turner's life. Winner of one of the top American closed-course air racing trophies and holder of significant record-setting speed marks by 1934, the flamboyant, uni-formed pilot with the ever-present smile topped by a needle-point mus-tache had piloted the Boeing 247D twin-engine transport more than 11,500 miles from Mildenhall, England, to Melbourne, Australia. He placed third in elapsed time in the "world's greatest air race" behind a British de Havilland racing plane and an American-built Douglas DC-2 transport piloted by two Dutch pilots. Roscoe and his two-man crew—Clyde Pangborn and Reeder Nichols—were the only Americans to complete the strenuous trip.

The race was known in Australia as the Centenary International Air Race but was more popularly called the MacRobertson Air Race, sponsored by Sir Macpherson Robertson, wealthy owner of the MacRobertson confectionary empire. To Turner, former balloonist, barnstormer, and record-setter in the United States, this race had been

1

the chance of a lifetime to spread his name to a world-wide audience and enhance his sincere belief that the future of aviation was tied to speed and safety. *Time* magazine reported that "U.S. aviation enthusiasts were little concerned that a British racing plane had won the world's greatest air race. What pleased them greatly was that in second place was a U.S. transport plane powered by U.S. engines [flown by the Dutch crew]; that not far behind, roaring over Australia, was another U.S. transport plane flown by U.S. Pilot Roscoe Turner."[1]

The public did not know the administrative and financial difficulties that Turner had to overcome in order to enter the race—from not having a birth certificate so he could obtain a passport to having to reduce the fuel load on his aircraft to meet stringent race requirements. He also had to provide full insurance coverage, which he finally obtained through Lloyds of London. And few knew that he had conquered the greatest obstacle of all: borrowing an aircraft from its manufacturer and the airline that had bought it by old-fashioned shrewd bargaining based on his reputation as a skillful pilot.

Turner and Pangborn had shown they were formidable competitors even before the race began by flying the new 247D transport from the Boeing factory in Seattle to Los Angeles in 5 hours and 10 minutes at an average cruising speed of 204.6 mph, the fastest long-distance flight ever made by a multiengine passenger transport up to that time.

Feted, dined, and honored in Australia for two weeks after the race, Turner, Pangborn, and Nichols supervised the loading of their plane aboard the *S.S. Mariposa* and the trio sailed for the United States. The long sea trip forced the ever-restless Turner to take time to think about his past and his future. Then thirty-nine years old, he had established himself as a world-renowned racing pilot who had survived the crashes and financial uncertainties of the barnstorming era and had helped extend the frontiers of flight by pushing the aircraft he flew and himself to their limits.

Although he had not won the London-to-Melbourne race, the worldwide publicity as the captain of the only American crew to complete the course meant that he was returning as a hero to the United States. As the *Mariposa* plodded northeastward from Australia with the big Boeing tied to its deck, Roscoe thought about those days in Corinth,

Mississippi, as the senior son of a dirt-scrabble farmer and his wife who had lost two children in infancy and reared six others—five boys and one girl. The parents had guided them to adulthood with the kind of old-fashioned, southern, turn-of-the-century discipline that gave them a desire to excel and prosper to the limit of their respective abilities and dreams.

The farming area around Corinth in northern Mississippi has been home to the Turner family since the mid-1800s. Roscoe's parents, Robert Lee and Mary Aquilla Derryberry Turner, both had Scotch-Irish ancestors who had arrived in this country before 1800. Born in 1872 in South Carolina and 1877 in Tennessee, respectively, they had married in 1894 and became a typical rural couple trying to eke out a living by farming in Mississippi's northern Alcorn County, a few miles south of the Tennessee border.

Roscoe was born on September 29, 1895, in the Jones School Community (also known as the Gift Community), nine miles west of Corinth, in a rustic house that was barely more than shelter. The Lebanon Cemetery in that community has the graves of Roscoe's paternal grandparents, a great grandmother, and other Turner kin. The oldest birth date on the tombstones is that of Fannie Turner: 1774.

After the first two children were born, the family moved first to a homestead in McNairy County, Tennessee, then in 1903 bought fifty acres of farmland in West Corinth. The Turner farm, on property known locally ever since as Turner's Hill, was located a mile west of the Alcorn County Courthouse. Corinth, the county seat, was a small antebellum town in the extreme northeastern part of the state that boasted 3,600 people in the census of 1900. It had a few stores along the main streets, but its early farm economy was enhanced by the fact that the town had the good fortune to be a busy railroad junction. The Southern Railway, Illinois Central, and the Gulf, Mobile & Ohio railroads criss-crossed each other there. The smoke from the old coal-burning locomotives stung the eyes; the train whistles, the banging and slamming of the freight cars being transferred may have kept the townspeople awake at night, but it was a reassuring sound since it meant the world knew that Corinth was important in the grand scheme of American industry. The

Chamber of Commerce advertises Corinth as "Mississippi's Gateway City" and "Crossroads to the Deep South."

Corinth was founded first as Cross City in 1854; the name was changed to Corinth two years later. It was a mobilization center for Confederate troops at the beginning of the Civil War and was occupied by Federal troops in 1862, after the nearby epic battle of Shiloh. In October of that year, the battle of Corinth, considered one of the fiercest and bloodiest encounters of the war, caused historians to say it was "the beginning of the end of the War in the West." During the war years more than one hundred skirmishes and raids occurred in the area.

The location of Corinth as a farming community with immediate access to rail transportation showed potential for growth and seemed to the Turners to be an ideal place to raise a family. Roscoe, the first of their eight children, was followed by Abe (1898), Cass (1905), Robert (1907), William (1912), and Mary Emma (1918). Two other sons— Roy and Roy Lee—died before their second birthdays. The main source of family income was from the cotton, corn, soybeans, sweet potatoes, and "enough peanuts to exercise our teeth on" that they grew on their farm. "The crops didn't bring in much but we never starved," Roscoe recalled. All heavy hauling and plowing work was done with mules, which his father preferred to horses. They also raised cows, hogs, and chickens, as did most farmers during that period.

Mary Emma recalls that they raised everything on the farm that they needed for subsistence. The only things they had to buy at the general store were flour and sugar. For extra family money, the boys sold milk, butter, and eggs to their neighbors and the general store. Their father also hauled lumber, was county road commissioner for a time, and did contracting work on the roads at 75 cents a day in the winter using his own mules and a wagon. He also served as a part-time Alcorn County deputy sheriff about 1909 and worked part-time on the railroads.

The six surviving Turner children, all born at home, were reared in the strict tradition of southern, church-going families. Women did all the housework, laundry, ironing, and cooking. The only occupations outside the home they were expected to follow in their adulthood were nursing, teaching, and secretarial work. The females were brought up to expect to marry, have children, and be deferential to their husbands.

The males in the family did the outside farm work as soon as they could hold a hoe or milk a cow. It was a "given" that all children had chores to perform for the family good or they didn't eat. Fathers were to be obeyed promptly and without question or their offspring could expect consequences that were often painful to their posteriors.

"From the time I was six as the oldest," Roscoe recalled, "I got more than my share of feeding the pigs and milking the cows. I never did learn to like sweet potatoes because they reminded me of the blisters I got from hoeing. I was graduated to plowing when I was eight. Looking at the rumps of two mules all day in the hot sun made me resolve that I didn't want to grow up to be a farmer."[2]

Roscoe remembered that in those days he would be

out of bed at four or five o'clock in the morning, feed the hogs and cows, chickens and mules, then to school and return at night, then the same thing as in the morning, plus cut wood for the stove and fireplace.

One day Dad got sorry for me and bought me a large billy goat and a little red wagon to carry butter, milk and eggs to the market. But the goat would sometimes butt me over, run away with the wagon, spill the milk and then Dad would tell me how careless I was so I would try to improve.

It hurt for Dad to say that to me. It just broke my heart to make a mistake or fall short of someone's expectations. As I grew up I always tried to do things better than anyone else around me. I wanted my every movement to be so good it would be outstanding. I began to follow this policy in everything, even to helping Dad shovel manure onto the wagon to haul it away.[3]

The elder Turner, an unsmiling but sentimental man, was strict with the five boys. Even though his formal education ended with the sixth grade, he wanted his children to get more schooling than he did. He was completely secure in the notion that he was totally responsible for family discipline and his offspring should obey him in all matters without question.

Mary Emma recalled that at school, one of Roscoe's classmates made fun of his brother Abe because he had on patched pants. "Roscoe was such a hornet that he just beat the devil out of the kid for taunting his little brother," she said. "Unfortunately, Roscoe, Abe, and I all have the thinnest skin you ever saw. The principal whipped Roscoe with a switch and Roscoe's skin was so thin it cut him. When he went home, Roscoe was bloody from the hips down. Papa said, 'I wanted to beat the principal so bad, I didn't know what to do. I knew if I took up for the child against the teacher, I'd ruin the child.' Papa said he walked miles around the place back and forth until he could bridle his temper."[4]

Although there was singing in the Christian Church denomination the Turner family belonged to, no instruments were used, and close dancing was not condoned. However, the elder Turner played the fiddle and called the square dances on Saturday nights. Mary Emma said, "he liked to have his whistle wet once in a while but he never took more than one drink.

"We were poor but we were taught to have pride in our work, in our appearance or whatever we did," she added. "We tried to do the best we could with what we had. We were all taught to be religious and all went to church without fail."[5]

Roscoe and his father argued frequently because they were both stubborn, determined, and emotional at times and each was easily annoyed by the other, according to Mary Emma. However, they could forget their differences quickly, each knowing that they hadn't changed the other's mind.

"The old GM&O mainline ran right through our farm," Roscoe recalled.

> Whenever I was missing from my chores, Dad would know where to find me—sitting on a little knoll down by the tracks day-dreaming that I was Casey Jones at the throttle of one of those locomotives. I thought of all the engineers as my friends because they would toot their whistles when they saw me waving. I told Dad when he threatened to whip me for wasting so much time watching the trains that one day I was going to drive one of those big locomotives. I'm sure every kid in Corinth had the same ambition. Dad always countered that railroading was too dangerous and that I should forget about it.

Roscoe liked to putter around with any kind of tools and machinery and said his father encouraged him to make a wagon for himself to satisfy the urge to "make something." He found four bent wagon wheels in a junk yard and straightened them out. His father gave him a few pieces of new lumber he had bought to "pretty up" the house. Roscoe was allowed to pick out a paint color and chose blue, a color that was to play a prominent part in his life but in a way he could never have dreamed of at the time.

The wagon became an obsession as he tried to make it go faster and faster down the hill on the farm. He piled rocks in it theorizing that they would increase the speed. He slowly began to realize that speed was what he needed to satisfy an increasingly mysterious inner drive.

As so many kids did in those days, Roscoe turned to flying kites. Starting with small ones, he learned the secret of lofting them and keeping them airborne. He built one six feet across, which he thought would be big enough to lift him off the ground. "My takeoff technique was simple," he said. "I hitched the kite with a rope to one of our mules. Then I hung onto a cross-member of the kite's frame with one hand and threw rocks at the mule with my free hand. The damned mule wouldn't move, so I tried jumping off the barn roof into a hay stack to get the kite some momentum and almost broke my neck when the kite collapsed. However, the fall didn't hurt as much as the whipping I got when Dad found out what I had tried to do."

Roscoe attended the one-room Glover School in West Corinth and liked it but always regretted that he never completed twelve years of schooling. School terms were only about five or six months then and farm children were expected to help their parents with the chores and crops in the good weather months. "It wasn't as easy going to school in those days as it is now," he wrote later.

School houses were few and far between and roads were mostly old red mud with an occasional little gravel stretch here and there. The school house was one large room. We had one big wood stove and we boys had to take turns cutting wood. Our seats were benches eight or ten feet long with no backs which were placed around the heater. Our teacher heard our lessons over in one corner of the room fartherest from the heater.

We used slates to write on and had some crude paper tablets. Our pencils cost one cent; a five-cent pencil painted red was a luxury. Our pastime during recess and lunchtime might be anything from chasing a rabbit with a stick to playing ball. The ball was mostly made of twine wrapped tightly around a rock.

Roscoe and his brothers walked together the three miles to school each day. At times the road was so muddy that they would take a longer way through the woods and fields.

> I liked to stay back with the teacher and the girls. The other boys always walked ahead and the big ones were always kicking the little ones or kidding them. I would take it when it came my way but my brother Abe, who was next to me in age, wouldn't; consequently, he was always fighting and sometimes if he wasn't faring too well, I would help him a little and when he got mad at someone, I'd lick him for not being more diplomatic. I never liked a fight and would not fight until I had to. I had several fights during my school years. One time I hit the other fellow and he hit the ground. The teacher whipped us both. It wasn't considered very nice to fight during my last three years of school.

Roscoe's favorite subjects in school were arithmetic, history, and geography, "subjects which were to play a very important part in my later life." He disliked English and his southern drawl was often sprinkled with improper use of plurals and tense, which he learned to correct over the years. Christopher Moreland, a teacher of the upper grades, was a strict disciplinarian who brightened up his classes with readings from newspapers and magazines about advances being made in science and current events. Roscoe remembered being shocked when he heard about the assassination of President McKinley in 1901 and of Vice President Theodore Roosevelt becoming president.

> Most people around Corinth thought the country would go to the dogs. Our little brains were much too young to know anything about politics. We were all from Rebel families and proud of it.
>
> One day Mr. Moreland told us about the Wright brothers and the flights one of them made at Fort Myer, Virginia, in 1908. Although they had invented and flown a flying machine in 1903, this was the first time we had heard about it. I remember everybody talking about it when they heard that one man [Army Lt. Thomas Selfridge] had been killed in it.

Roscoe completed the tenth grade, which was as far as he could go in the one-room schoolhouse. His military records show that he attended school in Corinth from 1903 to 1910. As Milton L. Sandy, Jr., a Corinth businessman and historian, comments, "There were no real educational standards in Mississippi then and if the teacher said you had completed the tenth grade, then you had. The teacher advanced students based on ability rather than years."

Although Roscoe still wanted to be a locomotive engineer, his father thought a business course would qualify him for a job in a bank. Roscoe earned the money to attend the Corinth Commercial College. The courses cost $65; books and supplies were free. An advertisement in the local paper counseled: "Buy now—use it any time later on."

> I started to business college taking shorthand, typewriting, penmanship, bookkeeping and commercial law for about six months. By this time there was one motorcycle and two or three automobiles in Corinth. The railroad had lost some of its glamour for me and I became interested in automobiles. The first one I ever saw was a one-cylinder, high wheel, solid tire buggy. The famous Glidden Tour of automobiles came by the farm one summer and I had the chance to see the great automobiles of that era. It was the most exciting event that had ever happened in Corinth. There was a Stanley Steamer, a Flanders, and an E.M.F. [Everitt-Metzger-Flanders] built by Studebaker.
>
> One of the more progressive citizens in Corinth had two old E.M.F. cars that he rented out for short rides, even though the roads would not permit going any great distance, especially after a rain. I was about to finish up my business courses and one day stopped by the man's garage in Corinth. I had been there before and had helped a mechanic repair a Ford Model T. He taught me how to drive it. The man knew of my interest by this time and asked if I wanted to drive the E.M.F. I said I did but he said I'd first have to put the rear axle back in it. The gears had been stripped and it had to be reassembled. I found a catalog showing a drawing of the gear assembly and put it together. Only trouble was it now had three speeds in reverse and one speed forward so I had to do the job over.
>
> I finally got it all together and drove home. My dear old mother, who said I always had a faraway look in my eyes, tried to help me when Dad got mad but when her patience ran out, she could do a good job on us kids, too. She said Dad would skin me alive if he found that thing there. I kept the car for one night and got my pants fanned a little over that.[6]

Aviation entered the life of Corinthians in 1910, when Ernest F. Waits, a local jeweler, optician, artist, musician, and inventor, built and flew a home-made "aeroplane," probably the first ever flown in the South. He had invented such items as toothpick and cigarette dispensers, an oil burner stove, and the first X-ray machine, which he gave to a hospital in Battle Creek, Michigan. Once he was satisfied with an invention, he went on to other things that interested him and never applied for patents. He experimented with electricity and made a lighted kite that he flew at night to the delight of the townspeople.

In 1909 Waits had constructed the first amateur wireless station in mid-America which attracted nation-wide attention. A Memphis newspaper commented: "So successful have been his [wireless] investigations and experiments in this mystical field of research and invention that he has no difficulty in receiving wireless messages from points as far distant as Puerto Rico."[7]

When Waits read of the Wright, Curtiss, Santos Dumont, and Farman flights of 1909, he immediately began to build an "aeroplane" along with Max Weesner, a former professional wrestler, on the third floor of a building in downtown Corinth. Using detailed plans and photos in *Popular Mechanics* of Santos Dumont's *Demoiselle* as a guide, they constructed a similar single-cockpit monoplane called the *Sea Gull*, which was powered by a 2-cylinder, 30-horsepower Detroit engine weighing 112 pounds. The frame was built of bamboo and weighed 100 pounds.

On its first flight from a field south of the city, Waits climbed to 100 feet and landed in a treetop. He suffered a severe cut on one hand from a piano-wire bracing and developed blood poisoning, which took several weeks to heal. The *Sea Gull* was first flown successfully from the Kennedy farm on Old Mill Road near Corinth in October 1910 and was put on display at the first National Aero Show in St. Louis the next month. A Memphis newspaper featured a photo of the plane in flight and boasted: "With the exception of the two wheels, every part of the machine has been constructed by Waits and Weesner, and it is a marvel of beauty and grace. Down to the most minute detail the construction is perfect, and while things are supposed to have a weakest point, this has none—no more than a one-foot square piece of boiler steel."[8]

The Corinth newspaper noted that Waits had financed the building of the plane and that Weesner made several "straightaway" flights in it.

Weesner said he worked 529½ hours building it over a period of 43 days. When the plane was returned to Corinth, a reporter commented more flights would probably be made in it, "in which event if you should see a monstrous-sized bat-like thing sailing overhead, don't be scared into a conniption fit, but just remember that it is Mr. Waits or Mr. Weesner out enjoying a few whiffs of pure altitudinous air."[9]

Roscoe was fascinated by Waits and his inventions and the two became fast friends, although there was a twenty-seven-year age difference. However, there is no evidence that he helped Waits work on the airplane or saw it fly. Roscoe recalled that "the first airplane I ever saw was in 1913. It was flown by a famous aviatrix of her day. She came to Memphis, Tennessee and flew at the old fairgrounds there."[10]

Meanwhile, Corinth was treated to another type of flying machine in the summer of 1910. Professor A. M. Nassar of Toledo, Ohio, arrived in town with a dirigible to demonstrate it during the Fourth of July celebration. The newspaper called it "a healthy-looking affair . . . made on the same style of the one used by Count M. Zeppelin."[11]

When Roscoe showed no inclination to seek a "white collar" job, his father helped get him work in Bramlett's Hardware Store at $30 a month. However, his interest was in the store's tools, not in the bookkeeping side of the business. With his entire first two months' pay, Roscoe bought his mother a Majestic Range, on which she cooked his favorite meals for many years.

Roscoe couldn't afford an automobile but did buy a motorcycle "at a dollar down and a dollar for the rest of your life. That's what made Dad mad." When he got a whipping for that, he ran away from home briefly but returned, determined to continue working with anything mechanical, especially automobiles.

Automobiles now became an obsession for Roscoe, and he read everything he could find about them and auto racing. The nation had been caught up in the automobile (at first called motocycle) races since the first national race in Chicago in 1895, Roscoe's birth year. In the racing of cars, technological change and improvement were constant; competition and emotion made it into a sport. The 500-mile races began at Indianapolis in 1911. The winner earned $20,000, the world's richest racing prize at that time. Roscoe couldn't know it then but his name and its association with speed in the air would also be synonymous with Indianapolis, and he would be connected many years later with the Indy 500 races for three decades as an honorary race starter and referee.

However much Roscoe was interested in automobiles, his father remained adamant that he should follow a business career. When brother Abe was old enough, he worked in the local bank, but Roscoe fought the idea, although he did work there for a short time collecting money from merchants for deposit. He began to hate to go home at night because he and his father would always get into an argument. When his father found him at the garage one day, he took the lad aside and gave him a serious lecture; strangely, he didn't get mad.

"Son, you won't be worth shootin' if you keep foolin' around with things that burn gasoline and pop!" his father said, trying to keep his temper in check. It was a conversation Roscoe never forgot. He realized that his father wouldn't change his mind so he decided then to leave home and strike out on his own. Now sixteen, he traveled the ninety miles to Memphis to seek his fortune. He boarded there with Mollie Bailey, an aunt.

There was a growing number of garages in Memphis but no one wanted to hire a teenage kid with no real experience as a mechanic. His tale of working on a Model T Ford and assembling the gears on an E.M.F. didn't make an impression. He found a job as a shipping clerk in a wholesale grocery at $7.00 a week. The job's main fringe benefit was that he was allowed to sleep in the back of the store. An unofficial benefit was that he could eat whatever foodstuffs dropped out of boxes that had split open in shipment.

There was another bonus benefit. He was able to meet many truck drivers who brought in the produce. One day an ice truck driver said he was going to quit and suggested that Roscoe go down with him to the ice house and apply for the job. "The truck driver's name was Joe and he must have liked me because he brought me some maps of the city and told me about short cuts and tricks of driving in Memphis with a big truck," Roscoe recalled. "He let me drive when I went with him on my time off. Since I was big for my age and knew his route, he thought I could bluff my way through an interview and I did. I got the job."

Driving a big, powerful truck was heady stuff to a teenager in the early 1900s. A theory that he had developed in his mind was proven when he applied for the job. "If you wanted to be somebody, you had to act confidently and put up a good front. This did not mean lying. You also had to be good at what you did. And I realized that you also had to dress the part. I really wanted that job and had spent my last $5.00 for a new pair of khaki trousers, shirt, and cap. I will always think that looking like a young man who took care of his appearance and their equipment would be good for their business." This attention to his clothing and general appearance stayed with him for the rest of his life.

During this period, Roscoe met a garage owner who sold Cadillacs, then being equipped with the first self-starters, and was hired as a junior mechanic. He also earned money by chauffeuring for his aunt, and then for Mr. and Mrs. Frank F. Hill, a wealthy couple who owned one of the first Cadillacs in Memphis. He also worked at odd jobs in the garage and learned about Cadillacs, Packards and other automobiles, such as the Star and Gray. The 1916 city directory shows him employed as a salesman while boarding with Lillie Mason, a cousin.

Following his personal policy of being outstanding at what he did, he asked to be taken on full time at a Memphis garage working on automobiles. The city directory for 1917 shows Roscoe working as a mechanic for the Jerome P. Parker-Harris Co., a Packard truck dealer. After several months he had saved enough money to buy parts to get a second-hand racing car into condition for possible racing. Now "of age," Roscoe wondered if the revolution in Mexico or the war in Europe would involve him in any way.

On the night of March 9, 1916, Francisco "Pancho" Villa, with a force of more than five hundred men, crossed the international border and raided Columbus, New Mexico, killing seventeen Americans. Considerable property was destroyed before U.S. Cavalry units drove off the marauders. A week later, American planes were ordered to support General John J. Pershing in pursuit of Villa by carrying mail and dispatches. Although the experience was short-lived, it proved that airplanes would have a role in future military conflicts. Proof of the awakening interest in military aviation came in August 1916, in the form of the first appreciable appropriation ($13.3 million) for aviation ever made in the United States.

While American troops were involved in chasing Pancho Villa and his renegades south of the border, there was much speculation that America would be entangled in the war in Europe, which had begun in 1914. Race car drivers and college kids were applying for pilot training in the U.S. Army Air Service, a branch of the Army Signal Corps. Some Americans were already flying with the Lafayette Escadrille in France.

Roscoe often stated that he first saw an airplane up close in 1913 and that it was flown by a famous aviatrix, believed to have been either Katherine Stinson or Ruth Law. He was able to get near a military aircraft for the first time when a group of Army planes landed at the Memphis Driving Park in 1916. After chatting with the pilots, he knew then that he had been bitten by a new bug that promised to replace his interest in automobiles.

Roscoe thought the Army would want to train a man to be a pilot who could repair engines, was in excellent health, and was an experienced automobile driver. He applied for flying training in the Army Air Service that year but was turned down because he had no college education. But the driving and mechanical experience were valuable to the Army. The United States declared war on Germany on April 16, 1917, and the following month he enlisted as an ambulance driver in the grade of private and was told that he would be shipped overseas immediately. He wasn't. He was transferred to Fort Riley, Kansas, for driver training, then Camp Dodge, Iowa, where he applied himself and was promoted to sergeant. Two months later, he was a sergeant first class in the Medical Department and assigned to an ambulance company preparing for overseas duty.

But Roscoe's heart was set on flying airplanes. In November 1917 he applied for training but, instead, on January 3, 1918, was accepted as a Flying Cadet for entry into the ten-week preliminary training course to be a balloon pilot at Fort Omaha, Nebraska. Balloons weren't airplanes but at least they got up in the air, and graduation would mean a commission as a second lieutenant.

Roscoe often told a story about his first balloon flight and first parachute jump. Since balloon observers might have to jump out of their observation balloons when attacked by enemy fighters, he decided to try it on his first day aloft. At two thousand feet in a tethered balloon, he put his parachute on and climbed up on the edge of the balloon basket.

> Then I got scared. The earth seemed a hell of a long ways off. Then I saw another balloon not far away with some men I knew watching me. I knew if I didn't jump they would say I was yellow.
>
> I didn't jump while I was sitting there. I simply fell out and down I went.
>
> It was the first time I was up in the air and the first time I was shooting toward the earth with a parachute strapped to my back. It seemed like a long time before the parachute opened.[12]

Roscoe almost hit a house just before the parachute draped over a telephone pole. He was unhurt but admitted to being "bewildered."

The course at Omaha was followed by an advanced course for "maneuvering officers" at Camp John Wise, San Antonio, Texas. The ground training included map reading, artillery observation, telephone communications, rigging and repairs, inflation and winching procedures, theory of ballooning, and meteorology. Flight training consisted mostly of free balloon flights and caring for the balloon before and after each flight. The students, usually in pairs, would be cut loose early in the morning and let the wind take them wherever it chose. By late afternoon, they would descend by valving off the hydrogen gas and be picked up by Army vehicles that had been following them all day. Sometimes the wind would be so light that they would sit over a farmer's house for twenty minutes or more, visiting with the farmer and his family until a breeze drifted them out of range.

A light rope was standard equipment on board balloons so that ground crews could help bring the basket down. When things got dull, Roscoe and his fellow students tried to lasso chickens in a farmer's yard as they drifted by.

On one occasion, Roscoe and a fellow balloonist drifted over a farmer plowing his field and called down to ask him how far it was to town. The farmer gave them directions as he would a lost motorist: "You go up the road a mile and a quarter, turn right for another mile, then make a left turn and the town will be about a mile ahead. You can't miss it."

They thanked the farmer and went drifting on but not in the direction of town. In a few minutes they heard the farmer yelling from below. He had unhitched one of his horses and galloped after them. "You crazy sons-a-bitches," he hollered, "I told you to go a mile and a quarter and turn to the right. You young whippersnappers never do anything you're told!"

Roscoe also completed the aerial observer course and was designated a Free Balloon Pilot on February 22, 1918. He was put on flying status and commissioned a second lieutenant in the Aviation Section, Signal Corps Reserve, on March 19, 1918. He was then transferred to Morrison, Virginia, and remained there until he departed for France in September.

Roscoe was transferred to Pont-a-Mousson and Colombey-les-Belles but didn't see any action before the armistice was signed in November 1918. He elected to remain with the Army of Occupation and was assigned to Dieblich, Germany, where he served with the Third Army; he was promoted to first lieutenant in March 1919. He returned to the States in July 1919 and was discharged at Camp Travis, Texas, on September 4, 1919.

When the National Aeronautic Association issued pilot licenses in later years, Roscoe received certificate no. 417 and was "brevetted" as a Spherical Balloon Pilot. The license was back-dated to February 27, 1918, and was signed by Orville Wright.

2

BALLOONS TO BARNSTORMING

During his service in Europe, Roscoe received some "unofficial" flying lessons in two-seat trainers from brother flying officers. Flying with them as an aerial observer during those freewheeling, carefree postwar days of the German Occupation, he persuaded them to let him take the controls and showed that he was an able, eager student. Possibly fearing retribution of some kind from his superiors for acquiring unauthorized flying lessons, he never logged these early days of his flying career nor chose to tell much about them.

What is known is that when he was discharged, he had no job to go back to, no civilian clothes, and no prospects. He returned to Corinth and lived in a small apartment briefly. He told his parents that he wanted to stay in aviation, a career neither parent felt held a future for their first-born. "It will bring you to no good end," his mother told him frequently. His father, still insisting that Roscoe should work in a bank or somebody's business in Corinth, had hoped he would also be available

17

to help out on the farm. There were many heated discussions around the family dinner table.

Roscoe's sister, Mary Emma, born while he was overseas, remembers his homecoming vividly. "I was frightened," she said. "He was a big man and I had never seen anyone in uniform before. And when he hugged Mama, she sobbed and I thought he was hurting her. It took me a while to realize that he was my brother."[1]

Determined to stay connected to aviation in some way, Roscoe went to Memphis job-hunting soon after his discharge in early September 1919. He met F. E. Young, an air show booking agent with the Memphis Aerial Company, who had advertised for exhibition flyers to fulfill contracts throughout the South. Roscoe promised that he would "walk on top of the wings, climb from one to another and do other dangerous acts." To prove he had the nerve required, he made a parachute jump from a Jenny at Memphis, which caused a reporter to comment: "While it is not the first time that it has ever been attempted, it is the first time that it has been put over with the wonderful equipment that was used yesterday."[2]

Young referred Roscoe to Lt. Harry J. Runser, then scheduled to fulfill engagements Young had arranged in North Carolina. Five years older than Roscoe, Runser had enlisted in 1917, had completed pilot training, and was commissioned a second lieutenant in July 1918 at age twenty-eight. He was discharged the following December without going overseas.

Runser purchased a Canadian JN-4 Cannuck, a two-seat Army training biplane derived from the American-designed Curtiss JN-4 "Jenny" for a reported $2,000 in April 1919. Although a large number of U.S.-built Jennys were sold after World War I for about $500 new or as little as $100 if used, they were not immediately available. Later there were so many available that it was often more economical to replace wings, ailerons, tail assemblies, and engine parts with new ones and make modifications to the original plane than to make repairs. One historian reported:

> Companies like Sperry, Sikorsky, Martin, and others developed "high lift" monoplane wings for Jenny. These bettered performance by introducing airfoils with more lift and less drag. For example, the Sperry-wing

Jenny was 10 mph faster than its biplane counterpart, and it landed at only 35 mph.

Clipped-wing Jennys next came into vogue and flourished until their uncertainties began clipping too many pilots. Before long Jennys were so scrambled that hundreds of different models, in every conceivable conglomeration, became combined in a single craft. These, quite logically, were called "Combination" Jennys, and so they were: the combination of too much enthusiasm and not enough knowledge. For the pilot of this miscegenation, the odds were plenty to one.[3]

Since the Jennys had a top speed of about 65 mph and couldn't fly much above 6,000 feet, most were flown in the areas east of the Mississippi or along the West Coast. With a gasoline capacity of twenty gallons, they could not remain airborne much more than two hours.

Runser departed in the Cannuck from Toronto, Canada, for Fort Wayne, Indiana, his hometown, where he intended to put on an exhibition to promote the sale of Victory bonds. He announced that his main feature would be "falling a mile in flames," which would simulate World War I combat. En route, with his wife as a passenger, he crashed into a barn at Defiance, Ohio; he suffered three broken ribs, but his wife was unhurt. The Fort Wayne newspaper, commenting that Runser had previously claimed he had never had an accident before in 250 flights, quoted him as saying, "Most of the accidents are caused by the fliers by staying too close to the earth. There is actually no danger if you are high enough to take care of yourself." The reporter editorialized: "The accident of yesterday was evidently due to the fact that the mishap occurred when Runser was too close to the earth to make a safe landing."[4]

While recovering from his injury, Runser told a reporter, "You can't become an ace by quitting, and you may well believe that it will take more than broken ribs and obstructing hay barns to keep me out of the air. People make such a fuss about an airplane accident that you might think the life of the flyer is in greater danger than that of other people, but, as a matter of statistics, it is shown that there are more deaths from automobile accidents than from airplane flights, considering the conditions."[5]

Runser bought another Cannuck and announced that he was going to continue his plan to put on exhibitions to acquaint the public with aviation. Like several hundred other Army-trained pilots at the time, he decided to go into the barnstorming business with a wing walker—in this case, his wife. When he reached Jonesville, Virginia, in late September 1919, he realized that he needed another wing walker to replace his wife when she could not perform. He also wanted a parachutist and a full-time mechanic, the latter proving sorely needed after Runser made a forced landing in a pasture, wrecking a wing and breaking the landing gear axle. Repairs would cost $600. When Roscoe arrived in Virginia, he said he would become Runser's "mechanician" and help repair the plane if he could be taken on as a partner. He proposed to do the wing walking and parachuting and offered $500 of his Army mustering-out pay to seal the deal. Runser wanted $1,500. Roscoe saw the opportunity to gain experience as a pilot so he offered to make up the difference by putting some of his earnings back into the partnership for the chance to fly. The Cannuck was painted red and white and named the Runser & Turner Cloudland Express. The two Army lieutenants, similar in personality and both with a flair for showmanship, were in business.

The duo performed first at Lenoir, North Carolina, in October 1919, and subsequently became newsworthy for their unprecedented exhibitions in a number of cities in Virginia and the Carolinas. They hired an advance man to seek out show engagements. The message they sent ahead to him said: "Expect to reach Lenoir before Saturday. Mark large fields with white sheet. Important. Must be 20 acres or more. Book as many passengers as you can for flights."[6]

One of the Runser-Turner duo's first spectacular shows in the southeast was at the Raleigh, North Carolina, State Fair in October 1919. Runser thrilled the audience with a few stunts and then put on his "falling a mile in flames" act. Under the headline "Lieut. Runser Stages Thriller," a local newspaper naïvely reported, "When spectators at the State Fair yesterday afternoon saw Lieut. Harry Runser fall a mile in flames after his thrilling air stunts, no one realized that the aviator narrowly missed a real crash. In executing his long tail spin, Lieut. Runser was able to straighten his aeroplane out after numerous attempts to work the rudder which had stuck during the long fall. The rudder responded to his efforts when the aviator had just enough space to fly above the trees."[7]

Two days later, Runser made headlines again. He was arrested for trespassing "by landing his plane in the pasture belonging to Mr. W. S. Murchison. The case resulted in the aviator being forced to get a new landing field and paying the cost of the action. Mr. Murchison was willing for the aviator to use the field longer upon payment of $50, Lieut. Runser stated."[8]

In a magazine story published many years later, Runser wrote:

> In those days, every city and town in the east wanted to see the airplanes and the stunts we barnstormers performed in them. I climbed, did nose-dives, rolls, loops and tail-spins, and my wing-walker did breath-taking wing-walking stunts between and on the wings. I also took people up in the trainer seat for a fifteen-minute ride for $15. In those days a fair wasn't a fair, a circus wasn't a circus, and a carnival a carnival without an airplane. For several years it was an exciting and lucrative business.[9]

During these undisciplined postwar days, gypsy flyers soon became familiar figures in rural America. There were no safety rules in existence then and no regulations concerning airfields. There was nothing to prevent a pilot from taking up an unsafe plane and there were no official standards for aircraft design or engine performance. Although it is looked upon now as a glamorous era, it was a time of many fatal crashes. But it was also an epoch when these flying gypsies focused public attention on aviation and initiated thousands of people into the world of flight.

Barnstormers would often be paid $1,000 or more by local businessmen to bring their planes for special events in small communities so there was considerable competition. They would fly from carnival to fair to circus in the northeast during the spring and summer months and work their way southward as the average daily temperatures dropped. Advance men would drive ahead to each town to negotiate contracts, pick out a landing area, make arrangements with the landowners, and generate publicity if they got the job. Getting the job depended on who could tell the best story as to what they promised to do. Each advance man or the pilots themselves would try to outdo the others with tales of the death-defying stunts they would perform.

Pilots usually did their own work on the aircraft and engines; however, auto mechanics were often hired locally who would do minor work on the planes, sell tickets, fasten passengers in the cockpit for local rides, and work the crowds for more passengers while the pilots were flying.

When they began flying together, Roscoe and Runser continued to wear their Army officers' uniforms until they were almost threadbare. They contacted the Brooks Uniform Co. in New York City and had new ones made to their own specifications. In a letter to an aviation magazine, Roscoe explained why they ordered their uniforms:

> The advantage of uniforms is that they are cheaper than civilian clothes from the standpoint of wear and cleaning. After a day's work is done you can take a towel and Carbona and clean all spots. Then you are ready to go to dinner or theater, dance or any place. Your dress is suitable for all occasions. It further stimulates and advertises aviation. It shows them you mean business and can command respect. It is then your duty to uphold the dignity of the uniform and calling as there is none any better. Opportunities are unlimited in the air.
>
> If you look like a tramp or a blacksmith, how can you expect to meet the people that are able to support your business? It is impossible to keep clean or pressed up all the time and work with an aeroplane. A uniform is your only hope to look presentable.[10]

The uniform manufacturer later inserted an ad in the magazine with their photo saying, "You'll like the new type uniform being universally adopted by pilots throughout the country." A caption under a photo of the pair noted, "They believe properly attired aviators will be a big boost toward stimulating and properly advertising aviation."[11]

For Roscoe it was the beginning of his wearing a self-designed uniform during all of his active flying years. Highlighted later with a pair of initialed wings designed by a jeweler, wearing a uniform became his trademark. He chose a beige officer-type cap, sky blue tunic, cavalry-twill fawn-colored jodhpurs, and highly polished riding boots. A Sam Browne belt was often added. This was later replaced by an ornate silver belt buckle of his own design made by a West Virginia jeweler. He grew a pencil-thin mustache and waxed it so it could be twisted to needle-like ends. It became a facial trademark that he wore the rest of his life to set off his ruddy face and frame his "stage smile."

In a letter to a magazine editor years later, he said he believed he was the first commercial pilot to wear a uniform and gave the reasons why he wore it:

[It was] the only way to look halfway decent when we were flying the Jennys barnstorming and were unable to carry any clothes along. If we got greasy we would take gasoline out of the tank and wash the spots off; then we were ready to meet anybody from the Governor down.

[A uniform is] a walking advertisement that instills confidence in your business and singles you out from the thousand others around you and tells what your business is.

[A uniform] gives a person entrance to *any place* you want to go with no questions asked.

[A uniform represents] economy, morning suit, afternoon suit, evening suit and full dress and [is] very easy on pressing bills, as about the only thing that ever goes to the cleaners are the britches.

[A uniform is] a business getter, because it makes people feel at liberty to ask you where you are located and whom you are with and then it is up to you to do the rest if you are looking for business and need the money.

I am damn proud of my profession and I want the world to know what my business is.[12]

Often chided by reporters in print and by other pilots behind his back about wearing a self-designed uniform, he would say many times in response to reporters' questions, "I'm a flier and I'm earning a living at being one. Publicity helps. That's why I wear this monkey suit. It makes people notice me wherever I go. Not that I like it. Nobody will ever know how much guts it takes for me to wear this circus outfit."

To Turner his fellow barnstormers always looked like tramps and grease monkeys. Although they shared a contempt for his affectations, he was convinced it put him a cut above them and gave him maximum effect with his audiences. The detractors were no doubt jealous of the attention he always generated whenever and wherever he appeared.

The Runser-Turner partnership flourished as they traveled from town to town throughout the eastern quarter of the country and in April 1920, they sold the Canadian-built Jenny and purchased a British Avro training plane at Roosevelt Field, New York, which could seat two passengers in the front cockpit instead of one. This doubled the passenger capacity and their potential income from sightseeing flights. New to this country, the Avro proved to be an added attraction because of its top speed of 90 miles per hour.

They announced a year-long, nationwide, 50,000-mile tour beginning that summer and said they would visit every state capital

> to educate the public that commercial flying is a present, practical achievement. In this way they are preparing the confidence of the public in large commercial lines. . . . To show the stability of an aeroplane Lieut. Turner, who weighs 190 lbs. walks out on the wings. This proves that the pilot has absolute control and that the aeroplane is a safe and dependable means of transportation.
>
> The policy of these aviators is to never stunt a passenger, in that way getting every passenger a booster for the aeroplane.[13]

They hired Lt. Eddie M. Freeland, also a former Army Air Service officer, as a manager to travel ahead of them to extol the quality of their show and pick out fields; he would then wire them the location. They expected the tour to take a year and planned to average one state a week.

Although they never carried out their ambitious plans for a nationwide tour, they did barnstorm all over the southern states in 1920 and 1921. They spent quite a bit of time giving exhibitions to attract attention in the larger towns of South Carolina and North Carolina. While Runser flew, Roscoe wing-walked and parachuted. In a typical news item, it was announced that "Lt. Turner . . . while descending will give a demonstration of an observer saving himself from the burning flames. Then Lt. Turner will jump from one plane to another in mid-air, while the two planes are making eighty miles an hour."[14]

The headlines were not always favorable. In Bennettsville, South Carolina, the *Pee Dee Advocate* ran an item titled "An Airplane Arrested" with a subhead stating "Runser and Turner in Trouble For Selling Chances For Rides." At Big Stone Gap, Virginia, in July 1920, they were detained by police and the airplane "arrested" on a charge of operating a lottery. They had sold photographs portraying their acrobatic stunts, which were alleged to have been numbered. Local authorities saw these as chances on an airplane ride and padlocked the plane to a post. It was not known if they escaped a fine.

A few days later, however, they were in the news again for flying on Sundays. One irate reader of the *Pee Dee Advocate* complained that

> the devil and his machines get in where angels dare not tread. . . . We got rid of the saloon, and most of its intemperance, but the good people of Marlboro [County] better take notice that we do not get into something that will do more harm to us in the end than the saloon would ever have done. The saloon would never have destroyed our nation and the church but this Sabbath desecration by the people of this nation, if kept up at the present rate of increase, will destroy both church and nation and send us all to destruction.[15]

Another letter writer, a traveling salesman, noting that cigars and soft drinks could not be sold on Sundays, complained that the authorities did not prevent the townspeople from driving out to a pasture and paying $15 for a fifteen-minute plane ride. "My God, friends," he said, "what are we coming to? Think of Sunday being spent by our Christian people in this manner, and most especially so in Dixie and dear old Bennettsville."[16]

Roscoe felt the criticism needed a reply and defended Sunday flying with a long article in the same issue of the paper. He pointed out that there was no law specifically prohibiting flying on Sunday

> and personally I cannot see why there should be. It is only a means of transportation, such as many other vehicles are used for and I see no more harm in flying in an air ship than in riding in an automobile.
>
> The people are not convinced as yet that aviation is here to stay and will not invest their money in ships, considering them dangerous and very impractical. In order to convince them, flyers will have to demonstrate the many advantages and teach the people to see the future of aviation. The flyers deserve much credit for the efforts they have put forth so far. The towns will not even prepare landing fields and almost all of the accidents that happen are caused by trying to use unprepared fields for landing and flying.
>
> I realize fully that there are many dangers connected with flying under certain conditions and it is not my desire to antagonize anyone or to influence anyone to take chances in any way. Neither do I want to keep the

people away from church. I am a member of the church and try to attend services at least once every Sunday. In fact, we seldom fly on Sundays
until the afternoon and there are no services held during these hours in
the churches.[17]

They were also criticized by a committee of ministers in Staunton,
Virginia, for "commercializing Sunday." In an interview with reporters,
Roscoe made a statement that he asked to be placed in the paper:

I feel that no flight is complete without a prayer to God for our safe return to earth and fully realize that if it were not for His divine protection
we would be in no position to fly.

However, I do not feel that we can take things into our own hands
and for this reason we are going to take a popular vote at the field today
and if the majority of the spectators are in favor of not flying today we
will fly Monday.

We are sanctioned by the War Department of the United States and
by the Aero Club of America and in the few cases that we have had to
appeal to them for a decision in a case of a city's disapproval of Sunday
flying, we have received word that it violated no laws of any kind.

A man operating a "for hire" automobile on Sundays for the passengers' pure enjoyment charges fees for their transportation. From a standpoint of taking money on Sundays what is the difference between car
riding and plane flying? As far as carrying passengers for money on Sunday
is concerned it might be added that the ministers the world over would
find it hard to make both ends meet if they didn't pass the contribution
box on Sunday when the congregations are all at their churches; therefore, we find it necessary to cater to our congregation also on Sunday."[8]

Runser and Turner also received headlines for "bombing" Columbia,
South Carolina, with leaflets announcing the big show to take place on
Armistice Day. To keep their names in the local papers, they delivered
the first sack of newspapers from Columbia to surrounding towns.
Runser's wife, known professionally as Katherine Webb, and called
"eighty pounds of pep" and "Venus of the Air" by reporters, also performed wing walking. The Avro they flew was billed as "the first British
plane to fly over Columbia."

In Winston-Salem during the 1920 Thanksgiving period, the Runser-
Turner duo promised even more thrilling stunts at a "fireworks carni-

val." In an interview Roscoe said, "I can truthfully say that I'm going to do stunts never before tried by an air acrobat. I'm going to do all the thrills that's possible for a man to do and still have a chance to live. The wing riding during a loop-the-loop and the hanging by my toes while Runser does his death trap dive are some things these people have never seen."[19]

Roscoe couldn't keep his promise about wing riding through a loop. Another pilot, Monte Rolfe, flew the Avro that day but Roscoe was so heavy that Rolfe couldn't get the plane into a loop. He and Runser did perform the "death trap dive," which consisted of Roscoe hanging by his toes from the plane's axle while Runser dove toward the ground with full power and pulled out at what appeared to be only the last second.

While the stunting attracted the crowds and received the headlines, it was selling rides in the Avro that brought in the money. The challenge was to see how much the traffic would bear. One day in June 1920 at McConnellsburg, Pennsylvania, they charged passengers $20 each for a short flight but only four paying customers took rides that day. The local paper ran an editorial entitled "Air Plane Lights Here" about a man and his five-year old son who were in the air nine minutes and a second flight with two adults that lasted only seven minutes: "Considering the time they were in the air and the price charged each for the flight, it was generally considered too expensive. Had they charged one dollar a minute many more people would have availed themselves of the opportunity of taking a flight, and no doubt they would have been busy taking flights all day Saturday."[20]

The crowds seemed to love noise and low flying, so Runser and Turner obliged at all their shows. Runser, calling himself "The Ace of Aerial Acrobats" on his stationery, offered "Bombing of Cities" (with leaflets) in addition to aerial photography, aerial advertising, and "Special Messages Carried."

As the competition by other barnstormers got stiffer, they worked up a new series of aerobatics and aerial acts. The major act featured in all their newspaper ads was "Falling a Mile in Flames." They installed smoke flares beneath the plane and after a series of rolls and loops, they would set off the flares and spin crazily toward the ground seemingly headed for a fiery crash. Roscoe would jump out in his parachute; Runser would then head out of sight of the spectators and disappear as if the Jenny had crashed with him aboard. It was a crowd-shocker most of the time and created news stories wherever the pair took their act until competitors outdid them with more risky performances.

The two men became widely known for their daring acts and their fame spread rapidly throughout the South. Before or after these shows, the two usually gave talks to civic clubs and public gatherings and gave rides at whatever price the traffic would bear, usually $5 for a five-minute flight. They were respected for their views about the future of aeronautics and were widely quoted in local papers. Each appearance was used as an opportunity to encourage the townspeople to come out to the local field for their first airplane rides and see their show for which the standard asking fee, always negotiable, was $1,000 in advance from the local promoters.

Operating from Columbia, South Carolina, but apparently short of cash, Runser and Turner put the Avro they had bought for a reported $6,000 up for sale for $3,500. A magazine ad stated, "Reason for selling, getting large limousine."[21] The "limousine" was a large unidentified plane to be used for air service between Columbia, Charlotte, and Winston-Salem.

In an article for an aviation magazine about his experiences during those days, Runser wrote: "I got good money. I never accepted a contract unless I did get it." However, when he nearly crashed because he had difficulty pulling out of a spin at the North Carolina State Fair at Raleigh in 1919, he said he refused to do any more stunt flying.

> Let's have Federal control, and do away with daring stunts and advance aviation by injecting confidence into the minds of the public instead of fear.
>
> I can do any stunt known but I feel as though it will get you somehow some day, so I'll continue to fly straight. Let's all get on the same side and let stunt flying alone.[22]

While Runser quit stunting in the aging aircraft they had bought, Roscoe did most of the wing walking and parachuting to gain continuing attention for the pair. In August 1921 Roscoe parachuted into a lake near Hendersonville, North Carolina. A pre-event news report stated, "People wanting to see something new, or who have a craving desire to see a man risk his life to thrill them, will have this opportunity next Sunday, rain or shine, it has been announced. Here is the one and only chance for the mountain folk to witness a scene really enacted during the late war."[23]

At the same time, Runser and Turner announced they were planning "a giant venture which, if successful, would bring them into world prominence as flyers." Runser told a reporter that they were having an airplane made in Italy which would be capable of a speed of 145 mph "and which will be the fastest commercial plane in the world for the purpose of going to Buenos Aires, Argentina, during the next Christmas season." They intended to start on January 1, 1922.[24]

According to Runser, "Our trip will be conducted for scientific research, in the mapping out of air waves and other physical phenomena between the Americas, thus bringing them closer together."[25] It would be a 10,000-mile flight requiring thirty stops. The paper also reported that the pair were the first aviators to fly over Mt. Mitchell in North Carolina, at an altitude of 9,000 feet, and were the only flyers who had flown the full length of the Blue Ridge Mountains from their northern extremity in Pennsylvania to Georgia.

They wanted to continue their shows to raise money for this venture, but the Avro was damaged when Runser hit a stump on takeoff from a pasture at Manning, South Carolina. On October 13, 1921, Runser and Roscoe were scheduled to put on an exhibition during the annual Savannah, Georgia, Country Club Day celebration. In addition to Roscoe taking a dive from the plane into the water, they proposed to crash it into a building specially constructed for that purpose.

While the Avro was being repaired, they made the city of Savannah an offer for a dismantled Jenny that was stored in the courtyard of the police barracks. The plane had been seized some months before carrying a cargo of liquor. However, they were unable to buy the aircraft and assemble it in time for the show. The local paper reported after the all-day celebration that "this interesting feature was postponed owing to a slight misunderstanding which arose between the officers of the club and the aviators who were to perform, and partly because of the high winds which would have made flying very hazardous."[26]

When they could not buy the interned Jenny from the police, Roscoe learned that a Marine sergeant named John L. McCoy, a rated naval aviator, had a Jenny for sale at Parris Island, North Carolina. On September 21, 1921, he called the sergeant, who promptly flew the Jenny to Savannah and gave Runser a few landings to check it out. McCoy asked $600 for the plane. They agreed and said they would pay him $300 then and $300 "as soon as possible." McCoy accepted the deal and returned to his base. On September 29, 1921, they refueled the Jenny and departed for Rincon, Georgia, where they painted their own logo on the fuselage and headed west.

It was to be expected that sooner or later, the fliers would perform in Roscoe's hometown. They flew the Jenny to Corinth, where Roscoe parachuted from three thousand feet over the high school building and landed five blocks away. The *Weekly Corinthian* reported the story in its usual, quaint writing style:

> The parachute leap was a success, and the aviators won the plaudits of from four to five thousand people who witnessed the aerial detour from the plane a few minutes after 3 o'clock Wednesday afternoon. It was the first airplane leap that ever occurred at Corinth and there was much excitement regarding it.
>
> . . . . Technically speaking it was not a leap. For the momentum of the airplane filled the parachute with air and pulled Lieut. Roscoe Turner from the wing of the machine. While every eye was strained in watching the man on the wing of the plane expecting a plunge into the air, like a flash the big bright yellow silk parachute spread open, there a cloud of circulars spread in the air and the man began dropping. Down, down, he came, drifting slightly with the winds toward the northwest. By throwing his weight this way and that Lieut. Turner managed to control the drop thru the air sufficiently to alight within less than 100 feet of the place he had chosen for that purpose.
>
> . . . . It was a wonderful exhibition of skill and daring, and showed that Mr. Turner is not a novice in air navigation by any means, and if he continues to exercise the same caution and judgment as in the past there is a great future for him. As an air pilot Lieut. Turner showed himself a master while here.
>
> They were a bit disappointed in the amount raised for the leap, only an amount sufficient to guarantee against the loss of the parachute being

asked, but rather than disappoint the people of his home town, and particularly the hundreds of school children for whom special arrangements had been made that they might witness the thrilling performance, Lieut. Turner decided to make the leap.

The air was favorable to the event and it was a success in every particular. The landing was made in a little rough place and Lieut. Turner's ankles were a little sore this morning as a result but he was walking without difficulty, and carrying his usual good-natured smile.[27]

Runser took aerial photos of Corinth that day which were believed to be the first ever taken of the northeastern Mississippi city. He also took a number of passengers up after Roscoe's jump, including Roscoe's brothers Robert, Cass, and Will. The paper dutifully reported that "those who made the trip into the air were delighted with the experience, and not one suffered any inconvenience or fright thereby. They said near the ground it was the sensation one experiences after they had gotten into the air a few hundred feet, and the view of the city was most interesting, and really it was quite an educational treat for those making the flight."[28]

The Runser-Turner duo had been engaged to participate in an air show at the Memphis Tri-State Fair Grounds after the Corinth exhibition. To add something spectacular to their repertoire, they announced that they would deliberately crash the plane into a building at 60 mph as a show finale. The plane would be destroyed and they told reporters that they would either give pieces of the plane to spectators as souvenirs or set fire to it. Huge posters placed all over Memphis before the show called Runser's act the "Crash" and a "Supreme Act of Dare Deviltry." The posters added: "Don't Fail to See the Airplane Actually Flown Into a Building In Front of Stand. The Pilot Actually Flies HEAD ON. See His Miraculous Escape."

Runser flew E. F. Waits from Corinth to Memphis because Roscoe had sprained an ankle a few weeks before during parachute drops at Hendersonville, North Carolina, and Columbia, South Carolina. Roscoe took the train. The Corinth paper said Runser and Turner "are scheduled to fly head on into a frame building, going at a high rate of speed, crashing the building and the machine also. Just how they expect to take care of themselves in the daredevil performance they did not disclose to the public."[29]

Beforehand, Runser "bombed" Memphis with leaflets advertising the show that was to take place on a Sunday. A policeman, representing the police relief fund to which some of the receipts from the show would go, accompanied Runser and helped drop the leaflets.

> Wingwalking and other feats of daring will be preliminary to the "crash" which the flyers declare has never been attempted before.
>
> A physician who happened to be at police headquarters yesterday offered to introduce Turner to the local undertaker and asked him why he persists in taking such risks. Turner . . . declared "it is necessary propaganda to demonstrate the value of commercial aviation."
>
> "We've got some big things in view," Turner said, "including a flight to South America. But we can't swing them until we raise the cash. And businessmen aren't investing in the possibilities of commercial aviation. So, it's up to the aviator to risk his life."[30]

A rival Memphis newspaper headlined the coming stunt as "They'll Crash Good Airplane Just To Thrill" and announced they would present their aerobatics as "playing tag with the undertaker" as well as their feature of the day, "the Crash."[31]

When questioned as to why they would deliberately damage an airplane, Roscoe replied, "Aviation demands something big so Runser and I decided to try this. It has never been attempted before. The public does not seem to realize that we will actually fly into a house at 60 miles an hour and wreck a perfectly good plane."[32]

For reasons not explained but probably because of the weather, the air show did not take place on October 30 as scheduled and was held on November 6. In the interim, Roscoe came up with a new idea to keep the public interested in aviation and keep their names in print. He suggested that the police request a scout plane be sent to Memphis "to detect illicit stills along the [Mississippi] river and in the swamps." Turner offered his services to the department free of charge, provided that he be allowed to take photographs and lecture on his experiences. He was quoted as saying that whiskey-making could be broken up in three states with the use of a scout plane working out of Memphis. " 'The surest way to spot stills,' declared Turner, 'is to go up and watch for that tiny film of white smoke. Then it is easy enough to map the location and go after the still on foot.' "[33]

The suspense about the deliberate crash into a building built up daily. The day before the show, a local paper said that Runser and Turner had obtained a supply of bricks and constructed substantial corner posts for the house as a climax for their upcoming show. "Among other things, they promise to wreck the building and smash their airplane just to give the crowd something to talk about. Although they have never tried the stunt, both Runser and Turner believe it will render the flying machine worthless, and probably give them a severe shaking. Turner will also give an exhibition of wing walking without the use of clamps or stays."[34]

Runser and Turner performed as advertised with Roscoe doing his wing-hanging acts. Then, before the scheduled crash, Roscoe made a parachute jump and landed in a street near the fairgrounds. Runser then dove into the structure and emerged on the other side. The wings caught on the corner posts while the fuselage smashed through the lightly constructed building without much damage to the rest of the plane and no harm to Runser.

Preshow publicity stated that some of the gate receipts were to be donated to the police relief fund; however, many spectators tried to see the crash without paying to get inside the fairgrounds. The next day, one of the Memphis newspapers reported:

Aviators Turner and Runser risked their lives yesterday afternoon to thrill a few hundred persons. Their flying exhibition, with its startling climax, failed to attract more than a corporal's guard, in spite of the worthy beneficiary, the police relief fund.

"The Crash," with which they plan to make a circuit of big fairs next year, had a tremendous punch. The brick-cornered cottage at the Tri-State Fair Grounds looked flimsy. Lieut. Runser circled the field, then flew low and straight for the cottage.

The impact was terrific, bricks and timbers were scattered for yards. The cottage was demolished. The wings of the plane, wrecked, hung limp from the fuselage, which, fortunately, remained intact. Lieut. Runser escaped without a scratch.

It was the first time the aviators with a record of several years of daring exhibition flying, had performed the crash. The result could not be determined in advance. After the wreck small boys were permitted to complete the destruction of the wings for souvenirs.

Lieut. Turner, in an address to the spectators, who rushed from the grandstand to the wrecked machine, declared American flyers are being forced to take risks, to give exhibition flights, in order to raise funds for the development of commercial aviation. Businessmen, victims of exploitation, he declared, refuse to take an interest in the airplane. Flying is the safest means of transportation, he declared.[35]

The competing Memphis newspaper was not as gentle in reporting the show. Under the headline "Crashed Plane But It Didn't Mean Anything," it noted that gate receipts were only $200 but that the plane was worth $5,000:

Lieuts. Runser and Turner Monday were trying to figure the percentage in their aviation meet Sunday at the fairgrounds during which they wrecked their flying machine while a small crowd looked on in wonder.

The flyers didn't see what they were up against until they ascended for the parachute jump, and then they understood why so few were inside the grounds. The crowd was parked outside in automobiles.

Well, Turner did the parachute jump, landing in Central Avenue. Then Runser bumped the machine into the house, which looked so fragile. When he stopped, the house was scattered all over the infield and the plane [was] a pretty fair sort of wreck.

A gang of urchins finished the work of destruction by tearing off the wings for souvenirs. It was a great day for the kids.

"What's the use?" was Turner's reply, when asked why he allowed the crowd to demolish the machine. "The wings must be replaced before the machine is ready for use. We didn't make enough to buy a good steak, much less a pair of wings."[36]

Despite the disappointment, a Pathé News motion picture team had photographed the act and the pictures were shown on screens across the country. Runser later showed a film at local theaters where he appeared in person, which featured the crash and wing-walking stunts and parachute jumps performed by Roscoe. Titled *The Airmaster*, the preshow publicity flyers called it "the most sensational film ever attempted" and promised that "$1000 in gold will be paid to any person that can prove any of these scenes were faked!" Hollywood stunt pilots copied the stunt for a number of motion pictures, and Runser later claimed that he made some of these flights for the Fox Studios.

When the Memphis show was over, Roscoe contacted Earl Bailey, a cousin, and paid him ten dollars to tow the wrecked plane to his garage in Memphis and dismantle it. Bailey removed the engine and salvageable fuselage parts and boxed them for shipment, and Roscoe returned to Columbia, South Carolina. Ten days later, Roscoe wrote to Bailey requesting that he keep the plane in his garage until he notified him what to do with it.

Meanwhile, Runser returned to Fort Wayne, Indiana, to wait until the next show season. To prepare for the future, they advertised in an aviation magazine that they wanted "Connection with aircraft firm, selling, advertising, experimental or test work, or can do it all. Successfully flown through 22 states and over hundred thousand miles."[37]

While Runser and Roscoe were in Corinth and Memphis, an investigation by federal and military authorities was being conducted in Savannah. A newspaper account in the *New York Times* tells the story:

> Investigation by the Department of Justice and the Marine Corps has resulted in charges that an airplane belonging to the corps was sold by a gunner to a former army officer and another man. The two men in question, both civilians, have been arrested, and the Marine Corps is conducting a further investigation into the case of the gunner, who will probably be tried by court-martial.
>
> According to details revealed by the Bureau of Investigation, John L. McCoy, the gunner, obtained permission about September 21, 1921, to take a flight from the training station at Parris Island. He returned to the station a few days later with a story that the plane had been wrecked in marshes near Savannah, Ga., and that he had abandoned it. Suspicion was aroused, but there was no investigation.
>
> Some time later the Department of Justice and the Marine Corps began a dual inquiry, with the result that McCoy, who had left Parris Island, was traced to the Marine Corps Hospital in New York City. There, according to the Bureau of Investigation, he confessed that the plane had not been wrecked, but that he had landed near Savannah and sold the machine to two men, Roscoe Turner and Harry Runser.[38]

According to the indictment filed in the U.S. District Court for the Southern District of Georgia in February 1922, Runser and Turner were charged with conspiracy and receiving stolen government property; the plane was valued by the government at $6,000. Roscoe was arrested on January 24, 1922, at Columbia, where he was working as an automobile salesman and taken to the Richland County jail. Unable to post a bond of $2,000, later reduced to $1,500, he remained there until he was transferred under guard to Savannah to face the federal charges. Runser, arrested in Fort Wayne two days later, unsuccessfully resisted extradition to Georgia and was indicted on the same charges in Savannah. Before his transfer there, news accounts stated that Runser proclaimed his innocence and attempted to place responsibility for the purchase of the plane on Roscoe in an effort to relieve himself of blame.

Meanwhile, Sergeant McCoy was located in a military hospital in New York and returned to Parris Island, where he was tried by general court-martial for "wrongfully and knowingly selling property of the U.S. intended for the naval service thereof." He was also charged with stealing government property, embezzlement, falsehood, scandalous conduct tending to the destruction of good morale, and conduct to the prejudice of good order and discipline. He pleaded guilty to all the charges and was sentenced to be discharged from the Marine Corps and imprisoned for five years. However, when his case was reviewed, the sentence was reduced to three years, which he served at the U.S. Naval Disciplinary Command prison, Portsmouth, New Hampshire.

Roscoe maintained he did not knowingly do anything wrong and refused to wear his uniform in jail. He asked the public, through a newspaper interview, to withhold judgment until his side of the story could be explained. Roscoe said,

> The airplane which they accuse me of stealing was bought right here in Savannah. I bought it from a Marine, John McCoy. All that time hundreds of government planes were on the market, and I had no reason to doubt that McCoy was not the real owner. It was nothing out of the ordinary for a Marine flier to own a plane, hence I did not hesitate to buy it from him. My partner, Harry J. Runser . . . and I bought it together. We were innocent of any knowledge that McCoy may have stolen the plane from the Marine Corps. He was in possession of the plane here; when he named his price, my partner and I bought it. We concealed nothing. We operated the plane in this vicinity without any fear. Doesn't it seem logical to you that if we had any knowledge that the plane was stolen

we would have hopped off to the other coast and not given exhibitions throughout the south?[39]

There is no indication that Roscoe had any legal counsel; however, he had contacted a number of people in Corinth who sent the court a letter of endorsement that he hoped would be considered when his case was tried.

> This is to certify that we, the undersigned officials of Alcorn county, state of Mississippi, have known Roscoe Turner from his infancy up, and there has never been a charge of any kind made against him in the courts here. He comes from a good family, a family noted for its observance of the law. The father of this young man was deputy sheriff of this county for four years, and served the county fearlessly.
> We cannot believe that a young man reared in such a good family as this young man has been, would depart from such rearing and resort to crime.[40]

It was signed by the officers of three Corinth banks, the county prosecuting attorney, county sheriff, county circuit clerk, an attorney, and a U.S. commissioner.

The letter of endorsement and Roscoe's claim of innocence were to no avail. Taking the advice of the U.S. assistant district attorney but maintaining his innocence, he decided to plead guilty and rely on the leniency of the court. He was sentenced on February 24, 1922, to serve a year and a day in the federal penitentiary at Atlanta and to pay a fine of $50. Runser received the same sentence.

After the sentence was handed down, Roscoe told a reporter, "I'm going to Atlanta and serve the sentence like a man. I am innocent of any crime but I thought that this was the best way out, and when I leave the iron doors of the pen behind, I'm going in again for commercial flying exhibitions."[41]

Roscoe was released on parole on July 27 and returned to Corinth. Runser was also paroled at the same time and returned to Fort Wayne. Roscoe sent the $50 fine with a letter to the Clerk of the U.S. Court at Savannah on December 27. Two days later he was declared "finally discharged from custody."

This was an episode in Roscoe's life that he never discussed afterward with anyone outside his family and close friends, and little is known about his feelings during that period except that he said he never wanted to see Runser again. If he kept any pilot logbooks of those early days, they have disappeared. There are no clippings about this interlude in his personal scrapbooks or in Runser's. It is believed a Corinth attorney, now deceased, helped him to obtain the parole and to initiate a review by the Department of Justice, which ultimately found "it satisfactorily appeared that he had conducted himself in a moral and law-abiding manner." Roscoe was granted "a full and unconditional pardon" by President Calvin Coolidge "for the purpose of restoring his civil rights." The pardon document was signed by Harlan F. Stone, U.S. Attorney General, on August 29, 1924.[42] The Department of Justice has no record that Runser ever received a presidential pardon. It is known that Roscoe was very bitter about whatever role Runser had in the episode or may have said to the press after his arrest, and they went their separate ways after being released on parole. Runser eventually started a flying school in Danville, Illinois, and then a charter service at Toledo, Ohio. He ultimately retired to California and died in Georgia in January 1981.

In retrospect, there is no doubt that they paid the sergeant $300 for the plane and promised him another $300. It is also clear that the plane was still government property when the transaction occurred. However, what seems apparent is that they were taken in by a smooth-talking, persuasive Marine who convinced them that the Jenny was no longer owned by the government. At that time, hundreds of the venerable World War I trainers were being declared surplus and many had been deliberately destroyed overseas by the military services for economic reasons and because sales to the Germans were forbidden. It was also reported that many were destroyed because their easy availability hindered the demand for new aircraft.

It may be that the pair naïvely rationalized that they may as well have one of the aged Jennys and destroy it as part of their act at the Memphis show. On the other hand, they may have been duped into believing that the plane was surplus to the needs of the government and that the sergeant had the authority to deliver it to them for the agreed price.

In any case, it was a much-subdued Roscoe who quietly returned to

Corinth after his incarceration. He opened an auto repair business there in partnership with Earl E. Cobb. City records show that he registered with the state and paid a "privilege tax" to operate a business in August 1922.

In the two-year period of flying with Runser, Roscoe had accumulated several hundred hours of time at the controls and was increasingly confident of his own flying ability. Intent on continuing to fly, he began barnstorming on his own with a patched-up, aging Jenny he had rebuilt with parts he probably obtained from government surplus and other wrecked planes. Surplus OX-5 engines could be bought then for as little as $25 and wrecked and reparable Curtiss Jennys were available for less than $100. He could easily have bought one of those offered for sale by the government after World War I at Park Field, an Army flying training field located near Memphis.[43] Or he could have retrieved the wreckage of the Marine Jenny from Earl Bailey's garage.

After Roscoe restored the plane to flying condition and was literally teaching himself to fly it, he made a number of local flights from a pasture on the Suratt family farm. His sister recalled that, knowing their father's total lack of enthusiasm for flying, Roscoe would deliberately fly over the family farm, frightening the family mules when their father was plowing. Several years later, Roscoe persuaded his father to fly with him but was able to get him to fly around the field only one time. In later years, his mother found that she enjoyed flying and Roscoe took her on several trips, including a flight to California in 1932.

Local flights with paying passengers and performing for local fairs and special events became routine for Roscoe in order to keep his name in the news and attract attention to his availability. However, in those postwar days, the general public didn't think flying was safe and only the brave or the reckless would dare to get in the front seat of Roscoe's rattling Jenny. The newspaper items noting the names of local people who did fly with him helped instill confidence in Roscoe's flying ability. But Roscoe knew he had to do more than just give people five-dollar joyrides to make enough money to live on.

While continuing to fly, Roscoe became a salesman for the Gray automobile agency in Corinth. He felt that his success as a salesman depended on his ability to attract potential buyers to the agency through his flying and any newsworthy stunts with the Gray automobile that would establish its dependability.

To prove to skeptics how much power a Gray had, Roscoe would take potential buyers to Turner's Hill and show that it had the ability to go all the way up the incline without stalling. On one occasion, long remembered by older Corinthians today, he drove it up the courthouse steps, a feat that few cars of that era could match. The publicity was good for the Gray automobile and enhanced the flair for flamboyance and self-promotion that would be a standard in Roscoe's future.

To pay the expenses of his flying, Roscoe was able to borrow $100 from his brother Abe without their father knowing about it. "Papa wouldn't have given Roscoe the money for that purpose if he had had it," Mary Emma said. She added that Roscoe always had to borrow money, mostly from people outside his family, in order to buy or repair his airplanes.[44] E. F. Waits, the local jeweler and inventor whom Roscoe had known since his preteen years, was one of those who provided funds so Roscoe could tinker and buy parts and fuel. Waits recalled:

> When he came back from the World War, his first adventure was to thrill a multitude of the residents of this community with a parachute jump. Soon he set up an automobile machine shop and just to keep the flying pot boiling he experimented with an old Jenny which we constructed from scraps. Parts of two or three obsolete motors were used in making the motor for the plane. With what he had picked up about flying during the war he coached himself for the first hazardous solo flight in this makeshift machine.
>
> In one of his early flights to the nearby town of Savannah, Tenn. with me as passenger, he nosed the machine over and broke a wing. Later he flew to Saulsbury, Tenn. and broke a landing gear.[45]

In the fall of 1924, Roscoe teamed up with Arthur H. Starnes, a parachutist and stuntman, and formed the Roscoe Turner Flying Circus. Starnes tells of their first meeting after he was introduced to him by Luther Doyle, a Corinth restaurant owner.

> From this introduction on, Turner impressed me. He was a powerful, pleasant, smooth-faced man who towered more than six feet in height

and weighed about two hundred pounds. His captivating smile, his southern accent, and his firm handshake delighted me. His suit was a showy
one with a dark blue coat, decorated with gold braid and gold wing em-
blems, while his trousers were of light whipcord, accented by black shoes
and puttees. At his side, in one hand, was his snow white tailored cap. I
quickly sized him up as a man with showmanship and appearance. Next,
I had to convince myself of his ability as a flier, because now, more than
ever, I realized what it meant to have a skilled pilot at the controls of the
plane when I was doing stunt work.[46]

Their first air show together was at Corinth when the city inaugurated a Trades Day just before Christmas 1924.

We had several thousand attractively-worded circulars printed describing
our death-defying feats. These were mailed on the rural routes to the box
holders. The businessmen signed up for amounts in keeping with the volume of business each merchant was doing. The leading merchants contributed as much as fifty dollars, and so on down to the little hamburger
dealer who contributed as little as a dollar. Our plan was a rather easy
method of getting cooperation for the merchants did not hesitate to sign
up when they knew their own business would benefit, and that they did
not have to pay until after the show was over. We soon became businessmen in the world of flight.

Our first show was staged amid a surging crowd of Christmas shop-
pers. The weather was cold enough for the cotton farmers to be off duty
and ready for a little excitement. Black and white watched the wonders
of the home town boy who was well on his way toward becoming a noted
flyer. In most respects the show was a success. Of course, financially, it
was not successful, nor did we expect it to be. We wished only to make
a good impression in Corinth before we started a Trades Day tour through
the south.[47]

Although Starnes thought the show was mostly successful, the editor of the local paper was not especially impressed:

As The Corinthian is closing up the forms for the issue of today there is
a flying machine stunt going on in the air above the city. A big plane piloted by Roscoe Turner is carrying a passenger named Starnes. Starnes
walked the wings of the big airplane, hung from the wings by his legs,
climbed under the body and swung his legs from the axle of the truck,
swung on a rope ladder and then climbed back onto the plane.

Just what is to be gained by thus flirting with fate and giving hope to the undertaker is hard to understand, but there are a great many who do these things, and as long as they are done, though no one is profited thereby, there will be those who will watch and the members of The Corinthian force belong to that curious throng.[48]

During this time, Roscoe used a pasture on the Suratt family farm as his airport. Located about four miles from Turner's Hill, he often walked the distance if he couldn't get a ride. "The Suratts loved him like a brother," his sister said. "They let him do anything he wanted to with his airplane on their property."

This remembrance was confirmed by Mary Emma Hardin, whose grandparents owned the farm, now the site of Shiloh Ridge Golf Course. "To me, Roscoe Turner was a big brother which I did not have," she said. "When I was a small child, he carried me on his shoulders almost every day. He was so proud of the airplane but one day he walked out to find the cows had chewed the cloth covering from the wings. He came back to the house, sat down on the back steps and cried like a baby. He and a friend had spent days putting the fabric on and spent many more days repairing the damage."[49]

Roscoe had learned to tell wind direction by looking at the cows in the pastures where he wanted to land. Cows are nature's weather vanes since they usually turn their tails to the wind. However, they could be a big problem because they had a penchant for eating the nitrate dope on the fabric surfaces of a plane. He never forgot how his Jenny was nearly stripped clean of fabric by Suratt's cows, and thereafter he avoided staying in cow pastures overnight. His brother Bill also remembered how Roscoe cried when he saw the skeleton of his Jenny the next morning.

"Another disappointment Roscoe had was when taking off in his newly repaired plane with the friend as a passenger," Mrs. Hardin said. "As they lifted off, the tail hit a fence and they hit the ground. Fortunately, they were not hurt seriously. The passenger received a broken nose but the plane did not fare too well."[50]

Roscoe taught Starnes how to fly the Jenny and allowed him to solo after three hours and forty-five minutes of dual instruction. After a reasonably good season, they decided to look for two more planes. Starnes describes what happened next:

> He knew a man in St. Louis who had offered to sponsor him whenever Roscoe wished to add to his planes. The sponsor, millionaire S. H. Curlee, was a former Corinth boy who had gone into the clothing business there and later in St. Louis, and was an airplane buff as well as a close friend of Roscoe. He was willing to finance the material needed to complete our circus. In turn for the interest on the investment we agreed to carry Mr. Curlee's advertisement painted on the lower wings and fuselage of the two new ships that were to be added. For the initial investment there was an understanding that we would pay our sponsor as soon as business made it possible for us to do so. To further assist us, Mr. Curlee gave us permission to carry his sales representatives to distant towns at the rate of 80 cents per mile. Thereby, the advertising campaign for Curlee Clothes was greatly enlarged over the whole Middle West, and we were aided in making money in our otherwise idle hours.
>
> The two ships added a great deal to our passenger business. One of them was like the first one we owned, an OX Standard. The second plane was a larger ship, known as a French Breguet, powered with a Renault motor. The French ship had been built originally as a bomber by the French Government during the World War. After the war closed, an aircraft company in Chicago bought some of the planes and remodeled them for carrying passengers. Our Breguet was large enough to accommodate four passengers and a pilot. With a plane of such great proportions and the two small planes we did a rushing business.[51]

In addition to hopping passengers from farmers' fields, it was the stunt flying at the state fairs and trade days that enabled them to keep relatively solvent in the feast-or-famine business. The tab was usually picked up by local merchants who used the flying circus for advertising their respective businesses. The fairs were always publicized extensively in the local papers and Roscoe never failed to get top billing as a main attraction. The weeklong Tennessee Valley Fair in 1923 is an example. A local paper noted on page one that "Roscoe Turner, who has thrilled the crowds at the fair this week, will stay in Tuscumbia over Sunday and

carry passengers in short flights. Flights will be made from Funke's
Pasture on the Russellville Pike."[52]

Roscoe had stationery printed during this period that implied he
headed a large organization with extensive "exhibitional" and "com-
mercial" capabilities. Offices were established in Corinth, and in
Sheffield, Alabama, and operations were conducted from flying fields
in Corinth and Ford City, Alabama. The letterhead for Roscoe Turner's
Flying Circus identified A. H. Starnes as "The 'Safety Last Boy.' "
Under the exhibitional heading on the left side of the stationery, it read
"Single, Double and Triple Parachute Jumps; Changing Planes in Mid-
air; Change from Auto to Plane; Wing Walking; Death Swing and Death
Roll; Falling a Mile in Flames; Flight of Destruction." On the other
side of the letterhead under "Commercial" were listed "Passenger
Carrying; Advertising; Aerial Photography; Flying Instruction; Cross-
country flights a specialty any time, anywhere; and Airplanes and Parts
for Sale."

Locating their operation in the Sheffield, Tuscumbia, and Muscle
Shoals area seemed like an excellent move at the time. The area was
growing economically because of the federal government's plan to take
over and complete Wilson Dam, a hydroelectric plant on the Tennessee
River. Henry Ford had considered buying a nitrate plant there during
World War I, which would be used for manufacturing ammunition during the war and fertilizer afterward.

Roscoe used the OX Standard training plane to fly passengers locally
and offer flying lessons. In the spirit of the times and sensing a great opportunity, Roscoe teamed up with some local businessmen and formed
the Muscle Shoals Aircraft Corporation with E. C. Carter as president
and Roscoe as vice president and general manager. He flew many potential investors around the area as part of a campaign to encourage
them to invest in the region during the 1923–25 period. Advertisements
touted the strategic location of Ford City and Muscle Shoals: "You
should be interested and you should learn why your Government and
these great corporations are so deeply interested in seeking to operate
Nitrate Fixation and Hydro-Electric Plants at Muscle Shoals."[53]

Advertisements in the *Sheffield Standard* sought financial backing for

Muscle Shoals Aircraft Corporation from the public:

> This organization is formed on a purely business basis, and will be managed by experienced aircraftmen. It should pay well on the investment from the start, as the overhead is comparatively small, and the field of activity large.
>
> It is incorporated for $5,000, there being 500 shares at $10 each. There are numerous ways in which the corporation will make money— by taking up local residents and investors from a distance, photography, map-making and distributing advertising literature.
>
> This is the only corporation of its kind in Alabama. Being a pioneer in its field, it will undoubtedly prove a success from the start. It will be conservatively managed—that is sure.[54]

The ads were run in conjunction with a civic parade in Sheffield that prominently featured Roscoe and his airplane. The headline on page one of the local paper was "Turner's Aeroplane Leads Parade." A subhead read: "Sheffield Only City on Record Having Aeroplane in Street Parade." The article noted that the parade had been led by the plane "under its own power" and that when the parade was disbanded at the railroad, "aviator Turner ran his plane to the vacant lot south of the railroad track and took the air from that point."[55]

Like so many similar entrepreneurial ventures immediately after World War I, Muscle Shoals Aircraft Corporation did not last, if it ever really got started. Never one to place all of his eggs in one basket on such a speculative venture anyhow, Roscoe and Starnes continued their flying circus shows while maintaining their headquarters in the Sheffield Hotel. A standard contract was drafted to formalize their arrangements with the local sponsors:

> We, The Roscoe Turner Flying Circus, agree to do over the business section of _____ on ____ day, to-wit:
>
> ONE WING WALKING SHOW, INCLUDING THE SWING OF DEATH
> A PARACHUTE JUMP
> AN AIRLINE ACROBATIC FLIGHT, LOOPS, SPINS,
> WING OVERS, WHIP STALLS, ROLLS
>
> The undersigned hereby agree to give the amount set opposite their names after this exhibition.

They used the OX Standard for the show at Corinth and next performed at the first Trades Days at Sheffield, Alabama. It was the Swing
of Death that thrilled the crowds. Starnes would climb out to the tip of
the Jenny's wing with a rope attached to a brace around his neck and
lower himself until he was totally suspended by the rope. He would
swing in the airstream with arms and legs outstretched as the plane flew
by the grandstand. He never wore a parachute for these stunts.[56]

Starnes made a number of parachute jumps and performed wing walking but always tried to add something new to each performance. He
rode on the rear of the fuselage as if riding a horse and did the "one
hand swing" from a wingtip or the landing gear.

Facing ever-growing competition with similar "death-defying acts"
from other barnstormers, Roscoe and Starnes dreamed up a new feat
that was unlike any they had tried before. To get the job, they told the
city fathers planning an upcoming county fair that Starnes would hang
from the wingtip of the Jenny by his chin and would not be wearing a
parachute. When they got the contract, Starnes went to a blacksmith
and had a harness made that would fit under his armpits. A hook was
attached that he could hide under his flying suit.

At the fair, Starnes donned the harness where the crowd couldn't see
him and got in the front seat. When he crawled out on the wing, he
pulled the hook out, attached it to the wingtip's handhold, and dropped
free, so that from a distance he appeared to be hanging by his chin.
However, Roscoe had trouble keeping the wing up. At the same time,
Starnes realized that they could crash and tried to climb back up onto
the wing but between Roscoe having control difficulties and experi-
encing turbulence, he couldn't lift his weight onto the wing's surface.
Roscoe thought the only thing he could do was to land quickly and
hope that Starnes could climb up on the wing when he slowed down
for the landing.

Roscoe made a letdown to the field and tried to land as far away from
the crowd as he could with Starnes trying to get his body up on the
wing. When his dangling feet hit the ground, the sudden drag caused
him to drop off and roll up into a ball. As Starnes dropped out of sight
behind him, Roscoe gave it the throttle and went around, certain that
Starnes had been killed. He circled the field quickly and landed as near

to Starnes as he dared, but in his haste to see if he was alive, he hit a muddy hole, nosed up and shattered the propeller. He climbed out quickly and rushed to Starnes's side.

Starnes rose slowly and brushed himself off. He was bruised but otherwise unhurt. There was only one thought on his mind: hide the hook before the town fathers found out that he hadn't been hanging from his chin or they wouldn't get paid. Starnes stripped off the harness and hook and threw them into the bottom of the rear cockpit as spectators ran out to the scene. It was a stunt no crowd had ever seen before. Undaunted by this adventure, Starnes continued to be nervy and daring. Sometimes Roscoe would fly low in front of a crowd and Starnes would drop from the landing gear or a rope ladder and slide on the ground to a stop on his posterior.[57]

The initial agreement with the Curlee Clothing Company allowed Roscoe to operate from Muscle Shoals Air Junction in Alabama. Everywhere he landed, newspaper reporters and photographers were given rides, along with local dignitaries. The publicity for the Curlee company and Roscoe set a pattern of using an airplane for advertising that would intensify in the years ahead. Never failing to wear his uniform, he was always the center of attention and was invariably invited to speak at local civic club luncheons and dinners. He used these opportunities to promote commercial and private aviation and the development of local airports.

To supplement his uncertain income from barnstorming, Roscoe continued to operate an auto repair shop in Corinth. A typical advertisement in the local paper said, "Overhaul jobs on automobiles. Motors contracted for. Flying instructions from 5 p.m. to dark."[58]

He also continued to sell Gray automobiles in Corinth. An ad for Roscoe Turner & Company, entitled FAIR ENOUGH! in the local paper said, "If the demonstrations already made with the Gray Automobile have not fully convinced you of its superiority over all other cars in its class, to show you that we know it is superior, we offer six months free service with each car. We carry a complete line of parts and guarantee every job of work on any make of car that leaves our place of business."[59]

Roscoe listed recent buyers of the Gray in ads in the *Weekly Corinthian* and noted that the gas consumption of each owner's automobile was "averaging not less than 28 miles per gallon, and some of them 35 miles per gallon." He added that the Gray had "not a grease cup on the car, and only 14 oil cups—the simplest constructed automobile on the market."[60]

Although the flying was fun and he learned rapidly from his mistakes, it wasn't profitable. Roscoe gave their first plane rides to a number of local townspeople around the Corinth area but didn't always charge them if they were good friends and would pay for the gas. Articles in the *Weekly Corinthian* related his many local flights and trips to other cities. A typical news item was headlined: "Aviator Drives Over To New Albany and Attends Sunday School." The report stated: "A flying trip was made to New Albany, Sunday morning. Roscoe Turner left Corinth in his airship and in thirty minutes he attended Sunday School in New Albany. He also enjoyed the noon preaching service and while there was a guest in the home of Mr. and Mrs. Frank Lee. The air pilot found an excellent field in New Albany, and will make frequent flying trips to that town during the summer."[61]

An article in the same issue noted that Roscoe planned to fly to Meridian, Mississippi, to hear Gypsy Smith, an evangelist from New York City. Similar front-page articles in subsequent issues were headlined "Roscoe Turner Flying with Local Family" and "Several People Enjoy Flying In the Air Sunday Afternoon." One item noted that "Masters Robert and Willie Anderson, age 8 and 10 years, . . . have the honor of being the two youngest flyers in Corinth."[62] The paper later reminded its readers that Roscoe was going to make a trip to Sheffield, Alabama, and St. Louis on October 1–3, 1923 and added, "If there is anyone in Corinth who has the nerve and price, Mr. Turner will take you along."[63]

Another news story about a Bible class "picnic stew" given by the Corinth Presbyterian Church was reported in the same issue: "There were about 200 present . . . eighteen gallons of stew and six gallons of ice cream vanished. Aviator Roscoe Turner, who was enjoying an air flight during the time, must have scented the delicious stew, for swooping down on the party in several dives and circling the grove, furnished pleasure to the party, as well as demonstrating his appreciation of the Young Men's Bible Class of the Presbyterian Church."[64]

Roscoe liked to "swoop down" on Corinthians on his return after every trip out of town. It is said that he would fly over his house and drop a beef roast or a chicken for his mother to start cooking. When leaving, he would buzz the farm at Turner's Hill and then the downtown area. Wagging his wings in a farewell salute, he would then disappear over the horizon in true Hollywood movie fashion. Liline Dalton, one of his neighbors, seemed to speak for many Corinthian ladies of that era when she recalled that Roscoe was "the most dashing man I ever saw in a uniform."

Every air show in the area in which Roscoe participated was guaranteed to garner news space in the Corinth newspaper and the articles were written in the melodramatic style of the day. In October 1923 Roscoe persuaded Earl E. Cobb, a local ex-serviceman, to be a wing walker for him. After scoring a hit with the populace at Tuscumbia, Alabama, on his first attempt, Cobb became a local hero to Corinthians: "Mr. Cobb climbed a rope ladder, and hanging himself under the plane, while Pilot Turner motored over the city with Mr. Cobb hanging with his head down in mid-air, from the landing gear. There is nothing lacking in Cobb's nerve and skill for thrilling the public, and in putting on his additional stunt, contributed his services to Corinth and the thousands of spectators in giving this performance."[65]

Meanwhile, Starnes decided to take a job with another flying circus. Roscoe began barnstorming by himself with one of the planes. He lived briefly wherever he could make some money flying sightseeing rides. "As long as I could get passengers," he explained, "there was no reason to leave a town."

He experienced the usual problems of not making expenses and having trouble with his planes. When taking off alone from a field near Columbia, South Carolina, his engine quit at about 100 feet altitude, and he had to make a forced landing. He landed among a herd of cows and a few hogs. He thought he had missed all of them but found that he had hit one of the cows in the head and damaged his left wing. The cow, badly injured, had staggered away and fell on a hog. Both died.

The owner saw what had happened and came roaring toward Roscoe waving his arms. Shouting that Roscoe should have landed in the next field instead of the one with the animals, the farmer demanded immediate payment.

Turner apologized and tried to explain that he had no choice of landing spot and asked how much the animals were worth. As usual, Roscoe was broke and when the farmer told him the amount he wanted, he said he didn't have that much money. "Then leave that damned machine where it is and get off my property!" the farmer demanded. "And don't come back until you get some money."

Roscoe returned several days later and paid for the cow and the hog, both of which had already been butchered and the meat presumably sold by their owner. Fortunately, the plane was not so damaged that he couldn't repair it and the engine on the spot. Much to the farmer's disgust, a large crowd gathered to watch him make the repairs before he could fly away.

At another time, Roscoe flew into a pasture near Ripley, Mississippi, to drum up some business. There was only one horse in the pasture but the sound of the engine frightened the horse so badly that it ran into a ditch, broke its neck, and died. When the owner appeared and found his horse dead, he accused Roscoe of murder. Roscoe tried to explain that he hadn't done anything to the horse; it had committed suicide! The irate farmer threatened to call the sheriff and have the plane "attached" unless he was paid on the spot. This time Roscoe was able to pay, just barely.

The Corinth paper was not the only one to herald Roscoe's coming and goings. An item in a Bolivar, Tennessee, newspaper was typical. It noted that Roscoe "came over to our town from Corinth, Miss. in his airplane, accompanied by Miss Carline Stovall, and they were guests of Mr. & Mrs. J. H. Cornelius. In the afternoon, Mr. Turner made several flights, carrying with him several of our citizens, giving them the thrill of riding in an airplane, together with the opportunity of seeing how the country looks to those who travel the air route."[66]

The passenger who had accompanied him to Bolivar was to become Mrs. Roscoe Turner. On one of his trips home to Corinth during this period, Roscoe had met Carline Hunter Stovall, a petite, quiet girl six years younger, who formerly lived in Kenton, Tennessee. Her mother had died and her father remarried, but his new wife argued bitterly with Carline and her two sisters so the three girls moved to Corinth to live with relatives.

An accomplished musician and singer, Carline taught music at her home and played the organ at the local Methodist church. She was captivated by Roscoe, by now not only a local hero but a man who, by virtue of his publicity, had become well-known throughout the South for his daredeviltry in an airplane. He wore his uniform everywhere and few women could resist his charming wit, ever-present smile, and good looks.

After an on-again, off-again courtship because of his many absences, Roscoe asked Carline to marry him. When she accepted, they decided their marriage should take place on his twenty-ninth birthday, September 29, 1924, at the Suratt Farm, where he had been keeping his planes. It was exactly one month after he had been pardoned by President Coolidge for receiving stolen government property.

Ever-mindful of gaining continuing mention in the papers, he wanted to "do something different" and announced publicly that he was going to be married in an airplane. The event was held at 6 A.M. in the presence of a few friends, including Mary Emma Hardin, who lived with the Suratts. She had never attended a wedding before and vividly remembered those who attended despite the early hour.

The small group watched as Carline and Roscoe sat in the two cockpits of the Curtiss Jenny while a local minister performed the ceremony. Roscoe and Carline mentioned afterward in talks they gave before civic, social, and veterans' groups that they had been "married in an airplane." Roscoe always said he believed it was the world's first such marriage but never explained that the plane was on the ground.

Under the headline: "Married and Flew Away to Another Clime," the local newspaper gave front-page coverage to the event:

Just as the dawn came creeping across the field east of the city known as the airplane landing place there was a most unusual scene on that field. Roscoe Turner and Miss Carline Hunter Stovall, seated in an airplane were united in marriage by Rev. E. R. Smoat, who with some difficulty managed to stand on the wing of the machine, which was later to be their honeymoon boat on an air voyage to Dayton, Ohio.

. . . Clad in their aviation costumes and ready to go, they listened to an exceptionally impressive ceremony as the pastor, a warm personal friend of each of the contracting parties, pronounced them man and wife. There was no music of any character but the beautiful ceremony lost none of its impressiveness on that account. . . .

Mr. Turner is himself an experienced aviator of national reputation, some of his aerial performances being classed as the most hazardous attempts yet made by any air aviator, while his bride has ridden in the plane with him sufficiently not to be shy of the journey that was before them when they waved goodbye and the crowd waved bon voyage. It was the like of which has not been witnessed in Corinth and perhaps will never be again, and for that reason all the more interesting.[67]

Meanwhile, the Sheffield paper noted that Roscoe was flying to Dayton "to advertise Muscle Shoals, Sheffield and Tuscumbia." In a telegram to the Sumner Realty Company in Sheffield, he said: "I was married this morning just before leaving Corinth and my bride is with me." The paper noted: "This is a modern marriage and came quite unexpected to his host of friends in Sheffield, who wish the two all the happiness in the world."[68]

It is interesting to note at this point that Carline always referred to her husband as "Turner" when talking about him to others. The word "roscoe" was considered a mildly derogatory epithet during the 1920s because it was a slang word used in gang warfare movies to mean "pistol" or "revolver." There is no evidence that he was named after a relative or, as some have surmised, that his family had some connection with the town of Roscoe, Texas.

After the ceremony, they immediately took off in the Jenny for a honeymoon and to attend the International Air Races at Dayton. En route they were delayed in Nashville because of high winds and when they arrived in Dayton, Roscoe parked his plane on the edge of the field in the rain, causing one British visitor to comment, "You Yanks use aeroplanes like Fords . . . leaving them any old place. . . . On the other side we would overhaul a plane that sat out in the rain all night!"[69]

Soon after their arrival, Roscoe and Carline drew immediate attention from the national media. The *New York Times* ran their photograph in the rotogravure section of the Sunday edition with the headline: "The Honeymoon Special Arrives at Dayton: Roscoe Turner and His Bride." A clean-shaven Roscoe was wearing his self-designed uniform; Carline wore a helmet and goggles, and a leather overcoat with a ribbon attached that said "Mechanic" which enabled her to get inside the race course grounds.[70]

After the races, Roscoe and Carline flew to Chicago and then St. Louis to visit S. H. Curlee, owner of the Curlee Clothing Company, whose company baseball team was playing a championship game in Omaha. The team had forgotten their mascot, a bulldog, and felt they needed it for good luck. Would Roscoe and Carline fly the dog from St. Louis? They did, and when they arrived over Omaha, Roscoe decided to make his arrival known by flying low over the city's main streets. When he landed, he was promptly arrested and jailed. The chief of police, believing that Roscoe was the pilot who had been dropping advertisements for Curlee Clothing all over the city in advance of the game, was determined to extract proper punishment for violating a local ordinance. It took the persuasive powers of the officials of the baseball association, the Omaha Chamber of Commerce, and S. H. Curlee, to convince the chief that, although Roscoe had flown low over the city, he had not dropped any leaflets. The Corinth weekly newspaper duly noted: "The reputation of Omaha for hospitality was at stake and from subsequent occurrences it is presumed that all charges were withdrawn."

The return of Roscoe and Carline to Corinth was recorded in the local paper under the headline, "Back to Earth Came Turners This Morning." The news item was typical of the overblown reportage of the day: "After being feasted and toasted for more than fifteen days in as many large cities of the country from Nashville to Omaha, stood the test of hundreds of cameras, idolized by the flappers of both sexes everywhere, commented on seriously and otherwise by the newspapers from coast to coast, visitors in church, feted in social functions and the groom seeing his bride and flying companion through the bars of an Omaha jail . . . the aerial honeymooners are at home."[71]

To continue playing the air fair circuit, Roscoe needed a new stuntman to replace Starnes. He formed a partnership with J. W. "Bugs" Fisher, who advertised himself as a World War I ace who had served with the French army and told reporters that his name was spelled "Fisheur." Roscoe tells what happened on their first flight together at Athens, Alabama, on August 7, 1925:

Among the stunting equipment was a rope approximately 20 feet long which my former stunt man used to tie around his ankle and then hang down around the landing gear to make people think he had fallen off the airplane. We called this "The Dive of Death."

The occasion was a Merchant Trade Day performance, which we had promoted around to all the merchants getting small contributions to put it on over the town's square.

There were no specific acts but my man used to walk on the wings of the airplane and make a parachute jump. However, Bugs decided he wanted to put on the "Dive of Death." I told him to be sure not to get down at the end of that rope unless he was positive he could get back up to the airplane. I had no desire to be tried for manslaughter or crack up the only airplane I had, as a man hanging at the end of that rope acted just like an anchor. He would strike the ground first and slow the airplane in flight and change its direction.

Bugs assured me he could perform the stunt so we got over town and after Bugs had done his walking on the wings this was his next feat. He got down on the landing gear, tied the rope around his ankle and turned loose. I flew around and around waiting for him to get back into the airplane. He climbed up on the wing and slipped back to the end of the rope. The next time I looked he got halfway up the rope and then fell back and when I saw the anguished expression on his face I knew something was about to happen. He made another attempt halfway up the rope and then fell back again. Then he screamed that he couldn't make it.

Fortunately, I had a considerable amount of gasoline in the tank and immediately thought of a river about 15 or 20 miles away as I knew of performers being dropped into the river when they couldn't make the grade back up the rope. The river, however, was to do me no good as Bugs had nothing to cut himself loose with. I flew around trying to decide what to do with this guy.

Then I remembered there was some plowed ground right on the edge of the field that we were flying from. I decided it would be possible, perhaps, to save his life but I didn't expect to save my airplane. Without waiting around longer I flew the airplane very low and just at the edge of the field I dropped Bugs onto the plowed ground and started dragging him, just getting the wheels of the airplane over on the landing field and pulling Bugs behind in the plowed ground. The plane turned sideways but fortunately both wheels were on the hard ground and though we skidded along for a couple hundred feet, the only damage was a blown tire and breaking the leading edge of the wing where the rope that was dragging Bugs was tied to a strut.

After getting on the ground without cracking up, my next thought was to get back to the end of the rope to see how Bugs was. He was completely out and I didn't know whether I had killed him or not. I threw all the drinking water we had on the field into his face and he began to snap out of it.

The show was not over as the most important act—the parachute jump—was yet to come. I felt I was up against it because I thought Bugs would be through stunting for good but as soon as he came to sufficiently to realize the situation he said that he would make the parachute drop. So I took him up once more and he got out in an old crude balloon parachute and it opened all right but he landed on top of a house.

Just all in a day's work in the old barnstorming days."[72]

On another occasion, Bugs made a low altitude parachute jump and hit the ground hard. He thought he had broken his ankle and was taken to a local doctor for an X-ray. No one mentioned payment at the time but ten years later, after Roscoe had become nationally known, he received a letter from the doctor demanding $5.00 for Bugs's X-ray.

In the spring of 1925, Roscoe established a flying school at Gusmus Field, near Florence, Alabama. He now had three planes and added an unidentified seven-passenger model for commercial and exhibition purposes. He advertised in the Florence paper that his office was in the Sheffield Hotel, which could be contacted to make arrangements for local passenger flights at $5.00 each. Cross-country trips to any point in the United States could be arranged.

Business was reasonably good but entanglements with the law cropped up in Tennessee, where he was served with an arrest warrant for not having state and county business licenses. The licenses were $25 each, and the sheriff informed Roscoe that he would have to have a separate license for every county in which he operated. Roscoe was furious and said he could not believe it was the policy of the state to hamper aviation in such a manner. Roscoe pointed out that in Alabama, no such tax was imposed and even the two-cent-per-gallon state gasoline tax was refunded to pilots because of the fact that airplanes used none of the state or county highways. He probably paid the tax in the one county after calculating that he could more than make up for it in passenger fares and instruction.

The local paper stated that several citizens were taking lessons in "the art of flying" from Roscoe. "He takes aviation seriously," the reporter editorialized, "and believes he is performing a patriotic service to the country in teaching men to operate planes so they will be prepared in case of war or the development of commercial aviation, both of which he believes are future certainties."[73]

Always seeking to garner public attention by doing something novel, Roscoe decided to set an altitude record or at least say he had. On June 19, 1925, he "flew more than 10,000 feet into the sky. It was the highest altitude ever attained by an aviator in the state of Alabama and equalled by few in the southern states. At a distance of almost two miles from the earth, Turner's plane appeared about the size of a small bird. The flight attracted the attention of a large number of people in all parts of the district."[74]

In Lexington, Kentucky, at the city's sesquicentennial celebration in July, Bugs Fisher escaped serious injury when Roscoe was preparing to go aloft with a passenger. He hid under the wing and when Roscoe taxied out, he sat on the axle between the wheels. The extra weight was too much for the plane and it struck a fence on the takeoff. According to one report, Bugs was "projected" through the wing but luckily escaped without serious injury. The plane was repaired and he later parachuted to "a graceful landing within a few yards of the stadium."[75]

In their search for something new to entertain the crowds, Roscoe and Bugs put on their "Dive of Death" act at Lake Wilson near Sheffield, Alabama. Bugs thrilled the crowd by lowering himself on a rope swinging from beneath the slow-flying plane and dropped into the lake from a low altitude, where he was picked up by a speed boat. The next day he planned to transfer from a speed boat to the airplane. He then decided he could dive into the lake from the plane without injury. An ad sponsored by a local firm said, "This is no parachute jump but a straight dive from a speeding airplane. Something you have never seen and perhaps will not see again."[76]

The local paper reported, "New interest [in the upcoming celebration] was attracted yesterday by the application of several local people who want to win the $100 offered by J.P. Anderson to any citizen who will duplicate the Bugs Fisher jump from the airplane into the lake. One person will be chosen from the applicants to make the jump. One of the provisions of Mr. Anderson's offer is that no liability attaches to him for accidents or death occasioned by the attempt."[77]

Fisher didn't make his dive into the lake. He was injured the day before it was scheduled when his parachute was delayed in opening and he had hit the ground hard. He had jumped from an altitude of 500 feet but the parachute hadn't opened fully until he was only about 100 feet above the ground. He sustained painful leg injuries and was hospitalized.

Roscoe knew diving from a moving airplane was a dangerous feat, especially if the diver had not practiced and had little or no experience in high diving or stunting. He and Runser had an experience with Lt. B. R. China of Sumter, South Carolina, known as "Fearless Scotty" who, in 1921, had jumped from their Jenny at an altitude of 150 feet into Lake Junaluska, North Carolina. China had suffered severe bruises and was knocked unconscious for several minutes before he was picked up by a speed boat. Roscoe had heard that at least three other stuntmen had previously been killed attempting this feat.

Roscoe tried to back out of this part of the deal but the need for funds overcame his better judgment. Besides, he had heard that the townspeople were making bets that the act would never come off because either the man would back out or Roscoe would not want an outsider stealing the show.

Although Fisher had not made the dive as advertised, the man selected to try for the $100 offer still wanted to make his dive. He was Edward S. Etheridge, 41, an electrical engineer from Sheffield, who was said to be experienced in diving from the high masts of schooners. Roscoe briefed Etheridge thoroughly about how to get out on the lower wing and jump off when he was given the signal. Roscoe said he would descend to a few feet above the water and slow down as much as he dared without stalling.

The two took off and Etheridge climbed out gingerly on the wing but instead of waiting for Roscoe's signal, he jumped into Lake Wilson at about 100 feet altitude. The impact of his body hitting the water crushed his lungs and knocked him unconscious. He was picked up by a speed boat but died three hours later in the local hospital. The Sheffield newspaper noted that Fisher, who was recovering from the injuries suffered on his jump the day before, "was able to arise from his bed and visit the injured man in his room."[78] An editorial in the *Tuscumbia Times* noted, "The Fourth of July proved most serious to stunt fliers and the morbid crowds went home satisfied. Why is it folks love to see the risk of human life? Why can't we be satisfied without always demanding the spectacular?"[79]

The idea of jumping into a lake from a plane was not new. Earlier, when Turner and Starnes were flying together and arrived at a small town for a show, they learned that a competitor who had preceded them said he had a stunt whereby one of his men would drop off the plane's wing into a nearby lake. A local braggart had said they didn't need to pay someone from out of town to do that. He would do it for free. The show's backers offered the show contract to Turner and Starnes provided they would let their man do the jumping. Roscoe refused.

Starnes made a number of dives later when he worked for another flying circus. While making a movie at Huntington, Indiana, about two years later, he dropped into the Ohio River clothed in a heavy flying suit and football helmet. He was rescued and survived the fall but admitted, "My neck and chest muscles swelled to immense proportions. I was given medical care, but was told by the attending physician that there was no cause for alarm, and that I would be all right in a few days. I suffered agony physically, but was content. I was alive and *I had dived into the river.*[80]

Starnes continued parachuting for a livelihood and in October 1941 made the longest free-fall parachute jump made in history to that time. Bailing out of a Lockheed Lodestar airliner at 30,800 feet over south

Chicago, he delayed the opening until he was only 600 feet above the ground. He landed unhurt in a cow pasture near the Rubinkam Airport. The successful five-and-a-half-mile leap ended a year of test jumps to provide information to the Army Air Corps for its pilots, who may have to make parachute jumps at high altitudes in wartime.

Barnstorming in the first years of the 1920s was a time of few rules and great risks. Landing fields were always pastures close to a road near a center of population. They usually contained holes and ditches that could not be seen from the air. The planes, built of wood and fabric, aged rapidly; their engines were not designed to fly very long without maintenance. The pilots were vagabonds whose lives depended too much on luck. The whims of the weather, together with the quirks of the machines and the unpredictable fancies of the public, made for a life scarcely calculated for rest, comfort, or longevity.

The barnstormer learned early how to doctor a misfiring engine, patch a piece of ripped fabric, or use a packing crate to replace a piece of damaged wooden structure. There was always the possibility that he would be marooned in a remote area because of engine failure or lack of gas. The barnstormer's routine was to search for rural garages and land as near them as possible for fuel, which he would have to strain through a chamois to keep water out of the gas tank.

Roscoe Turner was only one of hundreds of energetic young men who had served in World War I and wanted to continue flying or become pilots. Flying mostly the Curtiss Jennys, of which ten thousand had been produced in the United States during, and even for a few months after World War I, they thrilled millions of people as they flew from one pasture to another, often staying only one hop ahead of the sheriff for nonpayment of local bills. Their survival depended not only on a lucky choice of a paying crowd but on their fragile machines that were always close to mechanical or structural failure. The men themselves, mostly outfitted with leather jackets, white scarves, leather boots, helmets and goggles were always greeted with awe and excitement as they climbed from their open cockpits.

In testimony before the Civil Aeronautics Board during World War II, Roscoe explained what it was like to fly a rattletrap airplane that was low on fuel and tied together with baling wire:

> There have been times during my career when I would fly into a town with only a few gallons of gas left and hunt around for a hayfield in which to land. Naturally, people would come running out. Among these people would be some ambitious bird who had a garage. We'd tell him we had to have some gas. He'd supply the gas. And without a dime in my pocket, I would persuade this fellow to take his payment in trade. I would take him for a ride, and he would be so happy to get back on the ground that he didn't charge me for the gas—and I was back in business again. It was a tough venture, but I finally made it go and made a living with it.[81]

It was the barnstormers who participated in the air shows and air races that helped to "sell" aviation to the public during those primitive days of heavier-than-air aviation. They created headlines in every city, town, or hamlet where they performed. Large posters were printed to drum up the crowds. Sometimes, however, the pilots would arrive unannounced and fly over a town at very low altitude at full throttle to attract attention.

Basil Lee Rowe, a World War I mechanic-turned-pilot, developed a system of testing a town for profitability as he barnstormed up and down the east coast. It was typical of what Roscoe and the others did to drum up trade. "I would buzz it a couple of times," he said. "If the people continued about their business, I did the same. But if the animals and fowl took off for the woods and the kids tried to follow me, I looked for a farmer's field from which to operate. When I found one, I buzzed the town to get the whole population following me like the children of Hamelin following the Pied Piper."[82]

Roscoe survived as a barnstormer during the first half of the 1920s but it wasn't easy. He had minor accidents and always owed somebody. The planes wore out and he managed to buy other planes but always "on the cuff" in one way or another. As the crowds grew jaded at the air shows and accidents were all too common, fewer people wanted to risk their necks taking a local ride in an aging plane. There was a growing push for federal regulations to bring order out of the chaos that resulted from the crashes that continually filled the newspapers. Roscoe realized the time was fast approaching when he had to either move up the scale of sophistication with his planes or look for another line of work.

The trip with Carline to the races at Dayton in 1924 eventually led to one new venture. Roscoe met William P. Mayfield and Fred Albert, staff photographers for a local newspaper, who had an idea. They thought factory owners in the Ohio, Indiana, West Virginia, and Kentucky area might pay well for aerial photos of their facilities for use in their advertisements. They were right. They made an agreement with Roscoe and took hundreds of aerial photos of factories, homes, stores, and business enterprises. After photographing more than five hundred sites over a ten-week period, they dissolved their partnership and Roscoe returned to Corinth.

He continued his barnstorming during the good-weather months and contracted for air shows in the southern states. As usual, he sought and gained mention in the newspapers of the towns in which he performed and his exploits were always reported in the Corinth newspaper. A typical report appeared in March 1925 when he hired a parachute jumper for a show at Water Valley, Mississippi. The man jumped out successfully but the wind carried him into a nearby pasture and he landed astride a cow's back. Fortunately, neither was hurt and the crowd thought it was planned that way. They wildly applauded Roscoe and the jumper for what "was one of the amusing features of the big exhibition."[83]

Roscoe developed big plans for the future in the spring of 1925. The Corinth newspaper reported that he had returned home from New York "where he went several days ago for a conference with capitalists interested in the establishment of an airline from New York City to New Orleans. He states there is a strong probability that there will be an organization of a company effected within the near future and that big passenger ships will be put into commission. His conferees are the owners of the largest passenger aircraft in existence and contemplate the construction of others of similar operating capacity. This ship will carry fourteen passengers."[84]

Roscoe probably didn't realize it at the time, but a new, exciting era was about to begin in his life.

3

FLYING THE S-29-A

Now married to Carline, Roscoe was confident that his future hinged on his ability to sell the public on the future benefits of aviation and in doing so, make a living for the two of them while promoting himself as its spokesman. He went to Birmingham, Alabama, in December 1925 and persuaded a group of local businessmen to finance the Roscoe Turner Airways Corporation. With Dr. Courtney W. Shropshire as president and Roscoe as vice president and director of flight operations, the announced purpose was to submit a bid to operate commercial air mail service between Birmingham and Chicago to begin in January 1926.

On February 2, 1925, President Calvin Coolidge had signed the Kelly Act, a law that provided for payment to private carriers to transport the U.S. mail, then being flown by Post Office Department pilots. The law was designed to give successful bidders for the various routes a financial incentive to hire the personnel and buy the planes that would carry passengers and cargo as well on a scheduled basis.

Roscoe and his associates decided that the Chicago-Birmingham route offered the best opportunity to enter the airline business. Birmingham was envisioned as a hub from which other air mail routes would be authorized to extend from there to New Orleans, Atlanta, and Miami. One early bidder for the Chicago-Birmingham contract was General Aviation Systems, which was turned down because the company lacked sufficient capitalization. Two late bids—including Roscoe Turner Airways and Sheffield Federal Aircraft—were submitted in December 1925. The latter was turned down because the company lacked the required bond. After planning schedules and working out details, the Turner bid was also turned down by Postmaster General Harry S. New because "the company did not submit sufficient proof of financial backing to carry out operations." The Chicago-Birmingham route remained authorized but no other bidders stepped forward.

This disappointment was only the first of many to come for Roscoe, but if he were to be given a middle name it would have been Persistence. He made a proposal to establish an air route from New York to San Francisco, but it was too ambitious a project for the backers to consider.

Roscoe had no way of knowing then, but his future would be associated with Igor Sikorsky, a Russian-born aeronautical engineer, designer, and pilot who had built the world's first four-engine airplane and other Russian aircraft before and during World War I. Sikorsky had emigrated to the United States via Britain and France in 1919 to escape the effects of the Russian Revolution and "because I thought this is the place which I would want to make my second mother country where I want to come and stay and work out my destiny."[1]

In Russia, Sikorsky had been designing a series of aircraft that were serially numbered with the "S" prefix. The first S-1 was a light biplane equipped with a 15-hp engine and built in 1910. It didn't fly but the "S" series established Sikorsky's reputation as a competent designer. It was his later work with small aircraft that convinced Sikorsky that larger aircraft could be built to carry passengers over long distances. His first large plane was the four-engine *Le Grand*, a significant breakthrough in aircraft design. Completed in 1913, it featured controls for two pilots and had plush cabin accommodations for four passengers. It was described by one writer as "a trolley car with ninety-two-foot wings."

His next, the *Il'ya Muromets*, named after a legendary tenth-century Russian hero, was a four-engine wooden bomber first flown in 1914. During its testing process, the three-man crew flew the giant craft 800 miles, an impressive flight for the time. One of the more than seventy built was converted into a passenger-carrying model that featured a spacious interior with wicker chairs, a table, and lights.

After Czar Nicholas was ousted in 1917 and Communism was introduced, Sikorsky went to France, and then to the United States in March 1919 with only $600. Unable to get work, he earned a marginal living as a teacher and lecturer. His first venture in an attempt to return to aviation was the formation of a company on Long Island, New York, with a group of other Russian émigrés to produce a multiengine plane that would carry 12,000 pounds of payload. However, sufficient financial backing was unavailable and the company was dissolved. Undeterred, Sikorsky next designed a four-engine bomber and submitted the drawings to the U.S. Army Air Service. His proposal was accepted and he submitted ten detailed drawings, but with military postwar appropriations cut drastically, the project was canceled.

Still convinced that the future of aviation lay in large aircraft, Sikorsky shifted to designing commercial transports. He had designed the S-28, a four-engine transport in late 1919 but again he could find no financing to make a prototype or get it into production. Living on beans and bread with only a dream to sustain him, he received a gift of $5,000 from Russian composer Sergei Rachmaninoff and eventually found a group of New York financiers who enabled him to form the Sikorsky Aero Engineering Corporation in 1923. Although weakly financed, he designed the S-29-A (A for America), which was built on a chicken farm near Long Island's Roosevelt Field. About 90 percent of the basic structure was fashioned with angle iron from discarded bedsprings, steel tubing, chicken wire, and wood salvaged from a nearby junkyard. The result was a strong, twin-engine, twin-ruddered sesquiplane transport two inches short of 50 feet long, with an upper wingspan of 69 feet and a lower one of 62 feet, 6 inches. With two Liberty engines installed, the top speed was estimated at 116 mph with both engines operating and 75 mph on one. Its service ceiling was 12,500 feet. As it had no brakes, it depended on the tail skid to provide the drag to stop it after landing. The engine throttles were used to steer the aircraft when taxiing.

The plane was operated by the pilot from an open cockpit situated in the aft fuselage. A mechanic was required to operate engine temperature controls in the enclosed cabin, which would hold fourteen passengers, comfortably seated in wicker chairs and a wide rear seat.

Piloted by Sikorsky, the S-29-A made its first flight on May 4, 1924, from Roosevelt Field with eight of his workers aboard. However, two Hisso engines had been installed which were not powerful enough and he crash-landed shortly after takeoff at the Army Air Service's nearby Mitchel Field. The first successful flight, with more powerful Liberty engines, was made on September 25, 1924. It was one of the first, if not the first, twin-engine aircraft in the country that could fly and even climb on one engine.

Many dramatic demonstration flights followed. One flight was a race between the 20th Century Limited train from Albany to New York, which the plane won. Another was a radio broadcast from the plane over New York City, one of the first successful such tests ever made from a commercial aircraft. The first flight for pay ($500) was made from New York to Washington, D.C., with two baby grand pianos aboard, one of them destined for Mrs. Calvin Coolidge at the White House, the other for a department store.

Sikorsky piloted the S-29-A more than two hundred times and carried 420 passengers during 1924. He had one accident when he crash-landed it at night and ran into a tree limb as he descended in the darkness. No one was hurt but thereafter Sikorsky kept the limb in his office as a reminder of how close he and his company had come to disaster.

During 1925, the S-29-A made more demonstration flights and publicity stunts such as aerial photography and more radio broadcasts. Dimitri Viner, Sikorsky's nephew, caused a sensation when he took photos of Sikorsky flying the plane while Viner clung precariously to a wingtip with one hand and his camera in the other.

While Sikorsky went on to design and build other "S" models, Roscoe saw the plane, the largest aircraft in the United States, as a chance to sell his services for advertising and charter flights, and possibly persuade others to back his plans for an airline. Despite its apparent success, there had been no buyers for the S-29-A until Roscoe offered $10,000. The exact financial details are not known, but it is believed that S. H. Curlee, a fellow Corinthian and president of the Curlee Clothing Company, provided a partial loan which was added to by anonymous Atlanta businessmen.

Roscoe paid Sikorsky $1,000 down and promised to pay the balance in monthly installments. Roscoe had only that down payment and it took him many months to pay off the balance. Meanwhile, he promised Sikorsky he would promote the airplane highly everywhere he went and serve as his southern sales representative. In the ensuing months he kept in continual touch with Sikorsky regarding the plane's performance and the hours he flew it. On one occasion he wrote that he wanted to raise the money to have Sikorsky build him a "round-the-world" plane that he hoped would be able to beat the record of 175 days set by Army pilots in 1924.

Rejected for the Chicago-Birmingham air mail route, Roscoe still had visions of establishing a passenger-carrying airline and thought Atlanta was an ideal location for its headquarters. He made his first landing at Atlanta's Candler Field in the Sikorsky on March 23, 1926. At the time the only building on the field was an old shack where oil and gas cans were stored; there was also a small tent where soft drinks were sold.

Continuing to use the name of Roscoe Turner Airways, he contacted financiers and merchants in Atlanta and New York and persuaded them to form a three-corporation combine for the operation of pioneer north-south air service. General Airways System and Sikorsky Aero Engineering were the two partners along with Roscoe Turner Airways. The plan was eventually to have daily passenger and cargo service between New York and Atlanta with four of Sikorsky's new trimotors then on the drawing board. Routes were also sketched out between St. Louis and Boston and from Atlanta to New Orleans and other southern cities.

One of Roscoe's contacts at Sikorsky was Col. Harold E. Hartney, a World War I pilot who was trying to organize an airline to run from Boston to Minneapolis–St. Paul via New York, Buffalo, Detroit, and Chicago. He wanted to join forces with Roscoe and Sikorsky and sell stock to get the airline organized. He contacted Roscoe in Atlanta who replied: "No one is in worse shape than I am for I cannot even pay my grocery bill at home today and I have got to figure how I can get enough gas to get out of town. . . . One or two more long flights will tell us just what we will have to do to get this plane to make her hold a scheduled run."[2] The sad state of Roscoe's finances was verified by Bishop Simpson, a frequent visitor during Candler Field's early days. "Turner was always required to pay before he was allowed to pump gas," he recalled.[3]

On the New York–Atlanta route, terminals were contemplated at several cities, including Philadelphia, Washington, and cities in Virginia and the Carolinas. Roscoe saw it as his job to publicize his own airline plan with the S-29-A, and he set off for an extensive round of promotional flights to cities en route that garnered reams of news copy. In the weeks following the announcement of his plan, he carried many passengers on flights over the cities he visited and never failed to get front-page attention, especially for flights that were unique and thus guaranteed to generate a news story. A sampling of headlines tells the tale: "Ball Player Hunts Crows from Airplanes, "Turner Will Make No Power Landing," "Mayor and Son Fly over City," "Aerial Photos Will Be Taken Here," "Capt. Turner to Fly under Bridge," "Air Pilot Brings Letters to Byrd and Others Here," " 'Sky Pilot' Given Air Trip by Captain Turner," "Plane Carries Dispatches to Opening of New Bridge," "Reporter Sprouts Wings and Takes First Flight," "Airplane Is Used To Deliver Papers."

Not all of Roscoe's flights received favorable publicity. After a trip with the director of the Richmond, Virginia, Chamber of Commerce, a cynical headline read "Chamber of Commerce Chief Sees No Thrill in Airplaning." The crow-hunting flight received this headline: "Hunting by Plane Proves Failure." An attempt to drop advertising cards and two footballs during what Roscoe thought was merely football practice, but was actually an important game between rival high schools in West Virginia, provoked: "Turner Apologizes for Dropping Cards."

The reporters' lack of familiarity with aviation in general and airplanes in particular is seen in the many clippings in the Turner scrapbooks. One caption for a front-page photograph of the S-29-A in Winston-Salem's *Twin-City Sentinel* was typical: "Above is the passenger cabin, on each side of which is located a motor, each capable of driving the car should the other go wrong." Another item in a Boston newspaper noted that the "great airship" had glided to an "anchorage."

The publicity resulting from the purchase of the S-29-A proved to be Roscoe's entrée to national notice. He contracted with the Davison-Paxon-Stokes Company of Atlanta to deliver the latest Parisian gowns there from the R. H. Macy Company in New York. On one side of the Sikorsky, Roscoe had "Davison-Paxon-Stokes Co." painted in large letters; on the other side, "The Macy Special." To promote the idea of regular service and "to demonstrate the practicability of commercial aviation," Roscoe and his backers made an agreement to fly the latest women's fashions to Atlanta in eight hours for the Easter sales. An optimistic headline in the *Atlanta Constitution* on March 28, 1926, read: "Beautiful Gowns Designed in Gotham in Morning Will Be Worn Same Evening in Atlanta."

Roscoe's flight northward to begin the service attracted Atlanta businessmen who wanted to be in on the publicity. They gladly posed with Roscoe and the plane for the local papers. On the return flight to Atlanta via Washington, D.C., with the Parisian gowns, Roscoe gave rides to local influential citizens along the route and made speeches extolling the commercial potential of the area and advocating the building of an airport at each city. At every stop, local politicians and businessmen vied for camera position with Roscoe and hoped for mention in the papers. One news account glowingly stated that Turner had flown 4,000 miles in the giant Sikorsky and had set speed records on every flight.

Upon arrival at Candler Field on March 28, a Sunday afternoon that was calculated to attract a great crowd, he was met by an estimated 10,000 spectators, who watched the gowns being off-loaded. Roscoe took the opportunity to tout his plan for making the Atlanta–New York run in eight hours. He especially praised Atlanta as a hub for commercial flying and predicted that the New York–Atlanta route "will be a model airway of the world." Atlanta, he said, had

> every natural advantage . . . to make it a place that would be restful and of interest to go out and spend an afternoon watching the greyhounds of the air come and go while local businessmen who own their own planes were going up and down on pleasure trips. In a few years' time, by proper development, Atlanta would have an air terminal from which planes would

be leaving for all parts of the country almost every hour, and mail, light express packages and other necessities could reach their destination in a few hours' time whereas it now takes several days. Air travel eventually will mean the same to humanity as automobile and train transportation does now. It will bring together big businessmen in a big way and will sooner or later be a necessity.[4]

It was the type of speech he would adapt for any locale whenever he was interviewed by reporters or invited to speak publicly.

While the future seemed to hold promise for eventual development of Atlanta as a center for air commerce, Roscoe had to seek more immediate opportunities to stay solvent. At this time, he still owned the French-made Breguet that was used for charter and sight-seeing flights. Never one to rest when he had a promotional idea, Roscoe made an agreement with a Firestone tire dealer to stimulate tires sales with the Breguet: "With every purchase of two or more Firestone tires and tubes, all next week we are giving a FREE ride in Captain Roscoe Turner's airplane. M.L. Dooley of the Madison County Auto Co. will drop from the plane a 29 × 40 inflated tube, and to the lucky person bringing the tube to the Madison County Auto Co. he will exchange it for a tube of the proper size to fit the car it is to be used on." The ad stated that those who didn't want the free ride could collect $3.00 instead.

So much interest was generated that the offer was repeated. This time, the ad said that another tube would be dropped over the courthouse square. It added, "This will be your last chance to fly with one of America's safest pilots, who has had nine years' experience without serious accident, Roscoe Turner, 'Safety First Pilot.' " Publicity was also gained when Roscoe turned his plane over to a tire dealer's garage for repairs, which a newspaper claimed was the first auto garage "to have an airplane pull in its door for service."[5]

Continuing an arrangement to make promotional flights for the Curlee Clothing, Roscoe agreed to fly their salesmen in the S-29-A from their 1926 national sales meeting in St. Louis to various cities in the north and northeast states as far as Maine. The 3,000-mile trip ended at Hartford, Connecticut, on April 17, 1926. During the flight it was reported by the *Hartford Courier* that he had carried about 800 passengers and transported 15,000 pounds of freight valued at $50,000.[6]

When the Curlee salesmen landed at Springfield, Massachusetts, the local paper published a full front-page story that was carried over inside. The unfamiliarity of writers of that era with aircraft can be seen in the description of aircraft operations:

> The powerful hum of the motors was unmistakable. It grew rapidly larger, settled toward the field, its two motors and their whirring propellers plainly visible, the great length of the fuselage reassuring. It circled about once, cannily, and veered off to the east to a disconcerting distance. "They've gone on," someone suggested. "It's too small for a landing."
>
> But suddenly it had turned again, headed straight back for the west, and then veering into the face of a stiff easterly wind dropped rapidly onto the field. At exactly the outer edge of the rough the great ship first struck ground, the tail hit just before the rollers, "a skid stop," to save distance in the short run. Gently but rapidly it sped across till close to the scrub pine wood at the other side, then it turned and taxied back to center.
>
> A big blue-eyed pilot in the cockpit tore off his helmet in disgust. "Oh, boy," he roared over his dying motors. "Never again! No more of these small town landings."
>
> People stared stupidly.
>
> "Did you see what I had to do?" he roared at them. "Turnin' like that to miss the woods, goin' like I was (a beautiful Southern drawl was creeping in) I might 'a cracked up this yer ship. Who said I could land here?"[7]

As the salesmen stepped off the plane and lined up for photographs with Roscoe and his mechanic James Maxwell, "All eyes were upon the pilot. The fact was he made a dashing figure. High-booted, in tan leather, coated trimly in sky blue, a broad chest lined with medals and other insignia, a tan buckskin topcoat over his arm, he looked fictitious. Anybody would have ridden in his machine in a minute, skeptic or otherwise. Several asked immediately."[8]

It was a typical reaction to Roscoe and one he fostered. Maxwell was interviewed by the *Union-Republican* reporter and added to the mystique of the moment. He admitted that during the flight to Springfield from Albany, he had to get out on the wing to make repairs on the engine. He "had nothing below him but 3,000 feet of air" and "tinkered with the cylinders on one engine and had them going full tilt, without a landing" while a passenger held on to him by his ankles. However, the paper editorialized that the moment was not as dramatic as it might seem because "the Sikorsky plane can keep its height and fly on an even keel with one engine dead. All the same, it was desirable to have both going, for speed, and in case of accident to the other engine."[9]

After Roscoe returned from New York, he and Carline, who was helping with the office work, planned for more publicity by staging an airborne tea party for Atlanta socialites under the auspices of Davison-Paxon-Stokes. Roscoe named the aircraft *Cloudcrest* for the occasion. The *Atlanta Georgian* headline stated that it was "a new wrinkle in Atlanta" and that the event would be "one of the most unique teas in the social history of the city." However, the tea party was canceled when Carline was suddenly stricken with appendicitis and rushed to Davis-Fisher Hospital for an emergency operation. When the doctors said she could travel, he announced that he was going to fly her from Atlanta to their home town of Corinth to avoid the long, uncomfortable trip by railroad. It was another plug for aviation and, as usual, received headlines and photo features in a number of southern newspapers. The May 24, 1926, issue of the *Atlanta Georgian* ran a photo feature across the top of its front page under the bold headline: "Makes Ambulance of Plane—Takes Invalid Wife Home." The photos showed her being off-loaded from an ambulance and lifted into the plane, plus "a closeup of the interior of the palatial Sikorsky with Mrs. Turner resting back among the pillows and her nurse, Miss Margaret Schultz." Dr. Troy Bivings also went along, as was often the custom in those days when patients had to be transported any distance. As soon as Roscoe landed at Sheffield, Alabama, where he had intended to refuel, he sent a telegram to the *Atlanta Journal*: "Arrived in two hours, fifteen minutes. Mrs. Turner took the trip well. Doctor and nurse delighted with their new experience. Will return to Atlanta Wednesday." The telegram provided still more grist for the news mills.

En route to Sheffield, Roscoe changed his mind about trying to land the big plane at the Suratt farm in Corinth with Carline, the nurse, and doctor aboard, and he instead opted for staying at Sheffield. Roscoe returned to Atlanta and Carline was driven the rest of the way to Corinth by automobile. The entire episode was duly headlined and covered in detail in the Corinth paper.

Continuing to try to sell the idea of commercial air transportation, Roscoe persuaded the Atlanta Junior Chamber of Commerce to fly a group to New York in late May 1926. The flight began at Atlanta's Candler Field with great fanfare and included five prominent Atlantans and a Fox News cameraman, in addition to Turner and James Maxwell. Over Calhoun Falls, South Carolina, near Abbeville, a water connection broke on one engine and Roscoe was forced to land in the wheat field of L. A. Jackson after flying about forty miles looking for a suitably level landing spot. An Abbeville newspaper reported the incident with large headlines:

> The nose of the giant plane was brought down gradually and the wheels touched first on the south side of a road running by the side of the field. The plane jumped the road and bounced into the field. Four deep ditches were traversed through the marvelous handling of the plane by Captain Turner before it was finally brought to rest in Mr. Jackson's backyard 25 feet from the house with one wing in an apple tree.
>
> Experienced fliers among the passengers said that "There are not three other pilots in the world who could have landed the gigantic plane as Captain Turner did without a fatal accident."[10]

No one was hurt, but the wing, one landing gear, and support wires in the tail section were damaged. "We were lucky to be alive," said John K. Ottley, chairman of the Junior Chamber of Commerce's aviation committee. "One wing nestled between the limbs of an apple tree only a few feet from the back door of the farmhouse."

When he saw the huge machine and the large group of well-dressed men descending from its side door, Jackson was too frightened to come out. "We just dropped in to pick up some apples," the Fox cameraman quipped. "Sorry, mister," Jackson said, "but they ain't ripe yet."

Thousands flocked to see the plane while it was awaiting parts. A refreshment stand was set up and Roscoe "was the toast of the town," according to one account.

Leaving Maxwell to make repairs, Roscoe took the train to Atlanta with some of his passengers and flew the Breguet back to the Jackson farm, with R. E. Condon, national vice president of the Junior Chamber of Commerce as passenger. Just as Roscoe was about to touch down, a man, woman, and child ran across the field in front of him. Unable to go around, he jammed the left rudder forward, ground-looped, broke off the right landing gear, and splintered the Breguet's propeller.

With both planes damaged on the same field, the publicity might have marred Turner's reputation but, despite the many newspaper accounts about both accidents, none of it was unfavorable to Roscoe personally and he was heralded as a hero. His wired response to a query from the *Atlanta Journal* gained him more fans: "Airplanes are cheaper than human lives so I crashed my Breguet to save a man and woman who ran across its path while landing here Sunday just one hour and twenty minutes after leaving Candler Field. Over ten thousand people were out to see the big Sikorsky transport and they covered the field."[11]

When the repairs were completed on the Sikorsky, Roscoe took off with Maxwell as his only passenger. A few minutes later, the right engine began to sputter and lost power. Roscoe landed shortly afterward in a field about two miles from Calhoun Falls. One of the pistons in the right engine had cracked and the engine had to be replaced, so Roscoe remained at Abbeville and helped the mechanic work on the plane. Meanwhile, the Breguet, still on the Jackson farm, had to be dismantled and returned by train to Atlanta.

It took more than two weeks for an engine to be shipped from New York and installed on the S-29-A. When Roscoe announced it was ready to fly, hundreds of spectators gathered to see it depart for Atlanta. A *Journal* reporter described the preparations and the "miraculous" take-off:

At dawn Saturday the wheat field was dotted with spectators who had driven from miles around to see the big plane attempt a takeoff. All the ditches had been filled for a short distance the night before and the filled portions had been marked at each end with improvised flags to aid Captain Turner in navigating his way down the rutted and furrowed hillside.

The tail of the Sikorsky was hoisted onto a wagon bed and pushed and dragged to the top of the slope with the aid of willing farmers.

Soon the motors were roaring and the propellers kicking up a whirl-wind of dust in a plowed field behind the roadway where the tail of the plane had been placed. Both motors were then opened wide and the big ship swept majestically down the field.

A sickening drop at the last ditch as the plane neared the clump of trees bordering the field drew screams from several women, but the big Sikorsky had taken the hop at the will of Captain Turner. The silver plane rose and headed towards Abbeville with a faint stream of smoke streaming from the two exhausts.[12]

By the second week in June, the Sikorsky was ready for the New York trip again. Stops were made in Anderson and Orangeburg, South Carolina, Washington, D.C., and other cities en route. While at Anderson, the Lions Club engaged him to fly a dozen-man delegation to a state convention in Orangeburg, 130 miles away, a flight which was reported as taking "only" 75 minutes. According to one account, the idea "was received with both awe and alarm" because "never before had such a 'mass haul' ever been attempted in South Carolina." It was the first time that one service club delegation had ever been flown to a convention.[13]

Roscoe flew on to New York, and on the return flight, one of the S-29-A's tires blew out while the aircraft was in the air. According to Igor Sikorsky, "The tire was so rotten that it could not stand the change in air pressure at altitude. The blowout was so loud and caused such a shock to the wing that Roscoe thought the end had come—that some vital part of the plane had failed. But he made a good, one-wheel landing with no further damage."[14]

Roscoe's domination of aviation news in the spring of 1926 led to his being considered to accompany Capt. René Fonck, the renowned French World War I ace, as relief pilot on a flight from New York to Paris in a new Sikorsky S-35 trimotor to capture the $25,000 Orteig Prize. The prize had been offered in 1919 by Raymond Orteig, hotel owner and philanthropist, for the first nonstop flight between the two major cities, a distance of 3,600 miles.

The S-35 trimotor was modified from its original design by having three self-compensating rudders and extra gas tanks installed. An auxiliary landing gear was added to help support the added weight of fuel that would be needed. Twenty-three test flights were made, far fewer than Sikorsky wanted; however, none were made at the total weight of 24,200 lbs. planned for the takeoff.

Roscoe's experience with the S-29-A made him an ideal candidate to be a crew member. However, he was not enthusiastic about making the flight and did not relish the idea of being a copilot for Fonck, who had no experience in flying multiengine aircraft. Although Fonck was a hero to the public in his native France, his brother pilots considered him cold-blooded and arrogant. He was officially credited with 75 victories by the French Air Force but always claimed 127.

Not only was Roscoe not overly impressed with Fonck's flying record as a fighter pilot but he did not like the hurry-up planning he saw taking place for the risky transocean flight. Despite the wide national publicity Roscoe received when he had been asked to participate, he turned the invitation down, although it might have been an opportunity to become world-renowned. "I had a hunch [about the outcome]," he told reporters later, but admitted it was the hardest "no" he ever said.

On the morning of September 21, 1926, with U.S. Navy Lt. Lawrence W. Curtin as copilot, Sikorsky employee Jacob Islamoff as mechanic, and Charles Clavier as radio operator, Fonck began the takeoff roll from Roosevelt Field with 2,500 gallons of fuel in the tanks. The S-35 never got off the ground. As it reached the halfway point with its tail still on the ground, Fonck was either unable to stop or unwilling to abort the takeoff. One wheel collapsed as the huge trimotor reached the end of the runway, ran down an embankment, and exploded into flames. Fonck and Curtin escaped; the two others were trapped and died inside the blazing inferno.

Fonck was blamed for overloading the plane with fuel; he was also criticized for insisting that he needed a mechanic and radio operator, in addition to a copilot, for the flight. Roscoe's refusal to join the flight was vindicated when other flyers confirmed his assessment that Fonck was not competent to fly the giant Sikorsky.

Although Roscoe worked seven days a week to publicize his availability for charter flights, he was continually receiving letters requesting payment for overdue bills. One particularly persistent series of letters came from the Muscle Shoals Oil Company in Florence, Alabama, for $232.30

worth of gas and oil he had purchased in the summer of 1926 while operating from there. When payment was not received, the bill was turned over to a collection agency that asked him to make a partial payment if he could not send it all. "A remittance of even a small amount will show that you have some consideration for our clients who had to pay long ago for the goods for which you still owe them," the letter read.[15]

Roscoe did not take kindly to such letters and sent a check for ten dollars as a partial payment to Muscle Shoals Oil. He wrote,

> I will say that if you think you can get this money before I can you are perfectly at liberty to do so. I told you last year that I went broke for fifteen thousand dollars and that is not so easy to make a start again in so short a time and I am still trying to send you some. You are not the only ones I owe and I see no reason why I should pay you and not them and for that reason I sent you $10 and each of my creditors $10 a few days ago and this is the method I am going to use to pay these accounts provided you are willing to accept this method and if you are not you will have to wait longer.
>
> It is not my intention to beat you or anyone else but there are places in life when a man cannot meet his obligations. I know that you have been patient with this account but when a man can't, he can't. So now if you want to collect the full amount with interest you will have to give me my own time to pay it.[16]

Roscoe's need for funds to pay his debts was never-ending, but his enthusiasm for flying and his desire to prove how safe flying was remained undaunted as he continually sought money-making opportunities. Flying passengers on hops from local pastures could always be counted on to pay for gasoline and provide the bare necessities for himself and Carline. But it was at the carnivals and festivals where large numbers of people gathered that he could depend on making enough to tide them over and pay a few overdue bills.

At a county fair at London, Ohio, in August 1926, Roscoe resorted to one of his old barnstorming ploys which was designed to show how safe airplanes were. At his prompting, a newspaper reporter asked rhetorically, "What if the motor stops, like it does in a Ford?" Roscoe answered by going aloft and making a "dead stick" landing, "thus proving that a ship with a dead motor in the hands of the right person is as harmless as a dead Ford."[17]

Roscoe stayed in the Ohio area for ten days selling flights. He wrote a thank-you note to the townspeople, which was printed in a local paper. He said he appreciated the interest they had shown in aviation

> and also the business you have given me. In seven years of commercial flying I have never been treated any better.
>
> I want to thank Mr. Bridgman for the use of his field; also Mr. Boyd for a few trips out of his, and the Madison County Auto Co. for the assistance in repairing my little mishaps.
>
> London, Ohio, will never be forgotten by me and the work which I am doing is just the forerunner of a future passenger and mail service, because the people who have been up will not be afraid to take an air line any more than boarding a train when the service is put through, which it will be in future years.[18]

Always searching for money-making ventures with the S-29-A, Roscoe wrote to the president of the *New York Times* suggesting that he make a "Capital to Capital" tour of every state in the union as a publicity stunt for the *Times*. "The big plane we could letter AIR EXPRESS OF N.Y. TIMES and with a film of the History of Aviation we would spend a week in each city visited working in connection with civic organizations and high schools, calling the trip the Aeronautical Educational Tour of N.Y. Times Flyers, which would include my mechanic and Mrs. Turner, who is a singer and musician. This trip will cost $250.00 per week and I will make it for you if you can stand the expense."[19]

While Roscoe made local sight-seeing flights from Dayton in the S-29-A, he pursued new publicity ideas. He joined the Junior Chamber of Commerce and in September 1926 participated in an air circus to dedicate Junior Chamber airfield markers at Moraine Field, Dayton's municipal airport. The marking idea was a Junior Chamber project designed to enable pilots to locate and identify airports from the air through large rooftop and water tower signs indicating the local airport name and direction to it. Although Roscoe had said previously he was through with stunting, he agreed to put on his "Falling a Mile in Flames" illusion once more, which the local paper noted as "the most spectacular event of the aerial circus."

The stay in Dayton was followed by Roscoe's decision to move to Richmond, Virginia, which he now touted as "the gateway to the south." Invited by a group of businessmen to establish an airport, he flew a Standard biplane to Sandston, Virginia, on January 20, 1927, through a sleet and ice storm. After searching desperately for the designated cow pasture, he landed on a road parallel to it near a small building he was going to use as his headquarters. He came within ten feet of ramming the corner of the building. He recruited some men from Sandston and over the next few weeks helped them get the pasture in shape for operations.

Located about five miles east of Richmond, the building was modified to include sleeping quarters for six visiting airmen or "more in emergency." Runways of 1,150 ft. and 1,450 ft. were scraped and leveled. The field was officially named the Richmond Air Junction, with Roscoe listed in U.S. Department of Commerce aircraft-landing facility documents as the owner, operator, and caretaker. Two mechanics were available for servicing and meals could be obtained "in village one mile distant." The fire apparatus consisted of hand extinguishers. There was no hangar or workshop; all work was done outside under a large surplus Army tent.

Roscoe started his operation with the Sikorsky and Standard and then acquired a Waco 9, a Standard J-1, and a Curtiss JN-4 Jenny. He made a verbal agreement with the president of the Richmond Air Junction Association to give the association 30 percent of his gross income for permission to operate from there. The association was to furnish office and hangar facilities for the newly created Roscoe Turner Flying Service, and Roscoe was to be in charge of the flying field. He agreed to operate a flying school, carry passengers on sight-seeing or cross-country flights, service aircraft, and be a distributor for Waco aircraft. A press release stated:

> Flying instructions commenced on Thursday, February 17 [1927] and among those enrolled for lessons is a minister of the Gospel and a female student. Captain Turner says that in the future flying will be just the same as golf for the average person. A person will go to the flying field, wheel his plane out and fly wherever his business or pleasure call him, and then return to his desk. For flying today is rated the safest means of travel, next

to travelling by steamship, which is known to be the safest means of travel in the world. This, of course, does not include military or experimental flying, which is very dangerous.[20]

Shortly after he settled in at Richmond, Roscoe, accompanied by mechanic Bennie Kolgan in a new Waco, went on a "pathfinding tour" of cities in Alabama, the Carolinas, and Virginia with the objective of starting an air mail and passenger route that would link southern cities through Richmond with New York. To gain publicity for the idea, he brought letters from the mayors and chambers of commerce of the various cities and personally delivered them to Virginia governor Harry Flood Byrd.

Such ideas in those days took much time to mature. In addition to offering flying instruction, air taxi service, and aerial photography, he made sales flights in the Waco he had obtained as a demonstrator. He used it to gain publicity for the plane as well as his services by delivering newspapers to small communities within 100 miles of Richmond. When the announcement was made that he had opened a flying school, the *Richmond Times-Dispatch* noted that he had operated "every type of plane used in this country, including the giant Sikorsky twin-motored transport." The flying service "will operate a school for flying, where all who wish to may learn to operate an airplane, perform passenger-carrying, aerial sight-seeing, aerial photography, aerial advertising and emergency cross-country trips to any place in the United States with one-hour notice."[21]

The ads for the R. T. Flying Service in the Richmond papers cautioned readers, "Don't confuse our flying with military, experimental or exhibition, which are hazardous. Our service saves time and is pleasant and restful. The day of the airplane is NOW; we are equipped to teach you to fly, to handle fast commercial traffic, or to sell you a plane."[22]

Offering these services required continual promotions, which included giving local celebrities, influential politicians, and female citizens their first flights. Roscoe reasoned that if newsworthy people, especially women, could be convinced that flying was safe, the general public would also be reassured. On many of these flights, he illustrated the safety of the aircraft by making "cold motor" landings "to demonstrate the safety of a modern plane in the face of motor difficulties." He gently persuaded

Oliver J. Sands, founder of the town of Sandston, to make his first flight in the Sikorsky, even though Sands had refused the offer of other pilots because "I have too many other responsibilities to risk my life in an aeroplane." Pleased with the sight-seeing flight with Roscoe, Sands promptly collared one of the city officials and said, "We'll have to clean up Sandston's streets, since all these people are now flying over our town."

Once established, Roscoe was the host for a number of aviation personalities that flew into Richmond. Among them were Amelia Earhart, Clarence Chamberlain, Benny Howard, and Frank Hawks. Roscoe became good friends with Dick Merrill, a pilot for Pitcairn Aviation Company of Philadelphia, which had won the air mail contract for the Miami–New York route. Merrill made regular stops in Richmond and was later best known for his record-setting flights for Pitcairn's successor, Eastern Airlines.

Probably the best-known celebrity of the era that Roscoe took on a flight between two cities was Will Rogers, the famous comedian who was then mayor of Beverly Hills, California. They departed Richmond for Staunton, Virginia, for Rogers to make a speaking engagement, but Roscoe had to land thirty miles away on a farm near Fishersville because of a rainstorm. The headline in the *Richmond News-Leader* read: "Rogers Clamps Lid on Wise Cracks and Is Given Air Ride." The Staunton paper headlined its story, "Cowboy Mayor Is Forced to Drop in on Fishersville Folks."

After the flight with Roscoe, Will Rogers became one of aviation's greatest salesmen and was later named "No. 1 air passenger of the United States" by the two great transcontinental airlines. During his lifetime he made twenty-five crossings of the country by airlines and flew more than 500,000 miles. It was reported that his life insurance policy carried a double indemnity clause in case of death by violence or accident. The company refused to continue the policy because of Rogers' passion for flying. Rather than agree to stop flying, Rogers had the provisions stricken from the policy. He was killed on a flight with Wiley Post near Point Barrow, Alaska, on August 15, 1935.

The summer of 1927 brought a new opportunity to use the Sikorsky. Roscoe planned to make a flight to the West Indies to see if there might be any profit in providing passenger service between there and New York. Before he could fly to the islands, however, he obtained a $10,000 contract with United Cigar Stores Company to convert the S-29-A into a "Flying Cigar Store" for a ten-week tour of thirty-seven cities along the East Coast and as far west as St. Louis. When the conversion was completed to include a sales counter with cash register and eight passenger seats, Roscoe, his wife, two mechanics, and an entourage of five United Cigar sales managers, prepared to depart Curtiss Field, Long Island, on July 5. In addition to cigars, the ship carried clocks, watches, razors, lipsticks, and compacts for sale.

Piloting from the open cockpit in the rear fuselage, Roscoe taxied out into a strong wind. A sudden stiff gust lifted the plane off the ground and set it down squarely on top of a parked Curtiss Jenny. No one was injured but the Jenny was not flyable; the S-29-A's right engine and propeller were damaged and the flight was delayed until repairs were made. It cost Roscoe $1,000 and a week's delay to have the damage repaired.

In the following weeks, the flying cigar store received the hoped-for headlines everywhere it landed. Roscoe and Carline were invited to luncheons and dinners and both spoke on radio programs that gave Roscoe the chance to talk about his concept of aviation's future. He advocated the building of airports, encouraged the development of airlines to haul passengers as a logical follow-up to carrying the mail, and gave his predictions of things to come so that "America will soon lead the world in aviation."

Encouraged by the attention he was getting, he announced in Rochester, New York, that he and Carline were planning a tour of the world in the Sikorsky in the summer or fall of that year. Although the flight never took place, it made good copy for newshounds, who were always looking for interesting quotes to go with their stories about the flying store. In Grand Rapids, Michigan, telling how safe flying really was, Roscoe said, "More people met death in Missouri as the result of being kicked by mules than were killed in the entire United States in airplane accidents."

Large signs were painted on the S-29-A's fuselage advertising the plane as the "First Flying United Cigar Store." At every stop, crowds gathered to walk through the plane, buy the wares displayed and talk with its pilot. Roscoe handed out memorial plaques to local dignitaries commemorating the plane's visit. Parades were often held in which Roscoe and Carline rode to city hall to present a plaque to the mayor or other top local personages. Roscoe arranged advertising tie-ins with local merchants to obtain meals, lodging, and transportation. In Buffalo a local car dealer loaned the Turners Reo Flying Cloud and Wolverine automobiles for use during their stay. In Toledo a Nash dealer loaned them his latest model. Local hotels put them up free for the publicity their presence generated. The result was always photos in the local papers with the Turners posing by their "favorite choice" of autos.

Headline writers of city newspapers tried to outdo one another in gaining attention when the Sikorsky came to town. The *Peoria Star* ran a large photo of the cigar plane with the headline, "Could Lay Big Smoke Screen if Necessary." The next day, the paper referred to it as a "Smoke House." To ensure more press coverage, when the plane reached Washington, D.C., Roscoe contacted the Atlantic City Beauty Pageant and arranged for four entrants to accompany him to Boston, the last stop of the tour.

When the tour ended in September, Roscoe received a letter from the company calling it a "huge, worthwhile success" attributable "to the flying ability of Captain Turner, which, together with his fine executive judgment and knowledge of just what was to be done on this advertising, sales and good-will building tour, put it over in a mighty fine way." It was a letter of reference that Roscoe would use to obtain future promotional contracts.

Roscoe learned from newspaper accounts that a pilot "fond of lions" was being sought to transport the full-grown lion of Metro-Goldwyn-Mayer Pictures from Los Angeles to New York. With the United Cigar contract now completed, he immediately telegraphed film producer Louis B. Mayer and asked for the job. Roscoe said that, although he had little experience with lions, he believed he could get along easily with one. He received no response. In the years since, some writers have said that Roscoe had worked in a circus and had previous experience with lion taming, but there is no evidence to support this claim.

Exhilarated by his success but disappointed that his contract with United Cigar was not to be renewed, he contacted the G.H.P. Cigar Company in Philadelphia to see if they wanted to rent space "by the month or by the year" in the S-29-A but they declined.

Typical of Roscoe's never-ending, behind-the-scenes promotional activities was an inquiry from the Omaha Chamber of Commerce member on behalf of a member who sold Frigidaire refrigerators there. Would Roscoe be interested in helping him with some promotional stunt to advertise his wares?

Roscoe replied that for $2,500 he would carry the company's ad

> on each side of the plane and get a story with a photo showing the ad in at least one local paper of each of [ten cities] and three national aeronautical magazines, and for each city I fail to get a story and picture in the paper and each magazine he may deduct $200 from my contract. To show him I am willing to give him his money's worth I will carry the ad on the plane for a month after the trip to Omaha is over free of charge. . . . [He] can call me the "Flying Ice Man," "Frigidaire Flyer," or anything he wants to hang on me.

He added that he gave one to four luncheon and dinner talks every week "and over the radio once in a while."

While Roscoe was carrying out his attention-getting flights and gaining front-page publicity with each one, he was tireless in his pursuit of more business. He wrote personal letters to potential customers for future advertising assignments. Reviewing his successful operation of the S-29-A for the R. H. Macy and Curlee companies, he sent a letter to the Life Savers Company noting that a competing candy manufacturer, the Curtis Company of Chicago,

> has been using a small plane for two or three years and this year are putting out six small planes, so it must be good.
>
> Now we offer you this plane and a high class pilot which you may use as THE LIFE SAVERS SPECIAL, over the following territory, and we guarantee a story and picture of the plane in at least one local paper of each of the following cities and three national aeronautical magazines. . . .
>
> You are to bear the expense of painting and lettering in whatever colors you desire. The plane will have to be lettered and painted at Garden

City, L.I. Terms of the contract $1,000 upon signing of same and $500 more when half completed and the balance of $1,000 when contract is completed.[23]

Roscoe wrote a similar letter to newspaper tycoon William Randolph Hearst, offering to "take this plane on an educational tour for aviation" visiting all of the Hearst newspaper offices across the country. It would be called the "Hearst Special" and "would be of much news value following the course of the flight, which would take several weeks, consuming whatever amount of time you might desire." To add interest, he stated that Mr. Horace Ashton, explorer and lecturer, would go along to take pictures and make lectures at some of the stops.[24]

Another letter was sent to a New York representative for Barking Dog cigarettes saying that the same plan as was used for the Flying Cigar Store could be used to advertise Barking Dogs. He added, "we know of a dozen advertising planes on the road but we have the largest and we started first in the business so that gives us an advantage in many ways."[25]

None of these letters led to contracts, but a complaint letter from Roscoe to the Champion Spark Plug Company engineering department eventually did, in a roundabout way:

> I wish you could make me a spark plug that will stand up in my Libertys as I have told you before in my wires they keep breaking off the porcelains inside although they give excellent service otherwise. We have tried the nines and the sixes, your representative in New York thinking that the sixes would give better service than the nines. And I gave him the old plugs to ship back to you but he left them in my plane, so I have a full box of about forty broken plugs which I can send you if you can get any information from the broken plugs. Now I have had to put back in my Mosler plugs but as long as I am not going anywhere no one will perhaps know the difference, as I am still a booster for Champions.[26]

He received an apologetic reply which asked that the forty plugs be returned for testing. The following year, after Roscoe had gone to California and proposed an attempt to break the endurance record, Champion offered him a cash prize of $500 if he broke the record "and if you succeed in breaking the record by ten hours we will double the amount because that will increase the publicity value of the record to us." The letter noted that the plugs he had complained about had been improved and that the company would send him the newer plugs for his record attempt.[27]

By this time, Roscoe was getting more experience in advertising his flying skills and negotiating deals. He wired back that a competing spark-plug firm had offered him $1,500 if he broke the record and an oil company had put up $5,000. However, he noted that "I perhaps can switch to Champion plugs if you want me to try."[28]

Back in Richmond, Roscoe's business was dependent on obtaining aircraft for instructional purposes. He made an agreement with an airport operator in Huntington, West Virginia, to purchase a new Jenny with a new motor for $1,200 and hoped to establish a partnership. "I am incorporating next week for a hundred thousand and if you would be interested in joining me here in the school," he wrote, "I might also be able to join you in your projects to help put them over at least and superintend them for you if you desire."[29] There is no record that a partnership was formed.

The year 1927 had been an epic year for aviation. In less than a decade, the Atlantic had been spanned several times, first in 1919 by a U.S. Navy plane and in May 1927 by Lindbergh alone. U.S. Army flyers had circumnavigated the globe, America had been spanned nonstop, and dirigibles had remained aloft for nearly 100 hours. The North Pole had been crossed by air, and Hawaii had been reached by plane for the first time. Speed and distance records were being established and promptly beaten as airplanes and engines were continually improved.

Roscoe knew many of the American pilots who were getting press attention for their exploits and envied them their fame and whatever fortune they were able to garner as a result of the publicity. Still in debt for the Sikorsky and having to work hard continually to remain solvent and maintain his image and lifestyle, he wondered if he could continue in the flying business as a freelancer. As he was to say many times during his lifetime, "the greatest hazard I have had to overcome was starving to death while following this business. It is a profession in which one gets little or no encouragement. Your friends beg you to quit before it is too late; very few people will invest any money with you to help carry on the work; sometimes your creditors will try to collect from you before you take off."

The answer to what he was going to do in the immediate future came from a man he had never met and a place he had never seen: Howard Hughes in Hollywood, California.

4

HELL'S ANGELS
AND NEVADA AIRLINES

Howard Robard Hughes, Jr., was a millionaire orphan who had inherited the Houston-based Hughes Tool Company, a corporation his father had built by supplying drill bits, tools, and dies to the oil industry. The young Hughes moved to California in 1925 and decided to become a motion picture producer. He amended the charter of the Caddo Rock Drill Bit Company of Louisiana, a subsidiary of Hughes Tool Company, to allow it to make movies as well as lease drill bits. The new company was called Caddo Productions.

Hughes financed several unimpressive pictures, beginning in 1925 with *Swell Hogan*, which was so bad that it was never released. The next year's *Everybody's Acting* was better, and it was followed by *Two Arabian Knights* in 1927, which won an award for its director, Lewis Milestone. Then came *The Mating Call* in 1928. Hughes did not take an active part in directing these films or writing the scripts.

Despite his unlimited funds to finance the films, no one in Hollywood took him seriously, except Hughes himself. Ben Hecht, a famous writer

87

of the time, called him "the sucker with money." However, Hughes quietly learned all he could about the technical side of filmmaking. He had taken up flying in 1925 and bought a two-seat Waco biplane, which he was taught to fly by J. B. Alexander. Exhilarated by the experience, he conceived a plan to produce and direct an epic film about the flying aces of World War I that would establish a reputation for him with the cynics. He already had a title: *Hell's Angels.*

Hughes chose Marshall "Mickey" Neilan as director; Ben Lyon and James Hall played brothers who fell in love with the same girl: Greta Nissen, a Norwegian actress. The story was written by Neilan and Joseph M. March. Shooting of the indoor scenes began in October 1927. For the outdoor flying scenes, Hughes began to assemble pilots, mechanics, and flying machines on a scale that impressed even the Hollywood skeptics. He passed the word that he wanted the flying scenes to be realistic with actual World War I British, French, and German fighters and a few bombers. Throughout the spring and summer of 1927, his scouts scoured the States and Europe and bought or leased eighty-seven vintage planes at a cost of $562,000. Thirty-seven of them were authentic wartime combat planes; others, such as American-built Travel Air 2000s, were modified and painted to look like warplanes. The assemblage was the largest private air fleet in the world.

The final scene was to be the shootdown of a German Gotha by Allied fighters, with the giant bomber spinning earthward to a fiery crash as a symbol of the Allied victory over the Germans. There was one problem: No flyable German Gotha bombers had survived the war. Someone told Hughes about Roscoe Turner and the publicity of his many Sikorsky S-29 flights. Since few Americans had ever seen a Gotha and the S-29 was the largest aircraft then flying in America, could it be modified to look like the German bomber? Hollywood staging advisors said it could. One of Hughes's agents contacted Roscoe and drew up a lease agreement, which he quickly signed but later admitted he should have looked at more carefully.

Roscoe did not know exactly what a Gotha looked like but he agreed to fly the S-29 to California for Hughes, believing that he would be compensated if it was damaged or destroyed. He signed a contract for his firm leasing the Sikorsky to Hughes for $11,000, plus $1,000 for gas when he arrived in California. Roscoe's nine-man board of directors in Richmond objected and demanded $15,000 but Roscoe prevailed.

Roscoe expected to be on the West Coast within thirty days. The Sikorsky would be changed to look like it *could* be a Gotha, and he would fly the "bomber" when required for the movie for the same wages as the rest of the pilots. Meanwhile, Hughes's publicity men told West Coast and movie industry reporters that they had found a Gotha and it was being flown to Hollywood by no less a personage than Roscoe Turner, "one of the world's greatest pilots." Press releases stated that the plane had been imported from Germany at a cost of $50,000.

Roscoe turned the business in Virginia over to associates and departed the East Coast in February 1928 in the Sikorsky, with a mechanic and Carline as "navigator," ostensibly to set an east-west speed record. It was not an easy flight and record-setting was out of the question. After leaving New York, one of the engine's radiators sprung a leak and Roscoe had to find a large enough field to put the plane down for repairs. As they resumed the trip, rain, sleet, and snow storms and muddy fields intervened to slow them down. They proceeded to Atlanta and near Newman, Georgia, Roscoe became lost and had to buzz a railroad station to read the town's name. Engine problems developed en route but Roscoe and his mechanic managed to solve them. Meanwhile, Hughes's minions in Los Angeles were threatening to call off the deal if he didn't arrive soon.

Typically, everywhere he stopped, reporters descended on Roscoe and Carline seeking photos and quotes. It was no coincidence that they were always met by a crowd. Roscoe would telegraph or telephone ahead to newspapers where he intended to land and tell them he was coming with the giant "Gotha." No one ever questioned the plane's authenticity. He asked what the best time would be for his arrival so that he could make their next editions.

Continually delayed by weather and being bogged down in muddy fields, they arrived first at March Field, the Army Air Corps base at Riverside, California, where engine repairs were made. Hughes had his publicists plan a grand reception and on March 26, 1928, led by Hughes in his Waco and three German Fokkers, the "Gotha" was flown to Van Nuys, where Roscoe and Carline stepped out to a huge crowd, including a number of movie stars and newspaper reporters. Photographers focused on Carline, in helmet and goggles, and indicated her role in their captions was as the "navigatrix" for the "German Gotha." "The flying couple made a big hit with the public following their spectacular arrival," a trade newspaper reported. "They are being widely feted already and are in big demand for personal appearances at various public functions."[1]

The "German Gotha" was touted by Hughes publicists as the "largest plane ever flown on the West Coast." No newspaper ever referred to it as a converted Sikorsky and the secret remained safe from the media. After the initial press briefing, it was promptly hidden away, painted dull brown with a German cross on the tail and skull and crossbones on the fuselage. The open cockpit in the rear fuselage, from which Roscoe operated the controls, was outfitted with a machine gun to simulate a rear gunner's position. A cockpit was fashioned in the front of the cabin for the actors who sat before dummy controls. Simulated machine gun positions were built in the nose and cabin entrance door.

Hughes hired more than seventy pilots, with Frank Clarke as chief pilot; he later gave Frank Tomick the responsibility for the camera planes. At first Hughes hired novice pilots at $10 per day but when they cracked up three planes in quick succession, he hired only experienced professionals at $200 per week, a nice sum for the times. A large plot of ground had been leased and cleared at Van Nuys, which was named Caddo Field and re-created as a World War I American airfield in France. Another field was acquired near Chatsworth in the San Fernando Valley, where a reproduction of the airdrome was built called "The Jolly Baron's Nest," the home of Baron von Richthofen's Flying Circus, the *Jagdstaffel I*. Smaller fields were leased at Inglewood, Encino, Santa Cruz, and San Diego.

The eighty-seven planes that Hughes acquired included Fokker D VIIs obtained from the U.S. Air Service, which were shipped from Germany; American planes such as Travel Airs, which were dubbed "Wichita Fokkers" by pilots and painted to simulate others; and a number of British SE-5s, Sopwith Camels and Snipes, and Avro 504s purchased in Canada.

For realism, Hughes insisted that all aerial scenes had to be shot against a backdrop of white, puffy clouds. He moved a production crew of a hundred people in October 1928 to Oakland because the area around Los Angeles was often too hazy. At this location, after six months of training and practice, and much idle time when no clouds appeared, the spectacular air battle in which fifty planes took part was finally filmed the way Hughes wanted it. The idle time on the ground disgusted many pilots. They posted signs reading "Today's War Postponed: No Clouds." According to Hughes, the total cost of this one dogfight alone was $250,000, a staggering sum in those days.

In his insatiable desire for authenticity, Hughes often demanded that his pilots do some dangerous flying. At times, the pilots rebelled and tempers flared. On one occasion, a pilot who had performed a number of low-level passes over a stationary camera had enough of Hughes's orders for flying ever lower. When Hughes signaled that he wanted another pass, lower than any of the others, the pilot dove so low that his landing gear smashed the expensive camera off its tripod. Hughes finally said he was satisfied.

Roscoe flew the S-29 many times from Caddo Field while "enemy" fighters made their simulated passes at it. He recalled,

> We would take off and climb up through the fog where the camera ship and the fighters would make their attack. We used the old German Fokker D VIIs for the enemy and British planes for the defenders. In some scenes we would have as high as 35 pilots and airplanes, and naturally, there were occasions when they would get tangled up. One time a plane came down between my stabilizer and the trailing edge of the wing, barely missing the fuselage. . . . We had some scenes which were without clouds. We would get down in the canyons and mountains in order for it to be unidentifiable as part of the United States.[2]

Hundreds of aerial scenes were shot before Hughes would approve them. He was totally involved in making the air sequences and spent hours diagramming the planes' routes and using models to study camera angles. Flying his open-cockpit Waco, he directed some of the sky battles himself, signalling his instructions to cameramen and pilots from the air. One scene involved forty planes dogfighting in a melee that would set a standard for realism in future films. The scene of the ob-servation car hanging below a large model of a German dirigible sup-posedly hiding in the clouds over London was shot more than a hundred times before Hughes was satisfied.

Hughes was a rough taskmaster during the filming. When Roscoe was with the group in Oakland, he wired Hughes that the Sikorsky's propellers needed refinishing, which should be done in Los Angeles. Hughes did not want him to leave and wired back:

> I do not feel you should leave at this time under any circumstances. As you know we have tremendous expense with all these ships and if we get a good day of clouds we can shoot the whole works including shot with bomber. If the bomber props need refinishing that should have been done before we brought all those ships up there. I dont think you should sug-gest anything like this which you know would affect the morale of the troupe. At a time like this when I want everyone on their toes it is ab-solutely imperative that we get these shots right now and I am depend-ing on you not only to fly the bomber but to do what you can in every way to help get them. As you know we are having trouble with whole formation on account of lack of good pilots. I should think you could get in there and help keep them in line. Just as soon as we get the shots outlined in my memorandum to Harry Perry requiring the extra ships I will be glad to let you come down and take your plane into Los Angeles. Kindest regards Howard.[3]

Roscoe flew the Sikorsky regularly. A mechanic always had to ride in the closed passenger compartment while he flew it from the open cock-pit in the rear fuselage. Although he never tried to loop or spin it, he made wingovers and "flipper turns" like the other pilots were able to do in their Wacos and Travel Airs. In a letter to Sikorsky, he bragged, "the only thing that can catch it out here is a Fokker F.10."

On one occasion, seventeen-year-old Bill Eadie, fascinated by the plane, hid in the rear baggage compartment. When the plane was air-borne and Roscoe tried to maneuver, he found the controls binding. He yelled at the mechanic in the passenger compartment to look at the control cables to see if there was anything constricting them. The me-chanic found the frightened teenager holding on to them; he pulled the stowaway forward into the cabin while Roscoe landed. Instead of turning him over to the police, Roscoe gave him a stern lecture and sent him home. He told the waiting press that "the kid's been punished enough."

The S-29, apparently without Roscoe at the controls, was involved in a ground accident that nearly cost the life of a cameraman. Two expensive movie cameras had been set up directly in the path of the Sikorsky to catch the bomber as it appeared to be taking off. The airplane was supposed to taxi up to the cameras at a high speed into barriers that had been erected to stop it. Heading directly toward the cameras, it accelerated and smashed through the barriers and hit the cameras. One of the cameramen, Harry Perry, and a mechanic in the plane's nose were almost killed when pieces of a broken propeller spun by their heads. The Sikorsky, damaged but reparable, plowed into a bean field. It was out of action for a week.

With a large number of vintage planes involved, it was inevitable that there would be engine failures, midair collisions and ground accidents. The front pages of local newspapers were emblazoned with news of the forced landings, bailouts, and crackups. One of the most spectacular of these occurred while a German Fokker, piloted by Al Wilson, was flying over Hollywood returning with some twenty other planes after filming a dogfight over Redondo. They were flying high above a thick bank of clouds and the ground below was obscured. Without warning, the propeller of the Fokker suddenly spun off the engine shaft. Believing he was somewhere above the Hollywood mountains, Wilson bailed out and descended through the clouds. The aircraft dove past him and crashed into the backyard of movie producer Joseph M. Schenk's palatial residence on Hollywood Boulevard. Wilson landed safely on the roof of another house nearby. The propeller crashed onto a sidewalk narrowly missing several pedestrians. Schenk and his actress wife, Norma Talmadge, left the plane in the backyard exactly where it had crashed for several years as a joke and conversation piece.

Hughes himself had a crackup during the filming that nearly killed him. He was unhappy with one pilot who was supposed to take off and make a steep, low altitude turn at 300 feet with a Thomas-Morse Scout plane equipped with a rotary engine that revolved with the propeller. The pilot refused, saying that he would do it at about 1,000 feet but not 300. Furious, Hughes jumped into the plane, which he had not flown before, and roared into the air. When about 400 feet off the ground, he started a steep climbing turn, which was exceptionally dangerous in a plane with a rotary engine because of the torque. He immediately stalled out, fell into a spin, and crashed. About a hundred pilots, stuntmen, and mechanics watched in horror, certain that he couldn't have survived. They found him unconscious with one cheekbone crushed. He was rushed by ambulance to the Inglewood Hospital and spent about a month there. He was transferred to St. Vincent's Hospital and subsequently underwent minor plastic surgery. The smashed cheekbone gave him considerable discomfort for the rest of his life.

Four men were killed during shooting of the film. Two pilots died while trying to make forced landings when their engines quit. The third occurred while a stunt pilot was putting on a show for the ground crews. Diving straight for the ground with full power, he intended to pull out at the last second. He didn't.

It was the final tragedy that caused the most repercussions and cost Roscoe his airplane. The script called for the Gotha to appear to be spinning out of control to a fiery crash. It was first planned to install two dummy engines on the lower wing of a Curtiss Jenny so it would appear to be the bomber from a distance. The Jenny was then to be put into a spin; the pilot was to set it afire and then bail out. Three camera planes would then follow it through its death dive to a spectacular finish.

Before the scene could be shot, the Jenny's fabric caught fire while it was in the hangar leaving only the carcass. It was refabricated, set afire, and pushed off a cliff with cameras situated so it would be filmed as it struck the ground. The result was unrealistic, so Hughes decided that the Sikorsky would have to be used.

Although the final shot of the Gotha spinning toward the earth had been made once with Roscoe at the controls, Hughes was not satisfied. Roscoe had made a mild spiral with the power off. Hughes wanted a tight spin with full power on. Roscoe balked. To his dismay, he learned then that the contract he had signed with Hughes had cost him control and ownership of the plane. The fine print was interpreted by Hughes's lawyers to mean that ownership would be transferred when the lease payments equaled the value of the Sikorsky. When the agreement was made, apparently no one, including Roscoe, thought it would take as long as it did to complete the flying sequences.

Meanwhile, Roscoe wrote to a vice president of Sikorsky suggesting that Sikorsky might want to sue Hughes for damages because all of the movie's publicity had been made "without your permission or mentioning the Sikorsky name" and left the impression that the plane was built in Germany. Roscoe suggested that he be considered a salesman for Sikorsky and be put on the payroll.

By this time, the S-29 had been through much strenuous flying and Roscoe thought it may have been weakened internally. He had made 122 flights and flown it over 10,000 miles between March and September 1928 and said he would spin it only if Hughes would pay an experienced aircraft mechanic to check the plane thoroughly from nose to tail, which would take about a week. Hughes was infuriated about the delay, not the cost. He would find someone else.

While Roscoe was away from the field, Hughes asked several pilots to fly the plane but they refused. Noted stunt pilot Dick Grace was offered $250, but he said he wouldn't do it for less than $10,000. Army Air Corps pilots at Rockwell Field near San Diego were also contacted. One of them was Lt. Irwin A. Woodring, who had visited Roscoe to ask his opinion about spinning the Sikorsky. Roscoe replied by letter:

First, the people in this picture have been disposed to give everything a trimming who has any dealings with them, if possible. They took my plane away from me through one of their trick movie contracts and then promised me that if I would stay with them and help make the picture that they would let me have it back. So as I had lost so much money in the deal and my business back in Virginia I decided to stick with them until they asked me to spin this big plane. When I refused they have been giving me the go-around ever since and I am thoroughly convinced now that I have lost all the way around.

The reason that I would not spin it is because the weight of the ship as you saw it today is 11,000 lbs. The covering of the ship is the original that was put on four years ago with the exception of the upper wing; both front and rear spars on the lower wing have buckles in them under the engine mounts; all of the fittings are very rusty and I have pulled one out

at the fuselage since I have been flying it out here. Frankly, the ship is in
terrible shape and owing to its size I don't think it would be possible to
clear it with a parachute in a spin.

   . . . Now if you want to spin this baby, I would suggest that you watch
everything very closely both as to the airplane and as to dealing with
these people because, frankly, they think that whoever spins it will get
killed and they won't have to pay. Bear in mind that you can't fly this
ship without taking a mechanic along as he controls both the spark and
radiator shutters and has all the oil and temperature gauges in the cabin
with him.[4]

Hughes contacted Al Wilson, one of the most experienced pilots of
the group, and offered him a $1,000 bonus if he would put the giant
Sikorsky in a power-on spin. The money was enticing and he said he
would. Phil Jones, a mechanic, anxious to earn a $100 bonus, volun-
teered to ride in the cabin to set off smoke equipment to simulate a
burning plane. The aircraft was then to pull out of the spin and go out
of sight behind a hill while ground explosions were set off to simulate
a crash. Roscoe had flown all of the Gotha's aerial sequences thus far
himself and Wilson may never even have sat in the cockpit before. Most
of his flying experience had been in light, single-engine planes.

   On March 22, 1929, Wilson and Jones climbed aboard with their
parachutes. Three de Havilland camera planes plus Hughes in his Waco
took off from Caddo Field; Wilson then took off and climbed to 7,000
feet as the camera planes maneuvered for position. At first, Wilson
seemed to be testing the Sikorsky as he stalled it and let it fall off briefly
on one wing. He recovered and then apparently changed his mind about
putting the gawky, unstable giant into a tight power-on spin. He also
may have been apprehensive about making a landing. After a mild trial
diving turn, he put the plane into a medium-angle spiral as the cameras
rolled. He claimed later that he then signaled Jones to release the lamp
black and activate the blowers, and shouted to him twice to bail out.
Wilson promptly leaped from the open cockpit and landed safely but
Jones, inside the passenger cabin, apparently didn't get the message. He
started the blowers and released several lamp black canisters before the
Sikorsky slammed into the ground in an orange grove in Pacoima, north
of Los Angeles, killing him instantly.

One of the most colorful aircraft in aviation history up to that time, shorn of its original identity, had performed faithfully to the end. It was a tragic finale for the one-of-a-kind airplane.

In the filming of the last moments of the Sikorsky, only the scenes of the bomber beginning its spin are shown in the completed picture; although the cameras were rolling and Wilson was seen leaving the plane from the open cockpit in the rear, these shots were not used.

One account of the tragedy, fostered by Hughes's press relations representatives to exonerate Wilson, stated that Wilson bailed out because the plane was old, the wing fabric had begun to peel off, and a piece of engine cowling had ripped away. He claimed that he heard the wooden wings buckle, although they were mostly metal. Pilots in the camera planes tried to substantiate his testimony, saying they saw the wings start to buckle, but many doubted their testimony. One of the camera plane pilots who was closest to the Sikorsky stated he believed that Wilson had done all he could under the circumstances.

Evidence was submitted during an investigation that Wilson had left the plane from the open cockpit only five seconds after starting the spin. As a result, Wilson's fellow pilots expelled him from the Professional Pilots Association. The Department of Commerce fined him $500 and suspended his pilot's license for three months. The district attorney investigated the incident on suspicion of negligent homicide, but no charges were brought. Few moviegoers ever knew that the final crash scene in the picture was an actual accident in which a man was killed.

Whatever the complete terms of Roscoe's agreement with Hughes were, Roscoe had received $7,000 for the plane but had to spend $2,000 for engine repairs when he arrived in California. He received no extra compensation for the loss of the Sikorsky. His total salary for flying as pilot for the year 1929 as reported to him by the Hughes organization was $2,000.

Roscoe's bitterness at losing the plane was expressed in an exchange of letters and telegrams shortly afterward. In one telegram he displayed his resentment:

> Have hoped for the best but it happened as I expected. You had destroyed the thing I loved and slaved nite and day to obtain. My business is completely lost. I cant understand why you with your millions have always

taken advantage of me in every way you could from the minute I entered
contract services at an honest price. Life and its pleasures are just as sweet
to me as to you. It is difficult to get financial backing in my profession.
The fruits of my labor helped you accomplish your desire. I hope you are
satisfied. But remember there will always be one promise you never kept:
that was letting me have back my plane.[5]

Referring to the Curtiss Jenny made up to resemble a German bomber
that had burned up on the ground, Roscoe showed the intensity of his
feelings at how he had been treated in a memo sent to Hughes before
the picture was completed:

> Well, Howard, it seems like you are having considerable bad luck with
> the picture. I hear your Jenny Bomber burned up. I do not know what
> you think or if you have such a thing as a conscience, but I believe in the
> law of retribution, and this applies to the rich as well as the poor. Just re-
> member this little note from me and sum up all the delays in the past and
> the money you have spent unnecessarily. Also, watch how many more
> disappointments you are going to have, not alone on the picture, but to
> yourself. All because of the law of retribution. Just because you never
> wanted to play fair with me, and because you took undue advantage of
> me and even let your organization humiliate and insult me.
>
> You have even played big-hearted and extravagant with everyone else
> but when it came to the man and his plane that your picture is built
> around, you always had on a conservative program and talked like you
> were ready to go to the poor house for your next meal.
>
> You have always told me how you felt about me, but you never of-
> fered me a chance to do any more flying when you had the gang out in
> the past few weeks. I did not go hungry because you overlooked me but
> I am just telling you that I noticed it.
> JUST REMEMBER THE LAW OF RETRIBUTION.[6]

Hughes called Roscoe to his office and disagreed vehemently that he
had treated Roscoe badly. In a follow-up letter, Roscoe said that he was
now

> thoroughly convinced that you or the Caddo Co. has no respect for me
> personally or my ability as a pilot and no consideration for my personal
> rights and possessions.
>
> I have had to stand for being cheated, defrauded and insulted by your
> company and I came to you man-to-man and asked justice which you

have refused to give me. . . . [This] proves to me that you and your company has not and will not treat me any better in the future than you have
in the past except to accomplish your own selfish ends. . . . You have broken me and taken my plane but you cannot take me, so my services end
with this.[7]

Hughes responded immediately:

I have just received your note which hurts me very much. I am very sorry
you take this attitude and I feel it is unjust. . . . I have tried to be fair in
my dealings with you throughout the picture and the only thing I know
of that you can criticize is the deal for the purchase of the bomber and as
you know I didn't make that deal with you and any misunderstanding is
not my fault.[8]

Reviewing what had happened during the flying sequences of the film
and how he had saved Hughes's airplanes several times by pushing them
in the hangar so they wouldn't be damaged by storms, Roscoe wrote
one more bitter letter:

Just remember, Howard, I always did the work you asked me to do and
I never advised you wrong in one single thing, and that you always got
the truth straight from the shoulder from me. I don't have to tell you
that my experience is above the average pilot and that my name and in-
fluence has some meaning in the aeronautical world. Your publicity department used it quite well for you. I have been successful to a certain
degree in aviation, and I like you personally, but I cannot understand why
the experience you have had with men and with your intelligence why
you will let a few leaches misadvise you so badly when all they are trying
to do is see how long they can stay on your payroll.[9]

The filming of the indoor scenes for *Hell's Angels*, which had begun in
October 1927, was finally completed and Hughes planned to release
the film in 1929. However, his planned release coincided with the first
showing of *The Jazz Singer*, starring Al Jolson, a film that brought sound
to the movies for the first time. "Talkies," at first considered only a passing fancy by the movie-makers, were immediately successful with the
public.

It was a severe jolt to Hughes, who had completed all the interior
shots without sound. Not to be outdone, however, he filmed all the

talking scenes over with sound and dialogue and dubbed engine sounds in the flying sequences onto a sound track. The original cast was reassembled except that Greta Nissen, who had a strong Norwegian accent, was replaced by Harlean Carpenter, a braless, blue-eyed blonde, who had been a bit player in several minor films. Hughes changed her name to Jean Harlow and coined the phrase "platinum blonde" to describe her bleached hair. *Hell's Angels* launched her career as a "sex goddess" and superstar.

It took three years to complete the filming of *Hell's Angels* to Hughes's satisfaction and cost $3.8 million. More than 20,000 persons had taken part in its making and more than 3 million feet of film had been run through the cameras; only about 15,000 feet were finally used. It was estimated that the planes had flown 227,000 miles for the flying sequences. It was the most expensive film ever made until David O. Selznick's *Gone With the Wind.* Although Hughes always claimed a profit, the film lost $1.5 million, but the loss had no effect on his financial status. The tool company had ample profits to cover it.

Before the premiere of the film, Hughes booked a theater for a private showing alone. However, Louella Parsons, noted Hollywood columnist, sneaked in and refused to leave, becoming the only other person to see the film before its release.

The world premiere was held on May 27, 1930, at Grauman's Chinese Theater in Hollywood. Roscoe, in uniform, attended with his wife. The prologue to the showing was a song-and-dance show in the "Sid Grauman tradition." A few days before the opening, a bogus German fighter plane was placed in the intersection of Wilshire Boulevard and Western Avenue with its nose buried at a steep angle in the ground to call attention to the upcoming event. A formation of old open-cockpit planes painted with Maltese crosses flew over the theater beforehand and stuntmen parachuted onto Hollywood Boulevard. Huge searchlights beamed across the sky that night and hundreds of movie fans strained against police barricades to see their favorite stars, who entered the theater on a long red carpet spread from the curb. A genuine Fokker biplane was suspended in the lobby.

Stretching the truth in the printed program, Hughes's publicists wrote:

For the first time in history a colossal film spectacle is presented without faked or processed shots. In 'Hell's Angels' when you see someone in the air, he is actually in the air. And when you see a person flying a plane, he is actually flying it. There is no pilot concealed in a hidden cockpit to give the false appearance of an actor doing the flying. Nor are there any faked shots where the actors and planes photographed on a studio stage, and the background double-exposed in later.

The truth was that a large model of the Zeppelin was used as were models in some midair collision scenes. In Roscoe's case, he flew the "Gotha" from the open cockpit, which had been made to look like a rear gunner's position, while Ben Lyon, one of the heroes, was inside the passenger cabin with false controls. The program also noted that "more than 50 wartime ships, including a giant German Gotha bombing plane, were purchased outright and re-conditioned for service in this single picture." The Gotha's secret was never revealed and few moviegoers ever knew that it was actually Igor Sikorsky's first plane made in America.

The aerial photography and Jean Harlow got the biggest raves from the critics. A *Photoplay* magazine writer commented, "Nothing like it has ever happened before and probably nothing like it will ever happen again."[10] The authors of one Hughes biography wrote, "*Hell's Angels* set the theme for all of Hughes's movies—rich in entertainment, low on philosophy and message, packed with sex and action."[11] Despite the criticism of a few, the film broke attendance records at Grauman's and ran to full houses for nineteen weeks. In an unprecedented occurrence, it opened in New York City in two theaters simultaneously; Hughes attended both of them.

Although Hughes used only a fraction of the footage shot during *Hell's Angels*, he was able to recoup some of his costs by selling aerial scene rights later to other producers. He used some of the dogfight and bomb sequences in his own *Sky Devils* film, and more footage is known to have been used in at least six other motion pictures.

Since the filming allowed much spare time for the pilots, many found Hollywood a place for fun and frolic. Roscoe, never one to sit around when he could be flying or negotiating a publicity stunt for pay, was attracted to the movie stars. He and Carline lived in the Hotel Bonnie

Brier on Hollywood Boulevard in the heart of the movie colony. Fun-loving and always a center of attention wherever he went, he had a new uniform made similar to the old one. He ordered new cavalry twill britches from the Cincinnati Regalia Company, a new powder blue tunic, a "Pershing" cap embroidered in red silk and gold bullion, and a Sam Browne belt for a total of $110. He had a jeweler design a pair of wings studded with thirty diamonds ("worth four or five thousand dollars") bracketing the initial "T" with a superimposed, intertwined "R." In the air he flew with a gold-and-crimson helmet with powder puffs stuffed into the ears to deaden the engine noise. On the ground he switched to a blue officer's cap. Whenever he was razzed for his ostentatiousness, he just smiled and said, "At least they're talking about me." He had no intention of changing his dress or appearance.

To supplement the income from Hughes, he gave flying lessons in a borrowed plane to Ben Lyon, his wife, Bebe Daniels, and several other Hollywood stars. He gave sightseeing flights to others, like comedian Joe E. Brown and actors Fred MacMurray and Clark Gable, who enjoyed their first flying experience. Each flight was designed to focus media attention on the stars, their studios, and Roscoe.

Roscoe became fast friends with Wallace Beery, one of the few major actors who was already an accomplished pilot. Beery, who played rough-neck comic parts, owned a Bellanca and kept it in the hangar along with Roscoe's plane. Beery wanted the engine overhauled one day and the mechanic had the cylinders out to grind the valves. A Santa Ana storm began to blow, filling the air with sand and debris. Roscoe happened to walk by and saw the engine with the cylinder ports open and unprotected from the sand and dust. He found the mechanic and, shouting mad, ordered him to get the engine covered up and the ports stuffed with rags. The mechanic knew it wasn't Roscoe's plane but Turner's size and commanding voice could not be ignored. Roscoe told him he would never work on an engine of *his* and he "had better damned sure get Beery's covered up."

Beery taught Roscoe a lesson about the teenage kids who always pursued Beery for autographs when he came to the airport. Roscoe asked him, "Wally, doesn't it bother you to have to stop and sign things for those kids?" Beery replied, "Sure, Roscoe, but don't ever turn those kids away. You can ignore the old folks sometimes but you always gotta take care of the little kids." From that time on, Roscoe did. In later years, he appealed to their sense of adventure in a number of radio programs. He was an avid supporter of the Boy Scouts, other youth organizations, and the Civil Air Patrol.

Whenever he was anywhere near the movie stars, studio photographers took photos that were given to the news media. Leading actors like Edward G. Robinson, Robert Montgomery, Joe E. Brown, Clark Gable, Eddie Cantor, and James Cagney, as well as glamorous actresses like Miriam Hopkins, Mary Pickford, Carole Lombard, and Constance Bennett, were pleased to have their photos taken with the ever-smiling Roscoe wearing his uniform. It enhanced their image to be associating with him, and he certainly didn't object, because it "was good for business."

Gregarious almost to a fault, Roscoe attracted movie executives, politicians, and prominent Californians who engaged him for flights to popular vacation spots in Mexico, northern California, and Nevada. He is credited with creating the Aerial Police in Los Angeles as a part of the County Sheriff's forces, believed to be the first in the country.

As one friend commented, "Roscoe couldn't move without being front page news. He meant it to be that way." Elinor Smith, a racing pilot of the 1920s, confirmed this in her memoirs when describing the day she arrived at the Metropolitan Airport in Van Nuys, California:

> We had just entered the hangar when the noisy blasting of an automobile horn and the high-pitched squeal of protesting brakes heralded the arrival of Roscoe Turner, an old friend from Roosevelt Field. As flamboyant a pilot as ever graced a cockpit, Roscoe ranked with the best.
>
> Roscoe believed firmly in the value of self-advertising and no one within a five-mile radius was ever unaware of his presence. If he wasn't roaring in over your head in an ear-shattering power dive, his personal attire was guaranteed to rivet audience attention and stop traffic in the middle of Sunset Boulevard. Today he was tastefully turned out in a sky blue tunic and matching overseas cap, each heavily embroidered with gold wings in varying sizes. Creamy whipcord trousers, enhanced by a red stripe edged in gold that started under his armpits and continued down to boot tops, drew attention to the highly-polished riding boots and snappy Sam

Browne belt that lent a military flair to his ensemble. His meticulously-waxed mustache, deep tan, and flashing white teeth provided the correct finishing touches to this vision of male comeliness.[12]

Roscoe developed an increasing fondness for using the telephone and sending telegrams at this time. When he landed anywhere, he would head for the nearest telephone and call someone he had been thinking about during a flight. When he called home and his wife read the mail to him, he would often reply immediately to the sender by telegram. His sister and friends in Corinth remember him sending telegrams to them at a time no one else in town ever received any except when a relative or close friend died.

On a clear summer morning in 1928, a group of aviation dignitaries was having a breakfast at the Los Angeles Breakfast Club. Someone suggested that Roscoe and Ben Lyon fly over the hotel and drop some flowers for the ladies attending. They borrowed a Ryan monoplane, similar to the one that Lindbergh had flown to Paris. After making a second pass, the engine quit from lack of fuel. Roscoe crash-landed in the Los Angeles River. Neither he nor Lyon was injured and the plane received only minor damage.

When Capt. Walter Perkins, chief of the Aeronautics Branch of the Department of Commerce in Washington, heard about the crash, he instructed Roscoe to report how the accident happened. Roscoe replied:

> On the morning of Friday, July the 13th, I was flying the Sikorsky S-29 about an hour and half in a movie production for the Caddo Co. When I landed I immediately stepped into the Ryan belonging to Roy Wilson with Ben Lyon as a passenger with some flowers to be dropped over the Breakfast Club honoring the pilots of the National Reliability Tour. I turned on the gas above and below but Roy Wilson tells me that it required six turns of the lower valve to get a full flow of gas from the main tank but we left the field near Van Nuys with motor working nicely.
>
> We flew down the Los Angeles River to the Breakfast Club and dropped one bunch of flowers and were circling to drop the second bunch when the motor cut out which sounded to me like a magneto or ignition failure but I cannot say whether it was gas or ignition. When the motor stopped, I set my glide for the river bed on which I could have made a

safe landing but there happened to be water in it softening the ground and on landing I turned over but neither I nor my passenger was hurt.[13]

The crash gave Roscoe added publicity in the local press, but he never heard any more about it from Washington. Considered a hero for being able to bring the plane down without much damage to the plane or injury to anyone, Roscoe shrugged off the accident casually as not worth further mention.

Roscoe and Carline were absorbed into the Hollywood scene and made friends everywhere they went. Happy-go-lucky and jovial in public, Roscoe was well-liked by the motion picture actors and executives. They not only wanted him to fly them somewhere and wait, they wanted him to accompany them while they visited or discussed business. He made so many friends in the press in Los Angeles that he couldn't move without being front-page news.

Roscoe fully intended to return to Richmond at some time during 1928 to carry out his plans to build a better airport and continue to promote some kind of airline operation along the East coast. It is not clear what arrangements he had made to regain control of his business, but he had heard that things were not going well. In a letter to a friend, he confided that he was so busy that "I can't even get a vacation to come back and straighten things in my business there which has been wrecked by my double-crossing associates whom I left in charge."[14]

Roscoe was informed by letter from the Department of Commerce that his Transport Pilot License had expired in April but the notification, forwarded from Richmond, didn't reach him until the end of May. He promptly took a physical exam and wrote to Major Clarence Young, head of the Aeronautics Branch of the Department of Commerce. Chafing at the government interference with his life, he replied that "it would be appreciated if you would set me straight as I am attempting a new world's endurance record in about ten days as my new plane will be ready next week."[15]

Young replied that he could not renew the license because Roscoe had not submitted an affidavit showing his flying time for the previous sixty days as required by new Air Commerce Regulations. He was ordered to return his license immediately. Anxious to proceed with his

plans, Roscoe contacted some of his friends in Washington who inter-
ceded on his behalf. Furious with the new red tape that was enveloping
aviation, he apparently continued to fly even though the license was not
officially renewed until later.

Roscoe visited all the local plane manufacturers frequently and tried
to borrow money for a new airplane so that he could pursue his quest
for profitable ventures as well as enhance his lifestyle to that which he
envied and saw all around him. The only way to do this was to keep flying for pay in any way that he could devise.

Roscoe had become infatuated with the Lockheed aircraft being produced and on the drawing boards during his visits to the plant while
filming *Hell's Angels*. He made many visits to the factory to watch them
being built. Of sleek design and powered by the latest engines, they represented speed to him and, as he said many times over the years, "speed
was the only excuse for an airplane." It was an era of record-setting and
he wanted to be a part of it. It was the most glamorous epoch in aviation with many air races conveying the excitement of the era. The focus
on speed was contagious and captivated those willing to risk everything
to be the fastest to span the distance between two points or chase around
pylons.

After *Hell's Angels* was filmed, he wanted to go to New York to drum
up some business but couldn't afford the $400 plane fare. He asked the
Lockheed factory if they by any chance had a plane going east that he
could ride in as a passenger. They said they had a plane to be delivered
there but had no pilot. They would pay expenses both ways if he would
deliver it. Roscoe recalled:

> I had never flown a Lockheed and they were so much faster than any-
> thing else in the country that I was just a little bit afraid of it. A friend of
> mine came out from New York to have his plane overhauled at the fac-
> tory and told me his Lockheed was so easy to fly that it was much easier
> than pushing little ducks in the water.
>
> He took me for a hop in his ship and I liked the performance but since
> there were no dual controls I couldn't very well fly it. So we landed and
> I took the ship up myself. I didn't have any trouble flying it but had a
> tough time getting it back into the field [because it landed so fast]. I
> started across the continent with some sand bags strapped to the back

seat to keep it from turning over in soft fields. It was my first transcontinental flight alone.

The farther I progressed, the better I liked the plane so I decided to drop off my course a bit and go by my home town and show them a real airplane. They didn't have a satisfactory landing field yet but I knew of a few hay fields I could land in. Being a farmer myself, I knew at that time of the year the hay would be off the fields. But I didn't count on it raining and making the ground soft and it had done just that.

I didn't turn over but I had to take down a few fences and push the plane for a mile and a half to a cow pasture. Then we had to cut down some trees and level off a runway. I just missed cracking up.[16]

Typical of a newsmaking, profitable enterprise was flying big-spending speculators over the California mountains on "ore inspection" flights while they looked for possible mineral deposits. Flying with G. Ray Boggs, a Nevada mining operator, Roscoe would go hedgehopping through the countryside looking for signs of possible claims. When they found a potential area, Boggs would sketch a map of it, file a claim and go back later with a mule pack train to check the area further.

Aviation record-setting was the rule in the late 1920s. One of those was an aircraft endurance record of 65 hours, 26 minutes, then held by German pilots. Roscoe persuaded Shell Oil Company to lend him a Timm biplane, which he named "Golden Shell," for an attempt to set a new one. With William Stapp as copilot, Roscoe stayed airborne for more than a day but had to make a forced landing in the mountains between Oakland and Glendale because of engine trouble. He made several attempts afterward but never did set a new endurance record.

He also flew several parachutists aloft who wanted to set altitude jump records. One of them was Bert White, a nationally known parachutist, who wanted to break the altitude record for a parachute jump, which was then 24,402 feet. Flying a Lockheed Air Express and using oxygen, they climbed to more than 24,000 feet, where the temperature dropped below zero. It was not high enough to set a new record, but the attempt kept Roscoe in the public limelight.

In the spring of 1929, Roscoe became interested in a firm that proposed to make flying safer by installing parachutes on aircraft so that when a plane had engine failure, it could be lowered safely and softly to the ground without injury to passengers or damage to the plane. Several experiments had been tried previously at Englewood and Oakland, California, and by the U.S. Army Air Corps but without appreciable success.

The Russell Parachute Company of San Diego believed it had the answer with 50-, 60-, and 70-foot parachutes and asked Roscoe to pilot the aircraft for an experiment with the 60-foot type. Roscoe was named an officer in the company and agreed to test a 60-foot Russell "Valve" type parachute on April 14, 1929, using a Thunderbird single-engine biplane weighing 2,400 lbs. The chute was concealed in the center section of the upper wing and was catapulted into the air by means of six coil springs with a mechanical release for the door, which fitted over the packed parachute.

After reaching 5,000 ft. over Santa Ana, California, Roscoe turned the engine off and pulled a lever that released the chute from the upper wing. He felt a violent jerk and the ship was hauled "backwards like a toy, to swing once or twice before beginning a gentle descent," as he described it. He dropped to a hard landing in a farmer's field narrowly missing trees and a power line. Although Roscoe was not hurt, the plane suffered a smashed landing gear and splintered propeller.

The drop took approximately five minutes and was witnessed by the press and newsreel cameramen in an accompanying plane. Replying to an inquiry about the parachute, the company president was confident that

> the large parachute will come into general use as a safety appliance in connection with small aircraft especially, and that the larger parachute will also eventually be used in connection with very large airliners where the parachute will be attached to a releaseable cabin in which the passengers or valuable freight is located. This releaseable cabin can be raised by the pilot in an emergency, thereby causing the large parachute to withdraw from the rest of the airplane and landed without injury to passengers or freight. The pilot, then being in a position to either land his ship, freed from a heavy load, or save himself with a personal parachute.[17]

The idea never caught on and Roscoe severed his connections with the parachute company claiming he had been "hooked" when he did not receive the agreed sum for his services. The aviation press considered Roscoe's parachute drop just one more of his bids for attention and thereafter referred to it as the "parachute stunt."

Aviation historians agree that Lindbergh's epochal flight to Paris in 1927 awakened national and world interest in aviation as nothing had before. If a lone pilot could fly nonstop from New York to Paris, surely airplanes were safe enough for people to fly in as paying passengers.

In the mid-1920s, a race began to set up passenger airline operations as a natural follow-on to flying the mail, which had been pioneered by the U.S. Post Office Department. The year 1928 was described by the U.S. Aeronautical Chamber of Commerce as one of "phenomenal expansion" for aviation. The airlines flew twice as many miles as the year before, tripled the poundage of mail they flew, and carried four times the number of passengers. An estimated 4,500 commercial planes were flying.

By the beginning of 1929, no fewer than forty-six airlines had attempted to offer service but only a handful survived after brief periods of operation. One of the first in California was Pickwick Airways, which began service between San Diego, Los Angeles, and San Francisco in March 1929 with a Bach Air Yacht ten-place plane.

Several businessmen from the Los Angeles area, including former Lockheed officials Ben S. Hunter and G. Ray Boggs, Roscoe's ore-hunting friend, pooled their resources to start Nevada Airlines, which began triweekly service between Los Angeles, Reno, and Las Vegas on April 15, 1929. The motivation for transport between these cities, besides the opportunity to gamble freely, was the liberal marriage and divorce laws of Nevada, which required only three days' advance notice for a marriage license and three months' residence to get a divorce.

Hunter and Boggs decided to purchase four Lockheed Vegas—fast five-passenger planes that would lend themselves easily to passenger service for the rich clientele of Hollywood. Roscoe was hired as chief pilot and operations manager for the fleet. He had given Bebe Daniels flying lessons, so he asked her to christen the first plane *Alimony Special*.

Roscoe was placed immediately in the forefront of publicity for the airline. He called it the "fastest airline in the world" because, at a 135-mph cruising speed, the Pratt & Whitney Wasp-powered monoplanes were the fastest passenger-carrying aircraft of that day. The flight from Los Angeles to Reno was just over three hours, compared to twenty-two hours by train. Shortly after the flights began, Bishop, California, and Tonopah, Nevada, were added "for the convenience of passengers and accommodation of sportsmen who wish to enter the high Sierras at this gateway point."[18]

Referred to by the press as "the line to freedom," the "liberty special," or the "matrimonial special," depending on a passenger's reason for a flight, the airline flourished for a short time chiefly because of Roscoe's flair for publicity. Although some reporters liked to refer to it as the "gin line," in promotion talks Roscoe called it the "the first high speed airline in the world." While other airlines were averaging about 90 mph for their flights, Roscoe said his Lockheeds averaged 141 mph. "Everyone laughed at me then and said it was impractical because of the limited carrying capacity of high speed airplanes," Roscoe said years later.

In an effort to plug Christmas as a vacation time in 1929, Roscoe advertised the "Santa Claus Special" in the *Glendale News Press* and flew such Hollywood luminaries as Loretta Young, Clark Gable, Joan Bennett, and Fred MacMurray to Reno for carefree weekends.

Writing in the Pratt & Whitney's company magazine, Roscoe colorfully explained how travel in the mountainous areas of Nevada had developed:

> Nevadans could hardly be expected to turn to air travel without a certain amount of resistance. Their transportation had been very slow until airplanes arrived. Speed has increased in two decades from two miles an hour to 135.
>
> When the now-historical mining town of Tonopah appeared on the horizon of mining investments, the best travel that could be extracted from a burro with the aid of a club was 2 mph. A prospector not impeded with a burro could cover three miles an hour. Later, a stage coach, drawn by three animated horses, could annihilate distance at the rate of eight miles an hour. A light mail coach might achieve a speed of 10 miles each hour.
>
> Then the automobile. Early benzine chariots, wobbling and entirely uncertain, under the best conditions could cover 100 miles in a single day. Now the planes. . . .[19]

Emphasizing the safety of the operation, Roscoe explained that his mechanics, R. O. Pecht and Omar Rhuble, and their assistants had extensive experience with the Wasp engine and had full responsibility for their maintenance. "This has been accomplished through the simple psychological expedient of requiring all members of the mechanical staff to be ready to fly over the line without warning. None of these men will postpone work on an engine when it should be done today. He does not care to fly knowing some worn part or maladjustment may bring him down on a mountain peak!"[20]

The schedule for the operation required four pilots and the aircraft to fly a total of about 1,000 miles per day. The one-way fare from Los Angeles to Reno was $60.00; the round-trip fare, $110.00. Pilots were paid $75 every two weeks plus 7 cents per mile. Mechanics earned $100 and helpers $70 every two weeks.

On August 19–20, 1928, Art Goebel and his mechanic, Harry Tucker, crossed the continent in a Vega named *Yankee Doodle* in 19 hours, 58 minutes, marking the first time a commercial plane had flown coast-to-coast nonstop. In February 1929 Capt. Frank Hawks, superintendent of aviation for the Texas Company (Texaco), with mechanic Oscar Grubb, started a year of record-breaking flights in a Lockheed Air Express with a west-east nonstop flight of 18 hours, 21 minutes, 59 seconds. Storms had forced them to fly almost the entire distance above a floor of clouds. Flying from 10,000 to 15,000 feet most of the way, it was a supreme test of Hawks' endurance and flying skills.

Not satisfied with the west-east record, on June 27 Hawks took off from Roosevelt Field, Long Island, on a solo nonstop flight to Los Angeles. He landed on the west coast 19 hours, 10 minutes, 32 seconds later. Turning his plane over to a ground crew, he rested for a few hours and returned to the field to take off for New York on another nonstop flight to break his own mark and set a record for the return trip. He arrived to a floodlit Roosevelt Field 17 hours, 38 minutes, 16 seconds later.

Roscoe was sure he could beat that record. Using a Nevada Airlines Vega named *Sirius*—outfitted with a new NACA cowling, one of the first three in the country to be installed on a commercial plane, plus a pair of the earliest style of streamlined wheel pants—he made a crossing between Metropolitan Airport in Los Angeles and Roosevelt Field on August 21, 1929. With him were Harold Gatty, later Wiley Post's navigator on the first globe-circling flight; Capt. Fred Trosper of the Los Angeles Police Department; D. R. Lane, a public relations executive; and one of the airline's mechanics. The flying time was 19 hours, 35 minutes.

After negotiating with Shell Oil to furnish the gas and oil for the flight, Roscoe called the plane *Flying Shell*. In an unsigned memo to the six airports where Roscoe might be stopping, depending on the weather, Shell notified its distributors that "every second counts" during the refueling process. The memo added, "We have no hesitation in saying that it is our belief that the name 'Flying Shell' and the two 24-inch Shell decalcomanias on the sides of the plane will give us no small amount of good publicity, which, of course, is quite apart from that which will accrue from the newspapers."[21]

With four stops on his return flight to Los Angeles, he completed the trip in 23 hours, 59 minutes, 42 seconds, after a battle with fog and storms. Roscoe hadn't broken either record, but it was the first time a plane carrying passengers in addition to pilot and mechanic had crossed the United States in less than 24 hours each way. It had not been an easy trip either way. Fighting fog, rain, and low clouds eastbound, he made stops at Albuquerque, Tulsa, Louisville and Cincinnati. On the westbound trip he made stops at the same intermediate points but was forced to land at Tulare, California, where he was grounded for three hours because of fog.

For good luck, Roscoe had carried a rabbit's foot, a small teddy bear, and a live turtle on the flights. A likeness of the turtle, that belied the plane's speed, was painted on the tail of the Lockheed. "I tried to get a more impressive cargo," Roscoe joked before an audience, "but no one else would ride with me on such an undertaking. Of course, those boys who did go, either didn't know what a chance they were taking by riding with me, or they didn't care."

Typically, Roscoe promptly announced that he had plans to capitalize on his feat. He told the press that he planned to establish "an aerial pony express"—a transcontinental service for freight and "occasional passengers" with three stops each way. "Thus a package leaving New York at the end of a day's journey would have traveled in four planes piloted by four different pilots and reached the Pacific Coast in less than 24 hours. He has not yet announced his exact route or the cities where he will maintain stations."[22]

Roscoe set up an ambitious schedule that called for flights of 17 hours eastbound and 19 hours on the return. He estimated that nine planes would be needed, plus six spare motors and three automobiles. Pilot pay would be $150 per month, plus 10 cents per mile flown. Mechanics would earn $200 per month. Each aircraft would be equipped with "radio phones, all the latest type of instruments, and an airplane parachute in upper wing to give absolute safety to airplane and cargo."[23]

Although the plans never materialized, it was good publicity for Nevada Airlines. During this period, while exploiting every possible approach to bolster support for the airline, Roscoe contacted Nevada lieutenant governor James G. Scrugham and offered him an orientation flight. In August 1929, with Scrugham and a state parks commissioner aboard, Roscoe made the first official flight between Las Vegas and Reno. It was not an uneventful flight. The Vega developed engine trouble after leaving Las Vegas and Roscoe made an emergency landing on a gravel road near Beatty. Roscoe and a mechanic made the necessary repairs to the engine and continued nonchalantly to Reno.

Nevada Airlines advertised that it had never had a forced landing, so evidently the unscheduled landing with the state's lieutenant governor was not counted. There was one incident that did make the newspapers, however, and that was the time an irate woman chased her husband into the cabin of the Vega beating him on the head with an umbrella. She was angry at him for gambling with their life savings at one of the casinos.

The airline operated until February 1930 and ceased operations because the Vegas could not make money except at high fares. Even trying to operate as an on-call charter company, there were not enough short-notice demands to make a profit. Roscoe, always optimistic about the future of the airlines as an industry, however, valued the experience. It was not to be his last venture in the airline business.

Roscoe continued to fly passengers locally in the Los Angeles area and occasionally flew for the movies. He was employed as an extra in *Dawn Patrol*, starring Richard Barthelmess and Douglas Fairbanks, Jr.

On January 2, 1930, one of the movie colony's most promising new directors, Kenneth Hawks, and nine others were killed in a mid-air collision of two Stinsons with cameramen aboard. The pilots were Ross Cook and Hallock Rouse. In accordance with the script, Roscoe was flying ahead of them in a Lockheed Air Express from which Jacob Triebwasser, a stuntman, was to jump and be filmed from the two camera planes. Roscoe told reporters:

> We took off about 3:20 from Clover Field. We were headed for a rendezvous off Point San Vincente. I was flying in the lead, carrying Triebwasser, Fred White and Fred Osborne. The other two ships were flying behind me and both to one side. They were to fly low over some speed boats that were waiting to catch the scene and pick up the 'chute man; then I was to turn back and Triebwasser was to leap out at a certain point in relation to the other two ships. I was still flying ahead of the other ships, when one of my passengers shouted, "They've hit!"
>
> I didn't see the actual collision. I turned back as soon as I could. The two planes were down on the water, locked together and all on fire. Nobody could have lived in that crash. They probably were dead before the planes struck the water.[24]

Roscoe was deeply affected by the accident. He and Kenneth Hawks had become close friends and he also knew the other two pilots very well. Roscoe wept bitterly when he stumbled from his plane.

Nevada governor Fred R. Balzar became an aviation enthusiast and made many trips with Roscoe during his term in office. In 1929 he appointed Roscoe as an aide-de-camp on his personal staff with the rank of lieutenant colonel. The tongue-in-cheek letter appointing him stated: "As a Lieutenant Colonel, he will be accorded the privilege of riding a horse instead of an airplane, can wear a sabre and plenty of gold braid but must buy his own uniform."

Not to be outdone, Governor James Rolph, Jr., of California also appointed Roscoe to his staff with the rank of colonel in August 1931. Rolph sent Roscoe a humorous telegram announcing the appointment: "I hereby appoint you member of Governor's staff of California. Now put on all the dog you want to and make yourself more picturesque than Emperor Norton of old, famous in California history. Three cheers for the flying gallant handsome colonel of the governor's staff of California. Congratulations."[25]

In early 1932 Roscoe flew Balzar and Rolph to a Republican governors' conference in Richmond, Virginia, and then to Washington for a second governors' conference. When visiting the White House, they asked Roscoe to present President Herbert Hoover with a heavy gold-plated chest, which, when opened, showed a replica of San Francisco and the Golden Gate bay area.

Roscoe's commission on the Nevada governor's staff was effective from August 25, 1929, to March 1934. It was at this time that Roscoe first began using the title of colonel. When Balzar went out of office, Roscoe was reappointed by his successor, Governor Griswold, on November 16, 1934. For many years afterward, Roscoe signed his letters over the title, "Colonel, Governor's Staff, Nevada and California."[26]

Some writers have said that calling himself a colonel in all of his publicity was a farce and that he had never had *any* military service. When such a statement was made over a major broadcasting network, Roscoe brought suit against the network for an undisclosed amount; the case was settled out of court.

Roscoe's financial woes continued to pursue him wherever he went and he never gave up trying to sell advertisers on using his name and plane for publicity purposes. Delayed in Texas by fog and rain on one occasion, he sent a wire to an assistant in California to contact the General Tire dealer there, "and tell him to form some publicity for himself on his set of tires I have with me. He can say I am delivering them to him but I get them back."[27]

One particularly persistent creditor was the Johnson Airplane & Supply Company, Dayton, Ohio, to whom Roscoe owed $130 for aircraft supplies that he had bought in 1928. He paid $50 as soon as he was billed, but by April the next year, after his Sikorsky had crashed,

Roscoe pleaded that "you are not the only ones I owe. It will be impossible for me to pay anything on the account until I make other connections now and if my creditors do not give me time to pay off my debts, there will be nothing left for me to do but take bankruptcy, which I do not desire to do."[28] The company continued to remind Roscoe of the debt and when Nevada Airlines went broke, Roscoe told them he was out of work "but as soon as it is possible for me to do so, I will send you the amount of this bill."[29]

Bills and dun letters from creditors were always answered and Roscoe never tried to dodge payment. However, most of the time he could pay only a small amount of the total owed. When his car had piston rings installed in Los Angeles in 1929, Roscoe was not happy with the work and refused to pay a $15 balance. The debt was turned over to a lawyer and Roscoe was threatened with an attachment. He made two payments during the next eight months. When he had reduced the debt to $7, the owner of the company wanted a check by return mail or he said he would be compelled to place the remainder for collection. Roscoe paid $5, but did not pay the remaining $2 until mid-1930.

Money problems, many generated by "handshake deals" that were never put in writing, would follow Roscoe almost his entire life as he fought to remain an independent freelance pilot. He borrowed small amounts of money from friends but many of these debts were shrugged off later if they weren't paid. The wide publicity he generated often prompted creditors to write for their balances because they viewed him as a wealthy pilot who was clearly able to pay even the largest bills, since he obviously associated with the rich and famous. Others, glad to be associated with a man so popular, never mentioned the debts to him; if they did, he would pay as soon as he was reminded or explain why not. Most of the problems that developed could be traced to honest misunderstandings and poor record-keeping on both Roscoe's part and his creditors. It was a fault that many pilots had who survived the barnstorming days and lived by their wits while trying to make a precarious living. Roscoe, impatient with mundane business transactions on the ground, would rather fly and leave the paperwork to others. Bored and often short-tempered about financial matters, he seemed at ease and content only when flying.

Roscoe (*left*) and his brother Abe pause in their plowing behind the family mules at the Turner farm in Corinth, Miss. Roscoe was more interested in automobiles and motorcycles; the many hours spent doing farm chores convinced him that he never wanted to be a farmer. Photo courtesy of Mary Emma Whitaker.

Roscoe's birthplace near Corinth, where he was born on September 29, 1895. Photo courtesy of Mary Emma Whitaker.

Roscoe as a teenager before World War I. He completed tenth grade in the Corinth school and briefly attended a business college but was more interested in working on automobiles. He never received any more formal education. Photo courtesy of Mary Emma Whitaker.

Although Roscoe wanted to learn to fly after the United States entered World War I, he was refused because of a lack of a college education. Experienced as a mechanic, he enlisted in the medical corps as an ambulance driver in June 1917. Photo American Heritage Center, University of Wyoming.

Sans mustache, Roscoe poses for press photographers after he was nominated to be a copilot for French ace René Fonck, who planned to make a nonstop flight from New York to Paris in 1926. Doubting Fonck's competence, Roscoe backed out. Photo St. Louis Mercantile Library Association. Photo courtesy of Mary Emma Whitaker.

The Turner family c. 1927. (*Left to right*) William, Robert, Cass, Abe, Roscoe, Mrs. Turner, Mary Emma, Mr. Turner. Photo courtesy of Milton Sandy, Jr.

Lt. Harry J. Runser (*left*) and Roscoe pose beside their *Cloudland Express*, a British Avro that could carry two passengers in addition to the pilot. The pair put on air shows throughout the south and southeast from 1919 to 1921. Photo American Heritage Center, University of Wyoming.

Poster used by the Runser-Turner barnstorming team advertising their air show at the Memphis Fair Grounds in 1921. Roscoe wing-walked and parachuted. Runser climaxed the act with a crash into a flimsy building. This was filmed by Pathé News and later copied by other stunt pilots. Photo by C.V. Glines.

Roscoe and Carline, his first wife, were married while standing in the cockpit of a Curtiss Jenny on Roscoe's birthday, September 29, 1924. The minister stood on the wing and administered the vows. Photo courtesy of Mrs. E. F. Waits.

The diamond-studded gold wings designed with Roscoe's red "RT" logo in the center. The unique red-and-gold logo was used on stationery and calling cards for a number of business ventures. Photo courtesy of Madonna M. Turner.

Roscoe and Will Rogers before they departed from Richmond for Staunton, Va., in 1927. They landed thirty miles away because of a thunderstorm. Although Rogers had flown in a local flight before, this was his first cross-country flight. Photo American Heritage Center, University of Wyoming.

A closeup view of the twin-engine Sikorsky S-29-A undergoing maintenance. The pilot controlled the aircraft from the open cockpit in the aft fuselage. A mechanic was required to operate certain engine controls in the enclosed forward cabin. The plane could carry fourteen passengers. Photo American Heritage Center, University of Wyoming.

The S-29-A (*A* for America) was the first aircraft that Igor Sikorsky built in America. Roscoe was using it at this time to advertise Edgeworth Tobacco products while based in Richmond, Va. It was the first plane built in the United States that could fly on one engine. Photo courtesy of Madonna M. Turner.

Howard Hughes greets Roscoe upon his arrival at Burbank with the Sikorsky in 1928. Carline Turner, called the "navigatrix" by the press, is shown with helmet and goggles. (*Left to right*) Lucien Prival, Wallace Beery, Carline, Hughes, Roscoe, Greta Nissen, and John Darrow. Photo American Heritage Center, University of Wyoming.

The Sikorsky S-29-A, outfitted as a German "Gotha" bomber for *Hell's Angels*, being readied for towing. Only one S-29-A was ever built. Photo James R. Greenwood collection.

The entire group of *Hell's Angels* pilots pose beside Roscoe's Sikorsky "Gotha" in November 1928. Roscoe is standing in the rear row, at left. Photo James R. Greenwood collection.

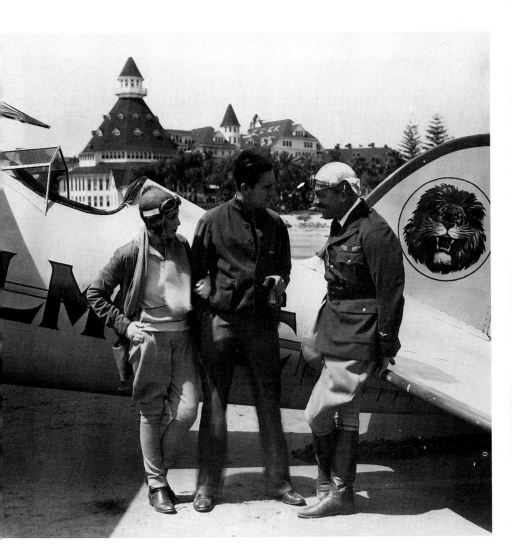

Movie stars liked Roscoe for his flamboyance and his piloting skills. He flew many of them from Hollywood to Mexico, Las Vegas, and Reno. Ben Lyon and his wife, Bebe Daniels, engaged Roscoe to pick them up at the famous Coronado Hotel, where Roscoe had landed the Lockheed Air Express on the beach. Photo American Heritage Center, University of Wyoming.

Cigar-smoking character actor Edward G. Robinson greets Roscoe, who was driving by in his 1929 Packard. Roscoe and Don Young, his mechanic, drove the Packard thousands of miles during the racing years. Photo American Heritage Center, University of Wyoming.

Actor Wallace Beery and Roscoe were good friends. Although Roscoe gave flying instructions to some Hollywood actors during that period, Beery was already a pilot and owned his own airplane. Photo James R. Greenwood collection.

Many of the pilots, mechanics, and planes used in Howard Hughes's *Hell's Angels* are arrayed for publicity shots with Roscoe's Sikorsky S-29-A as the centerpiece. Some of the planes were authentic World War I fighters and trainers; others were American planes painted to look like warplanes. Photo James R. Greenwood collection.

The inauguration of Nevada Airline's first flight from Reno to Los Angeles in April 1929 began with the smashing of a champagne bottle on the propeller of a Lockheed Vega by Judge George Bartlett of the National Aeronautic Association. Roscoe, general manager of flight operations, ducks as financial backers, movie stars, and airline officials look on. The Mississippi Valley Collection, John Willard Brister Library, Memphis State University. Press-Scimitar photo. Photo courtesy of Milton Sandy, Jr.

One of the Lockheed Vegas owned and operated by Nevada Airlines in 1929. Roscoe flew this one in the 1929 Thompson Cup race at Cleveland. He placed second in a closed-cabin race and third in a fifty-mile free-for-all race. Charles G. Mandrake Collection. Courtesy of Madonna M. Turner.

In 1929 Roscoe bought an interest in the Russell Parachute Co., manufacturer of parachutes designed to lower a disabled plane safely to the ground. Here he demonstrates the chute near Santa Ana, Calif. Roscoe was unhurt but the Thunderbird plane suffered a smashed landing gear and splintered propeller. Photo courtesy of Madonna M. Turner.

Roscoe holds a heavy gold-plated chest that was presented to President Herbert Hoover by Governor James Rolph, Jr., of California in 1932. The chest contains a replica of San Francisco and the Golden Gate bay area. (*Left to right*) Nevada governor Fred R. Balzar, Roscoe, President Hoover, and Governor Rolph. White House photo. Courtesy of Madonna M. Turner.

Al and Fred Key relax with Roscoe at the Peabody Hotel in Memphis while planning their stage appearance together at the Orpheum Theater. The Key brothers had just set a new world's endurance record. Mississippi Valley Collection, Mississippi State University Library. Photo courtesy of Michele Fagan.

While flying east to begin the 1936 Bendix race, the carburetor of the Wedell-Williams iced up and Roscoe crash-landed near an Indian reservation in New Mexico. The entire rear fuselage was destroyed up to the cockpit. A Zuni Indian guards the wreckage. Photo Charles G. Mandrake Collection. Courtesy of Madonna M. Turner.

This rebuilt Wedell-Williams was flown in the 1937 Bendix race after Roscoe had crashed it the year before. Roscoe lost the Bendix race by only 23 seconds and had to drop out of the Thompson race when his engine malfunctioned. Photo Charles G. Mandrake Collection. Courtesy of Madonna M. Turner.

The *Meteor*, shown being inspected by Roscoe, was designed to replace his Wedell-Williams. The original construction was begun by Lawrence Brown but was modified by Matty Laird. This photo shows the original straight-wing configuration as built by Brown. Charles G. Mandrake Collection. Photo Los Angeles Bureau, Wild World Photos. Courtesy of Madonna M. Turner.

Gilmore as a cub went on many flights with Roscoe in the enclosed cabin of the
Lockheed Air Express. In rough air, he would often try to climb from the cabin
into Roscoe's lap in the open cockpit. Photo B. F. Parrish and Son. Courtesy
Madonna M. Turner.

5

FLYING WITH GILMORE

Roscoe's double transcontinental flight of 1929 in the Lockheed Vega was an exhilarating experience and convinced him that the Lockheed designs were synonymous with speed and could be a ticket to the fame and fortune he sought. He decided to try to obtain a plane of his own and a sponsor so he could enter the 1929 Cleveland Air Races.

Roscoe had his eye on a Lockheed Air Express, a model that followed the Vega. Whereas the Vega's wing was attached to the fuselage, the Air Express had a parasol wing that sat about a foot away from the fuselage on cabane struts. Some considered it a rough flying airplane, one in which Herb Fahy, a Lockheed test pilot, in 1929 had tried and failed to beat Frank Hawks's transcontinental record. An open cockpit plane with a small enclosed cabin to accommodate four passengers, it was one of the first to use an engine cowling designed by the National Advisory Committee for Aeronautics (NACA) to help cool the engine and teardrop wheel pants designed to cut down on wind resistance, plus an experimental Pratt & Whitney Hornet engine.

The plane Roscoe wanted had been sold to the General Tire & Rubber Company, which planned to enter it in the National Air Races of 1929. However, the company could not find a competent pilot to fly it. At this time, it was the custom of the major oil companies to hire "name" pilots and have them advertise their products at air shows and races by setting records and otherwise getting their respective companies in the news in a favorable way. Among them were Jimmy Mattern at Pure Oil; Frank Hawks at Texaco; Eddie Aldrin at Standard Oil; Billy Parker at Phillips; and Al Williams at Gulf. Jimmy Doolittle resigned his regular Army commission in early 1930 and was hired by Shell Oil.

Ever alert to promotional possibilities for people and corporations that might back him, Roscoe called on Earl R. Gilmore, president of California-based Gilmore Oil Company, and persuaded him to buy the Air Express from General Tire at a bargain price of $15,000 so that Roscoe could advertise Gilmore's then-famous Red Lion petroleum products by making record flights. Gilmore was intrigued by Roscoe's flair for publicity and his record-setting efforts and put him on the payroll. In addition to whatever events or record attempts Roscoe wanted to make, the plane was also to be a flying test bed for the company's lubricating oils, fuels, and safety devices.

The company's trademark was a lion's head, which Roscoe had painted on the Vega's tail and wheel pants. Painted cream, with red and gold trim, the Air Express soon became a familiar sight at airports and public events in the west. The plane was christened the *Gilmore Lion* by movie starlet Carlotta Miles at the Los Angeles Metropolitan Airport before a crowd of five thousand people.

It was a happy coup for Roscoe because he was given unlimited use of a genuinely fast plane capable of setting records. Roscoe had a 450-hp Pratt & Whitney Wasp engine installed in place of a Hornet because of its proven reliability.

A newly designed NACA engine cowling was placed around the engine, which had its problems cooling the cylinders. The oil became too hot and the passengers roasted inside the cabin, as did the pilot flying in the open cockpit behind them. When the passengers tried to open the windows to cool off, the temperature rose to more than 100 degrees inside because the hot air from the engine hugged the fuselage and entered the open window. The solution was to pipe the air away from the cabin and out of the slipstream for passenger comfort. The cylinders were cooled by placing baffles between them and adding more radiator surface to cool the oil. "Of course, the pilot didn't matter in those days," Roscoe said. "We just let him cook. It wasn't until later that the comfort of the pilot was given much consideration."[1]

The Air Express was licensed to carry 52 gallons of fuel and 8 gallons of oil, but additional tanks were installed to carry about 20 more gallons of gas and 18 gallons of oil. It was certified to carry 18 pounds of luggage; however, Roscoe and Don Young, his mechanic, flew everywhere with about 600 pounds of luggage and tools; sometimes a full load of passengers was crammed in. According to Young, "the Civil Aeronautics Authority (CAA) inspectors knew that Roscoe was not carrying the load the plane was certified for but turned their backs and never questioned him."[2]

Air racing had become a popular sport in the United States by the late 1920s. It began in 1909 when wealthy newspaperman James Gordon Bennett established the first series of international closed-course air races, one of which was won by Glenn Curtiss in a biplane of his own design powered by a 50-hp engine. His average speed over the 6.2-mile course was 47.7 mph.

An air meet was held at Belmont, New York, in 1910, but there were no more races of consequence in the United States until after World War I, when Ralph Pulitzer, another wealthy newspaperman, sponsored a closed-course race held at Mitchel Field, Long Island, in November 1920. Prizes were Liberty Bonds in the amounts of $1,500, $750, and $500 for first, second and third places. Mechanics on each of the winning planes received Liberty Bonds valued at $300, $150 and $100. Sixty-five aircraft were entered; forty-four finished. It was won by Army Lt. Corliss C. Moseley flying a Verville VCP-R, first in a series of designs produced by Alfred Verville. Moseley's average speed was 156.5 mph.

Between then and 1925, there were five more Pulitzer races. The winning average speeds rose from Moseley's 156.5 mph to 248.9 mph in a Curtiss R3C-1 flown by Army Lt. Cyrus Bettis. Although each Pulitzer race was just one contest in a week-long show with as many as thirty events, they provided a focus on aviation for the speed-hungry public. Ever-greater speed was the paramount objective and encouraged the air arms of the Army and Navy and the manufacturers of military planes to strive to outdo one another in the various competitions. There were also numerous backyard mechanics who fashioned their own planes and entered them in the races in their respective aircraft weight and engine classifications.

Coinciding with the end of the Pulitzer races in 1925 was the founding of the National Aeronautic Association (NAA), which was affiliated with the Fédération Aeronautique Internationale (FAI), the international organization devoted to encouraging aerial record-setting and timing all attempts at records to ensure fairness and accuracy. In 1926 the first National Air Races (NAR) under the auspices of the NAA were held in Philadelphia. The races were heralded as a tribute to the business-like management by NAA of the many flying events. Spokane was the scene for the 1927 NAR; Los Angeles was the host city in 1928. A reported 100,000 people showed up for the 1928 events, in which three hundred entries had been filed.

The success of the races under NAA auspices led to the dedication of a group of businessmen in Cleveland to make their city the permanent home for the National Air Races. Beginning in 1929, the official national races and most later ones were held there. One of the features of the 1929 races was the nonstop cross-country derby from Los Angeles to Cleveland. Later known as the Bendix Trophy Race, it became one of the two prestige races. Roscoe entered the 1929 race with high hopes.

On October 31, Roscoe departed Los Angeles in the Lockheed Air Express with four passengers in the nonstop race to Cleveland. Two Lockheed Vegas streaked ahead of him to earn first and second places. Henry J. Brown garnered the first prize of $5,000 flying a Hornet-powered ship and spanned the distance in 13 hours, 15 minutes, 7 seconds. However, it was a miracle that he had won because about five miles from the Cleveland Airport, the engine sputtered and, out of gas, Brown made a straight-in approach to a spectacular dead-stick landing in front of the grandstand. Lee Schoenhair, flying a Wasp-powered Lockheed, placed second with an elapsed time of 13 hours, 51 minutes, 10.8 seconds, to win $2,000.

Roscoe, delayed by having to circumnavigate severe late afternoon thunderstorms over Missouri, placed third. He was disqualified from receiving any prize money because he arrived an hour and a half after the deadline of 6 P.M. However, he received more news mention than Brown and Schoenhair. Resplendent in his uniform, he was photographed as if he had won. One magazine writer commented: "A pilot with enough nerve to wear that uniform is bound to come in first eventually."

Disappointed but undismayed, Roscoe entered the Air Express in one of the closed-course races for open cockpit planes powered with engines of not more than 800 cubic inches piston displacement. He placed second over the 150-mile course to R. W. Cantwell, flying a Lockheed Wasp-powered Vega. Cantwell won $675 with an average speed of 152.7 mph; Roscoe's speed of 150.15 mph earned him a prize of $375. It was the first money award for racing he ever received. He was determined it would not be his last.

Another of the featured events was a "free-for-all" race of 50 miles around five pylons for the Thompson Cup, sponsored by the Thompson Products Company of Cleveland, manufacturers of aircraft components. Any type of plane could compete, military or civilian. The race was made from a racing start with all planes lined up waiting for the "go" signal. Roscoe later described how he felt about those racing starts: "I was so nervous that when the starter held up five fingers-indicating five minutes to go—my feet were shaking so I couldn't keep them on the rudder pedals. But by the time the starter got down to two fingers, I was as calm as a mill pond. When he fired his gun I was on my way. When those things happen to you it scares you but you can't afford to let them make you lose your head."[3]

What made the 1929 Thompson Cup race memorable was that it was won by Doug Davis flying a commercially made Travel Air Model R. He competed against Army Air Corps and Navy pilots flying the latest fighters and beat them all. Davis, flying the first of a line of Travel Air "Mystery Ships" that won many subsequent races, had a winning speed of 194.9 mph, which was nearly 50 mph faster than the average of the fighters. He pocketed $750 for the win.

Second place and $450 went to Army Lt. R. G. Breene flying a Curtiss P-3A pursuit ship; his speed was 186.84 mph. Roscoe, flying his Wasp-powered Vega, placed third with a speed of 163.44 mph to win $300. "Of course," Roscoe told the press years later, "I was just learning and I believed that better times were yet to come."

This free-for-all race for the Thompson Cup was an event that shocked the military services, then in the postwar doldrums because of lack of appropriations for aircraft research and development. Up to this time, the speed kings were the military pilots who had dominated the races flying high-speed pursuit models. The significance of these winning times was that aircraft manufactured by commercial plane builders and backyard mechanics had outflown some of the fastest planes the Army or Navy had in their inventories. It was a shock that was not overcome for almost a decade. Doug Davis's win was a significant moment in aviation history for the builders of civilian aircraft.

The publicity and public attention directed to the free-for-all speed contest encouraged Charles E. Thompson, president of Thompson Products, to sponsor a similar feature event beginning in 1930. The large, heavy Thompson Trophy he had designed was to be presented "to offer inspiration and initiative to the development of aeronautics in general, and faster land planes immediately adaptable to commercial and military use in particular."

It was to be a closed-course race of at least 100 miles with the winner garnering a $5,000 purse. There were no limitations on fuels, superchargers, or numbers or types of engines, and the competition would be open to civilian and military aircraft. Prize increases were promised for future years. The first race for the Thompson Trophy was held in September 1930 as part of the National Air Race program at the Curtiss-Reynolds Airport near Chicago. The course distance was only five miles around the pylons and the seven competing planes took off at 10-second intervals.

As Roger Huntington points out in his excellent book, *Thompson Trophy Races*,

> the first starter was almost in sight around the course before the last one took off. The spectators were thoroughly confused as to which plane was ahead, which planes were racing for second and third and so on. It was mostly a parade of fast planes making a lot of noise. These conditions were accepted in the more formal, military-dominated Pulitzer and

Schneider races of the twenties. The savvy Thompson promoters quickly saw there was no future for this new form of amateur pylon racing unless the spectators could identify closely with individual planes and pilots and follow their progress in a race.

The infamous racehorse start and the wild scramble around the first pylon were the gimmicks that took care of all this in later years. It was a bold new idea in the early thirties credited to NAR promoter Cliff Henderson, and was inaugurated at the 1931 races in Cleveland. It literally saved the sport."[4]

For the 1930 National Air Races held in Chicago, Roscoe entered his Lockheed Express in the Los Angeles-to-Chicago derby in competition with Wiley Post, Art Goebel, Bill Brock, and Lee Schoenhair, all flying Wasp-powered Lockheeds. Wiley Post won the $7,500 prize with Goebel and Schoenhair respectively finishing in the money. Post had made the flight in 9 hours, 9 minutes, 4 seconds. Brock was fourth and Roscoe last; all five completed the run within a 40-minute elapsed time span. The Lockheed factory at Burbank promptly adopted the slogan, "It takes a Lockheed to beat a Lockheed."

After the Los Angeles to Chicago race, Vincent Bendix, head of the Bendix Corporation, agreed to put up $15,000 cash, to be matched by the Cleveland Air Race Committee, for the first annual Bendix Trophy Race, nonstop from Los Angeles to Cleveland in the fall of 1931. The Bendix race would become a classic contest, along with the Thompson Trophy race, with enough of a cash incentive to make it worthwhile for plane designers and builders to gamble on their ideas, talents, and skills. Unlike the speed races around the pylons, the Bendix would require skillful flight planning and navigation for the pilots and the most efficient aircraft and engine designs that the aviation industry could muster.

The 1930 Thompson Trophy Race, which Roscoe chose not to enter, was won by Charles W. "Speed" Holman flying the Laird Speedwing *Solution* at an average speed of 201.9 mph. This plane was the only biplane ever to win the Thompson Trophy. Jimmy Haislip placed second in his Travel Air Model R at 199.8 mph, followed by Ben Howard, flying a tiny 90-hp homemade aircraft called "Pete" at 162.8 mph. Holman had been backed by Standard Oil and Haislip by Shell.

Acting on impulse one day when he saw the lion's head on a road sign advertising Gilmore Lion Head Motor Oil and Red Lion Gasoline, Roscoe wondered if he could acquire a lion cub and take it with him on the record-setting flights he planned to make. On February 7, 1930, a cub had been born at a lion farm in Agura, California, which could be obtained for $200. Roscoe couldn't spare that much money but persuaded Louis Goebel, the owner of the Goebel Lion Farm, to donate the cub for the publicity it would generate for his business. Goebel presented the three-week-old cub, then weighing 17 pounds, to Roscoe in a public ceremony well attended by the press. Promptly christened Gilmore, the lion was to become as much a part of Roscoe's image as his waxed mustache and flashy uniform. The image of Roscoe with Gilmore was to last far beyond their respective lifetimes.

Roscoe took the cub on a leash everywhere he went around the Los Angeles area, even to the golf links, where everyone wanted to pet him. He had no aversion to cats or dogs, although they couldn't figure him out. The Turner's dog learned to like him and they played cautiously in the Turner backyard. At the Lockheed factory, there was a stray hound of undefined parentage named Contact that had wandered in one day and allowed to stay. While Roscoe was in the factory enclosure, he would leave Gilmore to fare for himself while he conducted business elsewhere. Contact and Gilmore would roam the factory area together. Invariably, however, they would start a tussling match but when Gilmore got tired of playing, he would lie down, whereas Contact always wanted to continue. Gilmore would belt Contact with a quick swipe of his paw, which assured his friend that he required more time to relax. The two remained pals until Gilmore weighed more than 100 pounds and it was decided that continuing the match would be disastrous for Contact.

On April 13, 1930, when Gilmore was still a kitten and had been fairly well housebroken, Roscoe told Carline it was time to take him for a ride in the Lockheed Air Express to see how he fared. Roscoe recalled that "he was a pretty tired and nervous little cub when it was over. He was all right until we began to take off, but the minute the plane left the ground he made one terrified dive for Mrs. Turner's lap and stayed there. It was weeks before he stopped trying to scramble in someone's lap when we took off."

Despite his initial nervousness, Gilmore became "sold" on flying. During the next few months, Roscoe took him everywhere on his flights. To satisfy criticism from the Humane Society, he outfitted Gilmore with a small Irvin parachute and fastened the rip cord to the fuselage. If there were an emergency, Roscoe said he would throw the lion out first and then follow. He also had a small carrying case designed for ease in carrying Gilmore's chute. As he grew, two larger parachutes were made.

Gilmore became irritable when Roscoe left him alone for any length of time. Since he was such an attention-getter, Roscoe took him to public places, including restaurants and stores, where Gilmore would allow himself to be petted. After a while, he would become bored and curl up on the floor while Roscoe signed autographs and posed for photographs.

"At a banquet he generally sat quietly for a while then became restless, wandering around chewing and scratching at the feet of the guests," according to aviation writer Roy Rutherford. "He particularly liked shoes. When Eddie Cantor presented him on a New York stage he revelled in the spotlight, but when introduced at Graumann's Chinese Theater in Hollywood at the premiere of 'Hell's Angels,' he took a sudden fancy to the mop of hair worn by the orchestra leader and made desperate efforts to caress him. This stopped the show."[5]

The lion's appearance proved to be a trademark that even Roscoe had not figured on at first. Photographers could not resist taking shots of the two of them. A Dallas newspaper reported:

A sure method of dispersing crowds of aviation enthusiasts when they swarm about arriving planes was demonstrated at Love Field when Lt. Col. Roscoe Turner turned his mascot, a seven-month old lion out of his plane.

A small crowd of persons quickly thinned to three when Gilmore, the lion cub, scampered friskily across the field to greet the folk. Most of the crowd sought protection in the larger hangar. Gilmore, determined to extend his welcome, followed them in friendly fashion.

However, Colonel Turner of Los Angeles, called Gilmore to him. He took Gilmore for an automobile ride about the airport and then had him pose with a typewriter.[6]

Gilmore escorted Roscoe to the leading hotels, where Roscoe insisted on registering as "Roscoe Turner and Gilmore." Many hotels gave them free lodging because the photogenic pair always generated favorable publicity during their visits. The hotels would often have Gilmore's paw print put on the guest register to document his stay. When asked about their close relationship, Roscoe replied that he preferred the company of Gilmore to that of ladies, because "it is much safer. He never gets me into any trouble. He's always good company and always in a good humor."

Fred B. Collins, a Boeing sales manager, recalled an experience he had with Gilmore when Roscoe visited him in Seattle. "Roscoe was to stay at my house and he had that pet lion cub, Gilmore, with him. When I picked him up after a test hop he put the lion in the back seat of my car and we started for town. I was stopped at a traffic light when that goddamned lion started licking the back of my neck. It startled me so that I let out the clutch and we shot through the cross traffic narrowly missing several cars. A lion's tongue is about as rough as a rasp."[7]

Feeding Gilmore was always a problem. At first, Roscoe fed him a formula of a beaten egg, milk, and a little cod liver oil every two hours after heating a mixture with a stew pan and canned heat. At four months Gilmore was given a little ground hamburger with his milk; at six months he was eating meat alone. By the end of 1930, he weighed nearly 125 pounds and was eating 12–15 pounds of raw horse meat a day, an amount that was gradually increased as he grew older.

Gilmore was a sensation in New York. Roscoe would take him to night clubs and banquets and stroll with him through Central Park and down Fifth Avenue where traffic would come to a dead stop. Roscoe was asked on several occasions by the police to put him in a cab because they were obstructing traffic. At the Gordon Bennett Balloon Races in Cleveland when he was five months old, Gilmore charged a policeman's horse and gave the horse the fright of his life as the policeman tried desperately to hang on.

On flights to Corinth to visit his folks, Roscoe would take Gilmore around town on a leash to see all his merchant friends, especially Ernest and Eugenia Waits in their jewelry store. Mrs. Waits remembers him coming into the store and curling up on the floor while Roscoe chatted with her and the customers. Sometimes, Gilmore would put his front paws on the display cases and she was concerned that his weight would break the glass. She had to take display items off the counters and showcases when she knew he was coming.

Abe "Bud" Rubel remembers that the news of Roscoe's arrivals in town "spread like measles." Then in junior high school, Rubel says he and his buddies would get someone to drive them to the airport so they could see him and Gilmore. Roscoe always had someone ready a cage for Gilmore upon their arrival so the kids could see him. "After he got his pet put in the cage, he would come back to his plane talking to us kids and answering questions. We knew that within a few days, Roscoe would come to school and talk to us about his travels and experiences."[8]

On one occasion, Roscoe was driving in the rain in Los Angeles and suddenly skidded into another car. Gilmore, sitting in the seat beside Roscoe, panicked and leaped out when Roscoe opened the door to survey the damage. Pedestrians also panicked when they saw what appeared to be a mad lion charging down the street and ran for their houses. It took an hour before Roscoe could find him.

On another trip, Roscoe flew east to Hartford, Connecticut, with Gilmore, where they registered at the Heiblien Hotel. Roscoe and Stan Hedberg, a publicist, were scheduled to take the train to New York City, but animals were not permitted in the drawing rooms. Roscoe found a Carnation Milk box, stuffed Gilmore inside and the two men carried the box on board. Gilmore was extremely unhappy about this and clawed his way out, to the consternation of other passengers and the porter. When they arrived at Grand Central Station, Roscoe put him on a leash and walked him to the New Yorker Hotel with crowds following the trio all the way. At the hotel, Gilmore, apparently miffed at being treated like baggage on the train, nipped Roscoe in the leg; the result was a wallop that reminded him that was an improper move to make on Roscoe.

While 1930 witnessed the shrinking of distances between major cities throughout the country, the transcontinental record flights continued to hold the public's interest, principally because they measured the progress of aviation. Col. and Mrs. Charles A. Lindbergh opened the 1930 record attempts with a spectacular flight from Los Angeles to New York on April 20. With one stop at Wichita for fuel, they completed the flight in 14 hours, 45 minutes, 32 seconds, bettering Frank Hawks's record by almost three hours.

It was now Roscoe's turn. On May 1, with Gilmore as his passenger, Roscoe headed east in the Lockheed Air Express but encountered unexpectedly strong headwinds and extremely turbulent weather over New Mexico. Gilmore, frightened at the turbulence, tried to climb into Roscoe's lap while Roscoe wrestled with the controls. At one point, Roscoe thought he would have to jump but the thought of possibly losing Gilmore, even though he had a parachute, drove him on. He landed at Wichita but got stuck in the mud while taxiing, which delayed him getting to the gasoline pump. Because the mud slowed down his takeoff speed, he almost hit the telephone wires at the end of the runway.

Still bucking strong headwinds, he landed at Middletown, Pennsylvania, for oil but did not gas up. As a result, he ran short of gas and had to make a landing at Valley Stream, New York, for refueling before continuing the short distance to Roosevelt Field. Even so, he had made the trip in 15 hours, 37 minutes—only a little over three-quarters of an hour more than the Lindberghs.

Undaunted, Roscoe eyed Frank Hawks's east-west record and headed west on May 27. With a gas stop at Wichita, he landed at Grand Central Airport in Los Angeles in 18 hours, 42 minutes, 54 seconds, beating Hawks's record of 19 hours, 10 minutes, 32 seconds. It was an exhilarating victory over the clock.

Stimulated by the record-setting cross-country flight and the attention it generated with Gilmore, Roscoe flew to Vancouver, British Columbia, and announced he would establish a speed mark crossing three nations from Vancouver nonstop to Agua Caliente, Baja California, Mexico. The pair made the trip on July 16, 1930, in 9 hours, 14 minutes, 30 seconds. Gilmore got most of the press coverage.

It wasn't generally known but Roscoe and Charles A. "Slim" Lindbergh had a penchant for playing practical jokes on their friends and each other.

When Lindbergh was visiting the Lockheed plant in 1930, he pulled one on Roscoe. In his biography of Lindbergh, Walter S. Ross explains:

It started when Lindbergh wound a copper wire around the rubber cord stretched across the entrance to the hangar where his plane (the Lockheed Sirius being prepared for his trip to the Orient) was being built. The wire was attached to a booster coil. One day Turner came for a visit. He picked up the rope to enter the hangar. Lindbergh flipped a switch sending an electrical current through the wire. Turner's reaction showed that he had a command of speech as colorful as his costumes.

He got even a few days later by using the same coil. He wired it to a metal box of nuts and bolts. Then, when Lindbergh came to pick out some small part for his plane, Roscoe closed the switch and it was Lindbergh's turn to jump and howl.[9]

In his many visits to the Lockheed plant, Roscoe had met Donald A. Young, a competent young mechanic who worked in the metal fittings department and helped in the final assemblies. In those days, metal aircraft parts such as landing gear fittings, motor mounts, tail skids, and exhaust stacks were made by hand. He became highly skilled at welding fittings, sandblasting, and plating them and installing them on the aircraft. He learned by doing and never thought any job was too difficult in those days of linen, wood, and steel tubing. Young tells how his life-long association began as Roscoe's mechanic and confidant:

Roscoe was in and out of the Lockheed plant constantly. Often, as we started work in the mornings, Roscoe would be there going up to the main office to see Carl Squier, the plant manager, or chatting with someone on the assembly floor. I had worked on a Lockheed Explorer, a single-engine, single-seat plane and was loaned to a pilot named Roy W. Ammel, then flying for the Pure Oil Company, who planned to fly to Paris to try to beat Lindbergh's time across the Atlantic. He didn't make that flight because the weather never cooperated over a seven-week period. However, in order to establish some kind of a record, he made the first New York-to-Panama non-stop flight in November 1930.

Roscoe heard about me and when I returned from working with Ammel, Squier said, "Roscoe wants to see you" and gave me his address in Beverly Hills.

Young went to Roscoe's house and found him mowing the lawn; Gilmore was tied to a nearby tree. Roscoe handed Young a sidewalk

edger and as Young wore blisters on his hands, Roscoe said he wanted
to get into the racing business and needed someone to work with him
on his plane. He said he didn't have much money but could offer Young
$35 a week.

> I thought the excitement of racing would be well worth it so Roscoe
> asked me to come back to the house the next morning and help him bot-
> tle some home brew. This was during Prohibition. Although Roscoe did-
> n't drink very much home brew, I think he made it for the newspaper
> people and friends who were always coming to the house. Many times I
> found people sitting around his house drinking beer while Roscoe was
> out on a cross-country trip some place.
>
> We spent the whole day bottling the brew and dating the labels. He asked
> me to return the next day to make some more. I did but after that second
> day, I laid awake that night wondering if I had become a houseboy or what.
>
> I knew his Air Express had a bad oil leak in the tank and it had been
> in to the Lockheed plant several times to be repaired and they had never
> been able to fix it. So I got up real early the next morning and was at the
> field by 5 A.M. I took the engine firewall off the airplane, drained 300
> gallons of gas out of the tanks to get to the oil tank and had it out on the
> bench ready to repair it when Roscoe called from his home.
>
> "I thought you were coming over to my house," he said. I told him
> I couldn't and he wanted to know why. I told him I had the oil tank out
> of the airplane and I was repairing it.
>
> I guess he broke all records getting there. He stormed into the hangar
> and said, "Who in the hell told you to do that?"
>
> I said, "Roscoe, let's get one thing straight. I hired out to maintain
> your airplanes and as long as there's airplanes to be repaired, then that's
> what I'll be doing. I'm not too good at playing houseboy but I'll do that
> after the work on the airplane is done."
>
> Roscoe waited around all day while I was repairing the oil tank and
> never said another word about what my duties were to be.

Young resented being treated like a servant at Roscoe's beck and call.
When Roscoe wanted to fly somewhere and went to the terminal building to file a flight plan, he would yell to Young in a voice that could be
heard all over the field to get the plane ready for a flight. An understanding was reached when Young had enough of this treatment and
called his hand in front of some visitors.

One day, when I was standing out in front of the hangar talking to a couple of fellows, Roscoe was yelling for me. One of the fellows said, "Roscoe's calling you." I said, "Yeah, I know it." The other one said, "Aren't you going to answer him?" and I said, "No."

Pretty soon, you could hear Roscoe stomping toward us. He walked up to me and the two fellows spread out because they thought he was going to slug me.

"Didn't you hear me calling you?" he shouted.

I said, "Yeah, Roscoe, I heard you."

"Well, why didn't you answer me?"

"Well, Roscoe, you're going to have to stop calling me like a dog. You only make yourself look ridiculous and you make me appear ridiculous, too. After this if you want me, just go in there to the telephone and call or send somebody down to get me, or come down and get me yourself, but I'm not going to let you stand up there yelling at me."

He looked at me and said, "You know, they told me at Lockheed you were the orneriest son-of-a-bitch that ever drew a breath."

I looked back at him and said, "You know, that's funny. They told me the same thing about you."

He grabbed me in a bear hug and started to laugh. He said, "Boy, we're going to make it!"

Soon after the informal partnership was formed, Young learned that Roscoe had a bad habit that lasted all his life. He never felt he had an obligation to tell anyone where he was going or when he would return. Sometimes the absences would be for a week or more and there would be no apologies or explanations.

One time in early 1930 while I stayed in Burbank, Roscoe went to Atlanta for several weeks. Before he started home, he decided he wanted to check the valves and plugs on the airplane. He got a mechanic to help him and when they had the plugs out of the engine, Roscoe stooped down to get some tools out of his tool roll. The mechanic pulled the prop down just as Roscoe stood up. He banged his head on the prop and was flattened out on the floor. They had to take him to the hospital to get his head sewed up.

At that time, we had an oil pre-heater system on the Air Express that you plugged into a wall outlet in the hangar that a watchman was to plug in at a certain time early in the morning. The oil would be warm by the time you started the engine and you could take off without having to spend too much time and gas warming it up.

The night before Roscoe was to leave, he threw out the cord and told the watchman to hook it up at 6 A.M. in the morning. He also asked a mechanic to change the oil that night.

The oil was drained but instead of putting the new oil in the oil tank, the mechanic put it in the gas tank. When the pre-heater was turned on, it fried the oil tank because there was no oil in it. So Roscoe had to have the oil tank removed and replaced before he could start home.

When he got back from that trip, he told me what had happened and said, "Boy, make plans to travel because I'm never going any place without you." That's when Roscoe and I started traveling together.

There was another time when Roscoe's confidence in Young was firmly substantiated. Early one morning, Roscoe was scheduled to fly to San Francisco to pick up California's governor James Rolph. He wanted the plane gassed up immediately, so while Young was refueling the plane on top of the wing, he asked a helper to pass up a five-gallon can of oil. As Young poured the oil into the tank, he thought he saw something drop in along with the oil. He asked the helper if he had checked the can before he filled it and was assured that he did.

Roscoe always had a bunch of people—sometimes as many as 20 or 30—around just watching to see him off. While I was arguing with the helper who kept saying he had checked the tank, I got a rod out of the hangar and began to probe around inside. The tank had baffle plates in it and I couldn't find anything. I told Roscoe why I was concerned but when I said I couldn't find anything, he said, "OK, Don, button it up."

I laid there on top of the wing for a minute or so and said, "Roscoe, you're not going." He said, "What do you mean I'm not going?" I said, "I don't know what you're going to do but this airplane is going back into the hangar and we're going to take the oil tank out of it and find out what's in it."

He walked back to Mrs. Turner and said, "What in the hell am I going to do?" She replied, "Well, Turner, for once in your life, it looks like you're going to listen."

Roscoe walked back to me and said, "OK, Don, I'll call the governor and tell him I'll be there at 6 A.M. tomorrow."

We took the plane back into the hangar and it must have been midnight before Roscoe and I got the oil tank out of it. I was carrying the tank across the hangar floor and shook it but couldn't feel anything. I thought, "God, maybe I goofed." I put the oil tank up on the bench and while Roscoe watched, I turned a flashlight in the tank and there was a full cigar, oil-soaked, lying in the bottom. I fished it out and when Roscoe saw that, he couldn't believe it. If it had disintegrated and plugged up the screen on the engine, Roscoe could have gone down in the mountains somewhere. From then on, we were inseparable wherever we went.

Roscoe took Gilmore and Young with him as he established a number of other point-to-point speed records in the months following. Those who had never heard of Gilmore Oil began to know of "Gilmore, the Flying Lion." Gilmore flew over 25,000 air miles with Roscoe and was a sensation wherever they landed. But when Gilmore passed the 150-pound mark, his weight became a problem in the aircraft. The inevitable day came when Gilmore had to stay home and Roscoe knew he had to end their flying partnership.

The Turners received a permit to keep him at their home in Beverly Hills and put him in their garage for awhile but realized that wouldn't work when he leaped on top of their touring car and smashed the cloth top. They built a $2,500 house on a 30-square-foot fenced arena in their backyard. The house was built well off the ground away from drafts because lions are unusually susceptible to pneumonia. Gilmore liked the house. In the patio was a rubber tree with fine branches for gnawing and an automobile tire hanging from it that he would swat back and forth. A fishpond was built and he would watch the fish for hours, scarcely moving.

Indoors, Gilmore found it was great sport to take a running leap on small rugs and slide across the slick floor. He enjoyed pulling electric light cords out of sockets and turning floors lamps over. He loved the radio, preferring lively music. When he was outside in the yard, the Turners would park their car near him so he could hear the radio.

He kept his playthings under the piano and liked to cuddle a woolly dog that movie star Bebe Daniels had given Roscoe at a birthday dinner party. Roscoe allowed the lion to wander around the house and yard when guests were present. At other times, when they didn't want him there, he was tied to a post on the front porch. Although politely tolerant, the guests were always skeptical. Delivery boys and mailmen were understandably nervous about being greeted on the porch or at the front door by a full-grown lion. Roscoe often took Gilmore to actor Robert Montgomery's house and let the kids play with him.

Roscoe took him everywhere, including the golf course. He dutifully followed Roscoe's foursome for the eighteen holes, panicking the other golfers. A bright red-and-yellow portable cage was built for Gilmore by the company, and he was put on display at the United Air Terminal in Burbank. He was declared the official mascot for a Lion's convention in San Diego, where 20,000 attendees admired him. Later, they placed him in a cage as an attraction beside a Gilmore Service Station on the corner of the Earl Gilmore estate at Fairfax and Beverly Boulevard in Beverly Hills.

Roscoe and Carline visited Gilmore often to assure that he wasn't being abused. Even on these visits, Roscoe was able to garner press coverage because the lion, contrary to what animal handlers had said, seemed to recognize Roscoe and the pair would wrestle playfully as they had done when Gilmore was a kitten.

Not everyone appreciated Gilmore as time went by. In 1935 F. Hugh Herbert, a Warner Brothers Pictures executive living a half block from the Gilmore Service Station, wrote to the Los Angeles chief of police, declaring Gilmore "a public nuisance." "It roars right through the night," Herbert said, "in a loud and most distressing fashion, keeping me and my household awake. I have trouble enough with the Gilmore Stadium which was built practically in my back yard, without losing sleep over the Gilmore lion."[10]

The police were patient and contacted Roscoe and Gilmore Oil to see what could be worked out to prevent Gilmore from disturbing the peace. Gilmore was placed in his cage and moved by truck to a nearby garage at night. Roscoe personally canvassed the neighborhood and then replied to the police:

> The whole story is that these people are mad at (Mr.) Gilmore because he put up that Gilmore Stadium out there in that district and the noise antagonizes everybody. They think that if they can't make him move the stadium that they can make him move the lion, not knowing that he does not own the lion and that the lion is my pet and I keep him there for the entertainment of the kids who drive by there regularly to see him.

You will notice from the petition that I brought in to you that it was signed by everyone in that vicinity with the exception of two or three people. Those who signed told me personally that they enjoyed having the lion there, that occasionally he roared but it wasn't any louder than the traffic noises and nearby barking dogs so it did not bother them.

Of course, there are always a few old sore-heads in any neighborhood who would object to Christ if He were back here on earth again.[11]

Roscoe's plea for understanding went unheeded. An attorney with Gilmore Oil, C. S. Beesemyer, telegraphed Roscoe: "Lion at Beverly and Fairfax disturbing neighbors and is driving business from service station. We have been notified by police and city attorney to move lion. Necessary that lion be moved tomorrow as entire neighborhood up in arms against Gilmore. Please wire us where lion should be moved to and who shall move it."[12] Roscoe, unbowed, replied and reminded Beesemyer that Gilmore was still a drawing card for the company because of radio programs he was participating in at the time that were "worth money to you."

The demand from the neighbors to move Gilmore became too much for the company, which advised Roscoe that "it was imperative that the lion be moved immediately from Beverly and Fairfax." Roscoe replied that Gilmore would be moved by June 23, 1935. He wrote a final letter to the company saying that he had built a new cage but was not going to put the company name on the cage or paint it in the company's colors "so there will not be any confusion." However, he still offered to let the company use the lion and asked that he be allowed to buy the cage mounted on a truck they had built for him. He added,

You may also keep in mind that there is going on in the East at the present time three radio programs exploiting the name of Gilmore, and this fall there will be a national program on from coast-to-coast, so you can readily see that my lion is still doing a job for you. In fact, I did my job so thoroughly that 50% of the people still think I am with the Gilmore Oil Co. Only last week a newspaper man asked me if I was still flying for Gilmore and at the California Club last week, I was introduced as being with the Gilmore Oil Co. This is a handicap as far as I am concerned but an asset to the Gilmore Company, so don't forget to take cognizance of these facts.[13]

Roscoe also wrote to the police commissioners thanking them for permitting him to keep the lion at the service station location as long as they did. "After June 23rd," he wrote, "any lions that you may see at Fairfax and Beverly will not be my property."

When Gilmore and his cage were moved to the Burbank Airport, Don Young looked after him. Roscoe always visited and played with him whenever he was on the West Coast, even though he had been warned that lions cannot be trusted. Each visit was a news event. By 1940 Roscoe had moved to Indianapolis, and in August asked Louis Goebel of Goebel's African Lions, then in Camarillo, to take him. Roscoe sent a check for $150 to have a cage built and promised to pay $30 a month for Gilmore's food. "There is no one else in all the world I would trust my lion with but you, Louis, so take good care of him," Roscoe wrote.[14]

By October of 1940, Roscoe had a report from a friend that Gilmore was in a very small cage, his mane was coming out, and he was so thin his bones were showing. "Your cages are small," Roscoe wrote, "and naturally, if an animal stays in a cage with bars, they rub off their mane. I want to keep him just as beautiful as he always was, and I am willing to pay you for looking after him; so I expect some special care for my cat."

Goebel replied that he had a fire and was rebuilding the cages and barn. He had rebuilt Gilmore's cage under a beautiful oak tree "and (he) really has the life of Reilly." After an absence of eight years, Roscoe visited Gilmore at the farm in 1946 with reporters in tow. He weighed over 600 pounds by then and was in good health.

"That lion'll know me," Roscoe said.

And the lion did! As the keepers watched in fear and trepidation . . . the now full-grown beast leaned out and licked his former master's hand docilely.

W. J. Richards, keeper of the jungle compound, shook his head worriedly.

"I didn't believe it possible," he confided frankly. "I've heard of lions remembering their masters a year or even two years, but eight years—."[15]

When asked why he kept paying the food bills for Gilmore, Roscoe always replied, "For a long while he paid my bills; now it's my turn."

He predicted, accurately, that if anybody ever remembered him after he was gone, it would always be as "the guy who flew with a lion."

To carry out the lion theme on his flights after Gilmore had to stay home, Roscoe had a lion skin coat tailored that weighed 11 pounds. The first time he tried to wear it in the tiny cockpit of the Air Express, he couldn't get into the seat and had to put it aside. He also had a lion's tail swagger stick made and gloves that looked like lion's paws. When asked if the skin was actually Gilmore's, Roscoe replied that it wasn't. "It's the skin of a nasty uncle of Gilmore's who treated him badly," he said.

Don Young had many tales to tell about their experiences with Gilmore:

One time when we had to get a new parachute for him and Roscoe was fitting him with a new harness in the Lockheed hangar, he got nasty and bit Roscoe clear through the thumb nail with his needle teeth. Roscoe grabbed Gilmore by the mane and rump and threw him on the floor. He grabbed the lid off a large grease pail and really fanned him. He drew blood on Gilmore's nose. We all thought it was cruel at the time but realized later that Roscoe had to teach him who was boss—that he was not to get nasty with Roscoe.

He followed Roscoe everywhere and wouldn't leave him the entire day. It didn't matter if he was going to the Lockheed office or go flying, Gilmore would be right behind him like a dog. When Roscoe stopped to visit with someone, Gilmore would just lie down peacefully until Roscoe moved somewhere else.

A few times when Roscoe didn't take him on a cross-country and left him in the cage at the Burbank Airport, I would walk by and Gilmore would start to roar. All I would have to say was, 'Hi, Gilmore' and he wouldn't make another sound. All he wanted was recognition.

We learned from circus people that it was their custom to feed wild animals only six days a week. So that's what we did with Monday being the day he didn't get his meat.

Clyde Beatty, the famous lion tamer, told us that Gilmore was going to turn on us and kill us both some day because you can't trust a domesticated cat. No animals born in captivity will do exactly what you want them to do and they become vicious. He was right about Gilmore. He might do something ten minutes after you tried to get him to do it but he wasn't going to do it immediately.

When Beatty visited Gilmore with Roscoe on one occasion, he wouldn't even come inside the safety cage, not because he was afraid but because he didn't want to witness Roscoe getting hurt. And Roscoe was bitten badly one time when we visited him in the cage at Burbank. Gilmore always hated to see Roscoe leave and wanted to go with him. I usually went out of his cage to the safety cage first and this time I looked back and saw Gilmore's mane come up as I left. As Roscoe was about to follow me, Gilmore suddenly leaped on Roscoe and bit him on the arm. Roscoe had on a heavy flannel shirt and leather jacket but he put one tooth right through the jacket and shirt and probably about 3/4 of an inch into his arm between the muscle and the bone. But it didn't bleed; it was just a clean hole but I'm sure it hurt. Roscoe grabbed him by the mane and hit him on the nose. He said, "If you drew blood on me, you SOB, I'll kill you!"

When we looked at his arm, it wasn't good and he had quite a time with an infection.[16] After that, whenever I saw Gilmore's mane come up as I was going out to the safety cage, I'd go back in immediately and his mane would go down. We learned how to slip out quickly before he realized we were going.

We had a circus wagon built for Gilmore. It was used to transport him to various motion picture theaters when features like *Frank Buck Brings `Em Back Alive* was playing. We would park the cage in front of the theater which would always draw a crowd.

Lions have a way of relieving themselves sideways and Gilmore could direct a stream wherever he wanted to. When he felt like it, he would squirt onlookers with his peculiar urine, which was loaded with a pungent smell like ammonia. At one time in front of a Los Angeles theater, he let go on a woman and she sued Roscoe. When the case came to court, she apparently was too embarrassed to tell the judge that the lion had wet on her so she said the lion had spilled milk on her.

The judge knew what Gilmore had done and said it was a natural thing for a lion to do so he threw the case out of court. However, he told us to give people some protection so we installed pieces of plate glass about a foot high around the inside of the cage. The first time he tried to do his act, it splattered back on him and you'd have thought he had been hit in the tail with a 2 by 4. We didn't have any more trouble after that.

There were times when we had to give him castor oil which he didn't like. We'd take his meat, cut big slits in it and pour castor oil in them and rub it in with a knife. Usually, when we'd put the meat in his house, he was on it in a flash but the nights he saw us put in the castor oil, he'd just sit there and watch us and lick his chops. After we put it in the cage, he'd get up, stand there and stare at that piece of meat. When he couldn't stand it any longer, he'd pick up a corner of it with his two longest teeth trying to keep his lips away from it. Then he'd walk around the cage and try to drain every drop of the oil out before he'd eat.

Gilmore was never happy when Roscoe left on a trip and especially hated to be left in the car when Roscoe visited the Lockheed factory. Anyone who walked up to try to be friendly had to be careful because he would snap at them. However, if Roscoe let him out of the car to wander around the factory, that was all right.

Roscoe, Don Young, and Gilmore were staying at the St. Francis Hotel in San Francisco in 1931. When the three emerged from the hotel to go for a stroll, a mounted policeman came by and Gilmore started after the horse, just as he had done in Cleveland a year or so before. They had a 20-foot aircraft cable with a handle attached to the lion's harness. The cable would coil up quickly when there was no load on it to stretch it.

When Gilmore took off after the horse, Roscoe had difficulty holding the cable and had to let go. The horse departed with great alacrity down the street and Roscoe shouted to Don to grab the cable. Young remembered:

The cable had been coiled so long that it would snap back like a spring. I was running along the sidewalk after the coil and finally got it. I snagged it around a lamp post. The policeman finally got the horse to stop about a block or so away.

We rushed the lion back to the hotel and took him up in the freight elevator. The policeman came into the hotel looking for us but since Gilmore had been there before and the hotel workers liked the idea of him being there, everyone told him they hadn't seen any lion. He went away shaking his head.

That was the last time he was ever in a hotel.

Roscoe paid for Gilmore's upkeep until 1952, when he died at the Jungle Compound in Thousand Oaks, California, at the grand old lion's age of twenty-two. He was preserved by a taxidermist and kept in the

Turner's den until after Roscoe's death in 1970. He was displayed in the Turner Museum at the Indianapolis Airport until it closed and then was later sent to the National Air & Space Museum in Washington, D.C., along with other three-dimensional Turner memorabilia which are on permanent display at the Paul E. Garber Facility.[17]

In 1929 Roscoe bought a new Packard phaeton for a reported $1,900, which was his pride and joy. Having always been interested in Packards, he and Don Young used it extensively to haul baggage, parts, and people in support of his racing ventures. It became as much a vital support item for Roscoe's aviation activities as the aircraft. Young recalled,

> Whenever Roscoe was in a race, I'd fill the back of the Packard with spare parts and personal belongings and drive to meet him at the finish—places like Cleveland or New Orleans. There wasn't any room in those racing planes except for the pilot so we used the car all the time. Painted a two-tone gray and equipped with white sidewall tires, huge spotlights on the running boards, and a chrome trunk rack, it had an automatic lubrication system and other innovations that were new for that time period.
>
> We used the car so much for long-distance driving because in those days commercial airline service was pretty slow, and we could drive almost as fast as the trains went. We usually drove about 70 or 75 miles an hour.

The Packard was driven by the two of them from Los Angeles to Patterson, Louisiana, and to the air races in Chicago and Cleveland. Carline made two or three trips in it alone from California to visit their families in Corinth, Mississippi. Don Young said it made at least three coast-to-coast round trips that he remembered, and he estimated that he alone put 250,000 miles on it. He kept it in excellent condition and Roscoe never got rid of it. It was placed on display at the annual Indianapolis auto races. In the late 1960s, Don Young restored it to mint condition and said that it still had its original paint but that a small amount of chrome had to be replaced along with one seat cushion. It was displayed in Roscoe's museum at Indianapolis's Weir Cook Field and never driven again; it had traveled 351,000 miles. After the museum was disbanded in 1972, the Packard was donated to the Indianapolis Speedway Museum where it is on permanent display.

The Lockheed Air Express proved to be a moneymaker for Roscoe. Always operating between poverty and temporary riches, he was able to stay reasonably solvent by flying charter trips anywhere in the United States and Mexico. The movie stars flocked to him for charter flights because they had complete confidence in his flying ability and asked for him especially when they had to go back and forth between Los Angeles and New York. Many of them didn't trust the airlines and didn't want to fly with passengers who might bother them for autographs en route. Roscoe's charge for the one-way flight to New York was $1,600. If there were no passengers for the return trip, Roscoe and Young would promptly return. Young recalled:

> We'd land at Floyd Bennett Field at 2 or 3 o'clock in the morning after an 18- or 19-hour flight. I'd gas up and we'd be on our way back. Roscoe was usually OK for a few hours but when we'd get over Texas or some-where in the warm sunlight, he'd get really sleepy. I always kept a fire ex-tinguisher lying in the seat beside me to wake him up when he'd start to doze off. You would know right quick when he did because a wing would start down and the plane's engine would rev up, then he'd bring it back up. Then the other wing would go down and he'd repeat the process. Once in a while, he would bring the nose up and it would stall and he'd recover. I kept the fire extinguisher beside me so I could reach back and crack him on the knees if he got too far gone. He was always so dead-tired after these trips that he could sleep anywhere.

It was on his many trips with Roscoe that Young learned about Roscoe's sleepwalking, which was apparently a genetic anomaly. Roscoe and his four brothers all talked in their sleep, often to each other, and all had frequent nightmares ever since they were very young; also, all were sleepwalkers. Family members often told of the time in his early years that Roscoe sleepwalked to the barn and hitched up a team of mules.

Roscoe talked in his sleep continually, and from the time of his barn-storming days, it was almost always about flying. He would call the tower or make comments to an imaginary copilot. He would give orders in his sleep and exclaim about whatever was happening to the plane in his nightmares. He would often get up, go to the window and check the weather or comment about a plane's strange behavior. On a number of occasions, he apparently dreamed that his plane was on fire and he had to jump out of it. Once, while staying at the home of a movie producer in California, he had this kind of dream and dove through a glass window to get out; fortunately, he was on the ground floor and landed in the yard. He suffered minor cuts from the broken glass.

Those who roomed with Roscoe learned that they could talk to him about whatever he was saying in his sleep or dreaming and he would answer. He could often be talked out of whatever problems he was having in his dreams and would usually obey instructions to return to bed if he was sleepwalking. He rarely awoke and never remembered his dreams or walking next morning.

One time a group of pilots chained him to the bed in a hotel room as a prank, and he dragged the bed all the way to the window before he awakened. On another occasion, when he was staying at the Lincoln Hotel in Indianapolis, he walked in his sleep out on a balcony that went around the hotel. After walking around for awhile, he woke up but couldn't remember where his room was. He tried to find it and when he came upon a door that was cracked open, he cautiously went inside. He said, later, "Thank God, it was my room."

Roscoe admitted that a fire in the cockpit was his greatest fear, and he retained that fear in his subconscious even after he stopped flying in his last years. His anxiety about fire may have arisen from a time when he was smoking during a flight. He dropped the cigarette on the bottom of the cockpit and couldn't reach it. He was so frightened by the possibility of being blown up in flight that he quit smoking while flying and seldom lit another one, even though he later lent his name to advertise Camel cigarettes.[18]

On one occasion when he was on a commercial airliner flying from Newark to Toledo, it was said that several passengers recognized him and asked him for autographs. He obliged. Dead-tired and able to fall asleep anywhere, he quickly dozed off. Suddenly, he jumped up out of the seat and yelled, "We've got to get out of here! Something is wrong and we've got to get out of here!" The passengers were alarmed and the stewardess came running to calm him down. She shook him and he finally awakened. He couldn't believe what she said he had done but he apologized to her and the other passengers.

E. L. "Skip" Eveleth, a Pratt & Whitney executive, told of the time Roscoe stayed at his home in West Hartford, Connecticut:

> We all had a pleasant evening and had gone to bed when about 3 o'clock in the morning I heard a banging on the wall in the guest room where Roscoe was sleeping. I rushed in and turned on the light and said, "What's the matter, Roscoe?" He woke up slightly bewildered and said, "Oh, I had that terrible nightmare again. Do you remember when I broke that fuel line from the engine in the race? Well, in my dream I'm soaked with gasoline and the flames from the open short exhaust stacks of the big engine catch the fuel on fire and likewise catch me on fire with my soaked coveralls and I am trying desperately to get out of the cockpit." This was, of course, what caused his kicking and banging on the wall.[19]

Stories about Roscoe's sleepwalking, some admittedly far-fetched and which get better in every retelling, include the time during his barnstorming days when he and his stuntman were waiting for a haircut in a southern barbershop. A man walked in and shot one of the barber's customers. That night Roscoe got up in his sleep, wrapped his roommate in a sheet, and was about to bury him at sea when the "dead" man woke up.

Roscoe rarely ate any solid food while he was flying. On cross-country flights, he would wire ahead that, in addition to fuel and oil, he would want water to drink but no food. When he was relaxed on the ground and not planning to fly, however, he ate heartily and especially liked fried catfish. One night at Antoine's in New Orleans, he asked for a catfish platter and was brought a large serving. As he made it disappear, he asked if that was all they had. In quick succession they brought two more platters, which he also devoured. In memory of that feat, the owner featured "Catfish à la Turner" on the menu. Of course, this was picked up by the New Orleans newspapers.

Whenever Roscoe went home to Corinth, he would dive into his mother's pickled peaches and was known to eat a half gallon at once. He loved the sausage and hominy his mother made. His sister, Mary Emma, recalls that their mother saved the ashes from the fire to make lye, which was used in boiling corn outdoors in cast-iron pots to dissolve the outer shell on the corn to make the hominy.

Chicken and cornbread dressing were other favorites. Roscoe's craving for fried catfish was universally known, but it was not usually available outside of the South. He would fly many miles to visit friends in Louisiana and Mississippi just for a seafood dinner. As usual, news photographers took pictures of him eating catfish when he visited New Orleans and Meridian, Mississippi. As a result of his fondness for food, he liked to do his own cooking at home. His only problem was mastering the art of making cornbread, according to his sister. When he visited, she would always make some to take back home.

Whenever Don Young traveled with Roscoe, he could be sure of one thing: he wouldn't have much of a chance to eat en route. He tells what it was like:

> When we brought the governors back from Washington after their conference in 1932, Roscoe wanted to try to break the east-to-west coast-to-coast record, so I knew what that meant. Roscoe roomed with one governor and I roomed with the other. When we got up on the morning we were to leave, Roscoe and I gave the governors the opportunity to shave and get dressed first. When we joined them in the dining room, I ordered a substantial breakfast and when Roscoe saw this, he said, "Don, you're not hungry, are you?" And I said, "Why?" Roscoe said, "We'd better get out to the airport and get the plane ready to go."
>
> So, the two of us left for Bolling Field without so much as a cup of coffee. When the governors joined us, Governor Balzar said, "Don, I ate your breakfast, too." We arrived in Burbank 18 hours later and I hadn't had a bite to eat and nothing to drink.
>
> It was that way on all of our trips. When we landed, nobody had a chance to go in the terminal building. I would gas the plane and we'd be off again. On the trips with the Air Express, I always had a couple of Hershey bars, apples or bananas stuck in the side pockets. When we'd be flying along, I would hand a banana or an apple back to Roscoe and he'd yell, "Where'd you get that?" He just never thought of food while he was flying.
>
> On a trip in the Packard to Patterson, Louisiana, we drove straight through and it took us two days and nights. Before we left I bought half a stalk of bananas and that's all we had to eat on the entire trip.

Another of Roscoe's idiosyncrasies was the wearing of two wristwatches. He kept one on the time wherever he lived and the other on a time zone he intended to visit or was in at the time. In the early years, he used them to time his gasoline consumption and speed. Throughout his life, he was uncomfortable without two wrist watches and often carried a pocket watch as a spare. Mrs. E. F. Waits, wife of the Corinth jeweler, remembered Roscoe always seemed to have a watch there for repair or cleaning.

On their trips together, Young also learned about another side to Roscoe that didn't seem to fit his public persona. He read the Gideon Bible at night in hotel rooms before he went to sleep and read one every night of his life, if it was available. Although he never tried to impose his religious beliefs on anyone, he attributed his survival to "somebody up there" who continually watched over him.

C

WINNING THE BENDIX AND THOMPSON TROPHIES

The 1931 National Air Races at Cleveland represented a new era for high speed aircraft. Army Air Corps Capt. Ira Eaker chose to enter the closed-course races with a Lockheed Altair, the first Lockheed with a retractable landing gear, and Jimmy Doolittle arrived with the Laird *Super Solution* biplane with which he broke the transcontinental record. Lowell Bayles made his appearance with a Gee Bee (Granville Brothers) Model Z. "Jimmy Wedell showed up with a terrible looking old crate from Louisiana," Roscoe recalled. "He entered in his first Thompson Trophy race flying a plane of his own design with a 450-hp Wasp Junior engine. He had dubbed it the Wedell-Williams Model 44 and being a gun enthusiast, compared it to the famed .44-caliber six-shooter of the old west. Painted on the side of the fuselage was the inscription: 'Hot as a .44 and twice as fast.' "[1] Despite the homemade looks of his plane, Wedell placed second to Lowell Bayles, who won at a speed of 236.2 mph in the Gee Bee Z. Wedell had averaged a remarkable 227.992 mph in his original No. 44.

Wedell had already impressed the racing fraternity with his racing de-sign. The year before, he had entered the Detroit–Los Angeles–Detroit Cirrus Race, competing for a $25,000 prize. It was a grueling 5,541-mile, 16-leg race that tested men and machines to the limit. He arrived in Los Angeles second to the leader, Lowell Bayles. After some engine work was completed and new wheel fairings were installed during the night, he took off the following morning on the next leg, but the en-gine quit soon after takeoff and he crash-landed with damage to both wings and the landing gear. He worked all night to complete repairs; twenty-four hours later he took off again and finished eighth for a $1,600 prize.

Later that year, Wedell entered the National Air Races at Chicago. In the Los Angeles-to-Chicago derby, he was leading the pack until the Hisso engine broke an oil line and he had to make a forced landing in Texas. Despite the mishap, he proceeded to Chicago by commercial air-liner, where he had a second Wedell-Williams waiting for him. He placed second in the Thompson Race at 227.992 mph and second in the men's and women's mixed invitational race at 221.048 mph. To top off the meet's list of achievements, he entered a free-for-all race and, despite a malfunctioning engine, placed third with a speed of 167.106 mph. He followed these impressive performances with a "Three Flags Race" from Ottawa to Washington, D.C., to Mexico City in 11 hours, 59 minutes, to beat Jimmy Doolittle's earlier record of 12 hours, 36 minutes.

When Jimmy Wedell tried unsuccessfully to break Roscoe's east-west record, Roscoe decided he wanted a Wedell-Williams plane. He had heard that it had an aileron control problem, but Roscoe thought it could be cured. "I asked the Gilmore Oil Co. if they would advance me the money to build another speed plane and operate it under their col-ors. They advanced me $5,000 and I ordered a special Wasp Junior en-gine from Pratt & Whitney. We shipped the engine to Louisiana and Don and I drove down there in the Packard."[2]

Roscoe tells how his friendship for Jimmy Wedell had deepened:

He came to California in the winter of 1931 to try for my three-time record from Canada to Mexico and I was the only one he knew so I kept his little airplane under the wing of my big Lockheed, helped him cash his checks and get everything ready. In the meantime, I was quite impressed with Jimmy's honesty and straight-forwardness and I looked his airplane over very carefully and I could see where there could be a lot of improvements on it and make it a lot faster.

Jimmy was the kind of guy who couldn't lie. I asked him if he thought we could build a 300-mph airplane and he said, 'I think we can.' I said I would furnish the money and we made a verbal deal.

Then in January or February 1932, [Don Young] and I got into my automobile and drove to Louisiana to start construction of this 300-mph airplane. In the meantime, I started to consult with every builder in aviation as to what we intended to do and they said it couldn't be done; you can't get a 300-mph airplane in and out of an airport. I said, "Well, you fellows don't know any more than I do so goodbye."

My next problem was to get a power plant so I went to Pratt & Whitney and because the president was a personal friend, I told him what kind of power plant I wanted. He called in his engineers and they didn't want to build it. All it was, was a modification and a beefing up of their little 985 engine which is only 300 hp and I wanted it to develop 525 hp. To make a long story short, I got my engine and had it shipped to Louisiana.

When we arrived down there, we found nothing but a little tin hangar out in the middle of a cane field with two cross runways and I had expected to find some engineers and some people to build this airplane. I decided to make the best of it and I started to use my own barnyard engineering along with Jimmy's as neither of us had gotten out of high school but we had a lot of practical experience.[3]

Jimmy Wedell was one of those rare "eyeball mechanics," who had never received any military pilot training or college education. He was an excellent pilot and one of the most innovative designers and builders of racing aircraft during those relatively unregulated days of flying and cut-and-try plane manufacturing. Son of a bartender, he had lost one eye in a motorcycle accident during his teenage years, but like Wiley Post, he had learned to judge distances with one eye as well as anyone. Starting out as an auto mechanic, he bought two war-surplus single-seat Thomas-Morse Scout planes and rebuilt them to include an extra seat. He took flying lessons from Francis Rust, an old barnstormer, then taught his brother Walter how to fly and the two began barnstorming in Mexico and the southern U.S. Jimmy became known in Mexico as Señor Don Jaime, El Gavilán de la Noche (Sir James, the Night Hawk), because of his ability to attend a wild party, then depart at night for another air show the next day. He and his brother reportedly engaged in running illicit liquor across the border to Galveston but were never apprehended. The border patrol called his plane, painted black, "The Phantom."

During these wild days, Jimmy knew he had to have a better plane and wondered if, despite the lack of any formal education, he could design one. He met Harry P. Williams, a wealthy Louisiana lumberman, who wanted to buy an airplane and learn to fly. Jimmy became his instructor; the two became good friends and struck a deal. Williams would back Wedell to the extent of $2 million and allow him to design his own aircraft so he wouldn't have to try to earn his living by barnstorming. Williams bought more planes, incorporated the Wedell-Williams Air Service in 1928, and launched an air charter operation, in addition to backing Wedell in his plane-manufacturing enterprise.

Between 1931 and 1936, planes made by Wedell took a significant number of first, second, third, and fourth places in major air meets around the country. The planes he built were flown by winning pilots like Jimmy Haizlip, Doug Davis, Lee Gehlbach, and Roscoe Turner, but unfortunately the only big race he won himself was the Thompson in 1933.

Using only his intuition as a guide, Wedell was said to have chalk-marked his first plane on the hangar floor at Patterson, Louisiana. With his brother Walter and two mechanics, he eyeballed the profile he thought it should be and shaped the frame when he thought it looked just right. There was no wind tunnel or stress testing, just his concept of the smooth lines that a racing plane should have. Eddie Robertson, his shop foreman, thought his boss was a real genius. "Any man who could take steel tubing, wood, glue and linen and build the world's fastest airplane just out of his head. . . . I can't understand to this day how he did it. He said to me, 'Eddie I have too much surface there,' took a piece of yellow crayon and marked off how much smaller he thought it should be."[4]

Wedell's first racer, a sleek low-winged racer with a Hisso 180-hp engine, was named *We-Will* and later designated model number 44. It was modified twice and several more were built during 1930, all with slight changes in design from the original.

When Roscoe and Don Young arrived in Patterson to have Wedell build the racer, Harry Williams told them Wedell wouldn't have time to build it because he was constructing one for Jimmy and Mary ("Mae") Haizlip, the husband-and-wife racing duo. However, Williams said Wedell would lend them the drawings if they wanted to make one themselves. The problem was there weren't any drawings. Wedell had the plans and dimensions only in his head or in a little notebook he carried in his overalls pocket. As Roscoe and Young explained what they wanted, Charles "Frenchy" Fortrum, a draftsman, made some rough sketches so they would know what the structure would look like inside before it was covered.

Roscoe returned to California to continue his advertising work for Gilmore Oil, while Young stayed behind and borrowed sawhorses, tools, and tubing from Wedell and began to work. He proved to be as innovative as Wedell in following the sketches that Wedell and Fortrum gave him. "Once I got started," Young recalled, "there was no problem because I could visualize the finished plane. If I didn't have in mind what I was going to do, I'd just walk over to the plane Jimmy was working on to see what he was doing and make any measurements I wanted. I may not have done everything just as he did it, but the result was almost the same."

Wedell assigned Doug Worthen, a young apprentice mechanic, to help Young, and the two of them fashioned the plane by themselves. Except for the engine, gas tanks, pulleys and cables, and the wing panels, which had been made by Wedell, it was all their work.

When Young wired Roscoe that the plane was ready, Roscoe returned to Louisiana. Wedell tested the plane several times himself and Roscoe was ready to accept it. However, because Wedell weighed only about 135 pounds, Harry Williams suggested that Wedell make one more test flight with enough lead shot under the seat to equal Roscoe's weight of 220 pounds. He was then to make a low altitude pass at full speed. Williams, Roscoe, and Young went to the ends of the field to time the speed run. "It came across and hit the speed course at about 20 feet from the ground and we snapped the watches on," Roscoe said. "All of a sudden we saw one wing flutter and crumble up. Wedell's presence of mind saved him; he pulled the stick back and gained enough altitude to jump. His parachute opened at about 200 feet. When we got to him he said that this was one time when lead under the fanny certainly had pushed him out of the airplane and saved his life."[5]

The reason for the crash was believed to be the rigidity of the wings, which caused the guy wires on the left wing to snap off under the stress and collapse the wing. The plane had half-snapped when the wing buckled, which enabled Wedell to get out.

> The airplane was literally scrambled and dug a hole ten feet deep. In spite of the condition of the plane I saved the compass, the directional gyro and the artificial horizon which we sent back to the factory and I used them later on another racing plane.
>
> Since the plane hadn't been sold to us yet, I was out an engine. I asked Williams if he would hire an engineer who could tell us what happened to the airplane. There was obviously some weak spot somewhere; it was truly a beautiful plane and very fast. He agreed and I went back to California to continue my work for the Gilmore Oil Co.

It was believed that the problem was wing flutter that developed at high speeds and made the plane uncontrollable. Roscoe sought out Howard W. Barlow, a highly respected aeronautical engineer, who offered to analyze the problem and suggest how the racer could be redesigned. After working for the National Aircraft Engineers, a consulting firm in Washington, D.C., Barlow had joined the faculty of the aeronautical engineering department at the University of Minnesota in the fall of 1932. The plane was redesigned and built according to his specifications, loading schedules, and design criteria.

Young returned to Burbank while the finishing touches were being put on the new 44 model. He and Roscoe then flew the Grand Exalted leader of the Elks on a three-week tour of the United States in the Lockheed Air Express, followed by a trip with Governors Rolph and Balzar for a meeting in Richmond, Virginia.

Ever anxious to get work with his Air Express, in July 1932 Roscoe wrote to Franklin D. Roosevelt, then governor of New York, and offered his services to the presidential nominee. "It occurred to me that you would be interested in the tremendous advantages that could be obtained in the forthcoming campaign by use of the airplane in your travels over the country," he wrote. "I am confident that I am in a position to fulfill that possibility." He pointed out that he had made a large number of record speed flights and that he had not had a mishap with passengers for nearly fifteen years.

> It is not my intention to suggest to you a series of speed flights, although the plane which would be used, a Lockheed Air Express with a passenger capacity of four and baggage, could carry you with the biggest safety factor to any point within the country within a day. The fact that I possess a national reputation as a flier would, I am confident, aid you favorably in the public's eye. . . . The only expense to you would be the gasoline and oil and you may paint whatever campaign slogan you wish on the ship. The only reservation I would have to make would be that I am allowed to participate in the National Air Races at Cleveland, August 27th to September 5, as I expect, with a racing plane now under construction, to regain America's speed crown. . . .
>
> I am confident you will realize the enormous saving in time that could be effected, the great section of the country which could be covered, more than any other Presidential nominee has visited, the saving in physical energy and the deep popularity which could be added to an already favorable situation because of your unprecedented enterprise.
>
> My plane, at all times in perfect condition, would be available at the earliest possible moment should you find this offer satisfactory.[6]

The candidate didn't accept Roscoe's offer, but later that year he did fly to accept the nomination in Chicago in a Ford Tri-motor. During World War II, he also became the first sitting president to take advantage of aircraft for travel.

The 1932 National Air Races promised to be exciting as the three most successful builders of racing aircraft were planning to have their aircraft compete in the Bendix and Thompson races. Jimmy Doolittle planned to enter them with the Laird *Super Solution* biplane; the Granville organization had two new potential racers, one for each race; and Jimmy Wedell planned to fly one of his planes.

As the time for the races approached, Roscoe was disturbed because Don Young reported that Jimmy Wedell was actually building two planes that would compete with the one he was buying. However, when he learned that an additional 25-gallon gas capacity was being put in them he said he wasn't worried because, "All I wanted was a fast plane."

In the meantime, Mr. Gilmore had decided that he would not go through with his bargain for this plane but I told Don, Wedell and Williams to go on and build it just the same. Finally, Mr. Gilmore told me that he would buy the plane provided that I could sell the Lockheed Air Express. I told him that I would buy the Lockheed myself but he wanted at least half cash for it and I didn't have enough money to pay half cash. I told him he could take it out of my salary, as my salary was then running into four figures a month, but he wouldn't do this. However, since he didn't have a buyer, I took title to it in August 1932 and used it all during my racing years.

Then I got notice that the airplane was ready and the air races were only ten days away. I started hunting for some money and canvassed all my friends in Hollywood and was just about to give up. I had made a lot of friends with my Lockheed as I had flown almost all of the stars and executives for their first rides in the air, making $25,000 a year in the charter business.

I sat down and tried to think which one would be the most interested in aviation and would be willing to help me. I went to one star and she was willing to back me but her manager said he didn't think it was right for her at the time. However, he told me about another star there who might and he would introduce me. I went to the RKO Studios next day and met Miss Connie Bennett and her manager. We had a talk with her in her dressing room but she had had a terrible day on the set and was practically in tears because everything had gone wrong. After a few minutes, her manager and I excused ourselves and left.

Next morning her manager said that he had the money. You can imagine my rejoicing because no money or business was mentioned the day before. She said our visit was the only restful thing she had seen that day.[7]

Roscoe picked up the Wedell racer, had it licensed as NR61Y, and Young readied it for the 1932 Bendix Trophy Race from Burbank to Cleveland. Powered by the Wasp Jr. engine, which was rated at 300 horsepower, Young had it souped up to about 500 horsepower. It had arrived at Burbank unpainted so Young quickly painted it in Gilmore colors only a few hours before takeoff time.

Only the people who witnessed the takeoffs from Burbank could appreciate the hazardous feat it was. The takeoff sometimes was around midnight or one in the morning. The takeoff hour was established so the planes would arrive in Cleveland in the daylight hours and the spectators at the air show could view the landings at the finish.

The weather conditions could be perfect at Cleveland but not always so at Burbank. Besides, Burbank is situated in the heart of the mountainous area and it was always touch-and-go as to whether you would clear the mountains with a ship loaded with fuel. The sky could be black as ink and reliable instruments for blind flying and navigation were not available then.

After building only one model 44 for Jimmy Haizlip in addition to Roscoe's, Wedell built the third one for himself. It was to be a banner year for three of the virtually identical Wedell-Williams racers. All three were at Burbank getting ready for the Bendix race.

Roscoe, in NR-61Y painted cream and white, was first off from the Union Air Terminal at Burbank at 3:30 A.M., August 29, 1932. He made stops at Colorado Springs and Quincy, Illinois. Roscoe's time of 9 hours, 2 minutes, 25 seconds, was good enough for third place behind Haizlip, who crossed the finish line 8 hours, 19 minutes, 45 seconds, after his takeoff, and Wedell, who followed a half hour later. Haizlip won $6,750; Wedell, $3,750; and Roscoe, $2,250.

Haizlip and Roscoe continued to New York to try to set a new coast-to-coast record. Haizlip made the trip in a total of 10 hours, 19 minutes, after leaving Burbank; Roscoe trailed 39 minutes later. Both had beaten Jimmy Doolittle's record of 11 hours, 11 minutes, set the year before. Haizlip received $2,250 for the transcontinental flight. There was no prize for second place since the prize money went only to Haizlip as the record setter.

Roscoe returned to Cleveland and entered the Thompson race, which for the first time required the qualifying speed for entrants to be 200 mph. Roscoe placed third in the qualifying run at 266.674 mph, which earned him $525.

The subsequent race for the trophy was won by Jimmy Doolittle flying the Granville Gee Bee at a record-setting 252.686 mph. Roscoe and Jimmy nearly collided when they were flying neck-and-neck. "We came within a hair of piling into each other on a pylon due to lack of visibility," Roscoe recalled. "Buried down deep in your cockpit, one wing to the sky, you can't see the other fellow. We came within a few feet of getting it on a pylon. Jimmy pulled up, I pulled out and it's lucky we both survived."[8]

Wedell placed second, well behind Doolittle. Turner was third and Haizlip was fourth to make it a two-three-four placement for the Wedell racers. Roscoe pocketed $1,500 for this race. His speed was 233.042 mph.

The trio entered their planes in the race officially known as "The Shell Petroleum Corporation Speed Dashes (Men Only) for World's Record Over Three Kilometer Course." Doolittle won this contest with an astounding 296.287 mph, with Wedell, Turner, and Haizlip following in that order. Roscoe's take for third place was $525. Wedell and Haizlip won honorable mention for the Clifford W. Henderson Merit Award, based on points for placement in the various events.

Not one to pout because he hadn't finished first, Roscoe decided to see if his Wedell racer could set new point-to-point records. On September 25, 1932, he set a round-trip Los Angeles–San Francisco record of 2 hours, 41 minutes. On November 12, he departed Burbank for New York to set a west-to-east record. On landing at Columbus, Ohio, the Wedell blew a tire, which took too long to repair to have any hope of breaking the record. However, Roscoe continued to New York later and, two days afterward, attempted to set an east-west record. With fueling stops at Columbus, Kansas City, and Albuquerque, he landed at Burbank 12 hours, 33 minutes, after departing New York. It was a new mark for others to shoot at. Although the west-east record still eluded him, Roscoe was now considered one of the nation's premier pilots.

Over the years, Roscoe was often asked what it was like to fly nonstop coast-to-coast flights to set or break a record. He gave an excellent answer to veteran aviation writer Frank Kingston Smith:

> First of all, we knew that the flight would take almost a full day, so we waited until we had a good 24-hour forecast for the destination. If we took off at three o'clock in the afternoon from California, we had a couple of hours of daylight remaining so we turned to a heading of about zero-five-zero, climbed to 13,000 feet and held the heading. Until it got dark, we could correct for wind drift by the angle we cut across the high ridges. About five or six hours into the flight, we would be almost past

the Rocky Mountains, usually somewhere south of Denver, at 10 o'clock, their time.

The next visual fix would come up about four hours later, when, from experience, we could sometimes identify Omaha, Kansas City or Oklahoma City by their light patterns and compensate for drift. Of course, every hour we had to crank in a change of magnetic variation on the compass.

Our best navigation fix was about two-thirds across the country, when we came up on the Mississippi River, usually about four o'clock in the morning, locally. If we identified Davenport, or Hannibal, or St. Louis, or Cairo, or Memphis, we could really nail down our wind drift, compute our actual groundspeed and make a pretty good course adjustment.

A couple of hours east of the river, the sky began to get light enough to see the ground, and by the time we reached Indiana or Ohio, we could compensate for winds by using section lines all the way to the Alleghenies. From there, it was just simple dead reckoning and pilotage for a couple of hundred miles to the finish line.[9]

Always hoping to make improvements and try again to set a new west-east record, Roscoe had slight modifications made on NR61Y's fuselage and landing gear. In his next attempt, he left Burbank on April 29, 1933, but two and a half hours after takeoff, a wheezing engine forced him down near Prescott, Arizona.

Analyzing his chances for future record attempts and races, Roscoe decided to replace the Wasp Jr. engine with a Pratt & Whitney Wasp Sr., which developed 800 horsepower and consumed an extravagant 75 gallons of gas per hour. Howard W. Barlow traveled to Los Angeles and assisted in the engineering work needed to install the larger engine. He ran a weight-and-balance check and redesigned the engine mount, in addition to checking the entire structure to be sure that it would take the added stress imposed by the increased weight and higher speed that would be produced by the more powerful engine. The fuselage was smoothed up with new fairings and painted a gold-bronze color; the wings retained their red and cream colors. Roscoe made nine test flights in June 1933 and announced that he was ready to enter the Bendix race.

As usual, Roscoe was hurting financially. The cost of racing and maintaining a Hollywood lifestyle took its toll, and he owed a number of people. As a result, he was continually contacting potential sponsors with ideas for enhancing their public image through his flying. One of them was the Acme Battery Company, which agreed to manufacture automobile batteries exclusively for the Roscoe Turner Company, formed in July 1933 with Paul Laufenberg on a 60-40 basis. However, there is no record that any significant business developed from this partnership.

A few days before the National Air Races began at Mines Field, Los Angeles, an executive from 20th Century-Fox called Roscoe to ask if he would allow them to advertise a new film called *The Bowery* in large letters on the Wedell's fuselage. Roscoe, of course, had no objection and stated his fee. He was thus granted a reprieve from bankruptcy. The references to Gilmore Oil on the fuselage were quickly painted over.

Roscoe left for New York to be there for the start of the 1933 Bendix. He made stops at Albuquerque, Wichita, and Indianapolis for gas and headed for Floyd Bennett Field in New York. He tells what happened en route:

I found out later that as I was taking off from Indianapolis, the airport manager had come running out to tell me that the airport manager at Floyd Bennett had called to hold me on the ground because the weather was bad and fog was rolling in from the ocean. But I was on my way and with no radio they couldn't let me know.

I flew along for about an hour and a half and the weather began to look pretty bad ahead as I neared Allentown, Pennsylvania. By this time the ceiling was lowering and there were broken clouds and light fog under me right in the tree tops. I was able to stay above it but about half way between there and New York it cleared up and everything looked fine. Although there was a high ceiling and a little light rain, the fog below me had disappeared except in small patches. When I got over Newark, however, the fog was closing in again, and when I crossed the Hudson River, the Empire State Building was just barely sticking out of the fog. I thought there would still be an open place at Floyd Bennett so I flew on over there but found that it got worse. I turned around and came back, got under the fog and got over Brooklyn almost down in the streets thinking that I could gradually find my way to the airport.

Suddenly, the fog closed in on me and I had to pull back to get on top again. By this time, I had only 15 or 20 gallons of gas left and I thought it was going to be another case where I was going to have to take to my parachute and leave my beautiful airplane up there all by itself.

When I came out on top of the fog the compass was spinning and the only thing that saved me was the directional gyro. I turned around and started back west. By this time the fog had moved in and completely covered everything as far as I could see but when I got over the Hudson River, by a miracle of some kind, there was a little hole. I looked down and saw a sand bar. I cut the motor and spiraled down through the hole. Now, to land on a sand bar with a plane that lands at 90 miles an hour is not recommended. I didn't know how I was going to make it. To make matters worse, I saw a bunch of kids playing ball and a big pipe running across the sand.

I had no choice. I slid in for a landing and stopped the plane within about 800 feet from where the wheels touched down. Believe me, I was a happy man to get on the ground again.

All I did to the plane was bend one of the wheel pants a little bit. I left the plane there overnight and found out that this little sand bar had been used as an airport by Clarence Chamberlin in earlier days. Next morning I flew the plane over to Floyd Bennett Field to get ready for the transcontinental race.[10]

The night after Roscoe arrived at the field, a process server gained access to the hangar. He had a court order for Roscoe that had been obtained by someone Roscoe owed. Jimmy Wedell, who also planned to beat the record, happened to be in the hangar when the man arrived.

"Know where I can find Roscoe Turner?" he asked. Wedell, sensing that Roscoe wouldn't want to see the man, said, "Yeah, I think he's in the men's room." When the man left to find Roscoe, Wedell quickly located him and told him to disappear. Roscoe got into a pair of dirty coveralls and a sailor hat to cover up his distinctive uniform and evade discovery. The process server persisted, knowing from all the prerace publicity that Roscoe would be on the field someplace.

Roscoe was warming up the engine for takeoff when the man found out which plane he was in and started after him, shouting. Thinking that Turner didn't know who he was, he waved the papers and yelled, "Hey, Colonel Turner, I've got something for you!" Turner waved back, blasted him with the propeller and hollered, "See me in Los Angeles."

Roscoe taxied out to takeoff position and was off in the Wedell-Williams at 4 A.M. He flew at full throttle for awhile and was disturbed to learn that he was burning so much fuel that he wouldn't be able to make Indianapolis, his first scheduled fuel stop. He slowed down to conserve fuel but decided to land at Columbus to take on 50 gallons, enough for about a half hour's flying. He then left for Indianapolis where he was delayed because all the fuel trucks were refueling other aircraft.

Wedell, flying his redesigned racer with the smaller 450-hp Wasp Jr. engine, was no match for Roscoe's more powerful Wasp Sr. Both refueled at Wichita and Albuquerque and headed for Mines Field in Los Angeles. It was afternoon when Roscoe came barreling out of the eastern sky and roared across the field. He chandelled into the traffic pattern and landed before a huge crowd in the stands. He couldn't have picked a better time to land because the opening parade was forming and the first-day crowd was always the largest. Darryl Zanuck and Joe Schenck, representing 20th Century Pictures, Roscoe's sponsor, were in the stands cheering wildly. It was a sensational ending to a well-run race.

Roscoe landed 11 hours, 30 minutes, after his departure from New York beating Wedell by 28 minutes. He had also bettered his own previous record time of 12 hours, 33 minutes. Roscoe's average speed was 214.78 mph; the winning prize was $4,050. For having set a new speed record, he was awarded an additional $1,000. It was his first major victory.

Roscoe was confident that he now had the fastest airplane in the air and entered the Shell Speed Dash in the Unlimited three-kilometer category. He won easily with a speed of 280.247 mph and was awarded the $1,135 first prize. Wedell finished second, averaging only 1.3 mph slower than Roscoe.

The Thompson was next and Roscoe placed first in the qualifying trials with an average speed of 280.274 mph. The prize money amounted to $1,125. Now thoroughly convinced that he could win the Thompson and might even reach the 300-mph mark, he taxied out and took off with the others in the traditional racing start. He immediately took the lead at the scatter pylon with Wedell close behind. On the second lap, however, Roscoe cut inside the pylon and did not recircle it as required until the next lap. Despite this cost in time, he caught up with and passed the others to cross the finish line an apparent winner with Jimmy Wedell close behind.

Roscoe landed and was waved to the winner's circle in front of the stands. As he crawled out of the cockpit amid cheers from the audience, he was draped with flowers and posed smiling with the huge, heavy trophy, which was presented by actress Ruby Keeler. He was about to make an acceptance speech over the loudspeaker when an official raced up to him and interrupted the ceremony. "I'm sorry, Colonel," he said, "but you've been disqualified! You didn't circle that pylon you missed on the same lap like you were supposed to."

There had been a delay in reporting by a pylon judge that Roscoe had missed the No. 2 pylon and had not circled it immediately. The telephone line from the pylon judge's position to the main timer's stand had been disconnected, and he couldn't report what he had seen.

Turner protested. "I know I cut a pylon," he said. "The air was too full of airplanes. There could have been some midair collisions if I had tried to re-circle the pylon then. Somebody would have been killed. That's why I circled it on the next lap."

The race official could only say, "Rules are rules, Colonel Turner. Sorry."

Jimmy Wedell was the Thompson Trophy winner that year, with a speed of 237.952 mph. Roscoe's speed, including the extra time circling the pylon, was timed at 241.031 mph.

It was a bitter disappointment and it was embarrassing to have the disqualification announcement made before thousands of people. The rules stated that a missed pylon had to be circled on the same lap, not on the next lap. An onlooker commented, "Never did I see anything sadder than that husky fellow and his mechanic with bowed heads plodding across the field together." Despite the loss of the race on a technicality, Roscoe received the Cliff Henderson Trophy Merit Award as America's outstanding speed pilot during that year's races.

Not to be outdone by the organizers of the National Air Races, which was considered the World Series of competitive aviation, a group of promoters held the unsanctioned, controversial "maverick" American Air Races in Chicago in 1933. Sponsored by the *Chicago Tribune* and the Chicago Air Race Corporation, the races were held in conjunction with the Chicago World's Fair during the Fourth of July weekend.

Suffering from the humiliation of the disqualification in the 1933 Thompson race, Roscoe hoped to redeem himself in the eyes of his Hollywood backers by entering the Wedell-Williams in the three-kilometer Straightaway Shell Speed Dash. His previous wins brought him new sponsors: Macmillan Oil, Bendix, H.T. Spark Plugs, and Smith Propeller. He had the plane festooned with logos and ads for these companies and named it the "Macmillan Ring-Free Special."

It was another race dominated by the Wedell racers. Jimmy Wedell placed first with his racer now powered by the 800-hp Wasp Sr. Roscoe was second and Lee Gehlbach third. Wedell set a new world's speed record of 305.33 mph; Roscoe's speed was 289.9 mph. Gehlbach was farther back at 272.06 mph. Roscoe's prize for this event was $600. To average the speed of almost 290 mph, Roscoe also had to fly at more than 300 mph on some of the straightaway stretches.

Roscoe also entered the Frank Phillips Trophy Race. Jimmy Wedell won again, with Gehlbach placing second. Roscoe had to drop out on the eighth lap when the engine supercharger started to disintegrate but did collect $333.30 for a lap prize.

After the Wasp Sr. engine later broke a camshaft, and frustrated by having to follow the other pilots flying Wedell-Williams aircraft, Roscoe told Don Young to plan to install a new 1000-hp Pratt & Whitney Hornet engine for the next round of races the following year. Meanwhile, he had obtained a new sponsor—the H. J. Heinz Company—the food giant that boasted of "57 varieties" of soups, cereals, and other food products. The famous "57" logo was promptly painted as his racing number on the fuselage. The Macmillan logo was carried on the wheel pants.

Roscoe's near-wins encouraged him to keep on trying. Harboring a keen desire to capture both coast-to-coast speed records, he wanted to beat Jimmy Haizlip's west-to-east record. Still using the Wedell with the Wasp Sr. engine, he departed Los Angeles on September 25, 1933, and landed in New York 10 hours, 4 minutes, 30 seconds, later. He had beaten Haizlip's mark by less than 15 minutes, but he now held both transcontinental records.

Roscoe's achievements were rewarded by the presentation of the

Harmon Trophy in New York City by the American chapter of the Ligue Internationale des Aviateurs. It was transferred to him by Clyde E. Pangborn, who had won it the year before with Hugh Herndon for the first nonstop trans-Pacific flight.

Roscoe was so proud of the handsome prize that he planned to take it with him on his return to California. The rules of the League prohibited the expensive bronze trophy from being transported by air, but Roscoe persuaded the officials to let him fly it home in the Air Express cabin. When he arrived in Chicago, aviation enthusiasts urged him to pose with the trophy, but he refused to take it from the plane. Just after he arrived, he learned that his grandmother, Mrs. Mollie Derryberry, had been killed in a car-train crash in the Turner family auto and left immediately for Corinth. He told the crowd that the first place the trophy would be shown was in the window of the E. F. Waits Jewelry Store in Corinth.

The nation was in the deepest throes of the Great Depression in 1933. Public interest in aviation had throttled back as fewer and fewer people could afford to fly on the commercial airlines; it was a rare individual who had the money to learn to fly or own a plane. However, the one aspect of aviation that kept the average person focused on its promises and potential was the sport of air racing, which fascinated so many during those dark days of a faltered national economy. Roscoe Turner was one of the few freelancing entrepreneurs who was able to continue to make a living from flying. Every cent that he received from his sponsors and from winning races was put right back into maintaining his planes and helping to sell aviation. He never had any thoughts about getting into another line of work, despite the discouragements, the financial commitments, and the multitude of problems with flying machines that continually needed repair.

Looking ahead for new ventures and never reluctant to contact anyone he thought might be interested in backing him, Roscoe proposed to buy a Douglas DC-2 twin-engine transport in January 1934 to make a flight around the world at the equator with stops at Cairo, Calcutta, Manila, and Honolulu. In a letter to a financier in New York, he hoped to get backing from the Cities Service Oil Company and others to buy the plane for $75,000 and pay him an additional $75,000 for expenses. "If you and your associates do not choose to underwrite the full amount," he wrote, "you would have my permission to sell such other publicity as you might see fit—other than radio, newspaper syndicates or moving pictures." He added that upon completion of the flight he "would then be in a position to put into effect a round trip service between New York and Miami every day from December to March inclusive, making the trip either way in six hours. . . . Of course, I would have to be guaranteed a minimum of, say, six or seven passengers each way per trip."[11]

This plan never came to fruition but it indicated Roscoe's aspiration to run an airline again. When there was no positive response to this idea, he concentrated on preparing for more racing.

In a way it was a propitious time to be in the racing game. The two major aircraft engine manufacturers, Pratt & Whitney and Wright, would lend their engines to the builders of the experimental racers and especially to the pilots who had previously won some prestigious races and proved themselves a good bet to win future events. Since the manufacturers of the planes had to build them with their own resources, the engine manufacturers also depended on financial input from supporters who hoped they were backing a winning product. To them it was worth the expense and the financial risk to have the racing pilots test their engines for them in the various competitions.

Roscoe had to borrow money from a number of people during those days. His reputation for selling aviation favorably and his lack of trepidation about approaching anyone he knew to borrow money or equipment could not be denied. Lenders included some of the top names in aviation and business, such as William A. "Pat" Patterson, president of United Airlines, and William Randolph Hearst, famous newspaper tycoon. The debts were continually on Roscoe's mind and whenever he received prize money, he immediately paid his past debts or made partial payments, although he sometimes had to ask the lenders to hold his checks for a specified time.

When the new Hornet engine was installed in the Wedell, Roscoe flew to Detroit to do some publicity work for the Maxon Advertising Agency and H.J. Heinz. Wanting to keep his name before the public, he set a

Detroit–Pittsburgh point-to-point speed record. Several days later, he established a Detroit–New York record of 1 hour, 47 minutes, 21 seconds an average speed of 304.40 mph. He then established a new record for the 311 miles from New York to Pittsburgh of 1 hour, 19 minutes.

By the beginning of 1934, Jimmy Wedell had a new racer that sent a shock wave throughout the air-racing world. Designated the "45," it had an exceptionally thin cantilever wing (without any external wire bracing), retractable landing gear, and the Wasp Sr. 800-hp engine. Wedell entered it at the Pan American Air Races in New Orleans and won easily at 264.703 mph without using full throttle. The basic design, with the modifications required to meet new government standards, was later bought by the Army Air Corps as a possible pursuit plane and was designated the XP-34.

It seemed certain that Jimmy Wedell would be a winner of many of the future races he wanted to enter, but it was not to be. He was killed while giving a flying lesson in a training plane at his hometown of Patterson, Louisiana, in June 1934. Earlier, in February, Zantford Granville, one of the builders of the prizewinning but man-killing Gee Bees, had also lost his life, when he stalled out a Gee Bee on a landing approach at Spartanburg, South Carolina.

Although these two outstanding "name" pilots would not be participating in the 1934 races at Cleveland, there were others flying new, more powerful aircraft that had not been seen before. Roscoe had wanted desperately to enter the 1934 Bendix race and then make a clean sweep by continuing to New York for a new west-east record and crown this with a Thompson victory. However, the racer's fuel tank sprung a leak and had to be removed in order to be repaired. Working as fast as he could, Don Young couldn't repair it in time for the Bendix start.

The Bendix results were disappointing that year. Of the seven entrants, only two made the distance in the time required: Doug Davis, a colorful barnstormer and Eastern Airlines pilot, flying a Wedell "44" and Johnny Worthen, an associate of Jimmy Wedell's, participating in the new Wedell "45." A third plane, a Gee Bee flown by Roy Minor, straggled in too late to make the deadline. Davis received $4,500 and

Worthen, $2,500. Worthen in the new "45" would have won if he had not overflown Cleveland because of low visibility and landed at Erie, Pennsylvania.

Vincent Bendix, the trophy sponsor, was displeased with the race results and hoped the pilots who hadn't been able to fly to Cleveland would participate in an alternative race. He quickly offered another prize of $3,500 to the pilot who could break Roscoe's 10-hour, 4-minute, 30-second transcontinental record set the previous September.

It was an incentive for Roscoe to try again. He planned his flight to land at Cleveland as if he were in the Bendix run to show that he could have beaten Doug Davis's time and then proceed to New York, intent on setting a new transcontinental record. Departing from Burbank in weather that others did not dare to challenge, Roscoe landed at Albuquerque and Wichita for gas after plowing through the worst storm he had ever encountered. Roscoe relates what happened next:

Since I don't have enough gas to get to Cleveland, I have to stop at St. Louis. By this time I am out of the mid-western storms and have picked up some tail wind to compensate for the time lost in the thunderstorm.

We gas hurriedly and are on the way to Cleveland, running a little behind the schedule set on my previous transcontinental record flight, but now I have a nice tail wind and as I watch my time I can see that I am picking up most of the lost minutes.

About 40 miles out of Cleveland I run into another terrific storm and even after getting down almost on the housetops it is impossible to see anything. It seems almost impossible that the airplane will hang together through the terrific beating that it has taken in this storm, even after throttling down. But, within a few minutes that seem like hours, we are driving through the blinding rain and making a dive for the airport at Cleveland. I drop in to gas up and the storm is approaching the airport. The oil funnel won't fit and I am raising cain with the refueling crew, and it begins to rain and everything is all wrong.

It seems to me that if I have to stay here much longer there will be no point in going on—in pushing my racer and myself to try to shave minutes from that transcontinental record of 10 hours, 5 minutes I made last year. I do some rapid calculations as I sit there fuming in the cockpit and I figure that if they can refuel me in five minutes and I equal my old speed record from Cleveland to New York I will still miss the record by about four minutes. The five minutes go by and I am sitting on the ground. In the meantime the storm moves in and it begins to rain in sheets.

Finally, the refueling is completed and I don't see a thing but just the blur of the grandstand. I open the throttle and the wind changes at the same time. The plane is headed for the grandstand. I realize the seriousness of the situation. I just hang the load on those thousand horses and literally pull it off the ground on the prop, practically stalling. Then I bank the ship up on one wheel while it is running on the ground to turn its nose away from the people who fill that grandstand. . . . Just then I happen to think about the pylon that is in front of the grandstand that I am not high enough to clear. The rain is so thick that I can't see a thing, and my goggles are fogged up. Everything is just a blur and a squadron of Navy planes is coming by on the left. But I manage to miss everything ducking under the Navy planes, and in a few minutes I am once more on my way.

I give no consideration to gasoline consumption this time, as I have a sufficient supply to use all the motor will take.

The oil is getting very hot and I continue to take on altitude up to 12,000 feet. Counting the minutes and checking my speed, I find that I am doing far better than ever before across country, averaging 330 mph. If I keep up this pace, I will roll into New York between three and five minutes ahead of my old record.

And I do it, cutting off three minutes from my old time! That was the hardest transcontinental flight I have ever made, but, according to the reward that I received, these precious minutes were worth $1000 each.[12]

The successful takeoff from Cleveland had been pure luck. Thoroughly fatigued, Roscoe had landed at New York in the official time of 10 hours, 2 minutes, 39 seconds, to barely eclipse his own record. After greeting a small crowd and signing autographs, he went to the Half Moon Hotel nearby and slept for the next twenty-four hours before returning to Cleveland.

Roscoe had put his name on the list to enter the Shell qualification runs for the Thompson Trophy. Doug Davis qualified in a Wedell 44 at 305.215 mph; Roscoe trailed at 295.465 mph for a $625 prize.

The length for the 1934 Thompson race was still one hundred miles, but the course had been shortened to eight and one-third miles for each leg over a triangular track so the entire race could be observed from the stands. Davis was still flying the Wedell 44 that Jimmy Wedell would have flown, but it was now powered by a quickly installed 800-hp Wasp Sr. engine. At the beginning of the race, he leaped out in front of the eight-plane pack with Roscoe dogging him every inch of the way. Roscoe, with his more powerful Hornet engine, flew cautiously and made doubly sure he didn't cut a pylon. Davis opened a gap of about three miles while Roscoe hung back, fully expecting that Davis might burn up his engine trying to stay in the lead.

On about the sixth lap, Davis cut inside the second pylon. As soon as he realized it, he pulled up quickly—too quickly—into a high-speed stall. It was a maneuver that Roscoe had feared would be dangerous when he had cut a pylon in the 1933 race and chose not to circle it until the next lap. The Wedell 44 whipped over and spun wildly downward into a clump of trees. Davis was killed instantly.

Roscoe won the race easily over Roy Minor, his next nearest rival, at a speed of 248.129 mph to take the $4,500 first prize. *Time* editorialized later that "his rivals sneer at his clothes, at his brash statements that he is 'a bit of a hero to the boys in the country,' at his public swagger, but there could be no sneering at the flying records that he has won in the stiffest competition. . . . A temperamental prima donna on the ground, Turner is a cold, nerveless machine in the air."[13]

When he received the trophy in front of the crowds, Roscoe was not smiling. He and his fellow racing pilots had lost a formidable opponent in Davis, and racing had lost an outstanding pilot. Frequently emotional about losing friends, Roscoe was deeply saddened. The human price of high-speed racing was getting to be very steep. Jimmy Doolittle, who had quit racing after his 1932 win of the Thompson Trophy, said,

> I felt the time had clearly arrived to examine the role of the air races. They had served a useful purpose by arousing public interest in aviation. They had also become the inspiration and proving ground for new concepts in aircraft design and construction. Cockpit venting, retractable gear, and bold new wing and fuselage designs were born in the competition for the various trophies. But the price in planes and pilots had been high. I

thought aviation should now begin to serve world commerce rather than be considered mostly a sport. The racing planes were the guinea pigs of aviation—the machines in which we had done years of experimenting. I thought the time had come to give attention to safety and reliability so that commercial aviation could develop for the common good.[14]

Doolittle's thoughts were shared by many of the nation's racing pilots. Later that year, a number of them met to discuss changes in the rules that would make it safer for all. One of the major changes was the requirement that all planes entering the national races would have to pass an intensive inspection by qualified technicians. It was the beginning of rules and regulations for racing that encouraged good maintenance and safe flying.

After the 1934 races, Roscoe flew his Wedell racer to Detroit and stored it there for ten months. He returned to Los Angeles, hoping that he would have the new racer built in time for the 1935 racing season.

But there was a new adventure ahead. Months before the Cleveland races, Roscoe had begun negotiations with Boeing, United Airlines, and Pratt & Whitney Aircraft to borrow a new Boeing 247 airliner and enter the MacRobertson London-to-Melbourne Race scheduled to begin in October, only six weeks after the 1934 Thompson Trophy victory. It was to be an adventure that would put his name in the international news but would nearly cost him his life.

7

THE
TURNER-PANGBORN-NICHOLS
TEAM

His name was Sir Macpherson Robertson, a Scotsman and wealthy head of Australia's MacRobertson Chocolate Company. He was also co-owner of the MacRobertson-Miller Aviation Company of Australia. When he announced in early 1933 that he was going to sponsor a London-to-Melbourne air race the following year to celebrate the 100th anniversary of Melbourne's founding, he said an incidental objective was "to prove that fast communication between Australia and England is possible." He called it the Melbourne Centenary Air Race; the news media billed it as "the race of the century."

The MacRobertson Race was to take place during October 1934 with two categories of entries: a speed category and a handicap classification. The winner would receive the equivalent of $15,000 (in American dollars) and a gold cup for the fastest time in the speed category; second place would merit $7,500; and third, $2,500. The prizes in the handicap category would be $10,000, $7,500, and $2,500. Robertson would bear all organizing and publicizing costs.

Robertson, then 75, was noted for his support of Antarctic expeditions, and he had decided to encourage further development of aviation, then in the doldrums because of a worldwide economic depression. The Royal Aero Club of England agreed to organize the race and enforce the rules. Robertson insisted on two main terms: the race must be international in character, and everything reasonable must be done to reduce the risk of accidents. He also stipulated that the race had to be completed within sixteen days. The Aero Club made additional rules: takeoff had to be from Mildenhall, 55 miles outside London, and all aircraft had to stop at five control points, regardless of the route they chose, before landing at the Flemington Race course outside Melbourne. These stops were Baghdad, Iraq; Allahabad, India; Singapore, Malay Straits; Darwin and Charleville, Australia. It would be a grueling flight of more than 11,000 miles. They would cross nineteen countries and seven seas, and much of the flight would be over snake-infested jungles and steaming deserts, through blinding sandstorms and typhoons. Lloyd's of London gave participants a 1-in-12 chance of being killed. It would be a race that would test navigational skills as well as physical endurance.

The race was scheduled to begin on October 20, 1934, and it captured the imagination of a large number of the world's pilots. Among them was Roscoe who, after winning the Thompson Trophy, was now being referred to as "America's aerial speed king" by the international press. He had first heard about the race the year before from Joseph E. Lowes, director of advertising for Pratt & Whitney Aircraft. "I really think it is a very splendid opportunity for a few of our best American pilots to show the Englishmen just how swiftly the 10,000 miles between England and Australia can be clipped off," Lowes wrote.[1] Roscoe agreed and immediately began to contact possible sponsors. With this kind of encouragement from Pratt & Whitney, he was confident other sponsors would follow. He received added assurance from Don Brown, president of Pratt & Whitney, that the firm would back him with engines and technical help for the race.

The race announcement was greeted in international aviation circles with great enthusiasm. Sixty-five entries were received by the deadline of June 1, 1934, from the pilots of fifteen nations, most of whom had already achieved some measure of fame in their respective countries for long-distance flying or winning speed races. Seventeen entries from the United States were filed, including those of Capt. Frank Hawks, Wiley Post, Jacqueline Cochran, Ruth Nichols, and Laura Ingalls. Many entries, if not all, hoped their expenses would be borne by corporate sponsors, such as oil companies or aircraft and engine manufacturers, who would benefit from the publicity, a custom that had begun in the 1920s in the United States.

Roscoe made inquiries to Clairmont L. Egtvedt of Boeing and William A. Patterson of United Airlines, heads of their respective companies, to lend him one of their latest transports. At the time, Boeing was manufacturing the 247, a ten-passenger airliner powered by two dependable P&W 550-hp Wasp engines. Boeing publicists touted the 247 as "the world's first modern commercial airliner" and "the three-mile-a-minute airliner." First flown in February 1933, the 247 had a number of innovations, such as retractable landing gear, wing de-icing boots, elevator, rudder and aileron trim tabs, and controllable pitch propellers. It also featured vast comfort improvements for passengers, compared to the trimotored Ford, Fokker, Stinson, and Boeing 80A transports. United placed an order for sixty 247s at $65,000 each for its route system. Only fifteen more were sold to other buyers. The 247 was a big hit at the 1933 World's Fair in Chicago, and the company won the Collier Trophy in 1934 for making the plane's many engineering innovations.

Concurrently, the Douglas Aircraft Company was also developing a twin-engine airliner. The prototype was the DC-1, which also flew for the first time in 1933. It was followed by the fourteen-passenger DC-2, which represented a serious threat to Boeing; TWA was its first buyer.

Boeing was anxious to prove the 247's reliability and ruggedness, just as Douglas was. The London-to-Melbourne race would be the ideal test for both aircraft. Roscoe wanted to be the pilot who would make the Boeing name internationally famous as a manufacturer of transport airplanes. KLM, the Dutch national airline, sponsored two of its pilots, who would make the flight in one of the company's standard DC-2s, with paying passengers for part of the trip.

Roscoe's salesmanship paid off. Boeing agreed to modify a new passenger transport that it had sold to United Airlines, and United agreed to lend it to Roscoe for the publicity they hoped he would generate for both companies. The Boeing model was a 247-D—the first of the D models built—which was modified with extra fuel tanks to increase the fuel capacity to 1,125 gallons and thus extend its range to about 2,300 miles, which would be beyond that of the unmodified Douglas DC-2. The passenger seats were removed and eight vertical tanks were installed in their place in the passenger cabin, which could be fueled from the outside. There was a catwalk between the tanks in the cabin with cross-feed valves so gas could flow from one tank to another. Roscoe was assured that the race rules permitted the use of his passenger space "for petrol, provided of course that he does not exceed the all-up weight of the aircraft allowed in his certificate of airworthiness."[2]

When the deal with United and Boeing was announced, Roscoe told the press, "I have chosen this plane because it has been in service and tried out longer than any other fast big plane on the market. It has proven its ability to stand up in regular day and night transport service. Speed is not the only requirement for the forthcoming race. Dependability has to be there, too. This ship has both."[3]

The competition was actually to be two races run concurrently. The speed race had a minimum of restrictions; the winner would be the first aircraft to land at Melbourne. The handicap race measured an airplane's performance according to a carefully calculated formula involving gross weight, engine horsepower, wing area and payload. To win either of the races would be a tribute not only to the crews involved but also the aircraft, engine, and equipment manufacturers.

The England-to-Australia flight had been made before, the earliest in 1919, when Ross and Keith Smith made the trip in twenty-eight days. Others made it in successive years such as well-known British Empire pilots Alan Cobham, Charles Kingsford-Smith (twice), Amy Johnson, and C. W. A. Scott. The record of 6 days, 17 hours, 56 minutes, was set in 1931 by Charles J. P. "Unlucky" Ulm.

Long-distance flying had attracted the imagination of a number of European flyers and the MacRobertson Race gave many the incentive to consider attempting round-the-world flights; several had started, but none were successful. Roscoe had wanted to make such a flight ever since he owned the Sikorsky S-29 and thus become the first civilian flyer to circumnavigate the globe in a heavier-than-air machine. The Army Air Service aircraft that had circled the globe successfully in 1924 had extensive government cooperation and support. Roscoe had done some preliminary dreaming about making such a flight but there were no financial "angels" available then who had enough confidence in a successful outcome to consider risking their dollars. The race to Australia would give him good experience and, perhaps, an opportunity to obtain sponsors for such a venture.

Roscoe contacted a number of prospective patrons. Among them were the Hamilton Watch Company; Larus & Brother Company, cigar and cigarette manufacturers; and H. J. Heinz. He had previously written to Hamilton to obtain a replacement watch for one that had been stolen. He was offered a replacement watch gratis "in exchange for a few kind words from you telling of the years you have been using a Hamilton and a release that would allow us to quote you in a piece of advertising—perhaps a page in the *National Geographic Magazine*." Roscoe immediately responded, hoping for sponsorship but it never came. He did write "a few kind words," for which he received a free watch. Hamilton turned down the new request.

He asked the tobacco company for $1,000, saying that they could name the plane "the "Hi-Plane Special" or the "Edgeworth Special" or any name that they would like, but they weren't interested. He also contacted Cities Service Oil Company and asked for a loan of $75,000 to purchase an unspecified type of passenger plane for a round-the-world flight to advertise the company's products. He then proposed to have the plane modified with extra gas tanks so that he could depart Los Angeles and make stops only at Cairo, Calcutta, Manila, and Honolulu. He would then enter the MacRobertson Race and begin the New York–Miami flights afterward. Cities Service declined the opportunity.

One previous contact did pay off and that was with H.J. Heinz. As an incentive for Heinz, Roscoe pointed out that the Department of Commerce had given the Boeing the tail number 257Y and he was having the number "57" painted on the fuselage as his London–Melbourne racing number, as he had done previously on the small racer. He asked for $10,000 to pay for the tests of the Boeing 247 after the additional tanks were installed and to offset the costs of the flight itself. "If Mr.

[Howard] Heinz wants to be a real big shot in aviation," he wrote to the company's advertising director, "ask him if he will sponsor this flight personally and I will do anything he wants done in the way of advertising." He asked that the flight sponsorship be kept confidential from his ad agency "as I do not want to make them sore or think that I am doing any cutting in or chiseling."[4]

Heinz was only mildly sympathetic to Roscoe's need for funds, and by September he was desperate. The company made him a loan of $2,500, and Roscoe agreed to repay it out of the proceeds of the first contract that he entered into "for the exercise of my flying ability, either with H. J. Heinz Company or any other person or company."[5] Roscoe received a telegram from Howard Heinz wishing him luck but approved no further loans. "You have right to be confident," Heinz said. "So much luck enters into these things that I can only hope and pray for your success."[6]

Disappointed at not being able to borrow more money, he wrote to the advertising director: "I didn't look for another sponsor for this flight because I thought that if I was able to go out and get $80,000 worth of airplane, surely Heinz would pay the incidental expenses of the flight and taper off in a sportsmanlike way, and leave the impression that he was carrying through as I have said that he was, as no one would know but what he had purchased the airplane, too."[7]

Roscoe focused on preparing for the MacRobertson race. The modified 247 was registered as NR257Y (R for "restricted") and had the Boeing logo painted on the vertical stabilizer. The distinctive Heinz number "57" was painted in red and white on the fuselage and nose. The Macmillan Petroleum Corporation also added note of its sponsorship by publicizing its "Ring-Free Oil" on the aircraft.

During this time, Roscoe made frequent trips around the country in his Lockheed Express to visit potential race sponsors. Looking ahead, still wanting to start an airline, he also sought financial backing to start a daily six-hour "fast service" between New York and Miami which would begin after he completed the London–Melbourne flight.

To prepare for the flight, Roscoe asked Commander Harold E. Perrin, who was in charge of the race arrangements for the Royal Aero Club, if it would be possible for him to arrange a trip over the course for Roscoe as a "guest passenger" with one of the airlines. Perrin replied that he could not arrange free passage, and that the airlines went only as far as Singapore. However, if Roscoe wanted to pay for the trip, Perrin said he would arrange his reservations.

Roscoe sent in his race entry form and entry fee of £50 (about $250), but his secretary made a mistake by indicating the airplane was manufactured by the Douglas Aircraft Company. The Royal Aero Club accepted the entry, but when Roscoe tried to make a correction of this one word, Perrin cabled, "Deep regret rules prevent change of make and type entry form and cables specify Douglas this must stand."[8] Roscoe appealed the decision, but Perrin still refused to make the change or return his entry fee.

Roscoe was furious and expressed his unhappiness to his newspaper friends at being so summarily rebuffed. When several U.S. newspapers quoted his bitter remarks, the Australian Press Association in New York City wired him asking about the London Aero Club decision and requested his version of the story. An angry Roscoe wired back collect:

> Unfortunately in America we only have less than a dozen racing pilots in the major class and it has been the custom here that any racing events were purely from a sporting angle and it was my understanding the MacRobertson International Race was a sporting event and to build good will. The Royal Aero Club seems to think different. They have placed as many technicalities on the race as possible. Before the American pilots could find out what type of planes they could use the entries were ready to close. I cabled my money and entry and because my specifications and details do not conform with cable I am disqualified but I have plenty air in America to stir up. It will cost every American pilot from thirty five to a hundred thousand dollars depending on type of plane to enter this race with a possible first prize of fifty thousand dollars so it is easy to see they are not entering from a monetary standpoint. I feel that the Royal Aero Club in place of trying to help the American entries to get in the race they are doing everything they can to keep them out as there are always technicalities to tie up things with an airplane if you look for them and all the American entries will have plenty of trouble ahead regardless of how good they are. Evidently Sir Thomas Lipton was an exceptional Englishman.[9]

The pressure on the Royal Aero Club from the international press who were sympathetic to Roscoe's complaint was too much to bear, and the decision to bar Roscoe because of a mere one-word error on the entry form was reversed. Commander Perrin sent Roscoe a three-word cable: "Entry Boeing accepted."[10]

Roscoe immediately wired the Australian Press Association:

> Would like to retract statements in my telegram yesterday to you in answer to your wire regarding my entry in MacRobertson Australian race. I also apologize to Commander Perrin and the Royal Aero Club for my being a bit hasty but it was due to my utter disappointment. All my associations with English flyers have been most pleasant and I have found them to be every inch sportsmen in the highest degree. Am very happy and very gratified on receiving cable this morning from London stating my Boeing entry had been accepted. My best wishes for the greatest race in aeronautical history.[11]

A copilot was needed for the MacRobertson flight, and Roscoe chose Clyde E. "Upside Down" Pangborn, a former barnstorming stunt pilot with the Gates Flying Circus and "The Flying Fleet," who had flown almost completely around the world with Hugh Herndon, Jr., in 1931. Herndon and Pangborn did not return to Roosevelt Field, Long Island, their takeoff point, and had to crash-land at Wenatchee, Washington, Pangborn's hometown, after a tiring 41-hour flight. They were the first to fly nonstop across the Pacific from Japan to the United States.

Although it brought fame to both men, only Herndon received any substantial financial benefits from the flight. Pangborn received $2,500 of the $25,000 prize that had been offered by *Asahi Shimbun*, a Japanese newspaper. In 1932 and 1933 Pangborn ferried aircraft to South America and was a pilot for an East Coast overnight express service until it folded. Now thirty-five years old, unmarried, and broke, Pangborn looked for work in aviation and planned to enter the London-to-Melbourne Race with a specially built Gee Bee Supersportster, if he could get some financial backing. He couldn't, and the Gee Bee was turned over to Jacqueline Cochran to fly in the race if the supercharged Northrop Gamma she had chosen developed maintenance problems.

The selection of Pangborn as his copilot was an easy choice for Roscoe.

In addition to having a pilot license, Pangborn was a licensed mechanic. For several weeks Roscoe had been paying him $150 a week to fly Roscoe's Lockheed around the country on charter flights. Pangborn agreed to make the flight to Australia as copilot for Roscoe at a salary of $100 per week. He joined Roscoe and Don Young in Seattle as they prepared to test and accept the aircraft from Boeing.

Roscoe's plan was to fly the 247 to Los Angeles, have Young check it over thoroughly, collect the necessary survival gear and personal equipment, and fly it to New York. To avoid putting unnecessary flight time on the plane and risking the uncertainties of a transatlantic trip, the aircraft would be transported aboard a passenger ship to England, where Young would prepare it for the race. Roscoe, Pangborn, and Young would be accompanied to New York by Carline; Gladyce E. Lyons, Roscoe's secretary; and Whitney Collins, business manager for the flight. There they would be joined by Reeder Nichols, an experienced radio operator who worked for William Lear, head of the Lear Development Company. A friend from earlier days at Chicago, Lear had a newly built radio receiver/transmitter and a direction finder he wanted to publicize, and Roscoe asked to use them on the flight. Roscoe had also requested that Nichols be given time off to go. Reeder was hired at $100 per week plus expenses and a bonus of $1,000 if they placed first. Because of the weight restrictions, Roscoe was forced to exclude Young from the manifest. Although unfortunate, Roscoe did not consider this a problem since Pangborn was a licensed mechanic.

The 247 was flight-tested by Boeing in Seattle, but the engineers used water instead of gasoline to test the new fuel tank installations for leakage. When the engineers were satisfied with its performance, Roscoe accepted the aircraft and planned to see that the Boeing name would get in the papers immediately. He, Pangborn, and Young left Seattle on September 11 and flew to Los Angeles in 5 hours, 10 minutes, at an average cruising speed of 204.6 mph for the 1,120-mile trip. Boeing promptly put out a news release stating that the trip was "the fastest long distance flight ever made by a multi-motored passenger transport." Concurrently, United Air Lines announced that the acquisition of 247-Ds would mean a reduction in the company's $18^3/4$-hour California–New York schedule.

Continuing on the prowl for more sponsors, Roscoe made an agreement with Warner Brothers Pictures for $3,500 to publicize the company during the flight. According to the contract, "It is understood that the ship which you fly shall be known as 'Warner Bros. Comet' and that you will do everything within your power to publicize and make known the fact that your ship is so known, including painting such name in conspicuous letters on both sides of the fuselage."

After he signed the agreement, a bon voyage party was held at the Warner Brothers studios, where the stars turned out en masse to wish Roscoe good luck. The studio publicity director notified "all advertising and theater men" that Roscoe's "gigantic" Boeing would be streaking "across the longest ocean stretch of all" in another of "Warner Bros. mammoth promotional stunts." He also arranged for a christening of the aircraft by movie star Bebe Daniels as the *Warner Bros. Comet* and the two Pratt & Whitney Wasp engines as "Nip" and "Tuck."

Roscoe needed still more money or some kind of tradeoff to pay for trip expenses. He contacted his good friend Jimmy Doolittle, then head of Shell Oil's aviation department, to see if Shell would at least give him free fuel along the route. Reluctantly, Doolittle said that company officials had turned down all such requests for the race, but he sent Roscoe route maps and detailed airport information he knew he would need en route.

Roscoe approached Firestone Tire Company and other possible sponsors and was turned down by all of them. He then contacted William Randolph Hearst, wealthy newspaperman, for support. Hearst authorized a $6,000 contract that required Roscoe to submit seven articles, two before the race, one during the race, two after arrival in Melbourne and two after return to the States. There would be deductions for nonperformance. Concerned about being upstaged by rival newspapers, the Hearst contract specified that Roscoe not "give any authorized interviews or sign any statements for anybody." Roscoe's lawyer advised: "If either of you attend any banquets or dinners or any other reception either en route or after the race, make sure any microphone is removed if either of you say anything." Later, they were informed through Hearst's public relations firm that they should "not send any radio messages or broadcasts for newspaper or commercial purposes other than the dispatches intended for the fulfillment of their contract with us."[12]

Although she was not going on the aircraft during the race, Carline wanted to accompany Roscoe to London for the start, but neither could obtain passports because they didn't have birth certificates. When they wrote to the Mississippi vital records office, they learned that the state didn't have records on file for births before 1912. However, the State Department accepted an affidavit as to Roscoe's birth date from his parents; Carline, born in 1901, obtained a statement from her family physician.

Visas and overflight permits were also needed from about forty countries. It was no easy task and took weeks to get them from the various consulates and embassies involved. Many could not be obtained until they got to England.

After arrival at Los Angeles, Roscoe told Young to take the next day off and then get the 247 ready for the trip to New York. Since there were four persons beside the pilots aboard and no seats in the rear because of the gas tank installations, Young stowed folding chairs aboard. Thermos bottles of coffee and milk and baskets of fried chicken were purchased—enough to last for two days in order to eliminate the necessity for the passengers to debark for food while the plane was refueled at en route stops. Young recalled,

I worked a good two days and two nights around the clock. I had to check all the valves for clearance, synchronize the magnetos and get equipment stowed away in the plane. I was just finishing up on the third night, thinking I would have the next day off when Roscoe came in the hangar with Bob Montgomery and his wife and he was showing them through the airplane. When he came out, he said, "Don, I think we'll go tonight."

I couldn't believe it. Then he said, "You start gassing the airplane and I'll go home and round up the crew. When I come back I'll top off the tanks while you go home and pack."

I stood there for a few minutes and finally said, "Roscoe, I'm not going." He said, "What the hell are you talking about?"

I said, "Roscoe, you know Boeing wouldn't test this plane with a full load of fuel and you want to pull out of here tonight, over these mountains, with six people aboard and we don't even know if the airplane will pack 1150 gallons of gas."

I got my jacket and went home.

Roscoe had given me his license to have it renewed and I had forgotten to give it to him. He called me at home and asked, "Did you get my license renewed?" and I said, "Yes, I'll bring it right down."

When I got to the airport, Roscoe said, "Put 550 gallons of gas aboard while I go home and pack, then you go home and pack." I did and when I got back, there were about 15 or 20 people there to see us off, including Bob Montgomery who asked where my scarf was. I told him I didn't own one so he took his white cashmere scarf off and gave it to me.

When we got airborne, I was busy for about an hour or so running up and down the catwalk switching valves from one tank to another to be sure they would feed. Then I went to the back and everybody was out cold from carbon monoxide gas.

I rushed forward and told Roscoe to open the cockpit windows and the top hatch and I went back and held the door open with my foot to get the air flowing through the cabin. Then I went back and tried to get them awake but it was questionable whether I was going to get some of them out of it. I slapped them and did everything I could until they snapped out of it.

"The rest of the trip to Wichita, Kansas, our first refueling stop, was a nightmare for the three of us," Gladyce Lyons remembered.

Fighting to keep awake, fighting a growing nausea, not caring whether the ship flew on or crashed, we scarcely spoke a word to each other. It was not until after we had partially recovered our "land legs" by roaming the Wichita Airport, and we were on our way once more that we felt in the least like discussing our sensations. The three of us had the same general feeling of lightheadedness, the same aching throats and burning nostrils. All in all, we were as miserable as we might have been awakening from an anesthetic.

We got a bit of fun out of telling each other about our delusions. Mrs. Turner thought someone was trying to remove a needle from her forearm. Mr. Collins, the unfortunate victim of a hairpin which fell from Mrs. Turner's hair, found himself smothered in a sea of hairpins. Personally, I can remember nothing except the ever recurrent thoughts: "Why, oh why, did I ever imagine that I wanted to go to Europe?" "Why didn't I stay home?" and "I'll never live through this trip."

The weather became very bad after leaving Wichita and by the time we were over St. Louis it was really storming with a very heavy rainfall. We had flown beyond Pittsburgh when we were forced to turn back and land at an airport in Pittsburgh. There some reporter, who must have recently looked over the family album, grouped us all around the cabin door of the airplane, camp chairs, luggage, food and all, and made a real tintype picture. I mention this because it was one of the moments that seemed to touch Colonel Turner, for his voice was quite husky as he said, "Fellow ought to be able to win some kind of a race with this big a family."[13]

The 2,305-mile flight from Burbank to Pittsburgh was completed in 12 hours, 10 minutes, including a 20-minute stop at Wichita, for an average cruising speed of 189 mph.

It was not until the next afternoon that the storms cleared enough for us to get out of Pittsburgh, but as the weather was still bad over the mountains, Colonel Turner decided to go to Detroit to see some of his friends and pick up some more of the luggage that he has scattered around and about the continent.

We had an easy trip to Detroit, were there a few hours and then took off again for New York. Once again we had to turn back and this time we sat down at Buffalo. We curled up in the plane throughout the cool night and tried to get some rest. It was our second night in three days without sleep.

As dawn approached, we got underway. Visibility was poor and there was a very low ceiling. Don Young relinquished his position back of the pilots' seats and decided to sleep the last hundred miles into New York. He had just covered himself with a blanket in the aisle between the gas tanks when I saw him get up like a flash and dash to his post up front, just in time to see the oil pressure drop on our starboard motor. Apparently, "Tuck" had decided to tuck out on us.[14]

Young returned to the cockpit because he had heard a change in engine sound. Pangborn was sleeping and Roscoe, dead-tired, hadn't noticed. Young saw immediately that the right engine's oil pressure was dropping slowly. He awakened Pangborn and went back to the cabin to look at the engine through a window. Globs of oil were running off the right wing panel. He told Roscoe he had better shut the engine down or they were going to lose it.

"We didn't know if this airplane would fly on one engine or not," Young recalled. "Roscoe shut off the gas but the prop just kept on windmilling because we had no way to feather it. After about five minutes, it stopped suddenly and the plane started to vibrate. I just knew that I would have to pull that engine when we got to New York."

Strangely, after a while, the engine started to windmill again and Roscoe made the approach to New York's Floyd Bennett Field in Brooklyn. However, oil had saturated the brake drums on the landing gear under the dead engine, and Roscoe had no brake on the right wheel. "Roscoe took in the whole airport in one big crescent trying to stop it," Young said.

Pratt & Whitney engine experts arrived as soon as they were contacted and the engine was torn down. The problem was that the pistons were aluminum and couldn't cool as fast as the cylinders, which would shrink and stop the engine. When the pistons cooled off, the engine started to rotate again. Young installed a new set of rings in both engines hoping that they would not have any more trouble.

Reeder Nichols arrived and installed the radio and electrical equipment he would use on the flight. He was given time off by William Lear to prepare for and make the flight and went to Washington twice to obtain authorized frequencies and call letters (KHASH). He also obtained hydrographic charts from the Navy Department showing all radio stations along their route. In a letter to Roscoe, Reeder noted that there was no radio homing device available "which has been perfected to the extent that you could safely trust it over unknown territory with so much at stake."[15]

Before the plane could be loaded aboard the ocean liner, it had to pass a performance test given by an inspector from the Civil Aeronautics Bureau at Floyd Bennett Field because of its special fuel tank installation. An inspector arrived from Washington and required that Roscoe take off and land with a full load of gasoline within a given distance. On takeoff, he was instructed to clear an imaginary 165-foot obstacle. Roscoe got off in the distance required but when he landed the inspector said he hadn't attained the required height, even though there was no way to measure it. Roscoe, fuming and cussing, made another takeoff with the inspector standing at the other end of the field. Roscoe revved up both engines to full power while standing on the brakes. He let the brakes off and headed the plane toward the inspector on the takeoff run.

When he passed the required takeoff distance, he stood the airplane on its tail over the inspector's head, leaving no doubt that it could clear a 165-foot obstacle fully loaded. After landing, the inspector laughed and said, "Well, Roscoe, I've got to give it to you. You're cleared to go."

The 247 was scheduled to depart on the *S.S. Europa* on September 19 but failed to make that date, and so the plane and party were booked on the *S.S. Washington* for departure on September 26.

"Day and night, Colonel Turner worked to complete preparations," Gladyce Lyons said.

> There followed hectic days, days when he would return to our hotel and say to his wife, "I don't see how we're going to make it. This flight is going to cost me twice as much as I thought it would. I've just got to dig up some more money."
>
> There were days when we thought we would have to turn back, when we went around heartsick because we knew the tremendous disappointment it would be to Colonel Turner to have to quit after the months of planning. Each day we would hear of another of the 26 American entries who had planned to participate who either could not get his plane ready in time or who could not get financial backing. More and more determined to make the grade because of this, Colonel Turner kept making contacts. Finally, the glorious last day before we were to sail when some of his good friends came to his aid—Jack and Harry Warner.[16]

The Warner brothers donated $5,000 when Roscoe told them he needed that amount to pay the New York bills and continue to England.

The wings were removed from the 247 and the wings and fuselage were towed to dockside for loading aboard the *S.S. Washington*, a small passenger liner. As the fuselage was about to be hoisted aboard, it was found that the boom was not large enough to lift the plane the height required to place it on the sun deck. After many hours trying to figure out a solution, a lighter with a special derrick was chartered for $500 and the plane was carefully lifted aboard. It was only one of several delays that infuriated Roscoe and threatened to prevent getting the plane to England and ready by October 20.

Carline Turner recalled their departure day:

> It was a beautiful sight and hundreds of fans were on board to bid the flyers adieu. With them all crowded around, Turner and Pang said farewell

to America over the radio. The whistle blew and friends, fans, radio men, photographers and news reporters hastened down the gang plank.

Escorted way out to sea by Navy planes, piloted by friends of my husband, who dipped low over the *Washington* in a touching tribute to the American entry in this big race, our departure was indeed thrilling. The voyage was a delightful rest and relaxation. Captain Fried and his crew made the entire trip a celebration for the aviators sailing under the same colors they were to carry to Australia.[17]

The ship was first bound for Plymouth, where the Turner party, except for Roscoe, Pangborn, and Young, disembarked to a mail boat and were met by a young man who had made arrangements for the entire group to stay in the Grosvenor House in Cambridge. That is, all except Young, who was listed to stay in another hotel. Whitney Collins told the man gently but firmly, "Well, young man, you'll find that wherever Turner is, Young will be there, too. We will all stay in the same hotel." The young chap replied indignantly, "Oh, my, no! That isn't done in England!"

When Roscoe heard about this later, he turned down the quarters at Grosvenor House and rented three apartments on Berry Street in St. James.

After departing Plymouth, the ship was supposed to stop at Southampton to drop off the plane and crew, but the captain's sailing orders were changed en route and the ship proceeded to Le Havre, France, where the plane was off-loaded onto the dock. Arrangements were made promptly to load the plane aboard the *S.S. Roosevelt* and proceed back to Southampton. Young recalled,

> On the day we were supposed to put the airplane aboard the *Roosevelt*, there was a storm coming into that harbor that you wouldn't believe. And we knew we didn't dare let those Frenchmen hang that airplane up there in the wind. So, the ship went on and we were debating how we were going to get out of France.
>
> We never ran into so many buck-passers in our lives. They would have 15 Frenchmen standing on the dock arguing about what we would be permitted to do.

According to Roscoe, "When the *Roosevelt* pulled into the French harbor there was a 50-mile gale and they kindly waited three hours but the winds did not die down. Despite our anxiety to get our ship aboard, we had to be guided by perhaps wiser counsels from ship captains and harbor officials. The *Roosevelt* set sail for Southampton while we watched it forlornly sitting beside our plane on the quay."[18]

Young continued:

> They had a harbor master who was a terrific guy and stayed with us constantly trying to work with us to get us out of France. Time was getting short. We decided to see if we could fly the plane across the Channel. He drove us around in his Renault and we would measure the narrow streets on the way to the airport to see if the airplane would fit along them and around the corners. We had no measuring tape but Roscoe was wearing his lion skin coat and a walking stick with the lion's tail. When we would get to an intersection, Roscoe would jump out one side of the Renault and the Frenchman the other and they would rush over to the corner. Roscoe would start laying down the lion's tail, keeping count, while the harbor master was watching traffic.
>
> We found there was no way we could get the plane through the streets and out to the airport so we considered flying it off the dock but we had only maybe a foot and a half between the wing tip and the edge of the dock so we knew one little bobble and we wouldn't make that.

Roscoe considered transferring the plane to a barge that would be towed up a canal to a point near an airport but the French director of customs, who had never been confronted with such a weighty question before, said it couldn't be done unless Roscoe paid three million francs (about $100,000) in custom fees or bond. If the plane were merely transshipped to England without leaving the dock, there would be no duty or dock charges.

"Our pleas unmoved this stolid representative of the mighty French Republic," Roscoe said later,

> so we entrained for Paris and got the bond reduced to 500,000 francs. United States Lines stepped in nobly with an offer to provide the bond but that didn't settle the matter. Back in Le Havre we discovered that the locals wanted to weigh and evaluate every article in the plane and then weigh and evaluate everything collectively. Since we bought it as a whole

airplane we couldn't satisfy these demands. Hope in the shape of the good ship *Westerland* hove to in the harbor.[19]

"We were standing around the airplane in the rain when the captain of a small ship came ashore and asked us what we were doing there with the airplane," Young continued. "We told him about our problem and he said, "We'll put it on my ship." We looked at his ship and told him, "Thanks but no way. The ship isn't wide enough.' "

Roscoe and the ship's captain conferred. "This meant more telephoning, more haranguing, more measuring and when all was settled, we found we could just fit the plane on the ship," Roscoe said. "We began to load but only after rushing around money changing and document signing."[20]

Don Young told how the loading was accomplished:

He got his sailors busy bringing their mattresses off their bunks up onto the deck. He got a welder busy cutting off the big steel girders that supported the loading booms when they were at sea. They put the mattresses in between the hatches to protect the fuselage and they lifted the airplane on the deck with the nose sticking over one end of the ship and the tail over the other. We left in the doggondest rain storm we'd ever seen and made it to Southampton.

They were now three days late on their planned schedule. The plane could not be off-loaded directly at the dock and had to be transferred to a barge and then towed by tug to an auxiliary field near Hamble that had one hangar sitting on a sopping wet field. When it was off-loaded, thirty men were recruited by a Mr. Westbrook of Vickers Aircraft Company. They strained and pushed the fuselage to the hangar across the wet field, where Young installed the wing panels.

The plane was flown to Heston Airport. Roscoe, Pangborn, and Young made several test flights to check it out, then flew it to Martlesham Heath Airdrome, a Royal Air Force base, for weighing and inspection by race officials. Meanwhile, Nichols tested the radios using the code-transmitting signal of KHASH that had been authorized. When the officials checked the gasoline tanks and found that it had more fuel capacity than the aircraft would have been certified for in regular passenger service, Roscoe was informed that several of the tanks would have to be sealed off. With the total of 1,125 gallons the range would be about 2,300 miles. The plane was certified as an airliner to carry only 950 gallons and when the tanks were filled the Boeing was found to be about 500 pounds overweight. This was caused by the density of the fuel and the greater weight of British fuel, which was measured in Imperial gallons. About 100 gallons more had to be drained from the tanks to satisfy the rules, and the empty tanks were then sealed. The decreased fuel meant that Roscoe would not be able to fly nonstop to the five control points as he had planned and would have to make the trip in thousand or fifteen hundred-mile hops. He would have to zigzag and arrange for fueling at additional stops.

Frustrated, Roscoe facetiously told reporters: "Our ship's fine, and the weight is OK. She is absolutely grand and perfectly ready for the race. . . . But she'll have to fly without a crew!" In the cable language of the day, he wired the Hearst contact in New York: "Our only disappointment is that our tanks which should've contained distance-producing fuel are empty useless with the royal aero club seal on them but what's use squawking stop those are conditions race and we must abide by them stop."[21]

While at Martlesham Heath, the plane received much attention from the British press and visitors swarmed around constantly. Aircraft engineers and designers were especially interested in the Boeing because no 247s had been available for scrutiny in Europe before. Roscoe wired the New York Hearst office:

> They've examined it from nose to tail and even gone so far as to sketch the landing lights. I told them if they wanted the full specifications from the United States they could have them free. The thought struck me that it's time we ran some international races in order to bring some foreign competitors to the U.S. We could gain thousands and thousands of dollars of valuable technical knowledge.
>
> I'm sure that if any of our organizations wanted to start similar races in the United States they could benefit from Commander Harold Perrin, secretary of the Royal Aero Club, and his assistants who have done a very marvelous job. They've looked after everybody's comfort splendidly. Not only have technical arrangements for the race [been made] but they've assisted all nationalities in preparing maps, getting visas and giving ad-

vice as to the route. Every bit of data which has been collected on previous England-Australia flights has been placed gratuitously at our disposal.
So we who've never flown over the route have been given some idea as
to the conditions, climatic and otherwise.[22]

When the plane was ready, Roscoe flew it to Mildenhall Aerodrome,
the race starting point, where all the planes were housed until race time.
The Royal Aero Club provided hotel accommodations for the race crews.
At all hours of the day and night, crowds of designers, photographers,
and artists gathered around inspecting every last detail of the Boeing.
As Young remarked, "The visitors were getting millions of dollars worth
of engineering for the sum of the prize money of the race."

The Prince of Wales arrived in his special aircraft two days before the
race, accompanied by Lord Londonderry, chief of the Air Ministry. A
licensed pilot himself, the prince was keenly interested in the Boeing.
He sat in the cockpit for about forty-five minutes while Roscoe and
Young chatted with him about the aircraft's construction, fuel systems,
and the cockpit instruments. Before his departure, Roscoe presented
him with a model of the plane. King George V and Queen Mary, with
an entourage of reporters and members of Parliament, also visited later;
it was their first visit to an aerodrome, and the event created much comment in the British press. Queen Mary set foot inside an aircraft for the
first time when she entered the DC-2.

Carline described their visit:

> As is customary, Queen Mary walked behind His Majesty, as no one walks
> ahead of the King. Turner was presented to King George, who shook
> hands in real American fashion. He then asked my husband to present
> the rest of the party. When he shook hands with me, he said, "I hope
> you're not going with him." I answered, "No, I weigh too much."
>
> After the rest of the party were presented to King George, Queen Mary
> arrived. Very naturally, they both entered into conversation with us, al-
> though among their subjects it is not the custom for Queen Mary to con-
> verse at the same time as the King.
>
> They both looked into the plane and the King said, "I don't see any
> beds. Where and how are you going to sleep?" Whereupon my husband
> in his most natural manner, folded his arms and pillowed his head on his
> shoulder and said, "Just like this," causing King George to laugh aloud.[23]

During the trip to England, Pangborn had received a proposition by radio from an unknown sponsor with a tempting offer to fly an aircraft he had acquired. Although Pangborn never mentioned it, Roscoe learned about the offer and, concerned that Pangborn would pull out as his copilot at the last minute, had him sign an agreement the night before the flight to remain on the crew until Pangborn's return to the States, "in no event later than 60 days after termination or abandonment of the flight." In addition to his pay of $100 per week plus expenses, he would receive 20 percent of any prize money before Roscoe deducted any of the trip's expenses. There was also to be a division on a 50-50 basis of any money earned or received by either Roscoe or Pangborn for one year of any writings, movies, radio broadcasts, personal appearances, or endorsements for products used or in connection with the flight.

It was understood that Pangborn was not to seek any publicity from the flight because, even if they won, Roscoe knew that the sponsors he hoped to gain from postrace publicity would be his main source of income for a long time afterward. Pangborn understood this and never offered any objections or complaints about the arrangements.

While Young was preparing the Boeing, Roscoe was on the phone trying to get more sponsors. He autographed five hundred flight covers for a British air mail philatelist, for which he was paid £100 (about $500). Roscoe paid $200 to a man named Huntington, a map specialist, for the latest up-to-date maps of the countries along the course. Huntington plotted the entire course from London to Melbourne; Pangborn went over the maps to ensure the accuracy of Huntington's navigation figures.

Although more than sixty entries had been originally submitted, by race day only twenty planes were ready. They represented an unusual assortment of military aircraft, commercial airliners, and small, single-engine planes. Besides Roscoe and Pangborn, the only American entries were Jacqueline Cochran flying a Granville Supersportster and Jack Wright and John Polando in a Lambert Monocoupe, both American-built aircraft. The only other planes built in the United States were the Douglas DC-2, flown by Koene D. Parmentier and Jan Moll of KLM Airlines, and a Lockheed Vega, flown by Australians John Woods and D. Bennett.

Three adventurous passengers had bought tickets on the DC-2. Parmentier, the pilot, was no stranger to most of the course; he would be flying along his regular KLM route from Holland to Batavia. In a prerace press interview, Parmentier said, "Unlike the Boeing, which has had the seats removed to make way for extra fuel, I shall fly the Douglas just as it is and follow my regular route to Australia. We shall show our passengers the speed and comfort that will be commonplace on our new service."

The favored team was C. W. A. Scott and Tom Campbell-Black flying a de Havilland Comet, one of three Comets designed especially for the race. Both pilots had made many trips between England and Australia, and several other pilots had flown over much of the route. Of the Americans, only Pangborn had made any previous long-distance overseas flights.

In addition to the five mandatory stops, there were eighteen approved refueling stops en route that the shorter-range planes could use. At each stop, the competitors would have to make their own arrangements with the local gas vendors. The DC-2 flown by Parmentier and Moll would be refueled by their airline's gas and oil contractors.

The starting positions were determined by a drawing. Capt. James Mollison and his wife, Amy Johnson Mollison, flying one of the Comets, drew first place; Roscoe drew the second takeoff position.

Roscoe, Pangborn, Nichols, and Young went to sleep early on October 19, but just before midnight, they arose and went to the airport. At 3 A.M. the doors of the Royal Air Force hangar swung open and one after another the planes were rolled out and fueled. The planes were then lined up in two rows according to their takeoff sequence.

Since the Boeing had been stripped of everything that wasn't essential for the flight, the electric starters had been removed so the engines had to be started by hand cranks. Shortly before takeoff time, Young was preparing to crank the left engine:

> The Boeing was pretty high and we had to stand on a step ladder to crank one engine at a time. Anyone who isn't familiar with a hand inertia starter can't realize how much it can tear you apart after you've cranked it once or twice. Well, there were five of us there who could crank. One was Tom Hamilton of the Hamilton Propeller Company, George O'Brien, a

Hollywood film writer, Charlie Bunch from the Pratt & Whitney Company, Reeder Nichols and myself. We tried to crank one engine and we would crank and crank and crank and couldn't get it started. The officials were calling time and we had 15 minutes to be on the starting line for our takeoff position.

When we couldn't start one engine, we'd go over to the other one. Same problem. All of us cranked and Charlie Bunch tried so hard he upchucked. Finally, I called up to Roscoe and said, "Roscoe, are you pumping those throttles?" and he said "No" so we cranked and cranked some more.

While the others were trying, I went into the cabin and was standing there in the cockpit and when they yelled contact, Roscoe pushed the throttles forward. Pangborn, sitting right there beside him, said nothing. I said, "Roscoe, damn it, we're cranking our guts out and we're not going to start these engines if you keep pumping those throttles."

I called outside to Bunch, who was cranking, that the switch was off and to back the prop a couple of turns which he did. I told Roscoe not to touch the throttle. I then turned the switch on and on the first crank, the engine started with a blast. Then they went on the other side and that one started, just like that. Roscoe turned around to me with tears running down his cheeks and said, "You're the best God-damned friend I ever had."

Roscoe was using the throttle to pump gas into the carburetor which is what we had to do in those days to start most engines. He was just doing what he always did—pump the throttles. With those Wasp engines, you didn't have to do that.

The engines were started a mere six minutes before takeoff time. At precisely 6:30 A.M. on October 20, Sir Alfred Bower, Acting Lord Mayor of London, waved the Mollisons off in their *Black Magic*. Experienced in long-range flying, they were 12-1 favorites among the bettors. The nineteen other planes were to follow at about fifteen-second intervals.

Roscoe moved the Boeing into position to await the signal. One British writer noted, "Turner almost missed his takeoff spot because he overprimed his engines and arrived at the starting line like somebody late for church." Just as an orange sun edged upward over the horizon to the east, Roscoe eased the throttles forward, and the Boeing was off into the wind headed for Melbourne's Racecourse, 11,323 miles away. The first stop would be Athens, Greece.

8

THE RACE TO MELBOURNE

Reeder Nichols' radio log for October 20, 1934, shows the 247 was airborne from Mildenhall at 0630:45 Greenwich Mean Time (GMT). As it climbed, newsreel photographers flew alongside to take pictures. At 0650, still climbing to get on top of an overcast, the plane crossed the English Channel.

At 0751, Nichols wrote: "Flying on course 15,000 feet above France. Clouds now 10/10 solid overcast and no holes. Weather storming below and afraid that the boys who are not above this stuff are having a helluva time."

Pangborn had planned the flight to take them over the Matterhorn in the Swiss Alps because weather reports advised that only the peaks of the Alps would be visible above the clouds. When the Matterhorn was spotted, Roscoe altered course to avoid the high peaks. Nichols noted: "Motors running very sweetly for which we thank Mr. Pratt and Mr. Whitney as this certainly is no place to set down."

At 1110, Roscoe had Nichols send the first message to the Universal

192

News Service in London: "We have now left the mountains behind and are taking a straight course to Athens which will alternately take us over first land and then water. The temperature is more comfortable and Nichols, the radioman, is having less difficulty in operating his key. Shortwave schedules are being constantly kept with a Norwegian radio station."

Thirty minutes later, Roscoe messaged London: "Still on our course making good time. Ship is riding very smoothly and the two Wasps are purring away like two friendly cats."

At 1210, Nichols radioed Universal News Service: "Still going strong despite absence juicy steak." This was followed by a message to Athens Airport advising Shell Petroleum that they would be two hours late.

Before landing, Nichols noted in his log: "Sighted Athens some 40 miles away. Beginning to get dark and looks as if we are in for a night landing. If we gas up and get away in a hurry, will arrive Baghdad at night also which means that we arrive Karachi for daylight gassing and have to land Allahabad at night also. Altogether seems as if we are in for lots of night landings."

Roscoe landed the Boeing at Athens at 1641 GMT; all three were suffering from mind-numbing headaches. Nichols wrote: "Arrived Athens and immediately start to refuel among the jabbering of the Greeks who were very kind to us. . . . Had taste of Turkish coffee which seems to be okay if your teeth are close together and you can strain the coffee through them. Took about an hour and 15 minutes to gas and drink a couple of bottles of beer apiece."

When Roscoe climbed out from Athens, Nichols checked to see if he could contact London: "He answered back and damn near knocked the cans off my ears. This darkness must be good for something besides owls."

Instead of landing at Aleppo, Syria, Roscoe decided to fly directly to Baghdad. He sent a message to Universal News Service in London: "Due to rush in refueling and being behind schedule did not have opportunity to give much of story at Athens. Arrived there with splitting headache due to high altitude flying."

Nichols continues his running commentary of the flight, with customary humor mixed in, in log excerpts for the legs to Karachi:

1850   Called LGN [London] and told him to break schedules as I was very tired and expected to get some rest. Ship was riding very nicely and plenty of landmarks. . . . Have climbed to 10,000 feet and imagine our surprise at finding mountain which is uncharted approximately 13,000 feet. I thought we were going to run into it looking at it from my side of the cabin but Pang was watching it and we turned from our course to avoid hitting it. Most of the country we are now flying over has not been accurately charted and is therefore dangerous. This is one part of the world where a damn good compass is a good investment.

2136   Have been asleep sitting up in my chair. Pangborn is lying down underneath my feet snoozing away to beat hell. Roscoe is flying and my radio is quiet.

2150   Sighted Island of Cyprus through hole in clouds. Should be over Syria in another 30 minutes or so. Pang is still sleeping because there are to be some tough spots ahead of us where both he and Turner will have to strut their stuff.

2240   Must now be over Syria although clouds are solid underneath us. Called Baghdad Radio but made no connections . . . Can hear Baghdad working through static but very unintelligible.

2300   Baghdad giving weather report to Dutchman [Parmentier in the DC-2]. Also said that Mollisons had landed long time ago. Believe dependability of Boeing plugging along will win race so nobody is particularly worried about who is ahead at this early stage of game.

2352   Finally contacted Baghdad and got weather report of high broken overcast so everything is hunkydory and we are shooting through although cannot get weather reports beyond Baghdad. Asked for bearings but they have no direction finder and static so damn bad don't like to give phones to Roscoe.

2400   Another day another dollar.

0201   Landed Baghdad, nice little field complete with floodlights but very dry and dusty. Jumped out and directed refueling while Roscoe checked in and Pangborn checked oil. . . . All kinds of customs officials and immigration officers but did not even ask for passport, some mention of Roscoe's passport being all that was necessary. Dust is about three inches thick. One fellow told me that it hadn't rained here in two years and I believe it. It is getting daylight and notice some camels around. Strange, awkward looking things all loaded up with barrels of gasoline, one on each side. Took on capacity of gas and checked all tanks topping off each tank myself to make sure everything is okay. Roscoe has appointed me official in charge of refueling and Pang to plot course for next hop.

0231 [After takeoff from Baghdad] Weather is excellent and Roscoe is now sleeping. Left my radio and went up to front seat with Pang. Sun is directly in our eyes so took wheel while Pang fixed up compass cover lid in front of his eyes to keep the sun out.

0358 Passing over numerous small rivers and streams apparently rising out of the mountain range which is about 50 miles north of our course. The small streams we see below have few blades of grass on each side which looks green but ten feet from river bank the desert starts again . . . This country is certainly the most desolate place I have ever seen and surely is no place to set down.

0440 [Message to Universal News Service, London] "Unable to give story in Baghdad as unable spare time. Landed there just before daylight and took off in 30 minutes. Now headed for Karachi as cannot make Allahabad in one stop. Turner."

0544 Reeled in antenna and went up to cabin for few minutes. Roscoe still sleeping and Pang flying. Took wheel while Pang attended to some personal matters. Damn near fell asleep myself and asked Pang to shake it up before we went into nose dive. Over mountains about 12,000 feet and climbing to clear peaks of mountains which apparently haven't been charted. Awful hard to use these maps as they are terribly inaccurate even in large detail.

0600 Crawled in alongside Roscoe and went to sleep.

1010 Had a few hours of something that might pass for sleep for want of a better name. Felt awfully tired when got up and plenty sore. Every bone in my body ached. Think Roscoe feels same way although he is up front flying and Pang is navigating.

1110 Karachi . . . gave excellent weather report and said the Dutchman had already left. Too bad but maybe we will catch up with him yet. Anything can happen in a race like this and we will just keep on plugging along.

1115 Flying over country that is an absolute desert and no good for anything. Can't possibly see why the British are so damn proud of this country. Would hate to think of motors cutting out on this godforsaken desert.

1215 Sighted Karachi and the Indian Ocean which certainly looked good to all three of us. Somehow one associates water with civilization and this certainly is no metropolitan area we have been flying over as there is no sign of man, beast or even birds since we left Baghdad some 1500 miles back.

1229 After circling field and flying over the graveyard that is associated with every airport in the world and just missing a caravan of camels that seem to be everywhere in this country (except for the last 1500 miles), landed on a beautiful field and there were the Mollisons. They have been having some engine trouble and the landing gear is not functioning properly. . . . During refueling Roscoe and Pang had a long talk with the Mollisons. Their plane had been fixed up and they decided to go on.

1254 Turner made a very beautiful takeoff with the Mollisons right on our tail. They flew alongside of us while we were climbing and in the darkness which is fast approaching it looks good to see something living so close even if they are our competitors. This country we are now flying over is featureless with nothing but mountains and deserts and is certainly nothing to write home about.

The Boeing picked up a good tailwind as they headed toward Allahabad and fatigue was beginning to affect the crew. Pangborn came back and crawled under the blankets; Nichols threw a coat over him. Nichols noted in his log: "Can't afford to have anybody on the sick list with only half of the course flown."

1730 Haven't sighted Allahabad as yet. Can't get bearings from Allahabad and every time I ask him for few minutes of key so I can take bearing he answers with the same old story about beacon being visible sixty miles. Would like to get that operator around neck. Have been up front for last ten minutes helping Roscoe look for beacon. No soap.

1830 Called Allahabad and asked him to please give me bearing or hold key down few minutes so I could take bearing. He can't seem to understand that I can take bearing. He keeps telling me that beacon is visible for sixty miles. Must be a native on key and very dumb at that.

1930 No sign of beacon as yet and if it is visible for sixty miles we should soon be sighting it as we should be in Allahabad by now.

1935 Woke Pang up and he decided we had overshot Allahabad. I asked Allahabad to shoot rockets or flares into air. He hasn't got flares but his damn beacon should be visible for sixty miles. Pang turns ship around 180 degrees and try to get Allahabad to give us signal. He is now off the air but I hear Jodhpur telling him KHASH is calling. Called again and Allahabad answered. Told him urgent that I have his undivided attention as we were lost. Our gas is getting very low. He says okay and gives me about three minutes key down. We swing ship and establish course of 290 degrees but did not get good bearing as he broke off and starting calling Jodhpur and told them that he had heard me and that I was lost. This seemed a silly thing to do so in order to get his whole attention and also to close up stations that were interfering I sent out the SOS.

Nichols made no further entries until they landed at Allahabad. Roscoe tells what happened from his viewpoint on the flight to Allahabad:

We had plenty of gas to reach Allahabad but not much extra for detours. The route was totally strange to us. Visibility was poor. We knew it would be night before we landed.

In other words we had to fly by dead reckoning. We had to set a compass course, allow for drift, figure our speed, and from these calculations deduce when we would arrive at our destination. When the hour arrived we would gaze below [and] there would be Allahabad, pretty as you please. At least that's what we hoped.

So we sailed eastward over India. . . . Dusk fell and deepened into night. The hour arrived when Allahabad should be directly below us, but there was no beacon, no field light, no dark outlines of a city.

We didn't assume instantly that we were lost. Very probably we hadn't covered as much ground as we had supposed. We had complete confidence in our instruments and our alertness in staying on the course. Somewhere just ahead the beacon would soon pierce the black curtain of night. The thing to do was to stay on our course and barge straight ahead. This we did until a flash illuminated the horizon.

"That's it!" we decided and headed toward the flash. But it didn't reappear and we began to have that gone feeling in the pit of our stomachs. The flash was not a beacon after all—it was lightning!

Reeder Nichols, sitting in his chrome-nickel chair with green leather upholstery [it had been presented to him by a London automobile dealer], was sending messages to the operator at Allahabad.

"Give us a radio bearing," he requested. "Give us a radio bearing."

But for some reason we couldn't establish two-way communication. All the time we were requesting help, the operator at Allahabad was blithely announcing to the world, "Colonel Turner is lost. The Americans are overdue." We could hear him announcing it, but we couldn't get him to answer us.

In the meantime the needles on our gas gauges swung closer and closer to empty. Vainly we searched the ground for some check point, but there was nothing in the blackness below to give us an accurate indication of where we might be.

Very soon the motors would sputter and die. Before that should happen, however, it was important to have some plan in mind. We wanted to land on an airport. If that was impossible, we wanted to save the ship. Barring that, we hoped to save our lives.

"We can always bail out," was one pleasant suggestion.

"Yes," I replied. "Bail out at night into a jungle full of tigers. They tell me the tigers always go looking for fresh meat at night. Besides, if we bail out we'll lose our ship. The thing to do is to try to land on a river."

"Didn't they tell us at Karachi there were crocodiles in the rivers?"

I had forgotten the crocodiles and for the moment I actually visualized myself standing on the wing trying to unfasten a propeller to use as a weapon against the crocs. A sort of modern St. George battling the dragons with a sword of purest alloy.

Tigers, crocodiles, and no airport. Bail out and play tag with tigers. Land in the river and annoy the crocs. Do neither and die. One of the three fates seemed imminently to be ours. At that very moment, I think, all of us must have known intimately the state of mind of all flyers who have gone to their dooms in oceans and wilderness, blazing new trails for mankind to follow.

I looked at the gauges and saw with a shock that they read empty. We were a couple of hours overdue. Why couldn't we get a reply from Allahabad?

"Send out an SOS," I told Nichols. An SOS would silence all other stations on the air—even the Sparks at Allahabad who seemed to feel special delight in telling the world we were lost.

Nichols was aghast. "That's serious business. You only do that when you're on the spot."

"If we're not on the spot now we will never will be," I replied grimly.

So Nichols sent out the three famous letters. Then things began to break all at once. They had to, if we weren't going to be just another air casualty.

The Allahabad operator heeded our request and sent us the bearing we wanted. At the same moment we saw beneath us the Soune River. Feverishly we searched on our maps. Yes! We had located our position by the Soune—we were cruising over the only part of the river that took a due east-west course for approximately 50 miles.

We turned back, praying that our gasoline would last. As far as our gauges showed we were already riding on borrowed time. We caught a flash of light and hoped that it wasn't lightning.

"Flash your beacon on and off," Nichols radioed to the ground.

Allahabad obliged and when we saw the intermittent flashing we knew that our troubles were over. We coasted down to a landing and taxied up to the gas tanks in front of the hangar. As we slowed to a stop, our two motors gave their last gasps. But we didn't care—we were safely down, ship and all![1]

After takeoff from Allahabad, Nichols wrote his own version of the episode in his log as they churned on toward their next refueling stop at Alor Star:

2328   Did not try to keep log of what was happening when we were lost and will try to recite from memory the highlights of the adventure which has all of us a bit nervous and highstrung. After sending out the SOS, Allahabad apparently realized the urgent need of his radio and gave us his undivided attention from then on. Several times we established a course but it didn't exactly agree with the terrain we were flying over and inasmuch as our gas was running low we were constantly on the lookout for a decent place to land. To the north of us were hills and small mountains and altogether a very uninviting spot to have to set a ship down in. Pang's maps showed so many rivers and they all looked so much alike that it was very hard to tell one from another; however, we had overshot Allahabad something like 150 miles and over 50 miles to the south so we had no definite idea of exactly where we were and how far from Allahabad. For over two hours we flew with throttle back just beyond the stalling speed in order to conserve gas.

Pang had already decided that we were south of course and, in the meantime, Allahabad had arranged a crude makeshift loop and were attempting to take bearings on us. Allahabad informed me that we were in a southerly direction from them and I told Pang about this. He had already decided to go north and then is when we picked up the lights.

After sighting the lights I asked Allahabad to turn them on and off so that we could definitely establish whether or not we were right in our belief that we had sighted Allahabad. They turned them off and on for a minute or so and we knew that we were headed in the right direction but whether or not we had enough gas to get there was the question in our minds. The auxiliary tanks were completely dry and the right wing tank was also dry. The gas gauge showed that we just had about five or ten gallons left and sixty or seventy miles to go. We then decided that if we did crash to go down with the ship rather than risk the chance of being separated if we jumped in parachutes and being eaten by tigers or other wild animals. We kept the airport constantly advised of our position so that if we did crash they could send a rescue party out for us.

During the excitement of reaching the airport I forgot to turn off my dynamotor and when I grabbed the antenna to reel in, touched 2000 volts which gave me a nasty jolt and paralyzed my right hand and arm for 15 or 20 minutes. . . .

Believe me, we were damn glad to get down and a couple of stiff shots of whiskey sure felt good. We also had some excellent ham and eggs and refueled and were off for Alor Star [Siam] on the west coast of the Malay Peninsula.

The flight to the next refueling point was over the Bay of Bengal, but having to dodge thunderstorms and heavy rain took its toll in fuel consumption and time.

1054   Landed at Alor Star in one big sea of mud and water. Taxied up to gas pump and took two tanks of gas as it was inviting suicide to fill all tanks [which would make the takeoff through the water extremely slow] and only 400 miles to Singapore where we have to stop anyhow.

Immediately upon landing, officials wanted to know if we wanted flares set for our takeoff. Roscoe told them no, that it would only take 15 minutes to gas and it was broad daylight at the time. I was puzzled by their insistence on the flares but we finally convinced them that we didn't need them even in darkness as our landing lights are something to write home about.

After gassing and starting motors, received instructions from field superintendent who looked at his watch and said, "It will be dark in three minutes." We looked at him puzzled and he informed us that when it started to get dark here there was no fooling around. Hopped in and started to taxi down to edge of field in broad daylight. By time we got to edge of field which was about three or four minutes, it was pitch dark and we sorta wished we hadn't been so hasty about refusing flares.

1412 Landed at Singapore amid big crowd that had assembled. Lots of people in evening clothes which is gentle reminder that the English are down here in big numbers. Very efficient ground crew took over gassing and Pang and I hopped off to the tent where one of the nicest plates of ham and eggs I ever saw awaited us. Also some damn good coffee and beer. Had a couple of stiff jolts of White Horse whiskey to ward off colds and it sure warmed up the old system. A general feeling among the gang is that the hardest part of the flight is over being something like two-thirds through. These people are certainly enthused about the race and well they should be due to the fact that they are a week closer to England than they have ever been before.

1455 After very delightful time of little more than half hour, we took off [for Koepang, Netherlands Indies] with promise to stay longer next time. Learned that Scott had landed at Darwin but was having motor trouble so decided to gun her up and try to beat Scott to Melbourne.

1545 Sometime during last few minutes crossed equator. Being only shellback aboard felt the urge to initiate Roscoe and Pang into the Ancient and Loyal Order of the Deep but didn't feel such levity was appropriate at this time.

1800 Gave Roscoe shot of brandy and cup of good hot Ovaltine. Pang is back taking a well-earned rest and Roscoe is taking her into Koepang. Sat up front with Roscoe for few minutes but decided couldn't get much sleep in Pang's seat so cut in four tanks [of fuel] for Roscoe and laid down alongside Pang for some shuteye.

2310 Pang relieved Roscoe at wheel and we are now flying over the Flores Sea.

2400 Midnight on the ocean and not a streetcar in sight. . . . Another day, another dollar. Midnight according to our watches but sun is way up now. Can't figure out what day this is but believe it is Tuesday. Maybe I'm wrong.

0145 Sighted Island of Timor. Have been passing small islands for long time but not interested enough to find out. Just plain lazy or tired. Don't know which.

0213 After scaring lots of animals out of year's growth, landed at Koepang. Very officious Dutch officer dressed in white demanded 16 good dollars for the privilege of landing on his field and inasmuch as we had to have gas forked it over. Nothing but hand pumps here so decided only to fill three tanks and save a little time. . . . No gas or electricity on whole island and something like eight different tribes of natives. Big ditch all around airport to keep cattle and horses off flying field. The field was constructed entirely by native labor who worked one day a week in lieu of paying taxes. Soldiers would not let us smoke so had to walk across field while Pang took over my job of gassing up and I had a good puff.

0257   It is now just about high noon and the sun is sure beating down so was glad to get into air and get breath of air. Climbed to 10,000 feet and over the Timor Sea which we have heard so much about. Half way across old Tuck began to lose oil pressure so revved her back a little and decided to limp into Darwin.

0600   Sighted entrance to Port Darwin and knew we had safely crossed the Timor Sea. Old Tuck seems to be holding his own in the battle for oil pressure but believe Roscoe will take cowling off at Darwin and look her over.

0620   Landed at Darwin being two minutes less than three days from London. As was reeling in antenna the weight snapped off and joined fish in the bottom of the Timor. Had to be vaccinated at Darwin and crawl through tail of ship to restring antenna and put new weight on.

Roscoe is pulling off cowling and trying to adjust oil pressure relief valve on old Tuck. Learned that Scott and Black had landed in Melbourne so that leaves us out of the first money but the Dutchmen [in the DC-2] are still going strong and while there is life there is hope.

After almost two hours we decide to get into the air again, for which we will all be thankful because it is very, very hot here. Miss Cochran's mechanic gave us hand here which was very nice of her inasmuch as she was out of the race at Bucharest.

0810   Took off from Darwin and headed across a peninsula to the Gulf of Carpenteria to use as a landmark due to the fact that the country between Darwin and Charleville contains no landmarks that would assist in navigating. The oil pressure has dropped to 30 pounds on both engines and we are nursing them at reduced throttle. It is beginning to get dark although it is only 8 A.M. back in dear old London.

0840   Both Pang and Roscoe are at the wheel so went to sleep in the community bed. Woke up at 1115 to find Pang beside me.

1500   Raised Frisco and Bergen, Norway again. Believe this established record for consistent communication from airplane and also long distance record as absolutely impossible to transmit further because as near as I can figure we are 12,500 miles from Bergen and 8,500 from Frisco. Gave Frisco message for Universal News Service in New York and two personal telegrams for home.

2000 Have been getting bearings every ten minutes for last hour and half and advised him [Charleville] that we would be way behind schedule as we are nursing two very sick motors up here. They were somewhat worried about us due to fact we were long overdue in Charleville.

2200 Still getting good bearings now every three minutes and the transmitter hasn't been turned off for two hours. During last hour the sun came up and just as it was peeking over the horizon the (bearing) reports changed from 325 degrees to 360 which undoubtedly due to sun's rays bending waves. Pang was upset until I told him the trouble. Signals getting much stronger and we asked Charleville for some definite landmark but seems as if only landmark is dry river bed and there are so many of these that it means very little. Both engines still giving trouble but plugging along at reduced throttle.

2215 Landed Charleville after helluva night spent over Australian jungle. Everybody is tired and sore and we have just learned that the Dutchmen had forced landing at Albury and were stuck in the mud, so this gives us fresh encouragement to push along.

Old Nip and Tuck both need some serious attention but it seemed such a shame to have to tear into them when we were only a hop, skip and jump from home base. We gassed up and took on a bite of sandwich and some hot tea.

2314 In the air again and neither engine seems to be improved. Old Nip getting worse so throttled her back and flew on Tuck.

2400 Another day, another dollar. It is supposed to be midnight but it is about 10 A.M. to these people.

0009 Old Tuck started throwing oil out the breather pipe and looked as if it might catch fire so Pang started navigating for the nearest landing field which happened to be Bourke some 75 miles away.

0040 Landed at Bourke for forced landing and decided to take cowling off and load in cabin. Tightened up rockerbox nuts and then found out that cowling couldn't go in cabin so we put it back on again. Roscoe so damned tired that he was swaying back and forth and the heat was not helping the situation any either.

0200 Took off from Bourke for Melbourne.

0343   Passed over the finish line at Melbourne and 15 minutes later landed at Laverton Airport where big reception awaited us. Most welcome thing to my mind was American cigarette offered by American vice counsel, and four tall drinks of good old White Horse scotch. We were all very tired and showed the effects of 3 days, 21 hours, 5 minutes and two seconds of racing.

Thoroughly fatigued and unshaven, the trio was met by a crowd who wanted most of all to see Gilmore. Everyone assumed that Roscoe still flew with his pet and were disappointed when he did not crawl out of the cabin with his master.

When they checked in with the official timers, Roscoe learned that Parmentier and Moll in the DC-2 had landed just $2\frac{1}{2}$ hours ahead of them. Had they not lost about three hours when they overflew Allahabad and not had to land at the tiny outback town of Bourke, the 247 would have come in second to the de Havilland Comet flown by O. Cathcart-Jones and K. Waller, who had flown the route in 70 hours, 59 minutes. As it was, the Boeing had completed the race, according to the official timers, in 92 hours, 22 minutes, 38 seconds, flight time, and the Douglas had clocked in only 20 hours behind the Comet.

The KLM Douglas had entered both the speed and handicap races and opted to take first prize in the latter, rather than second place in the speed category. Cathcart-Jones and Waller received $15,000 and a gold cup for first place in the speed category; Parmentier and Moll earned $10,000, and Roscoe and Pangborn, $7,500, for their respective places in the handicap classification.

Word that Roscoe had reached Melbourne safely and in the money was flashed immediately to the States. Clair Egtvedt of Boeing wired Roscoe: "The boys are all proud of your outstanding accomplishment and fully appreciate what you and Pangborn have done by successfully completing so lengthy a flight over strange terrain. We also appreciate that you were flying a commercial transport plane where dependability was a first consideration in its design."

Although most of the British and Australian press featured the win by Cathcart-Jones and Waller in the de Havilland Comet, the fact that two commercial transports had placed second and third in elapsed time was significant. A British newspaper commented:

The results of the England-Australia air race has fallen like a bomb in the midst of British everyday commercial and military aviation. Preconceived ideas of the maximum speed limitations of the standard commercial aeroplane have been blown sky high. It has suddenly and vividly been brought home that, while the race has been a triumph for the British de Havilland Comet (the winner), British standard aeroplane development, both commercial and military, has been standing still while America now has in hundreds, standard commercial aeroplanes with a higher top speed than the fastest aeroplane in regular service in the whole of the Royal Air Force.[2]

When Will Rogers learned that Roscoe had finished in third place in the grueling race, he remarked in one of his radio talks, "In a race like that Melbourne hop, it's an honor to be third!"

After eighteen hours of sleep, Nichols wrote to Bill Lear from Melbourne:

> I want to express my thanks to the boys in the laboratory and the shop for the thorough manner in which they mastered every detail of the design and construction of what I honestly believe to be the best equipment ever installed in an airplane. It is a great source of satisfaction to me to know that among our other worries, I was not bothered by the thought that my radio would let me down. . . .
>
> The direction finder worked beautifully, especially when coming into Charleville. This country is absolutely featureless and every mile looks like the last 1,000 miles you have passed, so it was great to pick up bearings 450 miles away and run a chalk line over the jungles until we hit Charleville right on the nose. Never did the equipment fail me.[3]

Only nine of the twenty aircraft that had left Mildenhall eventually finished, and the race had not been without a tragedy. British Flying Officer H. D. Gilman and New Zealander Flight Lt. J. K. C. Baines, flying a Fairey Fox bomber, crashed in the Appenine Mountains near Foggia shortly after taking off from Rome; both were killed. Jacqueline Cochran, flying the unruly Granville R-5 International Supersportster with Wesley Smith, made two abortive attempts to land at Bucharest and damaged the landing gear severely on the third try; she was unable to continue. Jack Wright and John Polando, the only other Americans in the race, landed in Persia (now Iran) and were imprisoned for two days before being released. They elected not to continue.

Two other aircraft had damaging mishaps on landing; a lone British pilot who had strayed off course on his first leg and landed in Spain, was detained by authorities for illegal entry. He was later released but had damaged his plane beyond repair on the landing. The others that did not finish dropped out along the way because of engine malfunctions.

Shortly after his return to the States, Roscoe was invited to tell his story on the radio. Here is an excerpt from that program:

I want to thank you for your moral support, prayers and good wishes, for I know of a number of people who prayed for our safety who perhaps seldom ask for unseen guidance from the Creator of all things and Ruler of the Universe.

Personally, I thought once or twice that we would never see California again. I was debating in my own mind as to whether we would favor the tigers by jumping in parachutes—or land in the river and take our chances with the crocodiles. As you probably know, tigers aren't a specialty of mine. If it had been lions I would have felt a little easier.

We are very proud of our position in the race. We feel it is just as important to the United States as the position of Parmentier and Moll is to Holland, and Scott and Black to England. Naturally, we would like to have finished first, but it is impossible for any commercial plane to beat a specially-built racing job if the racer stays in the air. I know a thing or two about racing planes and I have nothing but praise for those great fliers—Scott and Black. They are regular fellows but I would not fly their plane, or any other racing plane, over that course and for that great a distance. Racing aircraft is mainly experimental and anything can happen. We think we are doing good to put a racer across the United States with engines of long tried and tested dependability. But to put one half way round the world with an experimental engine is something new in aviation and involves a certain amount of luck.

The Boeing and Douglas are standard stock transport models with commercial Wasp and Cyclone engines. The regulations under which our planes had to qualify were interpreted by us and our Department of Commerce to mean that our planes could not carry any greater load than was allowed on the airlines, so we used the combined mail, baggage and passenger weight allowance for gasoline.

Our engines on such commercial planes must go through 50 or more hours' test at full throttle before they can be used. The de Havilland people used all the finest engineering and designing skill in all of England to build three Comets and six engines, with four spare engines in reserve, for this race, and then the Comets were placed in the hands of the most skillful pilots in all the Empire.

Scott had broken the record three or four times from London to Australia. Parmentier and Moll have flown the course 15 times as far as Batavia, so you can readily understand why we offer no apologies or excuses for our position in the race, since we were the only representatives of the Stars and Stripes to complete the race.

Although we finished third, we received second prize money [for the handicap category] which, according to the papers was $7,500. However, when the rate of exchange was through with it, the total amount of six thousand American dollars was left, and that, with twenty thousand dollars more in cash, is what it cost me so that there could be an American plane and crew finish in the race. I knew regardless of how many planes there were, that with the strength of the Boeing plane to withstand the storms and the dependability of the Wasp engines, coupled with the skill of that great pilot, Clyde Pangborn, and with Reeder Nichols at the radio, we would be there sometime.

This may sound a bit egotistical but at the time we sailed [from the United States], the other American entries had dwindled down from twenty-one to three: Jacqueline Cochran, Jack Wright and myself. There was some question as to whether Miss Cochran or Mr. Wright would have their planes ready in time, and they just did make the deadline for their planes arrived at Mildenhall Aerodrome after dark on the last day that planes would be accepted. Miss Cochran was the only other American entry in the Speed Race, Mr. Wright being entered only in the Handicap Race.

Miss Cochran cracked up on the first lap of the race, and poor old Jack Wright landed in Persia and they picked him up and kept him over for several days.

Of course, things were not so easy for anyone in that race because of the great distances between landing fields and radio stations. If we missed any point on the course one stood a very good chance of never being seen again. Old Man Weather never seems to have any regard for races or racers either, and we had expected all different varieties of it on this race, so that every pilot was taxed to the maximum for skill, endurance and experience. How much of this one can put on an airplane depends more or less on the pilot's knowledge of his aircraft.

It was a great experience and without the help of our good friends, it would not be history now. The movie colony, in particular, has played a very important part in my career since 1932. I have had the pleasure of initiating most all the executives and probably half of the stars to the air, and most of them have been friends indeed. . . .

In my other speed ventures in this country I am indebted to Joe Schenck, Connie Bennett, Ben Lyon, Zeppo Marx, Rex Cole and Robert Montgomery. These good friends of mine have not donated to the cause of aviation directly, but they have enough faith in my skill and ability to take a chance with no security—and a big gamble on my neck. So far I have not failed them.[4]

Roscoe, Pangborn, and Nichols were entertained in Australia at garden parties and cocktail receptions for the next three weeks and refused invitations only when there was a schedule conflict. Meanwhile, in the States, Roscoe was the cover subject on an issue of *Time*. A lengthy article inside reviewing the race stated: "U.S. aviation enthusiasts were little concerned that a British racing plane had won the world's greatest air race. What pleased them greatly was that in second place was a U.S. transport plane powered by U.S. engines; that not far behind, roaring over Australia, was another U.S. transport plane flown by U.S. Pilot Roscoe Turner."[5]

The article reviewed Roscoe's life and his racing victories and added: "A temperamental prima donna on the ground, Turner is a cold, nerveless machine in the air. 'I am a speed merchant,' he likes to say. His showing last week in the race to Australia did his reputation and that of his merchandise more good than all the tricky publicity with which his name today is encumbered."

The Australian newspapers were intrigued by this unusual American pilot who wore a uniform all the time, topped by an ever-present smile and a bigger-than-life waxed mustache. The stories the Aussies had heard about his lion and his races had preceded him. One reporter wrote:

I like Roscoe Turner. His masculine ego erupts in colored shirts, diamonds, an entourage of pet lions, an unending flow of blushless swank. In a world where the theory that all men are equal now prevails almost universally, the art of swank, open and unashamed, is practically dead. I find it refreshingly stimulating. Showmanship is a gift not all who have something to show off display to its best advantage without arousing public suspicion, jealousy or scorn. Swank is a subtle art. When I see anybody carrying it off as well as Turner, I am consumed by envy.[6]

When the partying was over, Roscoe, Pangborn, and Nichols flew the 247 to Sydney and supervised its loading aboard the *S.S. Mariposa*. They sailed on November 14 and arrived in Los Angeles via Honolulu on December 1. They debarked but the ship proceeded to San Francisco, where the plane was off-loaded and reassembled.

While the plane was being unloaded, Roscoe met the Los Angeles press and issued a bylined story that he had prepared aboard ship. Without any idea how his next trip would be financed but hoping sponsors would come forward immediately, he boldly announced that he intended to fly around the world entirely by air, instead of partly by ship as he had just done.

It will be a scientific flight around the globe at the equatorial belt. Subsequently, I will fly from the North Pole to the South Pole, circumnavigating the globe in that way.

I hope to have Admiral Richard E. Byrd as navigator with me on that flight. And if Clyde Pangborn, the man who flew at my side in the London-to-Melbourne Race, will go with me, I'd like to have him on both flights. I am deeply indebted to him for his courageous and skillful aid. I consider him one of the finest fliers in the world.

The memory of our eventful trip from London to Melbourne still is fresh and glorious. And in that connection, I want to pay tribute to Reeder Nichols, our radio operator. He has promised me that he will accompany me on any flight I will undertake. He not only is one of the greatest radio operators in the world, but he built the finest radio set ever installed in an airplane. It was constructed especially for our flight and we established a few world's records for long distance communications.[7]

When the 247 was safely in the hangar at Burbank, Don Young removed the engines for overhaul and corrosion inspection. Concerned that he would have to return the plane immediately to Boeing for conversion to airline seating and lose the opportunity to fly it on a speaking tour, Roscoe wrote to the presidents of Boeing, United, and Pratt & Whitney companies. He reminded them of the amount of publicity his flight had generated and that he had returned the plane to the States in perfect condition.

> I am willing to cooperate and do anything that you want me to do as there are many more thousands of dollars worth of publicity to be obtained from this flight if we take advantage of it immediately. If we dally too long the story may weaken considerably as far as front page news is concerned. . . .
>
> Now, I have spent a little over one-third the price of this airplane to do all of these things, and I am very much aware that you, also, have spent considerable money. I have spent everything and am practically broke. The condition is not the same with you, so I would like to have use of this airplane from a publicity standpoint for a short while, or at least until I can get part of my money back. Any favors or suggestions will be gratefully received and appreciated, I can assure you.[8]

Boeing's Egtvedt responded immediately, agreed that the plane should be put back in a passenger configuration, and said that he knew United was contemplating an arrangement with Roscoe to publicize the plane's performance.

In a separate letter to Erik Nelson, a Boeing executive and former Army pilot who had flown around the world in 1924, Roscoe pleaded his case for being allowed to recoup his expenses for the flight. He reviewed the favorable publicity he had garnered for Boeing and reminded Nelson that TWA

> and the General Motors crowd are using Eddie Rickenbacker to push the Douglas and he isn't doing anything but the same old stuff that I have been doing for years. I feel that I have lent more color and can lend more color to Boeing than he ever can to Douglas because the general public knows that he is not flying the ship himself.
>
> Personally and confidentially, the Boeing is slower than the Douglas, so consequently I have to watch my "P's and Q's" on just what to do and how to do it. I have three friends who want to buy Douglases now and I am stalling them off.[9]

Noting that he was to go to New York for an official reception, he told Nelson that "I don't think it is a good idea for me to go into New York in anything but a Boeing. We flew to San Francisco on the airline and the fact we didn't have our plane just cut the Boeing publicity in half."

Since the image of both Boeing and United was suffering because of the DC-2's performance in the race and its apparent commercial potential, Roscoe was given permission from both companies to borrow the 247 for a short time. He immediately contacted friends and began to plan a speaking tour that would publicize his flight and the Boeing's achievement.

Roscoe was the featured speaker at an Aviation Day banquet in New York on the thirty-second anniversary of the Wright brothers' first flight. In his address, he paid tribute to Pangborn and Nichols and the people who financed the flight and included some self-effacing remarks:

> I am just a little country boy trying to get along and I am just learning a few things about aviation, so I asked one of the best pilots in the world to go with me and then I hunted for the best radio man I could find. He had to be a technician to make any repairs necessary, and the best I could find with the operating key, so Mr. Reeder Nichols got the job. There were plenty of fellows who wanted to go just for the ride; some wanted to pay me, and boy, was that tempting, for I needed the money, but I never economize where life and death are both playing side-by-side, and my profession is at stake.
>
> May I say that one of the biggest thrills I had on our way to Melbourne was when Mr. Nichols told me he was talking to San Francisco, more than 12,000 miles away. I believe this is a world's record for airplane communications.

Never shy about saying how much his flight cost, he told the audience that he could never have made the trip if it had not been for Boeing, United Airlines, and Pratt & Whitney. "They loaned me the airplane and engines, and I paid the rest of the bill to the amount of $26,000."

Money shortages were to continue, and he sought to publicize the flight and seek revenues to pay off his creditors. The radio manager for the Hearst news empire wired Roscoe after his speech and asked how much he would want for a radio broadcast. Roscoe replied: "We want a national hookup with one thirty-minute program a week at $2,500 per week. Figure includes my crew."[10] The arrangement was never consummated and Roscoe began to plan a nationwide speaking tour to tell of the flight. He hired an advertising agency, obtained motion picture films and photos from newsreel and photo services, and awaited bookings.

Years later, Roscoe was asked to reflect on the London–Melbourne flight, especially about the night they almost didn't make it to Allahabad. Although he was never thought of as a religious man, he was convinced, as so many pilots are, that the universe is dominated by some unseen force. Writing in a small, nondenominational religious magazine about the flight, he concluded: "I've a strong feeling of assurance about it, that life continues onward in a new dimension. To me, God emphasizes that assurance through His continuing presence. It's the presence I first sensed in the cockpit that night, a presence as strong as the air's invisible lift on an aircraft's wing."[11]

In late December 1934 and the following January, Roscoe remained in New York for a series of radio broadcasts that were carried over the Columbia network. Although he hoped to return to Los Angeles via Corinth for Christmas, he wired his parents that bad weather and plane trouble forced him to return directly to Los Angeles. He added, "May not get to see you until January. Must be in New York Jan. 7, and will either come by Corinth or return by Corinth en route back to California."

When he returned to New York, he and Pangborn were again on a nationwide radio program to tell of their experiences on the flight to Melbourne. Roscoe showed the first films of their trip at a banquet of the Society of Automotive Engineers, which was attended by Henry Ford, Harvey Firestone, and scores of other leaders of the automobile industry.

"We are known as the first pilots to cross Asia without seeing it," Roscoe said, referring to the night flight into Allahabad when they were lost. At this time, he announced their plans for a world flight "for which a big plane is now being constructed in Florida. We plan to start out from California in a westward direction around the world. We plan to refuel in the air and never touch the earth until we arrive back in the States."[12] The idea must have been a spur-of-the-moment thought because there is no evidence that either one had any backers for such a flight. And the type of airplane to be built in Florida is a mystery.

However, as far as can be determined, it was the first time any pilot believed it might be possible to fly around the world nonstop with in-flight refueling. It would be many years before a U.S. Air Force heavy jet bomber would be able to accomplish such a feat. Typically, his announcement made headlines, as he intended it should.

When he had finished the broadcasts, Roscoe and Don Young flew to Corinth, where Roscoe made more headlines: ROSCOE TURNER UNABLE TO LAND AT CITY AIRPORT. Scheduled to give a lecture at the school auditorium, he made several passes at the field in the 247 at the Corinth airfield where a large group of townspeople eagerly awaited the return of their hero. "Colonel Turner made five attempts to land, rolling the length of the field and rising again before reaching the ditch on the west side of the field," a reporter noted. "He was unable to cut down his speed sufficiently to stop inside the airport. On the last attempt he shouted to spectators that he was going back to Memphis to land. The plane was the largest ever to come to the airport here."[13]

A week later, referring to Roscoe's plan to fly around the world, the paper noted that

> Colonel Turner is searching for a motor which he believes equal to the strain of the trip—the longest possible route around the world and hopes that one of the new planes under construction will be suitable for the trip. A certain secrecy surrounds the operations and Colonel Turner could not afford to reveal more about the type of plane to be used. However, he said he planned to use a large plane and to take a number of persons with him on the trip.[14]

After he returned to Los Angeles, Roscoe began planning an itinerary that would take him to dozens of cities in the ensuing weeks. He hoped not only to make sufficient money to recoup his expenses for the Melbourne flight but to seek new sponsors for the races ahead.

9

ROSCOE'S FLYING CORPS AND THE TURNER SPECIAL

After Roscoe returned the 247 to United Air Lines it was used for several years on transcontinental flights and was then bought by a Missouri corporation as an executive transport. It was later sold to the Civil Aeronautics Authority (CAA) for use as an experimental aircraft at the CAA's Technical Center at Weir Cook Field in Indianapolis. Don Stewart, head of the center, with Roscoe as copilot, flew it to Washington in 1952 for enshrinement in the National Air & Space Museum, where it is on permanent display today. Painted on the right side are the United Air Lines markings with a logo showing the route flown to remind passengers that it was the plane that participated in the famous intercontinental race. The left side is painted exactly as it appeared during the London–Melbourne Race. The engine nacelles still carry the names "Nip" and "Tuck."

Disappointed that he could no longer borrow the 247 for continued trips around the country, Roscoe leased a Boeing 80A trimotor from United Airlines and arranged a sponsorship with United and

American Airlines to tour the country and encourage people to fly. When Roscoe and Don Young arrived in Oakland to get the plane, United's chief pilot, "Slim" Lewis, asked Roscoe if he wanted him to give him a check ride before accepting the plane. Roscoe looked at Young and said, "Oh, I think we can make it all right, can't we, Don?" He nodded. Both knew that it was a safe airplane and United had never had a fatality in it.

The 80A had a large passenger cabin, which could hold twenty-one passengers. It had wood paneling and wall light fixtures with lace shades on them. Young recalled their first takeoff: "When Roscoe pushed the throttles forward, the plane sounded like a ship's galley. Everything rattled and the instrument panel shook so badly that you couldn't read the instruments. After we got to Fresno, I went down to the dime store, bought a half dozen small rubber balls and placed them around the panel to keep the thing from bouncing so much."

Accompanied by a barker named Floyd Huff, they toured the United States and visited every city of importance along the United and American routes during the good flying weather of 1935. In addition to taking up passengers for pay, most for their first rides in an airplane, parachute jumps were made to draw attention to the availability of rides. They flew the 80A only on weekends, leaving it at the last airport of a weekend's activities, where they would have positioned the Lockheed beforehand. They would return in the Lockheed to Los Angeles, where Roscoe would pursue other publicity activities and Young would work on the racer.

In February 1935 Roscoe engaged Harold R. Peat, a New York talent agent, to schedule him for presentations telling about the MacRobertson flight. Over the next three months, he made about thirty appearances in the Southeast and as far west as Texas, for which he was paid from $200 to $350 each. In the fall, more dates were scheduled in the Northeast. A telegram sent from Peat's office was typical of the efforts to get him some appearances:

Hartford reports sale slow. So we must do something special Stop Is there any kind of stunt you can do between now and Friday to make front pages. Booked Wednesday night Manhasset Long Island and fine arts club here Thursday night as rehearsals at no fee except expenses.[1]

To assist in publicizing Roscoe's appearances and his availability for flights, Peat prepared a script for local hosts and as a guide for the barker hired to solicit passengers for the 80A at the airport:

> Money cannot buy any safer equipment for you to fly in, as this plane originally cost $100,000 to build. It carries 21 passengers and its crew. The plane is all steel, linen-covered. In addition to this superior equipment, Colonel Turner carries a crew of expert mechanics and the ship is carefully inspected each day. It is this superior service, which guarantees your safety when flying with him, that makes it necessary for him to charge $1.50 per passenger. You owe it to yourselves and to your children to take at least one ride in the air—the most modern type of transportation in the world today.

On one of his lecture tours in March 1935, Roscoe had an engagement in Cleveland. Accompanying him in the Air Express were Don Young and a friend of Roscoe's. Ceiling and visibility were almost nil in freezing rain. Roscoe made a pass at the field but couldn't find the runway. Unable to climb because of wing ice, he crash-landed in a field about six miles away from the Cleveland airport. He hit a ditch, broke the prop, and wiped out the landing gear. Fortunately, no one was hurt. Young stayed with the aircraft until it was repaired, and Roscoe returned to Los Angeles.

As usual, money problems developed on the speaking tours. Roscoe spent about $8,500 for motion picture film and equipment as well as travel expenses and had to pay 30 percent of his earnings to the agent. When the tours ran their course and the bottom line was totaled, it was not a profitable venture. It had, however, given Roscoe more national exposure.

During this period, Roscoe received a contract to advertise Camel cigarettes in national magazines. The ad quoted him as saying, "A speed flyer uses up energy just as his motor uses 'gas'—and smoking a Camel gives one a refill on energy. The way I notice this especially is that after smoking a Camel I get a new feeling of well-being and vim. I smoke Camels all I want. They never upset my nerves."[2]

In 1936 Roscoe was contacted by the Motor Glide Company of Los Angeles, manufacturers of a small motor scooter. Roscoe accepted a 25 percent interest in the business in return "for the use of your good name, time and effort" in publicizing the Motor Glide. Roscoe took a demonstrator model with him on his speaking tours and was photographed with it in hotel lobbies, where he reportedly had driven it from the airport. The newspapers, which were always notified in advance of Roscoe's visits, ran photographs of him with the scooter wherever he chose to go around town. Small enough to fit easily inside the Boeing's baggage compartment and weighing only 65 pounds, the handlebars could be folded down so it could also be carried in a car or boat. It was advertised that it could go five miles on one cent's worth of gas, "the lowest cost transportation available." The venture, like so many others, did not prove profitable for Roscoe and was abandoned.

The flights in the 80A were usually routine, but there were some that Don Young did not enjoy. En route home to Los Angeles after a trip to Washington, D.C., Roscoe decided to stop in Corinth to see his relatives and friends. The weather had been miserable with low clouds, turbulence, and blowing snow. Roscoe found the pasture that was still being used as the town's airport and made two or three attempts to land but couldn't slow the plane down enough to stop between the fences. He asked Young to go back in the cabin by the door so his weight would hold the tail down.

I didn't think it would do any good but I went back there and as he started more attempts to get into the field, I began to pray that he either get the thing on the ground or go somewhere else. I didn't care. Finally, he gave up and we flew to Memphis.

One of the car dealers there gave us a new LaSalle to drive to Corinth. The next day, Roscoe decided he wanted something in Memphis so we started driving back the 90 miles to Memphis over little two-lane country roads. Roscoe's dad went along and was sitting in the front seat. Roscoe always drove fast and his dad got worried. He said, "Roscoe, you'd better slow down because you'll come over one of these hills and find some farmer with a team of mules in the middle of the road."

The words had no sooner been said than we pop over a hill and there's not only one team of mules but two teams of mules and two farmers who had stopped to visit. Roscoe hit the brakes and the squeal of tires scared one pair and they ran away with the farmer which gave us room to get between them. It was close but we went on our way and nobody said anything.

We returned to Corinth and the next day we led a lot of friends and relatives back to Memphis to give them rides. I don't remember how many people went but we flew them all day long.

The late Cecil M. "Mac" Whitaker, Roscoe's nephew, remembered several trips Roscoe made to Memphis when he was growing up. "Whenever we picked Uncle Roscoe up at the airport," he recalled, "we would always stop and buy $100 worth of fireworks. We would then set them off that night at the farm and they could be seen all over the area. As kids, we always looked forward to his visits."[3]

One of the sponsors that Roscoe obtained during this period was a previous client—the Heinz Company, which paid him $3,500 for a five-episode test period on a radio show and, if successful, offered an additional $5,200 to be paid in weekly installments for a total of 52 episodes. While arrangements were being made, Roscoe took on the task of answering fan mail, paying bills, and seeking new ventures. He paid Pangborn $1,529 for salary, expenses, and his share of the winnings from the MacRobertson Race; Nichols was paid $1,844.

Typical of the nagging bills that arrived after the Australian flight was a dun letter from the Department of State asking for $6.34 as the balance due on telegrams sent via the American Embassy from Australia. Another was one for seven Australian pounds for piston rings purchased in Essendon, Victoria. And still another was a bill for $42 from the Norwegian government for radiotelegraph messages sent by Nichols via Norway's coastal station at Bergen. Roscoe refused to pay the last bill, saying that the Hearst organization was to pay for these. Hearst also refused, stating that the messages were never received.

The contract with Heinz proved to be a sustaining one. The company engaged him to lend his name to a cereal product campaign aimed at children. He was their spokesperson at air shows, exhibitions, and fairs where the Heinz 57 Varieties products were displayed. In 1934 the company introduced two sets of airplane cards. One was the "Famous Air Pilots" and the other was a set of twenty-five "Modern Aviation" cards, featuring famous planes of that era. These cards were placed in boxes of Heinz Rice Flakes Cereal. The No. 1 card featured Roscoe's "57" racer. Each box contained a different card and the idea was to collect every card printed. Two albums were printed in color to hold the cards and could be obtained by sending in cereal box tops to the company.

Later, for sending in the large trademark number "57" from a package of Heinz Rice Flakes, the boys and girls could join the Roscoe Turner Flying Corps and receive a set of wings, a pilot's license, and a certificate of membership signed by Roscoe, "Speed King of the Sky," along with a booklet with *Secret Instructions*, the *Secret Salute*, and *Secret Passwords*. A cartoon accompanying newspaper ads cited Roscoe as saying that Rice Flakes "helps me keep fit." Later, an album with twenty-five pictures, one in each package, was "distributed for the purpose of stimulating Young America's interest in Aviation" and was also offered for "57" trademarks.

The campaign was so successful that advertising and sales expanded rapidly. Roscoe became a hero in the eyes of young Americans during the Depression era and did much to focus their attention on aviation in general and Roscoe in particular. Two trademarks from cereal packages earned the collector appointment as a flying lieutenant in Roscoe's Flying Corps, a set of bronze lieutenant's wings, and a photo of a smiling Roscoe giving the corps salute: "Right arm across your chest with two fingers extended toward the Flying Corps Wings. When you see a wearer of our Corps Wings, salute and give the secret password: 'Eleven-thirty.' That stands for my East-West coast-to-coast flying time—11 hours, 30 minutes. If the other is a *genuine* member his answering secret password will be 'Ten-Four' for my West-East flying time—10 hours, 4 minutes."

Once a lieutenant, it took five "57" trademarks from packages of Heinz Rice Flakes to win promotion to captain and new silver-plated corps wings. When ten trademarks were sent in after becoming a captain, promotion to major followed, along with a set of gold-plated wings.

Other programs for children included a contest to name Roscoe's "Mystery Ship." Contestants had to include two labels from cans of Heinz Cooked Macaroni with their entry blanks. Today those wings and the other items are sold for hundreds of dollars at aviation memorabilia shows and auctions.

Another activity for the younger set was the Junior Birdmen of America, a national youth movement sponsored by William Randolph Hearst to develop an interest in aviation. Squadrons were organized in each town where interest could be stirred up, similar to the organizational efforts of the Girl Scouts and Boy Scouts of America. Roscoe accepted honorary membership and devoted much time to appearances with the kids. He considered it a continuing link with Hearst, but the relationship was never closer than correspondence with Hearst's assistants.

In June 1935 Al and Fred Key, brothers from Meridian, Mississippi, began a third attempt to set a world endurance record in *Ole Miss*, a Curtiss Robin single-engine cabin plane. They left the ground at Meridian's Municipal Airport on June 4, 1935, and landed on July 1. It had been a remarkable flight for the times and the record stood for many years. The pair received fuel and supplies from another aircraft 435 times, usually piloted by James H. Keeton and Bill Ward. During the flight Fred Key walked out on a catwalk they had added to the plane to service the engine and make minor adjustments.

When it appeared they were going to break the standing endurance record, the Meridians planned a Victory Day celebration and invited a number of famous aviators to be on hand for the occasion. Roscoe had known the Key brothers for many years. He had persuaded them to use Macmillan Ring Free Oil for the publicity and took a personal interest in their success. He was at the top of the Chamber of Commerce's list of invitees and promptly announced to the press that he was going to fly from California to attend the festivities and be on hand when they landed. Roscoe's planned arrival was headlined in the Meridian paper: COLONEL TURNER RUSHES HERE FOR BIG AERIAL DAY.

As the Keys remained airborne, they broke the previous official record of 553 hours set by John and Kenneth Hunter in June 1930 and then an unofficial record of 647.5 hours set by Dale Jackson and Forest O'Brine a month later. The *Meridian Star* reported that 40,000 visitors visited the airport on the record-breaking day and hundreds stayed to be present when either the brothers decided they had had enough or the engine failed. Among the acts that entertained the crowds who eagerly awaited the touchdown of the hometown heroes was the Army Air Corps acrobatic team of Captain Claire L. Chennault, who later become known for his leadership of the Flying Tigers in China during World War II. Mayor Clint Vinson informed the flyers while they were airborne that the airfield was renamed Key Field in their honor.

When the flyers landed with a new record in hand of 653 hours, 34 minutes, some Meridians were not pleased that Will Rogers and Charles Lindbergh had not responded to an invitation to greet the flyers. An editorial writer observed,

> Why should we worry over Will Rogers and Lindbergh ignoring our invitation to drop in and see us? We had a bigger man than either of them in Roscoe Turner, a native son, one of the greatest if not the greatest flyer of all times. Think of it, [he] left Los Angeles at 7 A.M., wired us he would be here on time and just five seconds before the record was broken, slipped over the trees from the west like a bullet, right on time. You can't beat that.[4]

Roscoe was genuinely happy about the record set by his friends; he introduced and then interviewed them before the audience at a large two-day vaudeville show at the Orpheum Theater in Memphis. The show was billed in advance as "The Scoop of the Year," to be held "less than three days after they set foot on this earth again." Roscoe told reporters he made the trip to greet them because he was "sincerely interested in seeing these boys get somewhere. They justly deserve it" after their long preparation and two previous failures. Afterward, Roscoe was criticized by some for trying to hog the limelight from their local heroes. One historian commented: [Roscoe Turner] "could sniff out a camera or reporter better than a prize blue-tick hound. . . . It was of little surprise that when Al and Fred Key did begin receiving publicity for their endurance flights, Roscoe Turner was there by their side soaking up accolades."[5]

Roscoe, Fred Key, and Lou Meyer, an Indy 500 auto race winner, made many guest appearances together around the country in the weeks following for the National Safety Council. Expenses were paid by Macmillan Petroleum Company because all three used its Ring Free Oil in their engines. Fred Key flew *Ole Miss*, Roscoe joined him in the Boeing 80A trimotor, and Meyer displayed his latest racer. Their tour lasted through the fall of 1936.

Roscoe announced he was going to enter the 1935 Bendix and Thompson Races and planned to use the souped-up Wedell-Williams Racer with a 1,000-hp Hornet B engine that had been almost completely rebuilt during the year. It was believed by most observers to be the fastest plane entered in the Bendix that year, although there was formidable competition. He was also favored to win the Thompson race and thus be the first to take the trophy a second time. His plans almost came to a halt when he had an auto accident in August. He was sued by the driver of the other car, and the judge ordered a $1,500 judgment against Roscoe.

There were nine entries in the 1935 Bendix, including Jacqueline Cochran and Russell Thaw in Northrop Gammas; Roy Hunt in a Lockheed Orion; and Benny Howard, with copilot Gordon Israel, in his *Mister Mulligan*, a beautiful plane of his own design, powered by a dependable P&W Wasp engine. Amelia Earhart and Paul Mantz entered with a Lockheed Vega. Another competitor was Earl Ortman, who entered with a Keith Rider R-3. There were also two Gee Bees, one was the "Q.E.D." entered by Royal Leonard, and the other, referred to as the Gee Bee R-1/2 hybrid, piloted by Cecil Allen.

There was a low ceiling and fog at Burbank on August 30, the starting day, but all aircraft departed without difficulty. Soon after takeoff, however, Allen disappeared into the clouds. He crashed the Gee Bee in a nearby potato field and died instantly. The last of the infamous small Gee Bee racers had killed its last pilot.

Roscoe sped eastward in his Wedell-Williams through storms and fog with stops at Albuquerque, Wichita, and Indianapolis. Howard and Israel, in the longer-range *Mister Mulligan*, had to stop only at Kansas City, Missouri, for fuel. They swooped across the rainy field at Cleveland in 8 hours, 33 minutes, 16.3 seconds. They seemed unbeatable, but since the race was won on elapsed time from takeoff, there was still the possibility that someone else could beat their time.

Just as Howard and Israel relaxed, Roscoe, in his gold-colored racer, dove out of the clouds and flashed across the finish line in the rain. The race officials could not tell exactly who had won until their watches were checked and Roscoe's takeoff time from Los Angeles was verified. The calculations were hard to believe. Roscoe had lost the race by a mere 23.5 seconds! Those few seconds meant that Roscoe was awarded $2,500 in second-place money instead of the $4,500 that Howard and Israel had won. But there was still the Thompson to be flown and Roscoe stood a good chance of winning. The race now required ten 15-mile laps.

In the racing start for the Thompson, Roscoe was off the ground first in a blast of speed and quickly led the large pack. It was on the last lap that the fates intervened to steal a victory. The supercharger impeller in the Hornet engine disintegrated and scalding oil gushed from the engine. Flying at treetop level, Roscoe couldn't see through the windshield and goggles as he struggled to gain some altitude so others wouldn't run into him and he would have some room to bail out. He leveled off at about 1,500 feet and, stifled by smoke, considered bailing out. However, he thought he could trade his excess speed for distance and looked around for a spot to land.

Below, the crowd gasped as the announcer shouted, "Turner's in trouble!"

Without any engine power, Roscoe had only one chance at a safe landing and decided to head for the airport. Barely clearing the airport fence, he hit the ground fast, bounced high and hard and braked to a stop directly in front of the grandstand. He climbed out unsteadily in his immaculate uniform, which was in stark contrast to his blackened face and oily helmet. He heard the announcer say, "Oh, my goodness, that Turner is putting on a real show today!"

A crowd of mechanics and rescue personnel rushed up to him and one commented on his bad luck. Roscoe, his hands shaking, said, "Bad luck, hell! When something like this happens and you can walk away from it, that's *good* luck!"

In his inimitable style, newspaperman Paul Gallico described what he saw in the next day's column: "He came in apouring, snicked the switch, bounced once, hung, hit at a terrific speed, and then was safe, rolling along the ground, the red fire wagon coming along at an angle to meet him. Always the perfect showman, he brought his dead, fuming ship to a stop, his wheels exactly touching the white chalk line in front of the grandstand."[6]

Roscoe explained why he decided to try to land the racer rather than bail out: "I said to myself, 'Hell, Roscoe, what are you doing? It's *your* ship.' It had cost me twenty grand. I decided to set it down." Looking back later, he said, "It's a good thing there were no autograph hounds there that day. I couldn't have signed my name with my arm strapped to a board. I was shaking like a V-8 engine with one bank out. I'm always like that at the end of a race. So is every pilot, if he has any sense. Because if he has sense, he knows that he's in a hazardous business and he's afraid. If you haven't sense, and therefore fear, they pick you up with tongs and a basket in the back stretch."[7]

Roscoe admitted he was apprehensive and wondered about the jinx that seemed to hover over him. He had laid awake most of the night before thinking about what would happen if a wing came off. An unidentified friend wrote: "Colonel Turner knows perfectly well the odds are against him and that most racing pilots die in their cockpits. He doesn't deny that the glory and money is worth it, though winnings are immediately thrown into some bigger, faster ship with which to try it all over again next year. . . . Racing is in his blood like a strong, intoxicating wine."[8]

In September 1935, apparently in preparation for Roscoe being killed in an aircraft, the Associated Press issued a biographical sketch that was to be used "primarily in event of his death." A friend sent it to Roscoe, who considered the obituary a joke, and its existence was one of Roscoe's favorite stories. It was a fairly complete review of his life up to that time, and newspaper editors used it in connection with later news events throughout his life. However, it contained some inaccuracies that were perpetuated by many writers who believed it was factual and used this false information as background for their articles.

The possibility of sudden death seemed to follow Roscoe as far as writers were concerned. Throughout his racing career, mention of risk, death, and undertakers was common among writers. An article in 1921 mentions an undertaker and on the Atlanta-to-New York flight in the Sikorsky that crashed in Abbeville, South Carolina, one of the passengers was an undertaker. Roscoe delighted in telling audiences that the man had handed out his business card to the other passengers as the plane was landing.

In 1934 Roscoe contacted Professor Howard W. Barlow, who had redesigned the Wedell to take the heavier Pratt & Whitney Hornet engine the year before, and asked for his help in designing a brand new racer that would be able to set a new world landplane speed record and put it in the 350–400-mph class. Barlow prepared some preliminary drawings and had a small model built. It was to be a cantilever, mid-wing design with fixed streamlined landing gear. The latter was to avoid the complexity and space requirements of a retractable gear.

Barlow's objective was to design a plane that would be fast enough for the Bendix but also be suitable for tight turns around the pylons of the Thompson race. Roscoe wanted to have the new ship use the new Pratt & Whitney Twin Wasp engine, which was said to develop as much as 1400 horsepower, and to have a three-blade, controllable-pitch propeller installed. It would be the first single-seat aircraft to be powered by the new Twin Wasp. The landing gear would be a combination of rubber compression pads and aluminum separators for shock absorption. The high-speed wing design chosen was such that it had the maximum ratio of speed to landing speed, was so stable that it would fly hands off, and responded softly to the controls. As Barlow commented later, "All of this was accomplished on an absolutely rock-bottom budget."[9]

The stress analysis and drawings were made under Barlow's supervision, assisted by John Ackerman and senior and graduate students at the University of Minnesota's Department of Aeronautical Engineering. Blueprints were mailed to Roscoe as fast as they were turned out so that construction could begin before all the drawings were completely finished. Seeing the shape on paper, Roscoe was more determined than ever to have the new plane built in time for the 1936 races and visited Barlow in Minneapolis when he had a model to show. Power would set the pace, and he wanted the most power that Pratt & Whitney could design into a new engine.

Lawrence W. Brown, head of his own aircraft company in Los Angeles, was engaged by Roscoe to build the plane to Roscoe's specifications and

Barlow's engineering data in the summer of 1936. Don Young was to be present to assist during its construction and represent Roscoe's interests and viewpoints. Brown had never built a plane with such horsepower. Without consulting Barlow, Brown made some changes that added weight to the fuselage. Much extraneous bracing was added to compensate for the heavier engine, which changed the aircraft's center of gravity. In addition, Brown also altered the gas tanks' position. As Young recalled, "it had enough steel in it worthy of a Sherman tank," and it was found that about 800 pounds total weight had been added. Roscoe also objected because the wing now looked too short to him. Roscoe wanted the fuselage lengthened and about 18 inches added to the wing span.

Pratt & Whitney, with a vested interest in the project, lent the expertise of Bill Gwin and Henry Igle. It was Gwin's advice concerning the new self-priming carburetor that eventually helped Roscoe at race time.

Brown refused to build the plane based completely on the Barlow specifications, and Roscoe was furious at the standoff. Brown and his chief engineer, Dan Halloway, finally convinced Roscoe that a major redesign had to be made. Although Roscoe relented, he insisted on reviewing the drawings before they started production. As the drawings were being made, Brown wanted Roscoe's approval but, typically, Roscoe was difficult to locate. He had begun a radio show on the NBC network in Chicago and could not take the time to fly to Los Angeles. Brown, without Roscoe's consent, began construction with many changes from the original Barlow design. When Roscoe was briefly written out of the radio program, he flew to Los Angeles, saw a mockup with which he posed for pictures, and had immediate disagreements with Brown about the wing design and the weight of the airplane.

Paul R. Matt, in an article about the racer, wrote:

"Oh, I knew it was a beautiful airplane," Roscoe related later, "but I began to make changes." He knew the plane would be highly unstable if the straight wing were used. Dan Halloway agreed and tried in vain to point out that it was the wing he had designed and wanted built for the racer. He said it was built according to the University of Minnesota drawings. He had approved the changes and redesign of the fuselage and tail but insisted upon retention of the original wing. The story that filtered through from the ensuing argument relates that Roscoe lost his temper, grabbed the emergency fire ax and began the series of changes by slashing away at the wing.

Halloway tried to cool the fiery tempers by suggesting that if Roscoe didn't want the wing as it was, he was confident a new one could be designed and built that would satisfy Roscoe's needs. The original spars could be used, it was only a matter of obtaining greater lift from more wing area and a thicker air foil. . . .

Suddenly, the colorful picture started to discolor and fade. There were "many pretty words," Brown would say, and too much 'charm' in the whole project. During May 1937, it was believed the design and construction were pretty well finalized and it was only a matter of solving the wing situation. Then came a serious misunderstanding and breach of confidence between Lawrence Brown and Roscoe Turner. No doubt it was intensified by Roscoe's inability to finance the work. Larry, who was already pinching pennies, discovered there were no funds to back Roscoe's project. Work stopped. Turner was furious.[10]

There was definitely a final disagreement between Roscoe and Brown, not only about finances, but also about requiring unnecessary overtime. Young explains:

Brown insisted on working men on overtime with the intent of completing the plane for the 1936 races. I told him it was needless to do that because even with overtime, it couldn't be done.

Brown ordered me out of his shop but I told him that as long as Roscoe pays the rent for the building and owns the shop, pays the salaries as well as buying the soap and towels in the washroom, he was talking to the wrong man. At that time, Roscoe had $46,000 in the project, not borrowed money, but his own. Brown left the premises with only his coat and I never saw him again.

I called Roscoe and told him that no matter what anyone told him, the plane, although it seemed to be near completion in the Los Angeles shop, was not ready to fly as it was. Roscoe flew to Los Angeles and agreed that it was not flyable.

Although upset that the new racer would not be ready for the 1936 races, Roscoe contacted Emil M. "Matty" Laird, owner of the E. M. Laird Airplane Company in Chicago. Laird had designed the *Solution*, which had won the 1930 Thompson for Charles W. "Speed" Holman, and the *Super Solution* with which Jimmy Doolittle had won the 1931 Bendix race. Roscoe asked him to take the Turner racer and finish it.

Young disassembled the plane and shipped it in a boxcar to the Laird Company in May 1937, along with the Wedell as Roscoe had requested. Young would work on the Wedell while Laird rebuilt the new racer.[11]

During the following months, the wingspan on the new racer was increased to 25 ft., 4 in., and the chord widened to 68 in. The airframe was lightened considerably by the removal of much internal metal. Laird's engineer on the project was Raoul Hoffman. He was assisted in the rebuilding process by Harold and Bill Laird, Matty's brothers; Larry Zigman; and Bill Kelly, the Chicago mayor's son.

According to Barlow, he did no further design work on the new plane, but "externally and internally, it was essentially the airplane I had engineered and designed." However, the Barlow wing design had been changed to a planform taper with a slight sweptback leading edge. The push-pull controls were changed to cable and the ailerons were lengthened to take care of the extra wing width. Another 50-gallon fuel tank was built into the fuselage.[12]

Disappointed that he would not have the new racer in time for the 1936 races but determined to compete, Roscoe had Young get the golden Wedell ready for another try at the Bendix. The races that year were to be held on the West Coast at Mines Field (now Los Angeles International Airport). Therefore, the Bendix would start from Floyd Bennett Field, New York.

Roscoe decided to take off from Burbank in late August 1936, about a week before the start of the Bendix. In a script he prepared for use on a radio broadcast, he tells what happened:

> I roll the plane out early one morning, warm it up and start down the runway. The motor starts to quit just as I am halfway down the runway. I turn around and go back to the end of the runway and start over again. It does the same thing. I attempt this four or five times and then finally take it back to the hangar. We take the carburetor off, we test the magnetos, we do everything. By this time it's too late to leave this day so the next morning we roll it out and everything is perfect so off we go for New York.

Since the motor is practically brand new, again we will take our time going over—just lope along at about 250 mph. We pass over the Colorado River at about 12,000 feet. The motor sneezes a couple of time and when a motor coughs or sneezes in one of these little racing planes, and especially one in which the motor is as powerful as this one, it really makes you jump as this engine develops a thousand horsepower.

I reach up and push the throttle to see what's wrong and everything seems all right. I check the RPM, the oil temperature, and everything still seems all right. I go for another few minutes and we are then over Flagstaff, Arizona. However, we are about 45 miles south of Flagstaff because we want to stay off the airway used by the airliners. The reason for this is that the motor is so large in front that we cannot see dead ahead and I am afraid we might overtake an airliner or hit one square in the face and that wouldn't be so nice.

The motor misses a couple more times. This time I reach up and move the throttle and nothing happens. We are losing RPMs but still at 12,000 feet. We lose more RPMs. The power is falling off rapidly so I decided to go north to get back on the airway in hopes of finding some kind of life somewhere because if we jump out in a parachute where we are, no one will find us.

We are back on the airway now and we have lost about 5,000 feet of our altitude. It is a shame to jump out and leave this beautiful little $40,000 airplane up here all by itself so we will just ride it down, and try to find out what is the matter with the motor.

We are over an Indian reservation now. We are still going down. I don't see any place to land. We are losing altitude fast and the RPMs of the propeller are down to almost nothing. I see a little green strip of land along two mountains so we will try to make that.

We slide in over the fence; the plane bounces a little. Whoop! Something is going to happen! I see the ground right over the nose and the plane is going to turn over. The thing that I have always feared is going to happen. We will catch fire and burn up right here.

The plane is upside down. My head is rubbing in the sand; the crank and a can of tomato juice is bouncing all over the cockpit. All of a sudden we are right side up again. The blue sky all around and we are standing still. The plane is standing on its wheels and its nose. Still a three-point landing but not the right kind.

I look around and try to take inventory of what has happened. The can of tomato juice is bent up a little and the crank is down between my feet and my side is hurting me quite a bit. I am still strapped in my seat. I look around behind me and I see that there is no tail on the airplane. Everything is gone clear up to the back of my neck. That is one thing I had done in overhauling it; I had reinforced everything right in back of my head in case I turned over so that it would keep from breaking my neck.

I look out the right side and the aileron is bent a little bit and so is the left aileron. The front part of the wings are all in good shape, and one blade of the propeller is not even bent. We are still standing up on the nose.

The more I move, the more my side hurts and I try to figure out what's happened. I'm trying to get out of the plane, but even with all the pain, I'm still very curious about what brought me down. I start taking off a little of the cowling and cutting into it to see if my mechanics had violated my orders so that in case the throttle came loose it would automatically open to full throttle. While doing this, I noticed there was a lot of liquid running out of the carburetor and I find that it's not gasoline but water. Then it dawned on me that my carburetor has completely clogged up with ice and that is what brought me down.

But we are still sitting out here on an Indian reservation and I don't know how far from the railroad and trying to make myself understood to the Indians that came over. I finally learned from one Indian that it is 17 miles to a telephone and that he has a couple of horses but only one saddle. Finally, he finds another saddle and we get on the two horses and start for a telephone.

My side is hurting me so badly by now that I can hardly ride and my neck is hurting also. I can hardly turn my head. We get to a telephone at the headquarters for the reservation and an officer there agrees to drive me to the railroad which is another 35 miles. I am still trying to figure out what happened that caused the airplane to break up from the back side.

Finally, I get on the train and there is so much pain now that I can't lie down and I can't sit up very well, so I just get in a half-reclining position in the Pullman. All night on the train I keep trying to rehearse again the whole procedure of the flight, and it dawned on me that I turned upside down once and the plane is going so fast that it sticks the tail in the ground and froze it all up clear to the back of my neck; then it turns over again back on its wheels and nose twice—so fast that it didn't spill a drop of gas or oil.

After getting back to Los Angeles, the doctors told me that I had broken a couple of ribs and fractured a bone in my neck. They said they couldn't understand why I didn't break my neck.

On picking up the plane, my mechanic found out that the control stick, which was about a one and a half inch of tubing, had been broken in two and the only thing that kept it from going into my stomach was my safety belt and my big silver buckle that I wear on my uniform which carries a dent from the stick today.

This is one of the closest calls that I have ever had in my whole racing career and the worst of it all is that I have no airplane now to run in the 1936 races so I will have to watch them from the ground.[13]

Don Young, waiting for Roscoe in New York, didn't know what had happened until he read it in a newspaper.

I called Los Angeles but they didn't know where Roscoe was. So, I got on an airplane and came home. By the time I got back, Roscoe was in the Good Samaritan Hospital in Los Angeles. I called him and he said, "Don, go to Macmillan [Petroleum Company], get a truck and go down to Arizona and get the engine and instruments. Don't bother to bring the rest of it home because it's all shot. There's nothing else worth saving."

I went down to Long Beach, got a truck with a winch on it. Cy Bench, the Macmillan chief engineer, and his nephew wanted to go along so we drove to New Mexico. When we hit the Arizona border, a guard there wanted $30 for the fee to bring the airplane across the state of Arizona. I said, "But we don't know what we're going to bring back because we haven't seen the airplane, so why don't we wait until we get back and then you can charge us based on what we have." He said "OK."

We went on and when we got to Navajo, Arizona, which was about ten miles from the New Mexico line, we went down a dirt road on the Arizona side and crossed over into New Mexico and went onto the Zuni Indian reservation in a big rainstorm. The storekeeper told us the wreckage was 11 miles from there but he said we would never make it because the adobe soil wouldn't absorb the water and it would just be standing in lakes until it evaporated.

Using the winch and driving stakes into the ground to have a base to pull against when they got stuck, they managed to get through the many lakes. It took the whole day to make the eleven miles to the airplane, where Roscoe had left an old Zuni Indian to watch over it. Young recalls that "there wasn't much left of the instrument panel because Roscoe had gone into it and bent it in."

> We decided because of the rains that we could save a lot of time and effort if we just sawed the landing gear off and hooked the winch onto the whole airplane and pulled it onto the truck. And that's the way we came out of there. We left New Mexico on the same road we had used going in which saved us the $30 fee in New Mexico. When we got to the California line, I told Bench if that border guard isn't out there, let's roll right across into California. He said, "No, we can't do that, Don." I said, "Let me drive."
>
> When we got to the bridge at the Colorado River, the border guard was standing there talking to somebody in a car and I rolled right into California and saved us $60. And that $60 was important then.
>
> Roscoe had told reporters that a bolt had come out of the throttle which is what caused his forced landing. I didn't think that was so but when I looked at it, sure enough a bolt was missing. When I visited Roscoe in the hospital, he had only his pants on and was pacing around the room like a caged lion and I said, "Roscoe, let me have the bolt." He reached into his pants pocket and handed me the bolt, nut, and cotter pin. I asked, "Why did you do this?" He answered, "Well, Don, I didn't want to give Pratt & Whitney a bad name." I said, "Yeah, but what about me?" He said, "You can take it but it would be bad publicity for Pratt & Whitney."

Young knew what had caused the power loss because it had happened to him when he was warming up the engine one day. The carburetor had a penchant for icing up and the engine muffs on the engine exhaust pipes would not produce enough heat to the carburetor to prevent icing. When the aircraft was rebuilt, Young made a mechanism that injected alcohol into the carburetor and dissolved the ice.

As he said he would, Roscoe attended the 1936 races at Mines Field as a spectator. Even though he wasn't racing, he still made news, but not in the usual sense. That year, Michel Detroyat, a French pilot who had put on spectacular aerobatic demonstrations at previous National Air Races, arrived in Los Angeles with a Caudron C-460. For several years, the National Air Race committee had been urging France, England, and Germany to send their best planes and pilots to compete. Detroyat was France's answer to the challenge.

In a qualifying run for the Greve and Thompson races, the Frenchman with his unimposing-looking Caudron stunned the crowd. His slowest lap—273.473 mph—was faster than any American plane had ever gone around a closed course up to that time. He won both races with a machine that had an engine rated at only 340 horsepower and walked off with a total of $14,450 in prize money.

American pilots were dazed by Detroyat's performance and grumbled openly. The press took up their complaint that amateur low-budget plane builders stood no chance against government-financed racers. Roscoe took it beyond grumbling. He mounted the speaker's stand and surprised the audience by loudly criticizing Detroyat over the public address system for his audacity in coming to the United States with a machine that the French government had paid to have built and flown, to the disadvantage of pilots like himself who designed, built, and flew their own machines.[14]

Roscoe received headlines for his tirade, but only a few "name" pilots stood up to support him. Detroyat, in a gesture of sportsmanship, withdrew from the Shell Trophy Race, "so that someone else would have a chance to win." Detroyat said he was planning to return to the National Air Races the following year and make attempts to set new coast-to-coast and intercity records but after the controversy got such worldwide press attention, no foreign competitors ever again showed up to compete or to try to set new American point-to-point records.

Roscoe was criticized by many for his stand but, if nothing else, the Frenchman's performance made Roscoe more determined than ever to have a machine that would be the world's best racer. The 1937 races were going to find Turner in the lineup with the fastest airplane that he could muster with his rapidly depleting funds.

Arthur Inman, co-owner of Inman Brothers Flying Circus based in Coffeyville, Kansas, had heard of Roscoe's bad luck and had offered to buy the Boeing 80A in August 1936 for $6,000 cash. The word "cash" had Roscoe interested, but he was obligated to fulfill a number of appearances first. In late fall, Roscoe had it stored in a hangar in Lincoln, Nebraska, where Inman looked it over and offered $7,500, which Roscoe accepted. The money came in especially handy because Roscoe had been sued by a man in Omaha for work done on the Boeing and had to pay him $750. Two years later, Inman suggested the two team up for an extensive barnstorming trip in the 80A. He thought they would "clean up on dollar rides if you flew the ship." Inman offered Roscoe a 50 percent ownership in the plane to Roscoe for $1,500. Roscoe was not interested.

He did need to obtain funds for the next year's races, though, so he began a vigorous letter-writing campaign to potential sponsors. One letter to the Gillette Safety Razor Company was typical. He was offered $500 to visit the factory and allow the company to run a testimonial using his name regarding Gillette razors and blades. Roscoe responded that he could not afford to visit for that small amount of money, but if they would "raise the ante a bit more," he would deliver his personal fifteen-year-old Gillette razor "that has been with me on all my record flights and went around the world with me on my London-to-Melbourne flight."[15] The company did not "raise the ante."

Life for Roscoe took a new turn when the National Broadcasting Company announced in October 1936 that they had signed him to star in their popular radio show, *Flying Time*, which was heard five days a week from NBC's Chicago studios. The original contract was for three months and the program was the story of aviation as seen through a boy's eyes. A radio trade paper touted the program highly, noting that "this is aviation from the inside—a story that pilots and mechanics see 24 hours a day—it is rainy afternoons in the hangars with the gang of old-timers telling about Roy Knabenshue and his acrobatic dirigible back when—and Frank Luke said to his squadron commander, 'See all those German balloons out there? I am going to go bust `em!' and he did. It is sparkplugs and spanners; it is parachutes and airfoils—it is flying!"[16]

Incidentally, it was during the 1936 races that Roscoe met a cartoonist named Zack Mosley, a pilot himself, who drew a syndicated cartoon strip titled "Smilin' Jack." Although many have said Mosley used Roscoe as the strip's main character, this is not so. One of the first and most enduring of all aviation-based adventure strips, it began as a Sunday feature titled "On the Wing" in October 1933. In December that year the syndicate ordered the strip's name changed to "Smilin Jack" and the main character's name changed from Mack Martin to Jack Martin. The strip assumed its flying adventure narrative form and lasted until 1973. As one biographer noted, "Mack Martin, the scared student-pilot, became Jack, grew a snappy little mustache, and acquired a suave smile that four decades of harrowing adventure were never completely to wipe off his handsome face."[17]

Although Mosley had met Roscoe at the 1936 air races, his "Smilin' Jack" character didn't sport a needle-point mustache until 1940. Mosley told the author the character's face was a composite of Roscoe and Duke Krantz, another pilot he knew who had a similar mustache.

In the middle of the Depression, the Works Progress Administration was established by President Roosevelt to help stimulate a stagnant economy. Many of the work relief projects included building airports. Mississippi's Alcorn County had obtained a $45,000 grant to build an airport at Corinth on the Suratt pasture where Roscoe had operated from during his early barnstorming days. The county paid $3,500 to employ an engineer and purchase the pasture.

E. F. Waits, Roscoe's long-time friend, had been one of the leaders in pushing the idea, despite some opposition from local townspeople who objected to the noise the aircraft would make. He had notified Roscoe in January 1934 that a plan was in the works to obtain the funds for the "Colonel Roscoe Turner Airport." Roscoe was pleased but asked Waits that it be named "Roscoe Turner Airport." He asked that the "Colonel" be dropped because, "it is not correct to use the military title in naming an object. As an illustration I will refer you to: The Floyd Bennett Field, New York; The Richard E. Byrd Airport, Richmond, Va.; and the Charles Lindbergh Field, San Diego, Cal."[18]

A ground-breaking ceremony took place in 1935 and the dedication ceremony was scheduled for October 15, 1936. The field was equipped with a beacon, floodlights, and a hangar. Two sod runways were bulldozed; at 600 and 2500 feet, they were thought to be of sufficient length for most civilian aircraft of that era.

The Corinth Chamber of Commerce secretary said that they were expecting 25,000 to 30,000 people to attend a week-long "aviation holiday," and other flyers had been invited to pay tribute to Roscoe on the official dedication day. Would it be possible for Roscoe to bring his racing plane there as well as the Boeing 80A?

Roscoe replied:

> If you expect me to bring my racing plane there, make sure that you do not let any flyers come in and operate off of that field before that date. If they should come in immediately after a rain they will make deep tracks which would be liable to upset my fast plane. As a matter of fact, I would like to have exclusive passenger-carrying rights during this program, as it is going to cost me something over a thousand dollars to bring both airplanes back there. Of course you can handle this as confidentially as possible . . . because I don't want it to look too commercial. At the same time, however, we have to figure some way of making our expenses as we go along.
>
> Should you be in contact with any of the other places who are going to open their airports this Fall, tell them that you can arrange to get me to come to their opening under similar conditions. I would like to stimulate aviation as much as possible back in my old home state.[19]

Later, Roscoe wrote that he was bringing only the Air Express to the dedication and, "I will take a few of the people up for a ride in it, so as not to disappoint everybody. Because I can carry only four passengers I will have to charge $2.00 per passenger."[20]

On October 15, 1936, Roscoe, accompanied by Fred Key, flew to Corinth from Chicago in the Air Express. Carline was already there to assist with festivity arrangements and report the condition of the field. Roscoe flew dedication covers for a stamp dealer to Corinth to help defray expenses. The city declared it Roscoe Turner Day and merchants closed their doors; Corinth schools were also closed and others in the county were dismissed early; a large parade was formed and marched through downtown with floats, marching bands, motorcyclists and horses. Mississippi governor Hugh White and Tennessee governor-elect Gordon Browning, riding in their official limousines, were escorted by police, along with local dignitaries and famed aviators Phoebe Omlie, Henry A. "Dick" Merrill, and the Key brothers, Fred and Al. The official dedication of the airport was made by Colonel J. Carroll Cone, assistant director of the Bureau of Aeronautics. Reporters and photographers were flown in from the larger cities in the surrounding area.

Small lapel buttons bearing Roscoe's likeness and name and surrounded with the words "Corinth Airport Dedication" were made to help defray the celebration's cost. They were sold by the Chamber of Commerce for 25 cents each for adults and 10 cents for schoolchildren. A special stamp cancellation was approved by the U.S. Post Office Department and used on outgoing Corinth mail during the week's celebration.

The airport was duly dedicated with speeches and an air show. Roscoe gave Governor White his first airplane ride, and during the ceremony was commissioned by the governor as a colonel on his staff. When it was time for Roscoe to speak, he commented that his "lion tamer's uniform was as much a part of me as my plane." He added, "Will Rogers had his slough hat, Al Smith, his derby, and Tom Mix, his white cowboy uniform. This lion tamer's uniform, though not so famous is, I feel, my good luck charm."[21]

When Roscoe was presented the key to the city by former Congressman Zeke Candler, he was overcome with emotion and tried to find words to express his gratitude. "I just can't take it, I guess," he said. When he recovered, he recounted how he had first flown from the field when it was a cow pasture and how he had been married there in 1924.

Tennessee governor-elect Browning told the audience that he resented the fact that Mississippians called him their own. "Roscoe belongs to America," he said, to a round of applause. That evening a banquet was held in the high school building. A proud Corinth citizenry had thoroughly honored a local boy who had put their town on the map.

A few days after the airport dedication, Roscoe wrote a letter to "My good friends in Corinth and Alcorn County," which he asked to be published in the local paper.

In this world of so much infidelity and make-believe, I have asked the editor of this good paper to bring you this message of sincerity from the bottom of my heart. I ask you to receive it in the spirit of unselfishness in which I have tried to live my life.

You have bestowed a great honor on me by naming your airport after me, and also by giving me such a tremendous ovation. Greetings have been extended to me from the four corners of the Earth but none have been so dear or so filled my heart with joy, as the homecoming planned for me by you dear people.

You have given me a new incentive to continue and I hope that my future will fulfill your expectations of me.

. . . I know there has been a great deal of opposition to this project but now that it is a fact I wish that one and all would get behind it, as you would any civic project, for through aviation lies advancement for your community.[22]

After the airport dedication, Roscoe decided he wanted to rebuild the Lockheed Air Express, which had been used strenuously for eleven years. But the wooden fuselage was oil-soaked and showed evidence of dry rot. Hugh Brewster, the CAA inspector, visited the hangar in Burbank when Young had it stripped down and asked him how it looked.

"It looks to me like a match would do a good job," Young replied, not knowing the effect his remark would have.

Without commenting or taking a good look, Brewster immediately went to a phone and called Roscoe in Chicago to tell him he wouldn't relicense the Air Express. Roscoe acknowledged the bad news and asked him to tell Young to fix it so no one else would fly it because he didn't want anyone to get hurt in it.

Taking Roscoe at his word, Young took the engine and propeller off, and removed the instruments and everything else that could be reused. He stripped the fuselage down, borrowed a United Airlines truck, and hauled the remains to an incinerator. He lit a fire under it and was amazed at how quick it blasted into flames. He took the wing, landing gear, and tail assembly to Paul Mantz for possible use in his movie work, knowing that he couldn't do anything with the pieces to build another flyable airplane.

Young flew to Chicago, where he was met by Roscoe at Midway Airport. As Roscoe greeted Young, he said, "Good news! I've sold the Air Express to a fellow in Mexico for $1,200, less instruments and engine."

Surprised, Young said, "Roscoe, there is no more Air Express. I burned the fuselage up."

Young recalled that "Roscoe came about two feet off the ground but he got over it quickly and we never said another word about it from that day on."

In Chicago, after Matty Laird took a look at the new racer when it arrived from Los Angeles in May 1937, he began to make changes to what Brown had done. Laird made some innovations and had it weighed after it was finished to his satisfaction. He had shaved about 400 pounds from the structure he had received from Brown.

Since it looked like his new racer would be ready in time for the 1937 Bendix race, Roscoe decided to lend Lt. Joe Mackey the Wedell, which Young had rebuilt in Laird's shop and put into racing shape. Mackey was to pay Roscoe $2,500, which was to come out of his expected winnings; Roscoe was also to receive 50 percent of winnings above the $2,500. In a letter to Mackey, Roscoe said, "In the event that something happens to my new silver racer I would fly the gold Wedell-Williams for one race and you would fly it for the other."[23]

The Wedell racer had had its tail section shortened and gear struts lengthened, which made it more difficult to land. Mackey flew it from Chicago to Los Angeles via Wichita, where he almost ground-looped it and dragged a wingtip. Later, Mackey said it handled beautifully in the air but he would rather drive a thousand miles than land it.

When Laird said the new racer was ready, Roscoe flew it to the Ford Lansing Airport, 21 miles south of Chicago, for test flights. Meanwhile, it had been registered with the Department of Commerce as the Laird-Turner Special, Model LTR-14, and was given the same NR263Y license number as before. Roscoe never liked this designation and wanted the name of Laird dropped whenever it was referred to by the press. As far as he was concerned, it was the "Turner Special" and, although he tried to have the designation changed on the records, he was unsuccessful. He had the race number "29" painted on the fuselage, reflecting his birthday of September 29.

Roscoe was pleased with its handling characteristics but late that afternoon, as the plane was being moved into the Ford hangar, a gas leak was discovered. The tank was removed, steamed out, and rewelded. Roscoe made another short test flight the next day and then took off for Los Angeles on August 30, 1937. When he landed at Albuquerque for gas, the engine was running rough and Roscoe needed help. Charlie Potter, a Pratt & Whitney engine specialist, flew from Los Angeles to check it over. It took three days to make repairs.

The plane proved to be a joy to fly, despite the landing difficulties, and Roscoe was ecstatic about its power. As he cruised along on September 2, the day before the races were to begin in Cleveland and two days before the Bendix start, he smelled gasoline in the cockpit but wasn't too concerned about it. When he landed at Burbank, observers saw gasoline streaming out behind the plane and flames shoot out of the tail section when the steel tailskid hit the concrete runway. The gasoline ignited and the tail section was engulfed in flames. Roscoe, sensing what had happened, headed for the grass, braked to a stop and let the propeller blast blow the fire to the rear as the fire trucks rushed to his side and doused the flames.

Roscoe followed the plane as it was taken to a hangar and was shocked to find the bottom of the fuselage dripping with gasoline. It was the same problem with the gas tank he had installed earlier. The tank was removed, the remaining fuel drained and the empty tank air-hosed dry. While a fire crew stood by and Roscoe watched, anxious to get the repairs completed, a welder began to spot-weld it. Then BOOM! The tank split open and Roscoe received flash burns on his hand. Luckily, no one else was hurt and not much damage was done but it was painfully evident that the plane, which Roscoe had now named the *Macmillan Ring-Free Meteor*, would not race in the Bendix that year.

Roscoe didn't want this bad luck to get to the ears of the race officials because he was afraid they wouldn't let him race if they knew his hand had been burned. But they did find out, and he was officially disqualified for the Bendix even if the plane were to be made ready in time.

Before the Wedell left Chicago, Young wanted to use a procedure he had used successfully for gluing the linen on the wings of the Wedell and the new Turner Special, but Laird had disagreed. When the Wedell arrived in Glendale, the linen was drooping down below the wing panel about two or three inches. Although Young had warned Laird's people about their gluing techniques, the glue wasn't holding, and he had difficulty repairing the linen when the plane arrived at Burbank. However, he finally got it ready only a few hours before takeoff time for Mackey to fly in the Bendix.

Roscoe saw Mackey off and wished him well. Unfortunately, Mackey was forced down at St. Louis by a loss of oil and was out of the race. When Young talked with Mackey later, he reminded Mackey that he had told him not to fly the engine at more than 2250 rpm because the oil scavenger pump was not sufficient to take care of the oil at a higher rpm. Mackey, ahead of everybody at that point, had pushed the prop control ahead and began to lose the oil. Mackey later said he had not been told this, but when nothing could be found wrong with the engine otherwise, he continued to Cleveland too late for the Bendix finish but in time for the Thompson. Meanwhile, Frank Fuller won the Bendix in a Seversky SEV-52 and pocketed $13,000.

Back at Burbank, the gas tank on the *Ring-Free Meteor* was removed, a new one was quickly fabricated, and Roscoe took off for Cleveland just in time to enter the new racer in the Thompson. During the dash from Albuquerque, Roscoe had a tail wind and had poured the coal to the Hornet. When he arrived at Cleveland, the Air Race Committee announced that he had just flown the last leg at 333.2 mph!

Just as on the Wedell, the fabric on the *Meteor's* wing was peeling off because Laird's people had not listened to Young's advice about gluing linen over a wood surface. Young, who had arrived in time to help, made repairs, redoped the area and had it ready in time for Roscoe to fly in the qualifying run. Roscoe completed the prerace qualification run, placing second with his best time of 258.903 mph, just a fraction slower than Steve Wittman in his Curtiss D-12-powered *Bonzo* racer. Roscoe was exhilarated and felt extremely confident that he would win the Thompson, because he knew he had the plane with the most powerful engine of all the competitors.

Nine planes leaped off in the traditional Thompson racing start and headed for the scattering pylon, with Roscoe neck-and-neck with several others. However, Roscoe skidded frantically in the first turn to avoid a midair collision with another plane and Wittman took the lead. Wittman led Roscoe and Earl Ortman for a number of laps, but on the seventeenth lap, with only three laps to go, his engine overheated badly and he was forced to pull up high and throttle back to stay in the race.

The fight was now between Roscoe and Ortman in his Marcoux-Bomberg, with Roscoe leading and Rudy Kling in third place with his Folkerts SK-3. With less than two laps to go, Roscoe, blinded by the sun and unable to see through his oil-stained windshield, thought he had cut inside the second pylon. Remembering what had happened to him in an earlier Thompson race, he desperately circled the pylon and headed for the home stretch behind Ortman and Kling. Ortman had the lead but didn't know it, believing that both Wittman and Turner were still ahead of him. Thinking he had third place comfortably won and could not do better, Ortman throttled back, entirely oblivious of Kling, who was flying high above him and only slightly behind in his blind spot. Kling made a bold, last-second move. He dove for the finish line and zipped in ahead of Ortman to take first place, a mere 50 feet ahead. Roscoe, who had been leading only a minute before, had to be content with third place with an average speed of only 3 mph behind the winner. He was awarded $3,000.

To add more disappointment to the loss, Roscoe found out from race officials that he had not cut a pylon and had given up the win through his own miscalculation. When the usually ebullient Roscoe was asked how he felt about it, he could only say, dejectedly, "I didn't fly it very well."

Mackey's luck was no better. Young had made some quick changes in the oil breather system that caused trouble in the Bendix, but Mackey had an engine failure during the race that forced him out; the engine had "swallowed a valve," which had nothing to do with any oil system changes that Young had made. Since Mackey had not won any money and Roscoe had only netted $3,000, Roscoe knew he was in trouble financially. He had agreed with Mackey to not only split the winnings 50-50 but also share the expenses. So, he owed $1,500 to Mackey off the top and knew almost everyone else who had helped him, including Matty Laird and Larry Brown, would be asking for their money.

Roscoe had tried to get sponsorship from a number of new sources for the 1937 races, which would have helped pay the overdue bills. He asked Curtis Candy Company officials to approve $10,000, but they declined. So did *Esquire* magazine, which replied that such publicity had not proved valuable to them. Undaunted, he never gave up trying to capture new backers.

Typically, Roscoe's disappointment at losing the Thompson lasted only briefly. He was sure he could run the Turner racer faster and shortly afterward entered speed competitions at Detroit and Cincinnati under the auspices of the National Aeronautic Association. Over the Detroit three-kilometer course, he soared to a new national speed record of 289.908 mph. But disappointment dogged him again when, two days later, Jackie Cochran flew a Seversky P-35 fighter plane over the same course for a new record of 292.271 mph.

Roscoe went to Cincinnati because he was offered an unusual deal: a share in the gate receipts. In accepting, he announced that he would break the Detroit–Cincinnati speed record and arrive over the Cincinnati Airport at precisely 1 P.M. Roscoe did exactly as he had promised. He did not fly during the air show and had the racer towed to nearby Lunken Field, the city's major airport, where it was put under wraps in a hangar to avoid creditors and process servers. Some Cincinnati businessmen and friends offered to help him by storing the Special there and promised to lend him money to prepare for the next year's races.

Several changes were made on the Turner Special during the next several months, including engine-cooling improvements by Don Young and a set of wheel pants made by metal expert John Hill of Hill's Streamliners. With the Wedell stored at Cleveland, Roscoe left to fulfill lecture dates and find other sponsors. He continued his work on *Flying Time*, which had begun broadcasting on November 15, 1936. The contract paid him $1,100 per week with the understanding that if NBC wanted to use him and a plane for publicity, his charge would be $200 per hour of flying. On weekends he flew a borrowed Boeing 80A "to pick up some spare change."

In his never-ending search for funds, he contacted automobile manufacturers (Dodge, Graham, and Nash), Gillette, W. K. Kellogg Company, and others. He also became involved with a group who was pushing a steam engine for aircraft, which Roscoe predicted "would not only eliminate the fire hazard but also eliminate practically all noise in flying, and give a far greater range of action for airplanes." He proposed to have a Lockheed modified to have the steam engine installed and make all the test flights if the group would put up $10,000 for construction of one unit and give Roscoe a one-third interest in the venture.

In addition to these initiatives, which never panned out, he wrote "Personal and Confidential" letters to the heads of companies who had supported him previously with contracts to advertise their products and asked for personal loans. He also wrote to the Navy, asking for permission to allow Pratt & Whitney to release one of their Twin Row 1830 Navy engines for use in his new racer. His request was approved

> provided that operation of the engine is conducted entirely within the continental limits of the United States. Your attention is invited to the fact that this engine has not been released for sale abroad and it is expected that you will not make information concerning it available to foreign interests.
>
> Your efforts to contribute something further towards the advancement of speed in our military planes is greatly appreciated and it is trusted that you will give the Navy the benefit of any important information gained in connection with your new racing airplane.[24]

This letter was about the only good news Roscoe received at this time. He and Carline moved to a small apartment in Chicago while he was under contract to NBC. He found that the program took more time than he imagined, requiring him to work all day with a writer and often in the evenings to prepare a daily script. This income and a salary of $500 per month he received from Macmillan Petroleum Company were his major sources of income at that time, but he managed to pay Don Young his salary and the bills for work on the new racer. He became disgusted with himself for being so broke and said privately he would never race again unless somebody paid to have the planes built and paid all his bills.

To help obtain more sponsorships, Roscoe hired Steve Hannagan, a publicity agent in New York, who tried to get him paying assignments that would also garner press coverage. Typical of his efforts was an offer to fly a trained seal from New York to Hollywood for a motion picture company. "Price should be kept as low as possible," Hannagan wired. "Naturally a lot of publicity involved in this. Confidential and rush answer."[25]

Roscoe's price may have been too high; there is no record that he accepted this opportunity. It appeared that he had reached a financial low point as 1937 came to a close.

To satisfy complaints by the humane society, Roscoe had a parachute made for Gilmore by the Irvin Parachute Co. in 1930. If the plane malfunctioned, Roscoe would throw Gilmore out and the chute's canopy, tied to the plane, would open. Here Gilmore poses with his chute and a oxygen mask. Photo courtesy of Madonna M. Turner.

Gilmore, here weighing about 150 lbs., was once too playful. On one occasion his sharp teeth bit into Roscoe's arm and caused a serious infection that doctors feared would cost him the arm. Roscoe's visits to see Gilmore always resulted in widely distributed photos. Photo courtesy of Madonna M. Turner.

The wingless Boeing 247 is loaded aboard the *S.S. Washington* in New York Harbor in September 1934. Off-loaded in France, it almost didn't make it to Great Britain in time for the race. Photo American Heritage Center, University of Wyoming.

The Boeing 247D flown by Roscoe, Pangborn, and Nichols in the 1934 London–Melbourne race is permanently suspended in the transport gallery of the National Air & Space Museum in Washington, D.C. Photo by Arnold Photo Syndicate. Courtesy of Madonna M. Turner.

FIFTEEN CENTS (IN CANADA, 20c) (Reason: Tariff)   October 29, 1934

TIME

The Weekly Newsmagazine

Acme

Volume XXIV   **ROSCOE TURNER**
His merchandise is speed.
(See TRANSPORT)   Number 18

Circulation Office, *350 East 22nd Street, Chicago.*   (Reg. U. S. Pat. Off.)   Editorial and Advertising Offices, *135 East 42nd Street, New York.*

Disheveled and tired, Roscoe manages a winning smile for a *Time* magazine cover after piloting the Boeing 247D to second place in the handicap division of the 1934 MacRobertson Air Race. Photo copyright 1934 Time Inc.

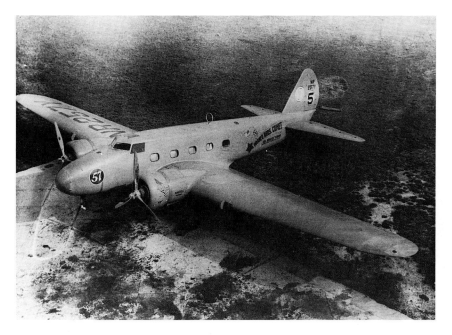

A view of the Boeing 247D named the *Warner Brothers Comet* before the 1934 London–Melbourne race. The various sponsors are noted on the left side of the aircraft. United Airlines, owner of the plane, had its markings on the other side. Photo Planet News Ltd., London. Courtesy Madonna M. Turner.

After completing the London–Melbourne race, Clyde Pangborn, Reeder Nichols, and Roscoe returned to California with the Boeing 247 by boat. They are shown here as they stopped off in Hawaii and received the traditional welcome. Photo American Heritage Center, University of Wyoming.

Roscoe poses with school children, who were impressed that the 220-lb. flyer
would use the tiny Motor Glide motorized scooter as a means of transportation
after landing the Boeing 80A trimotor at their local airport. Roscoe had a 25 percent interest in the Motor Glide firm. Photo American Heritage Center, University
of Wyoming.

The cockpits of racing planes were notoriously small and pilots could carry no baggage. Roscoe could barely squeeze into his Turner Special with a parachute on. Always flying in his self-designed uniform, he was ready upon arrival for interviews, dinners, or dances. Photo courtesy of Madonna M. Turner.

Roscoe attributes his success during the racing years to the excellent maintenance of his planes by Don Young, former Lockheed employee. Quiet, efficient, and with no desire for the spotlight, Young drove the 1929 Packard to the various races filled with aircraft parts and equipment. Photo courtesy of Madonna M. Turner.

Roscoe and Gilmore pose with Roscoe's Wedell-Williams racer (*foreground*) and the Lockheed Air Express at Burbank, Calif. Photo James R. Greenwood collection.

A chance meeting at the Lockheed factory in 1935 brought together Amelia Earhart, Wiley Post, Roscoe, and Laura Ingalls. Here they're looking over Post's Pratt & Whitney Wasp engine, which is destined for installation in the *Winnie Mae*. Photo courtesy of Madonna M. Turner.

Not all of Roscoe's flights ended with a safe landing. Here, with Don Young (*left*), he examines the damage to the propeller of his Lockheed Air Express after a forced landing near Cleveland. Roscoe is wearing a lion skin coat over his uniform. Photo American Heritage Center, University of Wyoming.

Proudly holding the Thompson and Bendix trophies, Roscoe poses with Charles E. Thompson (*left*) and Vincent Bendix. Roscoe and Jimmy Doolittle were the only pilots ever to win both trophies. Roscoe was the only three-time winner of the Thompson trophy. Photo American Heritage Center, University of Wyoming.

Always the center of attraction wherever he went, Roscoe poses with Capt. Eddie Rickenbacker, Amelia Earhart, and her husband, George Putnam, at the 1934 Indianapolis 500 races. Photo courtesy of Madonna M. Turner.

An in-flight emergency is explained to passengers by Roscoe in *Flight at Midnight*. Jean Parker played the role of flight attendant for Midway Air Lines. Photo American Heritage Center, University of Wyoming.

The Roscoe Turner Airport is dedicated at Corinth, Miss., on April 2, 1961. With a Southern Airways DC-3 in the background, Roscoe acknowledges the honor. The Mississippi Valley Collection, John Willard Brister Library, Memphis State University. Press-Scimitar photo. Photo courtesy of Milton Sandy, Jr.

Roscoe charms Senator Barry Goldwater at a meeting in Washington, D.C. Goldwater learned to fly during Roscoe's racing years. Photo American Heritage Center, University of Wyoming.

Appearing before Congressional committees on a number of occasions to testify for fixed-base operators and commercial aviation, Roscoe proved to be a formidable proponent. Here he is shown in an uncharacteristic pose pounding home an important point. Photo American Heritage Center, University of Wyoming.

The Roscoe Turner Aeronautical Corporation hangar and offices at Indianapolis Weir Cook Airport after World War II. A Beechcraft distributor, the company also operated a mechanics' school, an air taxi service, and provided maintenance for transient aircraft. Photo by Dean E. Timmerman.

Even on crutches, Roscoe attracted press interest. While recovering from an automobile
accident, he had turned his
hospital room into an office and
conducted business from his bed
until doctors decreed that it
interferred with his recovery.
Photo courtesy of Madonna M.
Turner.

When at home, Roscoe considered the kitchen his own domain. The black-and-
white tiles represented the traditional checkered flags used at air and auto races.
Photo courtesy of Madonna M. Turner.

Roscoe and Madonna pose with their pet bulldog in their award-filled den at their Indianapolis home while Gilmore stares in perpetuity. Photo by William A. Oates. Courtesy of Madonna M. Turner.

After his death in 1952, Gilmore was preserved and was one of the major conversation pieces in the Turner home in Indianapolis. Eddie Rickenbacker in a clowning mood in this 1961 photo, grabs Gilmore's ears while Mrs. Morrison, wife of Louisiana congressman James Morrison, looks on. Reprinted courtesy of the Indianapolis Star. Photo courtesy of Madonna M. Turner.

A year before his death in 1970, Roscoe, the Thompson trophy, and the Turner *Meteor* were featured on a float in the parade preceding the Indianapolis 500 races. Photo by H. C. Olsge Co. Courtesy of Madonna M. Turner.

10

WINNING THE
THOMPSON TROPHY—AGAIN

There were many lean days for Roscoe and Carline during the 1937–38 winter, but better times were on the way. In April 1938 Roscoe was offered $150 to appear on a radio show sponsored by Vitalis called *For Men Only*. He later received a contract to pose for advertisements of their hair products. He also continued to lend his name to ads for Camel Cigarettes, General Tires, and Ethyl Gasoline. Allsweet Margarine engaged Roscoe to sponsor a set of four model planes for advertising purposes, including a three-minute trailer that would include a résumé of Roscoe's life and an explanation about the model planes that Allsweet was giving away. He was featured in crossword puzzles and authorized a board game released in his name called the Roscoe Turner Air Race Game. For the latter he received a $500 advance and 3/10 of a cent for each game "delivered by the printer."

To add to this income, Frederick C. Crawford, president of Thompson Products, sent him a check for $500 "to help with the good work" and said he was going to increase the prize for the 1938

Thompson Trophy to $30,000. It was the incentive Roscoe needed to prove that his Turner racer was the best plane in the air. Despite the endorsements, Roscoe was still strapped for funds. His luck had been bad for three years; he felt he *had* to win big in 1938.

During the first half of that year, the Turner Special was modified to have two, large, well-streamlined spats fitted to its wheels and two oil coolers on the starboard wing to replace the single cooler below the fuselage.

The first racing opportunity for the Special came at the Pacific International Air Races held at Oakland, California, on May 30, 1938. The event he entered was the Golden Gate Exposition Trophy Race, which was flown over a 150-mile closed course. When Roscoe reached Oakland, he found he had a bad gasoline leak and the fuel was sloshing around in the bottom of the fuselage. The leak was caused by the high octane fuel decomposing the rubber hose leading from the fuel tank to the engine. A new type of hose was needed to prevent this.

Tony LeVier, a young racing pilot who was establishing a name for himself in the racing business, was working for Bill Schoenfeldt and flying his famous *Firecracker* racer. He recalled, "We were able to do a favor for Roscoe which paid off later for us at Cleveland. We happened to have a supply of the special rubber hose he needed to fix the leak, which we gave him. . . . Although Roscoe was a competitor of ours, Bill Schoenfeldt was willing to share whatever he had with Roscoe so he could race. That gesture cemented a lasting relationship between Roscoe, Don Young and our team."[1]

The race was flown over an extremely difficult five-pylon course. LeVier, flying a Shoenfeldt-Rider R-4, threatened Roscoe wing-to-wing for the first several laps but then had to slow down when his oil pressure rose to dangerous limits. Earl Ortman, flying a Marcoux-Bomberg, turned out to be a bigger threat. He and Roscoe dueled closely and the lead changed back and forth several times. On the eighteenth and final lap of the tight $8^1/_3$-mile course, Ortman crossed the finish line only about four plane lengths ahead of Roscoe in a time of 265.539 mph. Roscoe's speed was 262.402 mph; LeVier placed third at 260.762 mph and showed that he was going to be heard from again. Ortman had exceeded the world's closed-course record of 264.261 mph. Roscoe's consolation was that he had turned in the fastest lap of the race, being clocked at 278.8 mph on the ninth lap. This made him more determined than ever to win at Cleveland in September.

During 1938, President Roosevelt signed a bill to "put the nation's commercial aviation industry on a paying basis by eliminating free rides on airplanes." The airlines were reportedly losing an estimated $5 million annually because of issuing too many free passes in order to persuade people to fly. At the same time, he signed the Civil Aeronautics Act of 1938, which included the establishment of the Civil Aeronautics Authority (CAA). The top personnel would include an administrator, a safety board of three members, and a five-man aviation authority. When the plan was announced, about six hundred names were considered. A headline in the June 29, 1938, issue of the *Indianapolis News* read: COL. TURNER CONSIDERED FOR AIR CHIEF.

There is no evidence that Roscoe campaigned for the job nor would he have accepted it if it had been offered. He resented government interference in the business of aviation too much and had expressed his opinions bluntly on many occasions. Roscoe would also voice his convictions many times on behalf of the entrepreneurs who tried to make a living by furnishing training, sales, and service for private operators at local airports. Nonetheless, the Civil Aeronautics Act was the forerunner of things to come; the future growth of aviation in the United States would be dependent on federal policy.

The rules for the Bendix Race were changed in 1938. All pilots were required to possess instrument ratings and have radio equipment installed in their aircraft. Most important to Roscoe and other veteran racers was that no plane entering the Bendix could compete for the Thompson and other closed-course events at Cleveland; however, the rule change did not apply to pilots who could fly other aircraft. The change came about because of the concern that military fighter planes, like the Seversky P-35, would dominate all the races and discourage the low-budget, barnyard plane builders from competing. Roscoe decided not to participate in the Bendix race so he could compete again with the silver racer for the Thompson Trophy.

The winner of the 1938 Bendix race was Jacqueline Cochran. Competing against eight male pilots, she flew her Seversky to the finish line in 8 hours, 10 minutes, 31 seconds, for the $9,000 first prize and an additional $2,500 for the women's first place prize. Second place went to Frank Fuller, also flying a Seversky, who came in 23 minutes later.

The race for the Greve Trophy preceded the Thompson Race, and Tony LeVier was entered with the Menasco-powered *Firecracker*, along with Art Chester, Earl Ortman, and others with planes of their own design. On the first qualifying run for the Greve race, LeVier's engine blew up. He tells what happened:

> Only luck saved me from a bad accident. Inspection revealed that the No. 2 piston had a hole the size of a silver dollar blown through the head. The No. 2 cylinder was badly scored and required honing before it would be fit for use. There seemed no possibility of repairing it that afternoon and the deadline to qualify was the next morning.
>
> It was only a few minutes before Roscoe Turner learned of our predicament. In return for our assistance at Oakland he offered the services of his entire crew to help fix our plane. While we dismantled the engine he took his mechanic [Don Young] and the cylinder in his Packard and drove madly across Cleveland to find a machine shop before closing time. After working all night on the engine it was ready the next morning, and I flew and qualified for the Greve Trophy race a few minutes before the deadline.[2]

LeVier won the race by a bare four seconds over Art Chester in one of the most thrilling contests ever seen at Cleveland. "Roscoe Turner couldn't have been more pleased if he had owned the airplane," LeVier said. He had set a new record of 250.880 mph for the Greve race and won $12,000. However, after the race, the Schoenfeldt-built racer's 500-hp engine was in no shape to compete in the Thompson race that year. In addition, he had broken a wing spar on landing.

The Thompson Race rules were also changed in 1938. The race was lengthened to 300 miles and no more than fifteen planes could compete. There were no military planes entered; only eight planes built by the so-called amateur plane builders were ready for the racing start. Several were using 100 octane fuel for the first time to get extra power.

Roscoe objected to the extra mileage, a 50 percent increase over the previous year's distance of 200 miles. He predicted that the 300-mile race of thirty laps around the ten-mile course would result in a "Roman holiday" that would "kill off some of the boys." He contended the additional gasoline needed for the extra distance would overload most aircraft to an extent that it would be dangerous during the takeoff and early stages of the race. He also asserted that fatigue would be another element of hazard.

A number of pilots were queried about the distance increase, but only three responded, including Roscoe. Phil Henderson, business manager for the races, assumed that their silence indicated no objections to the new rule. When Roscoe was informed of this, he told a member of the press, "Oh, well, I don't give a damn for myself. Both my planes have motors that can take it, but I'm afraid it won't be so good for some of the other boys."[3]

A story circulated among the pilots that one of the competitors had bragged to a girlfriend that he was going to crowd Turner on one of the turns and force him into a pylon. When Roscoe heard about it, he was said to have called a meeting of the pilots and made a speech peppered with choice epithets and warnings about what he would do to anyone who tried. True or not, no one crowded him too closely on the pylons during the entire race.

Just before the races, the Turner Special was outfitted with Pesco oil and fuel pumps, and Roscoe leaped at this company's offer of sponsorship. He immediately renamed the plane the *Pesco Special*.

Roscoe and Don Young had souped up the Special and were able to get about 25 more mph out of it, as did Earl Ortman in his Marcoux-Bomberg and Steve Wittman in his *Bonzo*. Roscoe again allowed Joe Mackey to compete in his Wedell-Williams. Other entries were Army Air Corps pilot Lt. Leigh Wade, Art Chester, Harry Crosby, and Joe Jacobson. Roscoe described the race:

> There we were, lined up and waiting for the flag to drop. I felt confident. I was fit and knew the ship was in as good shape as an expert mechanic, Don Young, could make it. I had only one worry. I had taken on 55 gallons more gas than I'd ever loaded into the racer's tank before, and those pounds meant a great deal on the takeoff.

The flag fell. For just a moment I felt my ship shudder as it swerved to one side, then the tail came up and it straightened out. I held my breath as I eased off the ground. I wanted to get to the first pylon, round it and straighten out in the lead with a clear field; once in the lead, I intended to hold it. This was probably the most dangerous point of the race.

All the racers were heavily loaded and at no other time would they be so closely bunched as at the takeoff. I kept my eyes glued straight ahead and eased the throttle ahead. Ortman was leading me by yards, his lighter plane was taking advantage of the getaway and I knew Ortman was out to win and they didn't make any better racing pilots than he.

Almost before words can tell it, the first pylon flashed by and with the ship in a 90-degree bank and the stick in my belly, I turned the marker; still ahead of me was Ortman. I opened the throttle wide and slowly saw the ship ahead grow larger. Then came the second pylon.

The most difficult point of a closed course air race is turning around the pylons. Overshooting them means loss of time and trying to turn too soon means cutting the pylon and having to make a complete turn around it again before proceeding. I saw Ortman was going a trifle wide so I took the chance and shot inside his turn and away in the lead by a matter of a few feet.

During the first six laps Ortman and I passed each other at least six times. The one who got the edge at the pylon won the lead for our speed was so nearly equal and we were so close that with both of us in the same track, those turns were literally packed with death.

I wasn't satisfied. I expected greater speed from my thousand horse-power motor. I decided to step it up a bit. I pulled the mixture control gently back to get a leaner mixture into the carburetor. I held my breath for a moment. The airspeed indicator crept up a little and I sighed with relief. Figures show that I gained ten miles per hour by that adjustment of the mixture control. When I passed Ortman on that lap I never saw him again until the next to last lap.

Like a blur, the grandstands would flash past below and to one side of my plane. Out of the corner of my eye I'd see the dark mass of people, 270,000 of them. They were out to see the world's premier air racing event hoping, like people attending a bull fight or a boxing match, that they would have an added thrill. They won't admit they want to see a racer crash but if one does, they don't want to miss it.

For the next 40 minutes, I was hardly conscious of anything but the ever-recurring pylons. I climbed a bit higher and made diving turns at the pylons to add to my speed. Several times I passed planes and knew I had lapped someone but at a speed of over 300 mph, it was hard to tell whose plane it was. Out of the corner of my eye I saw a cloud of dust off to one side of the field and shuddered to think what had happened to someone.

I never concentrated harder on anything in my life than I did on that race. I saw the men in the corner of the field wave the number one sign so I knew I was in the lead position. I tore off tag after tag of adhesive tape [to keep track of the laps flown] and then I had only two laps to go. Then, all of a sudden, I blinked my eyes in disbelief and felt a sinking sensation in my stomach. There in front of me and a little lower was Ortman. How had be accomplished the impossible and taken the lead away from me?

For a few seconds, despair turned me cold. Then I took a grip on myself. I was going to win that race. On the next turn I shaved the pylon so close I could almost reach out and touch the stripes. I passed Ortman again and saw down on the field the numbers "1" and "29." I knew I was still in the lead and had only one lap to go. Then I realized what had happened. I had lapped Ortman, the one man I really feared in this race. I now had a 10-mile lead and could afford to go a little slower around the pylons and climb a little higher. If everything went well for just ten more miles—no breakage, no oil leakage to blind me, no cutting corners, I'd win the Thompson Trophy for the second time, something no pilot had ever done.

I never knew a greater moment in my life than when I saw the checkered flag go down as I crossed the finish line in front of the grandstands. I shouted to myself, "I've won! I've won!" In the joy of the moment, I made another circuit of the course.

But an air race is never over until you're safely on the ground. I nosed up to 3,500 feet and came into the field on a long glide. I hit the ground all right then began to bounce. I'd hit some rough spots and the ship made a half dozen bounces before I finally got it under control. I found out later that I had set a new world's record of 283.149 mph and had beaten the record of 264.261 mph set by the French flyer Michel Detroyat in 1936.[4]

Author Roger Huntington described the action from a different viewpoint:

The race started with Ortman, Wittman and Chester leading into the first lap in that order. Turner, confident of his superior speed, purposely took off easy and was very careful around the scattering pylon, applying more power down the long west straightaway. He caught up with the front-runners on the second lap, then eased back, letting Ortman set the pace in the 170-mph bracket. On lap six, Ortman cut a pylon and Turner took the lead when he turned back to recircle it. The order was then Turner, Ortman, Wittman and Chester.

But Wittman and Chester were both in trouble: Wittman losing coolant and Chester blowing oil out his engine breather vents. Then on the 13th lap, Ortman began blowing smoke. By the 16th lap, Chester had slipped back to 6th place. But Ortman and Wittman held on doggedly to second and third, even though they fell back gradually behind Turner, who was lapping easily in the 280 mph bracket. Finally on the 20th lap, Chester had to come down—out of oil. Ortman was lapped by Turner, and finally, on Ortman's 27th lap, an oil line ruptured and his pressure went to zero, spraying oil all over the fuselage and canopy. Still Ortman hung on, hoping against hope to finish the 30 laps before his oil supply was gone entirely. He just made it, finishing second at 269.7 mph to Turner's winning 283.4 mph.[5]

The win gave Roscoe more than a morale boost and a much-needed financial shot in the arm with the winner's prize of $22,000. He went down in the racing history books as the first pilot to win the Thompson twice. Joe Mackey in Roscoe's Wedell had placed fifth for a prize of $1,800. He had been clocked at 249.628 mph. Roscoe was always proud of the fact that he personally owned two prizewinning racers, the only pilot ever able to make that claim.

The award money enabled Roscoe to pay off some of his debts, but not all. It has been said by some that he never fully repaid Larry Brown and Matty Laird all the amounts that they claimed he owed them for their work. There is no correspondence or records in the Turner files to indicate one way or another. If he didn't pay what they asked, it was because he disagreed with them on the amount owed for the work performed. Don Young, who knew first-hand about all the work that was performed on both racers, supported Roscoe in his contentions. Always present when the planes were being worked on, Young was certainly in a position to know if Roscoe was being overcharged.

Young had a behind-the-scenes hand in helping Roscoe win his second Thompson Trophy. When the race was lengthened to 300 miles, neither knew for sure whether the racer would have enough fuel to make it. Young suggested that he fuel the plane with 50 gallons of gas in one tank and 50 in the other so the amount of fuel expended could be accurately measured on a test flight. Roscoe took off on one tank and when he was ready to fly the course for three laps, he switched to the other tank. He then changed to the other tank for three more laps and switched back to the original tank for the landing. Young measured the fuel left and they determined that, although it would be close, the Turner Special could cover the 300 miles with a little to spare.

Another innovation that Young introduced was a means of letting Roscoe know what lap he was on and what place he was in.

> I got a batch of 4-foot x 8-foot plywood panels, painted them white and put letters and numbers on them. One had an "L" and another a "P." I told Roscoe that during the race the "L" would show his laps, and the "P" will show his place. "If you're being pressed close, we'll have the 'P' and the 'L' boards close together. If you've got a good spread, we'll have them about 30 feet apart, so you know you can cut back on the power. We will keep stop watches on the closest planes to you so we can tell just by looking at their times whether they're picking up speed on you.

Young positioned the boards so that Roscoe could see them easily as he came around the home pylon. He also suggested that Roscoe fly the course in a slow, small plane before the race so he could study every barn, tall tree, house, and other landmark along the route and thus be sure he was on the outside of the pylons that were sometimes hard to see at high speeds in low-visibility conditions while having to keep an eye out for other aircraft. Larry Schmidlapp flew him around the course several times in a Waco cabin plane and this idea proved to be a great help.

It wasn't generally known but Roscoe almost didn't start the 1938 race. He still had a habit of pumping the throttle when he started an engine. But if it was done when starting the Hornet engine, it would flood quickly. When the signal was given to start engines, Roscoe had reverted to his old habit of pushing the throttle back and forth to get gas in the carburetor. As Young stood on the wing cranking the engine as hard and fast as he could, gas began running out under the airplane.

"Roscoe, you've got to stop pumping the throttle!" Young shouted.

"As usual," Young recalled, "he said he wasn't but I knew he had."

Young told Roscoe to close the throttle and not to touch it. There were only seconds left now before the race would start. After pulling the propeller through two or three times to clear the raw gas from the cylinders, Young yelled, "Contact!"

"It just so happened that it was on the right cylinder. It fired and boom it went. I ran up to the cockpit and Roscoe was crying. He said, 'Don, if I win this race, I'll make you a present of a thousand dollars!' and he did."

The prerace worries about having enough fuel to last the 300 miles at full throttle were unfounded. Roscoe landed with 40 of the original 206 gallons left in the tanks. He taxied in before the grandstand and climbed out smiling his broadest smile. If there were ever a jinx connected with winning the Thompson a second time, he had licked it.

The crowd gave him a standing ovation. Jackie Cochran and Fred Crawford, president of Thompson Products, greeted him warmly. Photographers yelled for "the trophy," and three appeared. One was the heavy bronze Thompson Trophy. Another was the silver Allegheny Ludlum trophy for setting a new record. The third was the Clifford W. Henderson merit award given on racing points. Roscoe got extra points over Cochran for the latter award because he had set a record in the event he had won, which she had failed to do. Several days after the races, Cochran sent Roscoe a note of congratulations for his Thompson win but asked that he repay her the loan of an unspecified amount she had made him the previous year because racing "takes plenty of money."[6]

To reporters clamoring for quotes, Roscoe said it was "the easiest race I have ever flown. The air was rough and I was afraid a couple of times that the jolting given the plane with its heavy load of gas would break a wing." Turning to Don Young, Roscoe insisted that race officials let him join him on the speaker's stand as the photographers crowded around for pictures. Roscoe received high praise from the aviation press for his second win of the Thompson. As one reporter wrote, "He has won the respect and admiration of all who once remembered him as a guy who wore loud clothes and talked big. The changed way in which Col. Turner was regarded by the crowd was noteworthy. He was the big favorite, justly so. Any man who had played about with so much tough luck and who had learned to take it in his big, lumbering stride, deserved to win."[7]

Typically, Roscoe responded optimistically to questions about his future plans. "I would like to build a ship that would do 500 miles an hour," he said, "and I think I could do it. The Thompson next year will be won at more than 300 miles per hour. With a new ship I could beat that speed in a 300-mile closed-course race."

In a magazine article, Roscoe explained what it was like to fly and win the Thompson:

Ten . . . Nine . . . Eight . . . Seven . . . seconds, the clock on the dash panel says, ticking them off. And you sit there in the cramped cockpit and sweat. Waiting for the starter to drop the flag.

The tiny racing plane trembles. The propeller clatters. The skin throbs.

You're in No. 2 position, next to the orange job with the taper wing, second from the end of the line. There are nine others, wingtip to wingtip, all rarin' to go. Stinging, snorting, little hornets.

And you've got to fly each one of them besides your own. Because you never know what the other guy is going to do.

This is the Thompson Trophy Race. The Big One. The National Air Races. The one that really counts. Aviation's "Kentucky Derby." You've got to win. Everything you own is wrapped up in this trim and powerful little racer. Everything. Even your spare watch is in hock.

For 365 days, since the race last year, you've been getting the ship ready. Wings clipped to cut through the air faster. Engine souped up to get more power. One thousand, 200 horsepower in your lap and a feather in your tail. That's what it amounts to. Enough to make any aeronautical engineer beat himself to death with his slide rule.

For what? For fame and glory and headlines and the prize money. So you can pay off your debts and come back next year.

Check your instruments. Fuel gage. Pressure gage. Oil temperature. Tachometer. Cylinder head temperatures. Glance at the chronometer. The clock has stopped. No, it's still running.

Six . . . Five . . . Four . . . Why is a second a year? Tick, tick, tick, it sounds like the bong of Big Ben in your ears. Tension, nerves, fear. It drowns out the roar of the crowd.

The grandstand: a kaleidoscope of colors. It'll be a blurred ribbon next time you see it flash by.

See that black and yellow job down the line? Keep your eyes on him. He's the guy to beat. Get out in front of him and try to stay there. No. 8, that's him. *Number Eight . . . Number Eight . . .* Beat him . . . Beat him. The engine sings it. A battle cry. Remember what your mechanic said—"They're ganging up on you. Look out! They're going to try to box you in." Just like they do in a horse race.

Three . . . Two . . . One second to go!

Why won't your feet be still? They're jumping up and down on the rudder pedals. Dammit! You can't stop them and your hands? Sticky, trembling on the stick and throttle. Shaking like you've got the DT's. Goggles streaming with perspiration. Your clothes are soaked. They're soggy. Itchy. Hell fever, that's what you've got. Scared-to-hell fever. You always catch it right about now—with one second to go. It'll go away. As soon as . . . There's the flag.

Slap the throttle. Wrrummm! The ship leaps forward. Your feet stop jumping. Hands? Cold and steady. Now, crouched in the cockpit, this is your world. Nothing else matters. It's up to you.

Faster, faster, faster, shooting across the field. Easy does it. You're free. The ship leaps forward again, like a shot from a gun. No more ground drag. Too much speed. You'll rip the wings off if you don't slow down the propeller.

Where are the others? Count 'em . . . one . . . two . . . three . . . they're all up. Don't get too close. One error and it's curtains for both of you.

You're no longer human. You're a machine. Every move is timed to the split second . . . There's the red roof. Pylon coming up. Left rudder. Left stick. Wing up. Wing down. You're around. The straightaway. More throttle. The wind whistles in your ears.

Brown roof. Big tree. Another turn. Here come the others. Who's that on the left wing? He's cutting in too close. You'll get his prop wash on the next turn . . . Here it comes, boy . . . Hang on!

Too sharp. Take 'em wider next time. Don't try to cut so short. Let the other guy kill himself. You're doing all right. There's the grandstand again. Swoosh!

Pull a strip of tape from the dashboard. That's how you count the laps. Thirty laps. Thirty pieces of tape. Twenty-nine now . . . Check it the next time you go by the crowd. The guy will have the big numeral card out. It should read 28 . . .

Where is No. 8? You can't see him. Red roof again . . . Turn . . . Straightaway . . . Throttle . . . Brown roof . . . Big Tree . . . Pylon . . . The grandstand. Okay, it says 28.

There he is! Just ahead. You're gaining on him. Faster. Faster . . . Pour it on. Pray this thing will hold together . . . Red roof coming up . . . Try to cut it real short this time . . . Take the chance . . . Maybe you can get him on the turn . . . NOW . . . Wing down deep . . . Snap back . . . Jerk . . . Shake, tremble, roar . . . But you made it. There's nobody in front of you.

Instruments? Oil pressure . . . Supercharger . . . Gas . . . Speed . . . Okay. If they only stay like that. Remember what happened last year— when the supercharger blew. It was only doing 2,000 rpm then . . . Now it's doing 3,000. You improved it. But that much?

Pylon. Grandstand. Tape. Round and round going nowhere. Brown roof. Red roof. Big tree. Straightaway. Pylon. Zoom room, zoom. Wing up. Wing down, Level off. More pylons. More trees, more roofs. It's hot. Like an oven. Is something on fire? Glance around? No, don't, you mustn't. At this speed you can't take your eyes off what's coming up ahead . . . Grandstand. Tape . . . There's one piece left. One more lap.

You're still out in front. If you could only look back and catch that number card for a recheck. It was so blurred. Maybe you missed a pylon. Maybe they'll disqualify you. No, not that, please. And let 'er hang together another two minutes.

It's over.

You won!

You're shaking again. You can hardly control the ship after she's on the ground. Your heart beats louder than the engine. Uniform soaked, sopping wet. Hands tremble. Knees buckle as you climb out to meet the reporters and photographers with a big, forced smile . . . Headache. Mustache ache. Exhaustion. Oh, for a great big soft bed . . .

Air racing is like that . . . It's the most dangerous profession in the world.[8]

Roscoe was awarded the Harmon Trophy as America's premier aviator for 1938. Disappointed that it had not been presented to him by

President Roosevelt as it had to previous winners and never too bash-
ful to ask, Roscoe sent a telegram to Louis Johnson, assistant secretary
of war:

> League of International Aviators awarded me Harmon Trophy Friday
> night and same is now in my possession. President presented it last year
> to Dick Merrill. Will you arrange official presentation to me as soon as
> possible, advising of the date arranged. Would like to have both you and
> Clinton Hester at the presentation.[9]

Roscoe also contacted members of Congress, who promised to take up
the matter with the White House but to no avail. He had won the
Harmon Trophy for the second time and it had been presented. No second ceremony would be held.

In April 1939 Roscoe was elected president of the Professional Racing
Pilots' Association by unanimous vote. As their representative, he recommended changes in the rules for safety reasons. Among them was a
request to have balloons lofted inside the pylons at a height of 50 feet
above the top of the pylons so the turning points could be more easily
identified. Also, he suggested that an emergency field be designated for
forced landings and policed so that it would be free of parked cars and
other obstructions.

In considering future work possibilities, Roscoe contacted a German
commission agent in early 1939 to obtain a Focke helicopter for $15,000
to demonstrate in the United States at the 1939 World's Fair. Obviously
unaware of the significance of the turbulent events unfolding in Germany
under Hitler, his thought was to buy the American rights and have it
manufactured in the United States. He was informed that it was "impossible for this year . . . to send a helicopter to America, in order to
demonstrate it during a world's fair. All other news which you may have
read in American periodicals or newspapers are not true."[10]

Concurrently, he wrote to the Kellogg Company saying that he intended to go to Germany to bring the Focke helicopter to the United
States and suggested that Kellogg either sponsor a tour of the country
with it or tie its products in with the release of the film *Flight at Midnight*,
in which he was scheduled to participate. "I can eat Corn Flakes as well
as any other breakfast food!" he said.[11] Hitler had already begun his

march to conquer Europe. There was no further correspondence with the German commission agent or Kellogg.

Although Roscoe planned to enter the 1939 Thompson race, he also wanted to compete in the Bendix with a different airplane. He contacted Floyd Grumman, president of Grumman Aircraft Engineering Company in May 1938. He said he had heard about a new military fighter that Grumman was building and asked to be appointed as a test pilot for it "at practically no salary except enough so that I could be classified as an employee, in order to get around any military objections."

He added, "Since there are going to be quite a few airplanes sold in the foreign market, both in South America and Europe, perhaps I could fit into this program also.

"In other words, I know that you have a plane that can compete and perhaps outclass the Seversky. I would like very much to fly one of your ships in the Bendix Trophy Race at Cleveland this year."[12] Grumman turned him down.

Roscoe turned elsewhere for a new racer but shelved the idea when no manufacturer came forth. He decided to make a few minor changes to the *Pesco Special* and take it back to Cleveland. Only this time it would be called something else if and when a new sponsor surfaced to finance him.

Roscoe offered his services to the Texaco Oil Company for a tour of the country advertising its Sky Chief gasoline. Among the many advertising proposals he presented was an unusual offer to modify his personal diamond-studded wings to reflect an affiliation with Texaco. The company was not interested.

In February 1939 Roscoe became vice president in charge of sales and advertising for the Porterfield Aircraft Company of Kansas City, Missouri, and demonstrated cabin and open cockpit models, which sold for $1,895; others with larger engines sold for $2,945. To capitalize on his name, it was called the Porterfield-Turner line of planes. His salary for 1939 was $3,125. He was not pleased with the airplane design and resigned in 1940.

Despite the turndowns of his many self-initiated proposals, the continuing press mention of his winning the 1938 Thompson race did spark some renewed interest in Roscoe for other product advertising. Immediately after the 1938 race, Firestone Tire and Rubber Company offered Roscoe a complete set of tires for all of his automobiles and airplanes and $1,000 for use of his name in advertising. Kellogg's Corn Flakes also offered him an opportunity to assist in publicizing the Cadet Aviation Corps, "a program to develop and sustain a healthy interest in aviation amongst the youngsters of the country."

Champion Spark Plugs became a sponsor and Roscoe painted out *Pesco Special* and had a large Champion logo painted on the fuselage, along with "29" the racing number that he felt would bring him luck because it signified his birthday. At the same time he inaugurated an idea he had first presented to Texaco. He had small cards printed with the Champion Spark Plug name which he would sign at his leisure, carry with him, and pass out when asked for an autograph. He bought a device that enabled him to sign six cards at once. These cards were especially handy because, as Roscoe admitted a number of times, his hands were so shaky after a race that he couldn't hold a pen to sign his name.

After the 1938 victory, Roscoe was notified he was going to receive another honor the following summer. On August 20, 1939, the citizens of Sheldon, Iowa, dedicated Roscoe Turner Field and held an air show for the occasion. In the dedication address by a prominent local attorney, Roscoe's contributions to aviation were reviewed and he was introduced as "the nation's foremost speed pilot." Tears filled Roscoe's eyes as U.S. Congressman Melvin J. Maas (R-Minn), representing the National Aeronautic Association, also paid tribute, saying that most airports were named after dead pilots and he commended Sheldon for naming its field after a live one. A large blue-and-white flag was raised on the flagpole bearing the inscription "Roscoe Turner Field" and aerial bombs were touched off to cap the dedication.[13]

Resplendent in his uniform but somber, Roscoe was uncharacteristically brief in his response. He lauded Sheldon's initiative in building the airport and holding the air show. However, he pointed out that air shows were for the purpose of showing the possibilities of the airplane and not to encourage pilots to attempt reckless stunt flying. His remarks were

prompted by an aerobatic display by several pilots who were danger-
ously trying to outdo each other and by a near-fatal batwing parachute
jump by "Batman" Zmuda. Zmuda had sent shudders through the audience when he had difficulty reaching the rip cord of his chute, which
was inside his flight suit, until he was only 400 feet from the ground.
He usually pulled it at 1,000 to 1,500 feet after gliding down with his
batwings from about 5,000 feet.

In October 1938 Roscoe had been offered a contract by Republic
Pictures for a forthcoming picture called *Flight at Midnight*, with op-
tions for future pictures. Roscoe was assured that the starring role he
would play would be that of "Col. Roscoe Turner." The stars were Phil
Regan, Jean Parker, Robert Armstrong, Noah Berry, Jr., and Roscoe.
Several months in the making, it was finally released in August 1939,
just before the Cleveland Air Races. The plot was typical of Hollywood
films during that period. It was summarized in the movie trade press
this way:

> Phil Regan is a crack flyer who takes his job too lightly, is a great guy with
> the girls and a constant source of worry to Pop Hussey, owner of the
> Norwalk Airport. Phil really falls in love with Jean Parker, transport host-
> ess being courted by Robert Armstrong, government inspector who
> grounds Regan for violating rules in flying the mail. Necessity of raising
> money to remove high tension wires from Hussey's field brings all in-
> terested in the field to urge Regan to test plane whose acceptance will
> mean capital for financing improvements at the airport. A celebration fea-
> tured by a broadcast from a plane flown by Roscoe Turner almost ends
> tragically when motors stall on Turner's plane, and Regan daringly flies
> into high tension wires to clear way for Turner's safe landing. This feat
> of heroism by Regan atones for his negligence in making a test in which
> his mechanic, Noah Berry, Jr., loses his life.[14]

Although Roscoe's role was widely advertised to attract audiences,
he is rarely seen in the film. The opening shot shows him climbing from
his plane and walking briskly out of the picture. He is not seen until
much later in the film when he unexpectedly appears in the middle of
a crowd and someone asks him a question. "Yes, that is right," he answers carefully and the camera abandons him until later when he ex-

changes unintelligible words with Jean Parker, acting as a flight attendant.

In a scathing review in a Cleveland paper after the 1939 races, the
headline read "Air Film Ignores Turner." A subhead said, "Picture Uses
His Name, Others Do the Acting." The paper's movie critic noted that
Roscoe's debut as a screen star "is dimmed by the scarcity and speedi-
ness of his strolls within camera range." The reviewer concluded that
"the world's outstanding speed flyer was obviously courted by the film
colony for the same reason it flirts with sports champions, chess experts,
dethroned royalty and broken-down orators."[15]

The New York Times summed up the film by asking if "something
[could] be done about providing filmgoers with their own anti-aircraft
batteries to bring down . . . such menaces to commercial aviation movies
as 'Flight at Midnight.' "[16]

The 1939 Cleveland Air Races loomed under a darkening world political sky. Hitler had seized all of Czechoslovakia, signed a nonaggression
pact with Stalin, threatened to invade Poland with a lightning campaign
of air and ground forces, and defied England and France to do anything
about it. The question in the minds of Americans was whether the United
States would be drawn into what was plainly going to be an all-out war
in Europe.

The question didn't seem to bother many in civilian aviation circles
in the United States at the time. The 1939 Bendix race took place as
scheduled and was won by Frank Fuller in a Seversky. Fuller also went
on to New York to claim a new record of 8 hours, 58 minutes, 8 seconds, for the west-east distance. It was his second Bendix Trophy
victory.

Contrary to what some writers have asserted, Roscoe and Young made
no changes in the Turner Special for the 1939 Thompson race. Still, it
promised to be the fastest Roscoe would ever fly as he made the qualifying runs at an average speed of 297.767 mph and made several laps
at more than 300 mph, a personal speed goal that he had hoped to
achieve for a long time. Joe Mackey, flying Roscoe's Wedell-Williams
again, qualified in sixth place at a relatively slow 251.221 mph.

As the racing pilots completed their qualifying runs, the world news was ominous. Germany had invaded Poland and Britain and France declared war on Germany. The crowds at Cleveland thinned as workers were called back to their jobs.

When the final race for the trophy began, Roscoe says he deliberately let the six others go ahead, planning to use his superior speed to catch up later. However, on the second lap he didn't spot the pylon and had to go back to circle it again, which put him farther behind. But Roscoe was fired with determination to gain the lead. Flying at nearly full throttle, he pushed the 14-cylinder Twin Wasp beyond its rated limits and roared in pursuit, passing the others one at a time until he was in the lead. By the ninth lap, he had lapped the entire field once. Exhilarated with the speed the engine gave him, he risked it all to prove his plane's prowess as the best in the sky and pushed the throttle to the stop. His airspeed indicator inched beyond the 300 mark and his speed was so commanding that he lapped the field a second time. One complete lap was clocked at 299.03 mph, the fastest lap ever flown over a ten-mile course.

Roscoe was the clear winner at an average speed of 282.536 mph which won him the $16,000 prize. Tony LeVier finished second with an average speed of 272.538 mph. Joe Mackey placed sixth in the faithful golden Wedell, originally built in 1932, averaging 232.926 mph and garnering the $1,000 prize.

LeVier might have been able to beat Roscoe if he hadn't miscalculated. He tells about his difficulties during that race:

> I had trouble on my takeoff. I was overloaded with a terribly dangerous rearward center of gravity problem and I was actually out of control from the time I took off until I reached about a thousand feet. I had the stick all the way forward and the stabilizer wound all the way to nose-down trim. If it hadn't been for the adjustable stabilizer, I would have crashed on takeoff.
>
> I made a huge circle of the whole course before I could get stability regained so I could race. I passed everybody but Roscoe. I didn't know it at the time but, apparently, he had cut a pylon early on and I didn't know it and he was behind me for many laps. When he came by me, I thought he had lapped me so I pulled back on the power and came in second. I do believe my airplane was faster but, of course, I can't prove it now.[17]

The race was Roscoe's crowning victory and made up for all the heartbreak and losses he had sustained over a decade. He landed to the greatest applause he would ever receive and the very welcome $16,000 purse. He just missed getting $4,000 more and the Ludlum Award because he had not bettered his 1938 record. But he had defied the odds of survival by competing for the Thompson Trophy seven times and winning it for the third time, an honor he never had to share with anyone else. He and Jimmy Doolittle were the only pilots ever to win both the Bendix and Thompson trophies.

When he found out what the timers said his speed was, Roscoe admitted that it was the only regret he had about the race. He had failed to break his own record and blamed it on the "bungled up start" and his failure to locate the first pylon so that he had to circle it. Although he won it decisively, it wasn't the best race he had ever flown.

As Roscoe taxied to the winner's line in front of the grandstand, his hands and legs shook nervously when he dismounted to receive the plaudits he deserved. Well-wishers crowded him to shake his hand. A wreath of flowers was placed around his neck as the trophy was handed to him. Reporters shouted questions at him. Roscoe shouted back, "Make way for the photographers! This is the last chance you boys will have to photograph me with the Thompson Trophy. I'm not going to race any more." The few who heard him did not realize that he really meant what he said.

Roscoe was escorted to the announcer's stand but refused to climb the stairs until Don Young joined him. When the two reached the microphone, Roscoe hugged Don tightly and said, "My life has been in this man's hands for nine years!" It was an emotional, heartfelt, and well-deserved tribute to a man who had devoted a decade of his life and his special mechanical skills to a man he revered.

In addition to the Thompson Trophy, Roscoe was also awarded the Henderson Trophy for the third time. A few weeks later, he received the Goddess of Victory Trophy from the American Legion for being "America's greatest speed flyer."[18]

When Fred Crawford presented the winning check to him, Roscoe confirmed what he had said to the photographers. He told the audience, "This is my last race. I'll be 44 this month. This is a young man's game."

The 1939 race was not only Roscoe's last race, it was also the last of the pre–World War II Thompson races. Many observers were disappointed at the scarcity of contestants when only seventeen racing planes competed in the four-day program and none of these were less than two years old. An industry magazine commented: "Some manufacturers feel that whatever the races may have done in the past to stimulate development of airplanes and engines, they are not contributing as much now, and many in the industry feel that the carnival atmosphere of ballyhoo, thrills, chills, and stunts does not inspire public confidence in aviation, although it admittedly pleases the crowds."[19]

The Professional Racing Pilots' Association seemed to disintegrate as the members agreed that there would not be any more air races as in the past. A committee was appointed to consider the possibility of having air races in Los Angeles the following year that would be a combination of midget airplanes and those eligible for the Greve and Thompson races. However, the idea died because the war was spreading in Europe and now greatly threatened to involve the United States. In addition, Cliff and Phil Henderson, who had managed the races for so long, resigned to pursue other business interests in California.

The consensus of the racing pilots was that if there were to be any races in 1940 and 1941, they would need some kind of subsidization or assurance that they could recoup their expenses, let alone make a profit from risking their necks. Generous as the prize money had become, the potential rewards did not warrant the heavy expense of building new racers. The "name" racing pilots of the past could not afford to continue to compete: Art Chester and Bill Schoenfeldt were reportedly trying to find buyers for their racers; Harry Crosby had been instructed by his sponsor to dispose of his plane; Keith Rider had a lien placed on his plane and owed a balance on the engine. Others had stored their planes or were being pursued by creditors for labor and parts charges.

The races were not resumed until 1946, mostly with highly sophisticated World War II Army and Navy fighter planes that could be purchased on the surplus market for relatively small sums compared to their original cost to the government. For example, a Bell P-63 King Cobra that had cost the government thousands could be bought for as little as $750, and Allison and Merlin engines could be bought for anywhere from $75 to $300. With aircraft parts so plentiful, many were encouraged to try their luck at racing. When the armament and other strictly military hardware such as armor plate was removed, the fighters could now reach speeds only dreamed of by racing pilots like Roscoe. There was no danger of structural failure on the pylon turns because military planes were strong enough to take stresses that were twelve to fifteen times the pull of gravity. As a result, the races flown by pilots who built their own planes and characterized the Golden Age of Aviation were no more. Of the eight pilots who had won the Thompson by this time, five had been killed. The remaining three were Jimmy Doolittle, Harold Neumann, and Roscoe, who through their racing and record-setting, had all helped push back the frontiers of aeronautical knowledge. And now Roscoe would move on to new challenges.

11

THE ROSCOE TURNER
AERONAUTICAL CORPORATION

In an interview with a *New York Times* reporter after the 1939 races, Roscoe revealed that he was going to start "the finest air school in the country" in Indianapolis. It was a plan that he had been exploring for a year. The decision to start an all-service aviation organization there was not based on a whim. Before his last Thompson race, Roscoe had carefully analyzed his next move after quitting racing and had decided that he wanted to settle down in a city somewhere in the midwest. During 1939 he had received an invitation from contacts in Dayton, Ohio, to open an airplane sales and service business there, but some Indianapolis civic officials heard of the plan and intercepted him. The Indianapolis Chamber of Commerce and City Council were trying to develop a major airport, and they thought Roscoe's presence would be a big attraction, so he was offered some valuable incentives to choose their city. Roscoe had drawn 350-mile-diameter circles around the candidate cities and decided that because of its location and the monetary encouragement of the city fathers, Indianapolis offered the best opportunity to transfer his knowledge and experience into a profitable business enterprise.

During the week following the races, he flew to Indianapolis to present a formal proposal to the Indianapolis City Works Board to build a hangar and administration building on fifty-two acres of leased land for the purpose of opening a fixed-base operation (FBO) and aviation school. The FBO would offer aircraft and engine repair facilities, radio sales and service, fuel, parts, supplies, and flight instruction.

Since there was no legal precedent upon which the board could base a decision to permit him to locate on city property, the board moved slowly. Roscoe, used to doing things quickly, strained and fidgeted. The board found that the lease and commercial property privileges he sought conflicted with the lease of the Central Aeronautical Corporation (CAC), which was then offering aircraft sales and services there. To solve the impasse, Roscoe, with Ray P. Johnson and William M. Joy, bought all of the stock of CAC, including assets and liabilities, for $20,000 on November 1, 1939. On February 8, 1940, the charter was amended changing the name to the Roscoe Turner Aeronautical Corporation (RTAC). The assets included four aircraft.

While negotiations were conducted during the winter of 1939–40, temporary offices were made available downtown at the Antlers Hotel for the construction of the hangar and school building. During this period, Roscoe used the back seat of his automobile as an office while at the airport. The makeshift nature of these accommodations was in part dictated by a shortage of operating capital, a continuing problem that Roscoe sought to improve by requesting small loans from a number of sources. One of them was Thompson Products, which loaned him $300 in December 1940 to be repaid within 120 days, but which he did not repay in full until 1943.

Roscoe's living and working arrangements were also affected by the state of the Turners' marriage, which had gradually deteriorated during the late 1930s. Residing in California, Carline made a brief visit to Indianapolis in 1941 and never returned. A divorce was made final a few years later, and she remarried shortly thereafter.

As he negotiated for space and construction began, he immediately started developing friendships with civic leaders and politicians. A long-time member of the American Legion, which was headquartered in Indianapolis, he became very active and served on its National Aeronautics Committee—first as a member, then as its chairman—which gave him a platform to advance his encouragement of aviation on a national scale. He let it be known that he was going to help make Indianapolis an aviation center that the citizens could be proud of.

Roscoe hired Col. L. B. Lent as general manager, recruited a staff of thirty-five experienced instructors and employees, and showed the board he was fully prepared to begin operations, but there were more delays. In June 1940, frustrated by the lack of action, he offered to relieve the Works Board of the task of operating the airport if the city would sell the property to him. He made the offer during a discussion of operating costs in which board members were trying to discover ways and means of increasing revenues. The offer was not accepted.

Finally, on August 9, 1940, after more than nine months of negotiations, the board agreed to give RTAC a twenty-year lease, renewable for twenty years. Ground was broken in the fall of 1940 and the RTAC building and an adjoining heated hangar were dedicated on May 29, 1941, with appropriate ceremony.

Valued at $150,000, the Turner building was built on two acres of land and contained a dormitory, two large classrooms, hangar space for forty small planes, a service and repair shop, control tower, and a row of offices along the structure's ultramodern glass brick front. The building would revert to the city at the end of the lease. A restaurant, called the Turner Cafe, was constructed nearby off city property to accommodate the students of the War Training Program because no satisfactory arrangements could be made to use the airport restaurant. The Civil Aeronautics Authority leased space in the Turner hangar, as did the U.S. Weather Bureau.

One of the Turner Cafe's problems surfaced early when the Indiana Anti-Saloon League asked the State Alcoholic Beverage Commission to void a permit to sell beer on the premises after it was opened to the public. Clayton N. Wallace, spokesman for the league, expressed the fear that the permit "might serve as an opening wedge for the return of roadhouses. It is no place to serve liquor or beer," he said. "We have a law making it an offense for a pilot to be drunk, so why should we permit places nearby to sell intoxicants?"

The permit was eventually granted by the state control board and Roscoe tried running it with a manager, then leasing it, but the venture was not successful and it was closed down. Although the restaurant had a ninety-nine-year lease on the property, the city wanted to purchase the ground surrounding it to expand the airport further. During this period, the Indianapolis airport had been enlarged and three airlines— TWA, Eastern, and American—served the city. The airlines had each agreed to pay $10,000 to extend the passenger terminal and construct a modern exterior to match the architecture of the Turner hangar. Roscoe negotiated with the city to relinquish the lease for an unannounced compensation.

When the Turner building was dedicated, RTAC operated sixteen aircraft for use in flying instruction and for charters that included ambulance service, aerial survey, and photography service. In addition, complete government-approved aircraft engine and instrument repair and overhaul shops were established. The students' dormitory could house eighty students. The Roscoe Turner Aviation Institute was incorporated as a subsidiary to offer complete ground school courses for aircraft and engine mechanics, welders, and control tower operators. RTAC also became a sales and service facility for Waco, Stinson, and Taylorcraft planes.

To publicize RTAC and the services it offered, Roscoe gave sightseeing rides over the city on Sunday afternoons for $1.00 per passenger. Youngsters who made these flights received a pair of gold-colored metal wings. In the middle of the small circle, where the wings joined, were the initials "R.T." in red letters, the logo he had used in his various business enterprises since the early 1920s.

Columnist Ernie Pyle summarized his impressions of Roscoe and his new operations:

For so many years Roscoe Turner was the central and glamour figure of aviation in Southern California, and I wondered. "Don't you get homesick for Los Angeles?" I asked.

He doesn't. In fact, he has not been back to the coast since he came here in November. He doesn't have time. He flies to New York once a week to broadcast. He makes shorter trips on business. He attends meetings, signs contracts, supervises his staff, sees people. He's the busiest one-man aviation industry I ever saw.

Already the Roscoe Turner Aeronautical Corp. is a big thing. It is a $225,000 institution. Roscoe himself doesn't have that much money, so he has backers. Three of them, but he's never told anybody around here who they are.

He runs a flying school. He has planes for sightseeing and for cross-country trips. He has a Link trainer for instrument flying. He has 75 students now, and will have scores more under the Government program. He has just been licensed as one of the few schools to train instructors, who will then in turn go out and train more pilots for the Government.

Roscoe is doing himself a lot of good. And the nice part is, he's doing Indianapolis just about as much good as he's doing himself.

Indianapolis has one of the finest natural airports in the land. For miles around, this country is flat as a board. There are no obstructions. The weather is good. This is a mechanical city. Labor conditions have always been good. The Government centers much air test work here.

Despite these natural advantages, there has never been a big aviation operator based here. Now Roscoe has come in and he's big. He says he'll make Indianapolis the aviation center of the Midwest. The city fathers say he will, too. They've just approved a contract for him to build a $100,000 hangar here. It looks as though he's going to town.

Roscoe Turner never did lay any claim to being a modest wall-flower. He loves acclaim and the adulation of his fellow humans. He loves to be a big shot. And now he has managed to step from the all-time winner's seat in the racing cockpit right into a little throne in the business world. I envy him.[1]

In a later magazine article, Roscoe succinctly explained that he chose Indianapolis because "there are more people, more railroads, more manufacturing, more agriculture and more money than you can find in any like area in America."[2] From a practical operating standpoint, the Indianapolis airport was flat, virtually obstruction-free, and with nearly unlimited possibilities for expansion.

As a final touch, in early 1940 Roscoe flew the Turner Special from Cleveland, where it had been stored, to Indianapolis on its last flight. After he landed, he had it suspended above the planes parked in the

Turner hangar where it remained as a racing icon to be viewed by visitors for twenty-eight years. It had never been flown by any other pilot. Meanwhile, the Wedell-Williams was stored in the Jim Borton hangar at Cleveland-Hopkins Airport. In 1940 Roscoe loaned it to the Thompson Museum for display. Today it is on permanent loan to the Frederick C. Crawford Auto and Aviation Museum at the Cleveland University Center, where it was moved in 1965. It is on display just as Joe Mackey left it after the 1939 Thompson race.

Roscoe continued to be busy on several fronts. He wrote a book entitled *Win Your Wings* (1940) with Jean H. DuBuque, a regional airport engineer for the Ohio Aeronautics Board. As the number of RTAC employees grew, he wrote and published a monthly newsletter called *Circles,* which he distributed to employees and used as a public relations medium. He also coauthored a newspaper column on aviation subjects.

Although he was launching himself in a new direction, Roscoe continued to seek other ventures and sponsors for promotions of their products. He negotiated a five-year contract with the Continental Baking Company to advertise Wonder Bread with the *Sky Blazers* radio program. It was heard coast-to-coast on Saturday nights on forty-eight stations of the Columbia Broadcasting System. He would fly to New York on Friday nights, rehearse all day Saturday, and return on Sunday.

To earn extra income and acquaint the public with flying, he flew an estimated 38,000 passengers, many on their first flights, around Indianapolis during the 1940–41 period. Many flocked to the airport on weekends to watch the planes, eat picnic lunches, and take airplane rides.

One of the sustaining arrangements Roscoe had was an agreement to fly the National Commander of the American Legion around the country on annual visitation and speaking tours. During these trips, Roscoe was given many opportunities to voice his opinions on a variety of aviation topics. Never one to mince words and always one who could be counted on to give quotable quotes to reporters, he merited space in the local newspapers wherever he went.

Another venture was an arrangement with William Schoenfeldt, a plane builder, and Keith Rider, airplane designer and racing pilot, who formed a company in Los Angeles to build military aircraft. They announced that their Twentieth Century Aircraft Company would turn out pursuit planes with the wings and fuselage of plastic "speedmold" construction, with veneer sheeting impregnated with synthetic material. Schoenfeldt was president and Roscoe was vice president. Rider had formerly been a designer with the Glenn L. Martin Company in Baltimore. The venture dissolved when the United States entered the war in December 1941.

Fate intervened at a time when Roscoe was trying to become firmly established as an entrepreneur. He was severely injured in an automobile accident in Indianapolis on July 21, 1940. Hit broadside by another motorist, he suffered a fractured pelvis; Marian Allyne, his secretary, who was riding with him, received a fractured collarbone, cuts, and bruises. Another passenger, H. W. Robinson, suffered only minor bruises. All three had been thrown out of Roscoe's convertible, which had its top down. The other driver, Graydon Hubbard, a state trapshooting champion, had reportedly failed to stop at an intersection; he and his passenger were also seriously injured. Roscoe filed suit against Hubbard and the Remington Repeating Arms Company for $150,000 for his injuries. Roscoe claimed his impairment kept him from renewing his pilot's license because he could not pass a physical examination, which in turn prevented him from participating in national air races. In addition, he was unable to fulfill a radio contract that he said would have paid him $86,854. He later settled out of court for an undisclosed amount.

During his recovery, Roscoe was still an object of much press interest. He established an office in his hospital room and news photos were taken of him dictating to secretaries Marian Allyne and Alice Haines and conducting business on the telephone. He also received news coverage when he presented awards to young model builders from his hospital bed. A long news story in the *New York Times* was headlined "Turner, Grounded by Injuries, Moves Office to Hospital." A subhead said, "Speed King Rueful Over Crackup on Ground After Flying 25 Years Without a Scratch."[3]

Roscoe had a desk, chairs, filing cabinets, and a radio brought in and two telephones installed. Arrangements were made for him to broadcast to the listeners of *Sky Blazers* from his hospital bed.

The doctors were not happy with Roscoe's insistence on doing business while he had weights attached to his legs to hold his bones in place. They ordered that a No Visitors sign be placed on the door and had the phones disconnected. More than a hundred bouquets of flowers and five hundred telegrams were received. Among those who sent the latter were Howard Hughes, Jimmy Doolittle, Major Al Williams, and officials from the Department of Commerce. The comedy team of Olsen and Johnson, noted for their unorthodox stunts, sent Olsen's mother to his bedside in Indianapolis with a large bouquet and a box of candy. President Roosevelt also sent a wire wishing him a speedy recovery.

When he was well enough to go home, but still bedridden, Roscoe had a hospital bed set up in his living room so he could continue dictating letters and make arrangements for future projects. By the time he could get around on crutches (he called them "sticks"), he was able to travel. Photos were taken at each stop, and he was sought out by reporters for comments on aviation affairs, especially in relation to the war and developing events in Europe.

In a 1941 interview with a Wichita, Kansas, reporter, Roscoe received bold headlines for his thoughts on the need for a separate Air Force independent of the Army. He recommended the establishment of a "mosquito air force" of 200,000 light planes for defensive use, capable of carrying 100-pound bombs, and the use of heavy bombers for the offensive campaign. Calling attention to the sad status of aviation in the country, he said that "50 percent of our veteran pilots in the nation believe Hitler will whip the world, including the United States, unless aviation is put entirely in the hands of aviation people, the same way Germany did." As a civilian beholden to no one for his views, he spoke out for an independent air force long before it became popular to do so.

Roscoe embellished his idea to use "flivver planes" for national defense in a later interview. He contended that each two-place plane could be converted into a single-seater with a rack for a 100-pound bomb or two 50-pounders and armor plate to protect the cockpit. Even without bombsights, he said, such planes would be effective with projectiles dropped from 1,000 to 1,500 feet.

"The cheapest military plane you've got is around $35,000," he added. "You can get these little ships in bunches like bananas for $2,000 apiece. Send them out in droves and you can blow any invading army to pieces before it got a start. You could fight off any ground forces from any direction. By creating this flivver-plane army, you could release all of the highspeed, high-powered fighting planes and long distance bombers for offensive duty."[4]

With quotable opinions like these at a time when national defense was on the public conscience, each of Roscoe's interviews merited reportage. Recovering satisfactorily from his accident and anxious to get back to flying, he relished any opportunity to expound on his thoughts. For several months, he wrote a weekly syndicated column that appeared in Sunday newspapers throughout the country, which was "designed to increase the interest of the youth of America in aviation." He received background information for his columns from contacts at American Legion headquarters and in Washington.

The progression of events in Europe appeared ominous for the United States. Although the war had begun in the fall of 1939, most Americans were still reluctant to see the country become involved. On September 5, the nation officially declared itself neutral. However, only three days later, President Roosevelt proclaimed a state of limited national emergency. When the Germans demonstrated that their air power permitted their ground forces to take almost all of western Europe, the predictions of General Billy Mitchell, America's premier air power advocate, seemed to be coming true. Before his death in 1936, he had prophesied that "neither armies nor navies can exist unless the air is controlled over them." Great Britain soon found itself alone to battle the Nazi ground forces slowly advancing westward to the French coast under an umbrella of first-rate fighter and bomber aircraft.

On May 30, 1940, President Roosevelt called for an American air force of 50,000 planes. This meant that men had to be trained to fly and maintain them. The next day, in an address to Congress, he referred to the possibility that the United States would be getting into the war.

On June 17, 1940, France surrendered. In America, the president signed
a draft bill, and on October 30, 1940, the draft registration numbers of
the first to be conscripted for military service were drawn and announced. He signed the Lend-Lease Act the following March, which
authorized the United States to provide food and war materials to
France, Great Britain, and other allies.

Meanwhile, the Japanese had rampaged through Southeast Asia and
seemed poised to take Singapore and Hong Kong, both then British
colonies, and invade the Philippines. Then, on December 7, 1941, "a
date that shall live in infamy," Japanese carrier-based planes bombed
Pearl Harbor. The next day, President Roosevelt signed the resolution
declaring that the government and the people of the United States were
at war with the Japanese Empire. A declaration of war against Germany
and Italy followed.

Besides being one of the first civilian aviators to take up the cudgel
for a separate air force, Roscoe also said that the buildup of an air force
"had been sabotaged by labor" because of numerous strikes that had
taken place, which he called treasonous. He added, "Labor should be
drafted if it doesn't volunteer of its own accord. Until we get someone
with authority in Washington with enough courage to make labor pull
into line, we are not going to win. And if we don't win, labor will lose
with the soldiers."[5] Roscoe was to echo this type of message many times
in the months and years ahead. Sought out more than ever by the press
wherever he traveled, his comments about military preparedness continued to garner space in the national press.

Roscoe's recommendation to encourage pilots in the civilian sector
to assist the military in a war that now involved the United States, was
in tune with what was going on in Washington. The Civil Aeronautics
Authority (CAA) had been created in 1938, and the following year it
established a Civilian Pilot Training Program (CPTP) to train private
pilots and instructors as a first step toward entering military pilot training. The idea originated with CAA member Robert H. Hinckley. It was
initially planned as an experiment in vocational training that would give
a boost to the small flying schools and light plane manufacturers, with
the added benefit to the armed services of a reserve of knowledgeable
pilots. The program began in thirteen colleges with 330 students. By

the summer of 1941, it was turning out 216 instructors a month and supplying them not only to CPTP schools but also to the Army, the Navy, the airlines, and the Royal Canadian Air Force. After the attack on Pearl Harbor, this unique government venture was named the War Training Service.

Roscoe had been watching the developments overseas carefully and knew that all kinds of training had to be increased to provide the manpower to fight a global war. He was ready to support the effort and made plans to enlarge his staff of instructors and administrators and expand his school under contract to the government. In April 1941 he applied to the Army Air Corps to have his base at Indianapolis established as a site for a primary flying school. He was turned down because "we must locate our fields in that part of the country where flying is least apt to be interfered with by weather."[6]

Next, he tried to get the Army Air Corps Ferry Command to route aircraft being transferred from the West Coast to Europe on lend-lease through Indianapolis as a fuel stop and for minor maintenance and servicing. This was also turned down. He then requested that he be allowed to set up an air traffic control tower operators' course, but this too was rejected because neither the Air Corps nor the CAA had any plans to train control tower operators other than by actual experience at active airports.

In June 1942 the CAA announced that the pilot training program was to be enlarged and that men between the ages of 18 and 37 would be given flight training to become flying instructors in the Army, transport pilots in the Air Transport Command, liaison pilots in the artillery, glider pilots, service pilots in the Army Air Forces, airline pilots, and pilots in the Ferry Command. In the initial stages of flying training and ground school, they were to receive no pay, only room and board. If they survived the preliminary flight training in light aircraft and subsequent cross-country training, they were to be paid $150 per month.

There were monumental headaches and fights, suits and countersuits involved in running a school under this program, as Roscoe could attest once he joined it. Before Pearl Harbor the program had been denounced as a boondoggle, a war-mongering scheme, and a waste of public funds. Wayne W. Parrish, owner and publisher of *American*

Aviation magazine, was a loud and frequent critic and unjustly accused the CAA of publishing false accident statistics to justify the program.

To represent the interests of the flight school operators, a group of them formed the National Aviation Training Association (NATA), later the National Aviation Trades Association. Roscoe became an active member and later its president. In an impassioned speech during the closing session of the first annual meeting, he said,

> the days have passed when an aviator was regarded as either crazy or unfit to associate with. Today we are working together in this flight training program with institutions of higher learning in all parts of the country. When we get together for meetings like this, it's different from an air race or an air meet. There we expect to take our fun as we find it.
>
> In these meetings with the college representatives, I am afraid we aviators have made some bad impressions. It behooves us to remember that we came here on a serious mission. All of us are crowded for time. We spent our money to come here. I believe we should try to govern ourselves a little better than was necessary in the greasy-coveralls days of flying.[7]

A few days after Pearl Harbor, it was announced that the Civil Air Patrol (CAP) was being established as an arm of the Office of Civilian Defense to "enlist, organize, and operate a volunteer corps of civilian airmen, with their own aircraft and equipment, for wartime tasks." It was believed that the CAP would immediately bolster national security and permit nonmilitary pilots to continue flying. Roscoe joined the Indiana wing staff of the CAP as a colonel but was unable to take an active part during the war. He became wary about the organization when it appeared to him to be in competition with the civilian pilot training program he and others were conducting.

In a bitter letter to a friend who ran an FBO in South Carolina, he feared that the Army "is planning on taking over these 17-year olds, putting them in uniform, and making us into a little Germany. . . . they'll probably have goose-stepping, too. In other words, they will be on a par with the schools and colleges, and do all the training themselves. We don't want that, of course, and our hope is to extend this C.P.T. Act and then steer it the way we operators want it to go when it comes time for appropriations."[8]

Anxious to be involved in the war in an active way, Roscoe wrote to General Henry H. "Hap" Arnold, chief of staff of the Army Air Forces, and asked for renewal of his commission in the National Guard. Arnold replied that he could not make such an appointment because the National Guard was under state jurisdiction. Later, Roscoe offered to pinch hit as a consultant to the government for Eddie Rickenbacker when he was briefly missing after a crash in the Pacific. This offer for service was also not accepted.

Seeing the potential for profit under the government programs, Roscoe thought about setting up a closed corporation to run a school for mechanics in Chicago to be capitalized at $50,000. He couldn't persuade enough backers to buy stock so the idea didn't come to fruition, which was just as well. Running a school and a fixed-base operation in Indianapolis created enough problems for Roscoe, from personnel matters to disciplining errant students. Trying to run a separate school in Chicago would have presented additional personnel management difficulties that Roscoe really didn't want to deal with.

When a few RTAC employees complained about working on Christmas Day in 1942, Roscoe posted a notice reminding them that his contract with the City of Indianapolis required that the operation be open night and day for 365 days a year. "If any employee is unhappy with his conditions of work, he should come up to the front office and ask for his check, because as I have stated before, I am not going to tolerate any griping in this organization."[9]

Another notice expressed his approach to student discipline: "I have been notified by the city that anyone jumping the fence is subject to arrest. I would suggest that you boys give this a little serious consideration because I don't have the time to come down and get you out of jail."[10]

When students were careless about leaving the airport gate open or unlocked, he posted this announcement: "The gates have been left open on numerous occasions. Therefore, we have changed the locks, and if this continues to happen, it will be necessary for us to lock the gates permanently and not permit any of you to park your cars inside. We are trying to protect your property as well as our own, and if you will not help to protect either one, there is nothing else for us to do."[11]

Roscoe's notices did not always carry a disciplinary message. The following was posted on the bulletin board as a reminder of the responsibility of the mechanics attending the school:

A flying man's life depends upon your hands, your heart, and your skill. A pilot is never better than the engine in front of him, and seldom as good as his ship.

The engine and plane are only as good as the mechanic. Good and reliable and skillful mechanics have kept pilots alive for 25 years of vigorous flying.

It is folly for an airman to attribute such an accomplishment to his own brains, skill or courage. Wings and an engine may be carrying a flying man into the air, but his life is actually riding on your character, your skill, and your reliability.

KEEP THE FAITH![12]

One of Roscoe's most vexing problems was the loss of instructors and students to the draft, and in a telegram he complained to the head of the training program: "All of my instructors are losing faith in me and the C.P.T.'s ability to get them deferred; therefore they are all planning on joining either the Army or Navy. What can you do about it?"[13] He also took his complaints to the press: "Any man who can fly any kind of ship doesn't belong in the infantry, tank corps, Quartermaster Corps or any place else except the Air Corps. We've got plenty of fighting pilots—in the wrong places." He cited the case of a flying school instructor who was drafted and "is now a clerk in an office somewhere."[14]

Qualified mechanics were scarce, so Roscoe made many trips to interview applicants. While at Chillicothe, Ohio, in April 1942 to dedicate a mechanics school at the federal prison, he interviewed several men who showed promise and whose jail terms were almost up. When they were released, he hired two of them. One turned out to be a good worker. "The other was so careless," Roscoe told friends, "he almost burned the hangar down."

To earn extra cash in the summer of 1942, Roscoe borrowed a Ford Tri-motor from W. O. Nichols of Columbus, Ohio, and flew groups on charter flights. He returned it to the owner at the end of the year.

In February 1943 the War Training Service contracted with Roscoe's firm to conduct the Cross-Country Course for thirty students. He was to furnish 20 to 25 hours of flight instruction per trainee in six aircraft of not less than 210 horsepower, of which three had to be not less than 240 horsepower. He was also asked to provide from 30 to 35 hours of flight instruction per trainee in twelve planes of not less than 65 horsepower. Classroom instruction was also required. In addition to nineteen flying instructors and a chief pilot, Roscoe was to furnish two mechanics and six mechanics' helpers. Lodging and meals were also to be furnished for Army Air Corps enlisted men who would be assigned to clerical duties.

Roscoe didn't have the prescribed number of aircraft so the difference was provided by the government. In addition to the Turner Special and the Wedell-Williams racers, the RTAC fleet now consisted of a Stinson Tri-motor, two Wacos, three Taylorcrafts, two Piper Cub Cruisers, one Fleetwing, and a Link trainer. It was the stimulus Roscoe needed to ensure his success as long as the training program lasted. Never fully supported by the CAA or the Army, however, the program was discontinued in mid-1944. Before it ground to a halt, 1,132 educational institutions had been involved and 435,165 trainees, including several hundred women, had been qualified by 1,460 contractors. RTAC turned out an estimated 3,500 students during its participation in the Civilian Pilot Training and War Training Service programs.

Realizing that the training program was not going to last past the end of the war, Roscoe envisioned a need for small towns and cities to have air service. In 1943 he proposed to the CAA in Washington that an "air feeder system" be established to serve 120 American towns with a population of 2,000 or more. He foresaw postwar public demand for passenger, air express, and mail service that would feed into trunk line stops of the larger airlines. Additionally, such a program would help meet the postwar need to employ the hundreds of fliers and mechanics who would have been trained in military service.

Another idea Roscoe proposed was for the government to give a pair of Jeeps and an airplane to every returning veteran after the war, just as it had been suggested to give every returning Civil War veteran forty acres of land and a mule. Typically, his remarks provoked mixed reactions and headlines. One editorial writer commented: "It would be a good way to dispose of and put to use a lot of surplus war machines which otherwise would be likely to stand idle and disintegrate. As for the airplanes, some folks think we are all going to be riding around the country in those contraptions right away after this war anyway."[15]

As Roscoe had predicted, the supply of pilots caught up with the demands of the military services and the War Training Service began winding down in late 1943. His operation was discontinued on January 15, 1944. By June 30, the Army had sent its last classes to the civilian contractors' schools and the Navy graduated its last class in August. Morale among the contractors, their instructors, and mechanics hit bottom as they faced an uncertain future.

The government eventually compensated the fixed-base operators for their overhead costs and allowed a reasonable profit. Many of the older employees were drafted and their expertise was lost as they disappeared into the Army in assignments unrelated to aviation. At the time the contracts were canceled, RTAC employed 94 people and had an annual payroll of $234,000. More than $62,000 had been paid to the city as its share of the revenue.

Roscoe was able to continue his school operation briefly by training Latin American students from seven nations. The seven-month course included 170 hours of flying instruction and 350 hours of ground school. The success he had with this training program convinced Roscoe that there was a need for continued pilot training for Latin American countries. He briefly considered specializing in training their pilots either in the United States or at some location in South America. He proposed to the Army Air Forces that aviation schools for the Latin American nations be established and that American operators provide management, instruction, and plans for a complete curriculum. General Arnold approved the idea and referred Roscoe to the air attachés of each nation to determine what could be worked out. In October 1945 Roscoe planned to head a goodwill mission to South America with the commander and staff of the American Legion, but the country was in too much of a turmoil with thousands of veterans being demobilized, and the trip never went beyond the planning stage.

Although he seemed outwardly satisfied with his role as a provider of pilots for the war effort, inwardly Roscoe had been anxious to get into action in uniform, preferably as a commissioned officer. He wrote letters to General Claire L. Chennault, commander of the Flying Tigers in China, and General Frank M. Andrews, second highest-ranking Army Air Forces officer. Chennault responded:

> I would like nothing better than to have you out here with me, but under the present setup, I am unable to commission anyone here and must take my personnel as shipped out from Washington. I appreciate your desire to get into active combat service, but, on the other hand, I think you are doing very necessary work in operating your school there. Someone with plenty of experience must conduct the schools for pilots and mechanics, while others employ the boys in combat zones. If I were not here, my next preference would be to have your opportunity of running a good school.[16]

Andrews replied similarly.

Roscoe volunteered to ferry B-17s to the war zones in Europe or the Pacific but was turned down. In desperation, he wrote to an Australian air force officer whom he had met after the 1934 London–Melbourne race to tell him that he was thinking about joining the Royal Australian Air Force. Roscoe assured him that, although he was running a flying school, "I have arranged matters so that I can leave it in competent hands and continue the training schedules without interruption."[17] His offer was politely refused.

Roscoe also sent several letters to his friend General James H. Doolittle, commanding the 12th and 15th Air Forces in North Africa during this period and later the 8th Air Force in England. Like the others, Doolittle responded that running the pilot training school was far more important to the war effort than having him assigned to Doolittle's staff.

This was not their first correspondence. One of the most-quoted stories about Roscoe and Doolittle was an exchange of letters in early 1942 before the Doolittle Raid on Tokyo. In January, after Doolittle had been assigned to General Arnold's staff in Washington, Roscoe wrote:

> If this thing gets too tough I think it would be a good idea for you and I to leave the country and go over there and organize our òwn fighting

squadron. I have made the statement several times that I was going to organize a fifty-plane group of B-17s with no pilot under forty years of age, and take some graduates from my school as co-pilots, get a volunteer gunner's crew, and I'll bet we would be the meanest outfit that ever hit the air. All the boys want to be counted in, so I think this is what you and I had better do.[18]

Doolittle was unable to respond because Roscoe's letter didn't catch up with him. He was busy planning and organizing his own top secret raid on Japan. In a second letter, Roscoe again suggested that Doolittle and he "have a large consignment of B-17s and go after Tokyo."[19]

After Doolittle's surprise attack on Tokyo and four other Japanese cities on April 18, 1942, he had returned clandestinely to the States and was presented with the Medal of Honor by President Roosevelt. He was also promoted to the rank of brigadier general, skipping the rank of colonel. A month after the mission, the War Department released the information that Doolittle had been the leader of the first raid against the Japanese homeland. Roscoe immediately wired him in Washington:

Congratulations you dog! Why didn't you take me with you? I could have been your co-pilot. Guess you have shown the world we old boys can still be of service as combat pilots. I made the statement more than a year ago I would like to have a group of 100 B-17s or something similar, with pilots from the First World War at the controls, and we could raise a little h---. How about making me your aide now, since you are a general? Phone me tonight if possible.[20]

As soon as Doolittle received the telegram, he called Roscoe, who shouted, "Jimmy, you son-of-a-bitch!"

Doolittle recalled, "He reminded me that when he had made a statement about a bunch of old men flying combat missions just after Pearl Harbor, I had told him we were too old to fight in the war. Wars were for young men, I had said, not old fogeys like us. He never forgave me after he found out that I had led the raid."[21]

Roscoe's long-considered dream to start an airline finally came to fruition when the Roscoe Turner Aeronautical Corporation announced the start of a "daily charter service" between Detroit and Memphis in July 1944. Robert H. Turner, Roscoe's brother, was brought in as company treasurer to help manage the operation. Stops were planned at eight intermediate cities for a total route mileage of 714 miles. Using four five-passenger Stinson Reliants, Roscoe claimed it was not a scheduled service, although the planes left within the hour that was announced. As soon as the plan was disclosed and operations began, Chicago & Southern Airlines filed a formal protest with the Civil Aeronautics Board (CAB) in Washington alleging the operation of a daily, scheduled service "is in direct violation of federal regulations. This operation can be conducted legally only as charter service."

Soon after he started, Roscoe received a telegram from a Memphis newspaper editor:

> Plans for Memphis Detroit services announced by Robert Turner unclear as to how a daily service can be offered in a charter business. Is line chartered in advance by weekly or monthly periods and if so who has chartered it. Or will there be no flights on days for which charter customers do not appear. Appreciate prompt reply collect."[22]

Although Roscoe complained bitterly about what he viewed as excessive government control over aviation, his inauguration of charter service on a scheduled basis was clearly against the CAB rules. To operate a charter service, no special approval was needed from the CAB, but to run a regular airline over a set route on preannounced schedules, hearings had to be held, a financial fitness investigation made, and approval given by the CAB. But Roscoe stuck to his belief that his service would not be illegal and added that he wasn't "trying to pick a fight with Chicago & Southern or anyone else."

The CAB regulators prevailed and the airline was ordered to discontinue service immediately or "take appropriate steps to place your operations within the terms of the Board's definition of non-scheduled service." Accordingly, Roscoe shut down after only forty days of operation. One hundred revenue passengers had been carried, not all of whom flew the entire route between Detroit and Memphis. Total expenses amounted to $5,600; the income was less than $4,000. According to Robert Turner, "We learned a lot of valuable things from an operations standpoint. We learned how many passengers are interested in long hauls and how many in short hauls—it's about 50-50."[23]

When the war ended in August 1945, there was general chaos in the aviation industry. There were thousands of surplus aircraft available and thousands of trained pilots to fly them. As of March 1, 1946, the government had made available for bidding 32,462 military and civilian types of aircraft. It was a situation similar to the post–World War I era, when hundreds of Curtiss Jennys and Liberty engines were sold to the barnstormers for a small fraction of their original cost.

As president of the National Aviation Trades Association, Roscoe cautioned that those who bought surplus aircraft might not realize that many of the planes would not measure up to CAA certification and safety standards and could not be flown without complying with certain mechanical changes, overhauls, or new parts. In addition, the military planes were usually not economical to operate because of high fuel consumption.

One of the important pieces of legislation that affected thousands of veterans and businesses like Roscoe's was the G.I. Bill. Veterans were authorized to go to college or learn a trade at government expense. In addition, they were authorized a small stipend for subsistence. RTAC was approved to offer flying and ground school training in 1946. At this time, there were twelve Taylorcrafts, five Vultees, three Stinsons, two Beechcrafts, one Piper Cruiser, and one Fairchild in the RTAC inventory.

Roscoe had studied the war-surplus aircraft market carefully and bought a Douglas B-23 medium bomber in April 1945, which he had converted to carry eighteen passengers "anywhere within the western hemisphere." He named the plane *Indianapolis Legionnaire* and told the press "we are happy over the fact that we have become the first established charter service organization in the world to provide such service."[24]

Roscoe learned that his divorce from Carline was final on December 5, 1946. On December 13, he married Madonna M. Miller of Sheridan, Indiana, an attractive, gracious woman who brought order and efficiency into his personal and business life. An accomplished musician, she was working as an accountant when they met. They were married in a quiet ceremony in the Lexington Hotel in New York City with a few friends in attendance. The ceremony was performed by New York Magistrate Charles E. Ramsgate, a World War I buddy of Roscoe's. Charles Rochester, president of the hotel, was Roscoe's best man, and his wife was matron of honor. Radio entertainer Arthur Godfrey, then living at the Lexington, attended.

The couple moved to a modest apartment in Indianapolis as Roscoe struggled to find his niche in the postwar business of aviation. In 1950 they moved to a large Tudor-style home on a four-acre estate in Indianapolis.

Madonna gradually took over some of Roscoe's duties to relieve him of the day-to-day business worries. When she became president of RTAC in 1950, the company was in financial trouble. A loan was obtained to retire the stock of the original three backers of RTAC. Other loans were negotiated, including one with the Small Business Administration, which were all later paid off in full. Under her careful watch over income and expenses, the business slowly began to show a profit. In 1958 she became treasurer: Roscoe was chairman of the board. She also became president and treasurer of Turner Hangar and secretary and treasurer of Turner Aero Supply, when these were incorporated as separate entities.

"I learned early in our marriage," she told the author, "that if I were going to see my husband at all, I'd have to go to the airport because that's where he was most of the time. So I decided to go to work for him.

"He trusted people too much," she added, reflecting on those first days of their marriage. "Everyone took advantage of him. Don Young knew this for years but couldn't do anything about it; for some reason, I could."

On one occasion in the early 1960s, when Madonna made out a statement of personal net worth for the bank, the bottom line showed a total of just over $1 million. She took the document to Roscoe to sign and said, "Roscoe, do you realize that for the first time in your life you're a millionaire?" Roscoe laughed and asked where to sign. He really didn't care about that title; being a millionaire didn't matter that much to him.

Now in his sixties, Roscoe was still possessed of boundless energy and had to be doing something all the time, no matter how trivial. At home, he was rarely quiet and always enthusiastic about a project at hand or the next one in the offing. He loved his home and for the first time in his life had time to enjoy it. Madonna recalled:

We would lock the gate and Roscoe would mow the lawn with a glass of wine in his hand; I would sit on the steps and refuel him. He was very proud of his lawn and spent a lot of time on the mowing equipment. A mechanic at heart, he acquired five automobiles and instead of trading a car in, he retired it. He built two garages to house them and a boat.

Roscoe especially considered the kitchen his own domain. It had black-and-white tile and white cabinets. I put his racing flags—green, white, and checkered—on top of the cabinets. He liked to cook and would broil steaks, fry catfish, and any other delicacy he might have in mind.

The kitchen was large with a rocking chair where he read the papers and often had a short nap. He would wake up alert and ready for another project. I sometimes thought this was the secret of his energy.

On one occasion, he decided to entertain his Legion Post with a catfish fry on our lawn. Since there were about 65 active members, we prepared for that many but 125 people came. We ran out of catfish and ended up serving hot dogs. It was a successful party that was enjoyed by all, including our Boxer dog, Penny, who imbibed too much from the beer keg and ended the evening leaning against the house barking.

On Saturdays, Roscoe would put on his old mechanic's coat—which was quite disreputable—and a red cap, put the dog in the station wagon, and go to the airport to putter around fixing things. He would then go to the grocery store to shop. He knew everyone in the store and had a personal greeting for all of them. He would come home with such interesting items as a case of caviar, artichoke hearts, okra, etc.

Sundays were often spent flying to airport dedications or civic affairs and sometimes having dinner with friends or family. Sometimes he would take me flying in the company's Beech Bonanza. He readily accepted invitations to speak and would fly any distance to fulfill his commitments.

During the week when we were at home, we entertained aviation friends who dropped in at the airport for cocktails and dinner. We never knew how many would be for dinner but enjoyed having them. Many stayed all night to exchange tales about their early-day flying experiences.

The one thing they shared in common was their dedication to aviation. Younger pilots were interested in Roscoe's racing career and especially enjoyed the den where Roscoe's trophies were displayed, along with Gilmore.

Roscoe's encyclopedic knowledge of aviation was legendary. One evening the Air Force Thunderbirds were weathered in at the airport and came to the house. As usual, flying was the main discussion topic. Younger pilots who had not shared the barnstorming days were always captivated by how Roscoe and his fellow barnstormers improvised and brought aviation to the small towns and villages for the first time. On one occasion, a young pilot asked Roscoe what he considered his most difficult experience. After a few moments of thoughtful silence, Roscoe said, "Wearing that God-damned uniform!"[25]

Roscoe was told many times by visitors, former students, and members of audiences where he spoke how his exploits had gotten them interested in aviation and encouraged them to be pilots. It was at these times that Roscoe knew the risks he had taken and the financial hardships he had endured trying to stay in the flying game and encourage public interest in flying were worthwhile. It was his enduring legacy to future generations.

12

THE CRUSADE FOR AIR POWER

Toward the end of World War II, there were imaginative predictions that everyone would own a small airplane and be able to fly anywhere they wanted with the greatest of ease. Roscoe envisioned that kind of future for Americans and was quoted in a speech in Jefferson City, Missouri, as predicting "flying automobiles" in the postwar future. "I'm not kidding," he said. "These things have already been flown. Some day when you go in to buy a car, the salesman will ask whether you want it with or without wings. You'll be able to drive to the airport, attach the wings and take off. When you come back, you'll check the wings and drive back to your garage."[1]

This rosy future was not to be forthcoming as the country tried to adjust from wartime to an economy reeling from uncertainty and unemployment. However, there was a slight breeze of optimism as many believed that after a year or so of adjustment, the pent-up desire for consumer goods would cause an economic boom and an eventual return to normalcy. In aviation, there was a wave of anticipation as aircraft manufacturers converted their assembly lines and geared up for orders from the airlines for new aircraft then on the drawing boards. The hundreds of military air bases could be used for municipal airfields; the small towns could be connected with larger cities by feeder lines as Roscoe had predicted.

At the time, Roscoe had twenty-four aircraft on his flying line at Indianapolis, plus one Link trainer for instrument training. The small two-seat planes could be used for flight instruction. Those with three passenger seats or more could be used for short-hauls on a charter or scheduled basis. He briefly considered making arrangements to fly freight for Slick Airways, an air cargo airline, but the deal did not go through.

During the first four years after World War II, some two hundred new cities appeared on the airline map of the United States. About half were authorized as additional stops on the regular routes of the trunk lines; the rest were towns that could be connected by new feeder lines. About 600 cities were authorized air service by 1950.

Roscoe was determined that he was going to share in the cheerful outlook for feeder lines by again trying to establish a scheduled operation emanating from his base in Indianapolis. The Roscoe Turner Aeronautical Corporation applied for and was granted authority in February 1948 to serve fourteen cities in Illinois, Indiana, Kentucky, Michigan, and Ohio with its main base at Indianapolis. Under the name Turner Airlines, he planned to use the four Stinsons, three war-surplus, six-passenger, twin-engine Beech aircraft and two twenty-one-passenger Douglas DC-3s as his fleet that would service a 500-mile route. He contacted friends in an attempt to get $2 million in capitalization, but the route was too short to interest investors. However, after much effort devoted to trying to obtain financing, Roscoe sold the franchise to John and Paul Weesner who were able to obtain approval for additional mileage.

Turner Airlines was formed on August 9, 1949, and service was inaugurated between Indianapolis and Grand Rapids on November 12, 1949. The airline was based at the RTAC hangars and Roscoe did public relations work for the airline, although RTAC no longer had a financial interest in the company. In November 1950 Turner Airlines changed its name to Lake Central Airlines. The Weesners experienced financial difficulties and later sold their interests; the airline was absorbed by Allegheny Airlines and eventually became USAir. Indianapolis thus lost its opportunity to have an airline locally owned and based in the city.

"Many of the companies were able to draw from experience as fixed-base operators," according to R. E. G. Davies, an eminent airline historian. "Some, like Turner Airlines, appear to have been inspired by the enthusiasm of an individual; all were characterized by a rugged individuality and determination which has enabled the feederline industry to survive as an entity in the face of many handicaps and much competition."[2]

During this period, Roscoe began to use the war-surplus Douglas B-23 extensively for charter work; it had been converted by Pan American to carry fifteen passengers and a crew of two. Advertised as "The World's Fastest Charter Service," Roscoe used it to transport American Legion officials and similar groups on tours of the country. The six-passenger Beechcraft and smaller Bonanzas were chartered to smaller groups or used for pilot instruction.

Roscoe's avocation after World War II seemed to be speech-making with a determination to keep the American Legion and the general public informed about the state of aviation in the United States. He would admonish his audiences not to let the nation's defenses languish. He told an audience in Rapid City, South Dakota,

> My main purpose from now on is to pound into the American people the vital importance of air power. If the American people had listened to Billy Mitchell after World War I, there would never have been a second war. And if the people don't realize the value of a huge air force now, there will be a third world conflict without a doubt.
>
> The people of America have a choice to make. They can either appropriate the money for a large, effective, hard-hitting air force, or they can save the money and pay for another world war. We'll have to pay the bill one way or another.[3]

In a rousing address at an American Legion meeting, he said,

> As a nation we dislike unpleasant things so we dismiss them from our minds. One of our troubles is that we will not move until we are mad or

scared. If from 1921 to 1941 we had spent one billion dollars a year on air power, Hitler and Hirohito would have remained quiet and we would have saved 360 billion dollars.

. . . It is wishful thinking to lull ourselves into the thought that there will be no more wars. Human nature does not change. We have always had wars and there is certainly no reason today to think this is the time when they are going to stop. The stage is set for the mightiest conflict of all times and this is not war mongering—America will be blotted out if we lose air supremacy.

He concluded his speech with a simple phrase that was to become a slogan the U.S. Air Force would adopt many years later during the Cold War: "Air power is peace power."[4]

In November 1948 Roscoe gave a speech that received considerable publicity. Entitled "Shall America or Russia Rule the Air?" it was delivered at a time just before the Korean War began when there was great public demand to cut the military budget. Roscoe said that a strong and powerful United States "is the surest guaranty for the perpetuation of a society of free nations. Air supremacy is the only way in which we can ever hope to lay the foundations for a permanent peace."

To maintain a strong America, Roscoe advocated universal military training, a strong National Guard and Reserve, and the establishment of the two service academies at West Point and Annapolis as postgraduate schools for professional officers "after they have learned a little about the economic side of our country in our regular universities and colleges." Although he endorsed having a strong army and navy, he warned about duplication and said that limitations must be placed on the budgets of these two services, "because they will fortify the moon as long as we give them money."[5]

One of the big aviation issues of the immediate postwar months was the proposal to create a separate air force and continue active research programs that Roscoe had advocated before World War II. He backed up the Army Air Force leaders seeking a separate service through his speeches and received assistance in the form of background information from the Pentagon and the American Legion. Concerned that Navy sympathizers would seek to get him fired from the legion's Aeronautics Committee and that he would lose his contract to fly the national commander around the country, he wrote to General Carl Spaatz. "I am willing to make any sacrifice necessary to accomplish our objective [of a separate air force] as long as I am assured that you will stand by me," he said.

General Spaatz and the proponents of an independent air force rallied to Roscoe's call because his presence always resulted in headlines wherever he spoke. As a reward for his efforts and a tribute to his past flying accomplishments, the national commander recommended in 1946 to W. Stuart Symington, then assistant secretary of war for air, that Roscoe be awarded the Distinguished Flying Cross. At the legion's request, Roscoe followed the recommendation with a letter of his own saying that he "would love to have this decoration." He reminded Secretary Symington that the award had recently been given to Army flyers for making speed runs across the country and that two civilians—Emory Bronte and Ernie Smith—had received them for making the flight from the mainland to Honolulu. "In view of these facts, it seems reasonable enough that I would be eligible for this medal, due to my many contributions to the advancement of aviation."[6]

Symington responded cordially that the Distinguished Flying Cross was reserved for members of the armed forces, including reservists. Although Roscoe had mentioned that he was "a Lt. Colonel in Nevada, a Colonel in California, and a Colonel in Mississippi and at the time a Colonel in Indiana," Symington said, "it would appear that the commissions to which you refer were honorary ones" and "we have to consider you a civilian." The awardees that Roscoe thought were civilians with no military affiliations were actually members of the Army reserve and therefore eligible. However, Symington pointed out that a few nonmilitary pilots had received the medal by special Act of Congress such as Russell N. Boardman and Jan Polando for a nonstop flight from the United States to Turkey; Harold Gatty and Wiley Post for their world-girdling flight; Amelia Earhart for her flight from Newfoundland to Ireland; and Glenn Curtiss posthumously for "advancing and developing the science of aeronautics."

Symington was well aware of Roscoe's personal efforts in the campaign to establish a Department of Defense and a separate Air Force. In a handwritten postscript, he added, "I would be glad to discuss with you who would be the best to introduce the request in the Congress if you thought advisable." Roscoe did not receive the medal at that time, but the thought did not die for those who wanted him to have it. After the Air Force became a separate service, Representative Carl Hinshaw (R-Calif.) introduced a bill in June 1949 for Roscoe to receive the Distinguished Flying Cross "in recognition of his meritorious achievements and contribution toward the advancement of the science of aerial flight." The bill was endorsed by Rep. Carl Vinson, chairman of the House Committee on Armed Services, after receiving a recommendation for its passage from Symington, who had become the first Secretary of the Air Force.

The legislation was eventually passed unanimously and Roscoe received the coveted flyer's award in a Pentagon ceremony on August 14, 1952. The award was made "for extraordinary achievement while participating in aerial flight." The citation accompanying the award noted that, in addition to winning the Thompson Trophy three times, he has

> placed first, second and third in the Bendix transcontinental race and has broken the transcontinental air speed record on seven separate occasions. During the interim war years between the two World Wars, Roscoe Turner traveled extensively throughout the nation, advocating his deep and unshakeable convictions in the potentialities of aviation. At considerable expense to himself, he converted his personal aircraft into a flying laboratory, and completed an intensive series of experiments to achieve higher degrees of speed and safety. The intelligence thus gained through sheer determination and courage was of inestimable value in the development of military combat aircraft. His contribution in training more than 3500 pilots and instructors during World War II is another of his many distinctions. By his pride in achievement, intrepid courage, and matchless skill, Roscoe Turner has materially advanced the science of aerial flight.

Presented by the Air Force chief of staff, General Nathan F. Twining, it was the first Distinguished Flying Cross awarded to a civilian in more than twenty years and was one of only six awarded to a nonmilitary person up to that time. Many civilian aviation leaders and high officials of the Defense Department and the armed forces attended the ceremony, including Secretary of Defense Robert A. Lovett and Air Force Secretary Thomas K. Finletter. President Truman sent a personal letter of congratulations, saying "You earned this distinction by efficiency and hard work."

Roscoe was honored further in 1956 when he was invited to Vienna, Austria, to receive the prestigious Paul Tissandier Diploma awarded by the Fédération Aeronautique Internationale. He was honored for a lifetime of contributions to private and sporting aviation.

In 1945 the Beech Aircraft Corporation had redesigned and newly type-certified the D-18S Twin Beech, which had been used as a small utility transport and trainer during World War II. The next year the single-engine Model 35 Bonanza was introduced and an approved type certificate was issued in November 1946. Roscoe had been a long-time friend of Walter and Olive Ann Beech and became a distributor for Beech Aircraft when they resumed commercial aircraft manufacturing after the war. Later, Roscoe was made the first enshrinee in Beechcraft's Hall of Fame as one of their outstanding distributors.

Roscoe's sales department was enlarged to sell Beechcraft. At the time, Beech required a deposit on all orders; in turn, Roscoe required a deposit from the buyers. Among the first customers was the Stokely-Van Camp Company and the Schwitzer Corporation, which hangared their planes and had them maintained at RTAC. RTAC was also a distributor for Collins Radio Company and many other aircraft equipment and parts suppliers.

The 1950s were difficult years for many FBOs including RTAC, but the company never missed a payroll or laid off employees. Although sometimes late in satisfying the accounts payable, creditors were always paid off eventually. According to Madonna Turner,

> It was difficult in those days to accumulate enough operating capital. We could not borrow on the buildings as the city had prior claim so we had to pledge our stock to get large loans. We also borrowed, using aircraft as collateral that we took in trade. However, we had a well-rounded operation with federally certified shops, a fuel concession, and hangar storage. Roscoe was a tremendous drawing card as everyone knew he was there. Much of RTAC's business came from out of state.

Roscoe's personal bills were beginning to pile up because a radio contract he had with Continental Baking Company had been canceled after the completion of a thirty-nine-week series. It was originally a five-year contract for $500 a week, which paid the agent an unusually high $200 from each paycheck. However, the contract was subject to cancellation at the end of any thirteen-week period if the sponsor so decided.

The high agent's fee arrangement was typical of Roscoe's personal business dealings, which never netted him a reasonable share of any proceeds. Madonna Turner recalled that he had once borrowed $3,000 from a friend to finance one of his winning Thompson races. Roscoe promised that he would triple the money if he won and paid the friend $9,000.

Although not a good money-manager, Roscoe was recognized for his realistic, down-to-earth approach to contemporary aviation problems. He was appointed as a special consultant to the House of Representatives Science and Aeronautics Committee in July 1960 and served for eight years during the 86th through the 89th Congressional sessions. He undertook a special study of the progress being made in the aeronautical sciences, "including a determination of whether government agencies have been pushing aeronautical research hard enough since the advent of the space age." He later testified before a Congressional committee about his findings and conclusions.

Roscoe already had experience on Capitol Hill; in 1958 he had testified as a member of the National Aeronautics Committee of the American Legion's National Security Commission in support of granting term-retention contracts to reserve officers who were being forced out of the military because of budget cuts. After the Korean War, there was an effort to reduce the size of the active duty force and thousands of skilled technicians and officers were dismissed from active duty.

"This intermittent pattern of retention and wholesale discharge of Reservists is not new," Roscoe testified. "Thousands of Reservists were induced to remain on active duty after World War II and by inference, if not by word, led to believe that they could count on making the armed forces a career." His appearance and testimony was representative of his activities in support of the legion's objectives to maintain a strong military force. Two years later the Indiana Department of the American

Legion honored him by dedicating the Roscoe Turner Airstrip at Shades State Park near Indianapolis.

The 1960s were kinder to Roscoe and Madonna financially. From the original six employees when RTAC began operations in 1939, the company had seventy-five people on the 1963 payroll. Roscoe became less involved in the daily business of the company and put Madonna in charge of managing all day-to-day operations. However, he was active in many civic organizations in Indianapolis, such as the Chamber of Commerce and the Convention and Visitors Bureau, and now had time to devote to them. He had many friends in the city and was happy to assist in promoting civic projects when needed.

Roscoe never sought public office but did think about it a few times. At an industry meeting in Wichita, Kansas, in November 1963, an Associated Press dispatch reported that he was seriously considering seeking the Republican nomination for governor of Indiana. He was quoted as saying, "The decision is right on the balance at the moment. It is contingent on several things."[7] He was also mentioned as a possible candidate for mayor of Indianapolis, but he was never endorsed for either office by a political party so the idea died a quiet death. According to Madonna, "Neither of us thought it was a good idea. We had enough problems at the airport." The subject was never mentioned again.

Roscoe always had things he wanted to do. He would often walk out on the ramp, get in an airplane, and take off in pursuit of an aircraft sale or a speaking engagement. Roscoe's secretary kept his and Madonna's daily schedules on their desks so each would know what the other had planned. One thing Madonna could be sure of was that Roscoe would call her every night whenever he was out of town. On one occasion, when she asked him where he was headed, he said "Hagerstown," so she assumed it was the town not far from Indianapolis. When he called that night, he said he would have to stay overnight because of bad weather in Hagerstown, *Maryland*. The dinner party she had planned went on without him.

In 1960 Roscoe negotiated with the Indianapolis Aviation Board to lease 4.5 acres of ground south of the RTAC hangar and the leased city hangars to build a large cantilever hangar. A separate corporation was formed under the name of Turner Hangar. The building was completed in 1962 and leased to Inland Container Corporation, TWA, and RTAC for additional hangar space. The office space was leased to Anderson Box Company, a subsidiary of Inland Container Corporation. Turner Hangar had the same lease rights and privileges as RTAC, and the building agreement was that it would revert to the city in thirty years.

Roscoe tried to visit Corinth to see his family and friends about once a year at Christmastime while his mother was living but seldom after that. In the spring of 1961, he received an invitation to attend a ceremony on April 2 dedicating a new Roscoe Turner Airport in his old hometown. The first one, built in 1936 on the Suratt farm, had been plowed up; the new one had been built in another location with a 5,000-ft. lighted runway and landing aids. When the letter arrived, Roscoe immediately responded. "I normally run a pretty tight schedule," he replied, "but because of my pride and love for my home town, I shall plan to attend the dedication on April 2 providing nothing unforeseen happens."

It was a memorable weekend for Alcorn County. There were parachute jumps, skydiving stunts, aerobatic flying, helicopter demonstrations, and static displays of military and civilian aircraft. Southern Airways inaugurated the first airline service to Corinth. On the dedication day, hundreds of automobiles clogged all the approaches to the airport. Parking was a problem that was solved by having school buses carry hundreds of spectators to the field. Governor Ross Barnett attended and made dedicatory remarks.

In his response to the honor, Roscoe said, "There was a time when I worked long and hard in an effort to get the idea across that an airport was necessary for Corinth. Corinth is in a central location for all surface transportation in northeast Mississippi and so close to the big industrial center in Alabama and the Tri-Cities."

In 1963 Roscoe received a surprise letter from Tony LeVier, then director of flying operations at Lockheed Aircraft Corporation, who wanted to nominate Roscoe for an honorary fellowship in the Society of Experimental Test Pilots, an organization of manufacturer and government pilots who had flight-tested aircraft. He apologized for not nominating Roscoe before, saying, "Dad, I just plain didn't use my head." He invited Roscoe to Beverly Hills for the society's annual awards banquet and added, "Please don't let me down on this, because you are number one in my book. You will be treated like a king while here for this gala occasion, and it is my guess that you will never remember being more pleased with yourself, unless it was beating me out in the 1939 National Air Races."[8]

Roscoe was genuinely gratified to be so honored by his peers. In his acceptance letter he recalled that he had done some test work with the first variable pitch propellers used on an airplane and was the first pilot to have a prop go into reverse in the air. "Mine got into reverse over Burbank and I was right over the airport," he told LeVier in his acceptance letter, "but I still couldn't get it into the field. I was in my Lockheed Express and I landed within two lengths of the airplane and I didn't bust up."[9]

By the mid- to late 1960s, it was a mellower Roscoe Turner who sat in his office, often wearing a western-style Stetson, while he concerned himself with routine company details and made many phone calls seeking new business. A large silk American flag presented to him by the Boy Scouts of America stood behind him. The old warrior was wearing down physically but wouldn't admit it. He loved to fly and was totally at ease in the air. As Madonna told the author, "Flying was as necessary to him as breathing." However, realizing he was not as sharp as in the past, he had Buford Cadle, a veteran pilot and good friend of the Turners, fly with him as a safety pilot. Roscoe had started a membership drive for the American Legion and made an aerial round-up seeking new memberships from the various posts around the country. It greatly eased Madonna's mind that Cadle went along.

Although he admitted to being nervous and shaky after a tough race, the only time Roscoe appeared nervous in public after his racing days was before a speech. He admitted he always felt insecure during public appearances because he had so little formal education. It was the single big regret of his life, which he never seemed to overcome. Always a happy person, he is remembered by all who ever met him for his smile and for having a kind word for everyone. He was also cheerful at home which Madonna attributes to the fact that they never took their airport business problems home with them. "This made for a successful marriage," she said, "with both of us working together."

Roscoe gave many speeches during this period and was kept abreast of Air Force developments through briefings in Washington as chairman of the American Legion's Aeronautics and Space Committee. In 1964 he made a trip to Europe with a group of industrialists, where he was briefed on operations of U.S. and NATO military forces.

Roscoe had foreseen the burgeoning growth in federal bureaucracy and a series of international events during the Cold War of the late 1950s and early 1960s shook him severely. He gave one speech entitled "Can We Save Our Capitalistic System and Our Way of Life?" which was highly popular with civic clubs and service groups. Firmly believing that the future of aviation rests with the young, he gave many stimulating talks to Boy Scout and Civil Air Patrol groups.

He also focused on airport problems, particularly the needs of Weir Cook Airport in Indianapolis. When another airport was suggested to accommodate growth in the area, Roscoe opposed it, saying, "We need a civic auditorium worse than a secondary airport." Instead, he advocated funds be spent on improvements at Weir Cook and a better road system to get people to and from the airport faster.

In 1967 Charles C. Gates, president of Gates Rubber Company, who was diversifying into transportation ventures, bought out the Lear Jet Corporation. This constituted threatening competition for Beech Aircraft and its distributors, which was heightened when Gates offered to buy out Roscoe's interest in his corporation. Roscoe wasn't ready to sell out completely yet. However, in March 1967, he did sell Gates controlling interest in RTAC with an option to purchase the balance of the stock in RTAC and Turner Aero Supply and with the agreement that Roscoe would remain as chairman of the board and Madonna as president until the option was exercised.

Officials of the Beech company were upset because, as a distributor for their aircraft, the Roscoe Turner Aeronautical Corporation had taken on Gates, a competitor, as a financial partner, which they considered a conflict of interest. Beech arbitrarily canceled RTAC's distributorship contract and refused to furnish any more aircraft or parts. RTAC sued the Beech company when it was learned that the "stop-sell" decree also went out to other Beech dealers from whom Roscoe tried in vain to get parts. The Turners decided to drop the suit, and the business relationship ended on a sour note, although they remained friends with Olive Ann Beech, owner of the company, and many of the Beech employees.

After such an eventful life and with an unending restless spirit, it wasn't easy for Roscoe to sit back and retire from the everyday aviation scene. Madonna Turner remembers his mood before they decided to sell the corporation's assets: "Roscoe and I went to the office one night at the airport. He stood and looked out the window and said, 'Honey, when I get so old I can't come here and look over the field and hear the engines, I want to die.' And at another time he said, 'I don't know what I will do when I get so old I can't fly, because that is the only time I can relax.'"

On September 28, 1968, the option was exercised on RTAC and Turner Aero Supplies, and two days later Madonna sold the stock in Turner Hangar.

After these agreements were consummated, the Turners decided to drive to New Orleans to attend the 1968 American Legion Convention. Roscoe wanted to stop in Meridian, Mississippi, to see the Key brothers, who were long-time friends. Roscoe had not been feeling well and thought he had arthritis but insisted on driving. They stopped at the home of Congressman and Mrs. James H. Morrison near Hammond, Louisiana. The Morrisons had often been the Turners' guests during the Indy 500 races in Indianapolis and, as Madonna explained, "Jimmy and Roscoe had fought some battles together in Washington."

While walking on the grounds surrounding their house, Roscoe became ill. Congressman Morrison suggested he go to the Ochsner Clinic in New Orleans, which Roscoe agreed to do. He was admitted and, after a few days of tests, the doctors told him that he had bone cancer.

Roscoe missed the fiftieth anniversary convention of the American Legion because of his hospitalization but had a steady flow of legionnaire visitors at his bedside. It was the first time he had not been able to attend a convention in twenty-five years to participate as a member of the Aeronautics and Space Committee. While recuperating, he was interviewed by reporters about his views on strategic air power and spoke out against Secretary of Defense Robert S. McNamara for reducing the nation's air strength at a time when Soviet military capabilities were growing stronger. He may not have been feeling well, but he was still capable of making headlines.

The Turners remained at Ochsner Clinic for a month while Roscoe had cobalt treatments. They had planned to build a house in Florida on the ocean and had already purchased a lot. Roscoe insisted they go ahead with their plans. Madonna rented a house nearby while the new one was being constructed. Building their new house kept Roscoe busy and he enjoyed doing it, although he was able to spend only a short time there. Meanwhile, they divided their time between New Orleans and Indianapolis. Roscoe's energy seemed to return after treatments, and he would be very active when his illness went into remission.

On December 9, 1968, the Wings Club in New York City made Roscoe an honorary life member, in a moving tribute to his many accomplishments and contributions to aviation. Club president R. Dixon Speas hosted the gathering of eagles, which included such pioneers as Jimmy Doolittle, Bernt Balchen, Cliff Henderson, Don R. Berlin, and Admiral C. E. Rosendahl. The honor was bestowed on Turner "in recognition of his imaginative racing techniques—to overcome public indifference to flying. . .and advance more rapidly the advent of high speed air travel—bringing the world to the threshold of supersonic travel." The next night, Roscoe and many other aviation pioneers were again saluted for their contributions to flight at a Night of Exploration at the Waldorf-Astoria Hotel sponsored by the prestigious Explorers Club. The awards were presented by honorary president Lowell Thomas.

In April 1969 Madonna had driven to Florida and Roscoe was to fly down and meet her there. However, she received a phone call that Roscoe had fallen off a stepladder while cleaning out a rain gutter on the Indianapolis house. He had landed on his back on a concrete walk and was again in the hospital. He had broken a few ribs but returned home after a few days. Madonna put a bed in the living room and he gradually regained his strength. He was soon up and resumed his activities.

The Turners were invited by President and Mrs. Richard M. Nixon to a dinner on August 13, 1969, honoring the Apollo 11 astronauts at the Century Plaza Hotel in Los Angeles. During the dinner the presi-

dent brought Michael Collins, one of the three astronauts on the first
moon-landing mission the previous month, over to their table. Later,
when Collins had become director of the National Air & Space Museum,
he wrote to Madonna that Roscoe had been the graduation speaker
when he had received his wings and said, "It was the best speech I've
ever heard."

The honors continued. Richard G. Lugar, then mayor of Indianapolis,
proclaimed September 9, 1969, as Roscoe Turner Day and asked all citizens to honor him as a great flier, sportsman, and citizen. That evening
he was surprised at the Indianapolis Aero Club dinner with still another
honor. William A. Ong described the occasion in an article in *Flight
Magazine:*

> Speeches and the introductions ended, the spotlight held the guest of
> honor in revealing brilliance. He stood calmly, the straight, husky figure
> and square shoulders stooped and rounded now with pain and the weight
> of 74 years. He accepted a plaque and a gold key to the city and a leather-
> bound book containing the signatures of all who had come to honor him
> that night. Sincerely he expressed his gratitude—without embarrassment
> but remotely, for many times in other years he had received similar hon-
> ors from other men in other places around the world.

The climax came when the Indianapolis Aero Club presented its own
gift. A curtain was drawn and the spotlight beamed upon it. The big
man looked and saw and was no longer remote. He brushed a hand
quickly across his eyes and his voice was husky when he spoke.

"Usually," he said, "a man must die before he is remembered like
this. But I have two doctors here and two in Florida and seven in New
Orleans and between them I think I'll be here a long time yet. So I accept your gift proudly but humbly, and in the name of all of you who
have been my friends."

The beautiful tribute was conceived in a great love for the guest of
honor from the hearts of friends who knew him best. It was a bust of
the big man and the sculptor had caught the piercing intentness of the
eyes and the exact angle of the jaunty, spiked mustache and the great
spirit of a pioneer. The bronze plate read: "In tribute to Col. Roscoe
Turner whose contribution to aviation has been exceeded only by his

dedication to God and country."[10] When the Turners returned home that evening, their house had been ransacked and many valuable mementos were stolen. It was a sad finale to a memorable evening.

Later that month, the Turners attended the Society of Experimental Test Pilots symposium in Beverly Hills, where Charles A. Lindbergh was given an honorary fellowship. Afterward, they returned to Florida. During the next few weeks, Roscoe made several trips to the Ochsner Clinic as an outpatient for checkups. The following November, he received the Distinguished National Veterans Award in Birmingham, Alabama, which had been originally created on the first official National Veterans Day observance in 1954 to honor outstanding citizens in the United States who have made the greatest contribution to the patriotic interests of veterans throughout the country.

Roscoe accepted the award "with great humility in the name of all veterans, those living and those who have made the supreme sacrifice, so that we could continue to be a free people." His remarks that night were aimed at the "crazy riots and demonstrations" then taking place all over the country, which he blamed on a lack of leadership "in both high and low places."

> Our educational institutions were established for learning and knowledge at great expense to taxpayers and private contributions. They were not established for students to take over, disrupt classes, and burn buildings. If the students knew how to meet the payroll and manage the place, we would not need chancellors, presidents, trustees and boards of regents.
>
> How can we change this situation? We should first dismiss students who are not satisfied with where they are. We should also not allow anyone to teach who will not take an oath of allegiance to our flag and the country for which it stands.
>
> We must make it our business to clean up this mess and continue in a position of leadership and strength. There has never been an instance in recorded history where appeasement has ever won a victory.[11]

Roscoe received a standing ovation. His remarks were memorialized by Congressman Bill Nichols (D-Ala.) by publication in the Congressional Record on November 18, 1969.

For several years it had been Roscoe's dream to open a museum that would display his Turner Special racer, his faithful Packard, Gilmore, and his flying memorabilia, as well as the many trophies and awards he had received. He wanted to do so not to satisfy his ego but to represent the era of flight in which he participated, to encourage the following generations to realize how their forebears had explored the realms of flight and made the advances that had kept the United States supreme in the aeronautical sciences.

In July 1968 the Indianapolis Airport Authority approved the construction of the Roscoe Turner Museum and Educational Center on airport property. It was to be financed by the Roscoe Turner Aviation Foundation with paid memberships and with profits going to charitable organizations. A land-lease agreement was made with the airport authority, and construction began with Roscoe overseeing the work. Roscoe returned from Florida in January 1969 to help move the airplane and the Packard into the museum building; Don Young came from California to help him prepare them for display.

During the last week of July 1969, Roscoe and Madonna officiated at the groundbreaking for the museum, an event that was covered by the press. Located on the corner of South High School Road and Roscoe Turner Drive, it was a modest building but large enough to contain the Turner Special, the Packard phaeton, and hundreds of trophies, plaques, and mementos that represented his racing and flying life.

Jimmy Doolittle invited Roscoe and Madonna to be his guests at the April 1970 reunion banquet of his Tokyo Raiders in Cocoa Beach, Florida. They were joined by Dick Merrill and his wife, Toby, and Ralph Evinrude and his wife Francis (Langford) Evinrude. Roscoe was introduced to the audience and received a standing ovation from the raiders, whom he so greatly admired for their epic flight in April 1942. When the dinner was over, Doolittle helped a weakened Roscoe to the car. It was the final meeting of two old friends who had contributed so much to aeronautics.

In the middle of May 1970, Roscoe returned to the Ochsner Clinic and was hospitalized. Madonna closed the house in Florida and stayed at the hotel adjacent to the hospital. Roscoe's condition continued to deteriorate and in June he asked to be returned home to Indianapolis. Dr. James Crane, an old friend; Bill Yager, formerly RTAC's chief pilot and then the Gates chief pilot; Roscoe's brother Bill; and Buford Cadle flew him there in a Lear Jet. He was met there by Madonna and her nephew Jim Miller who escorted him to the Methodist Hospital. His condition worsened steadily and he died there on June 23, 1970, three months short of his seventy-fifth birthday.

Services were held at Christ Church Cathedral in Indianapolis with entombment at the Crown Hill Mausoleum. More than three hundred friends attended, including General Jimmy Doolittle, Senator Barry Goldwater, Indiana governor Edgar D. Whitcomb, Dick Merrill, Scott Crossfield, and Tony LeVier with other Lockheed officials, plus many legionnaire associates and racing pilots. Governor Whitcomb ordered the flags at the state office building and atop the capitol dome flown at half-mast for two days in Roscoe's memory. The American Legion conducted a military funeral, and a fly-by of military planes in the traditional "missing man" formation was made over the mausoleum by the Indiana Air National Guard. Floral wreaths depicted a balloon topped by a single-engine plane and a lion with a "G" for Gilmore. A floral American flag and a floral checkered one, signifying the Indianapolis Speedway, where Roscoe had been an honorary starter and honorary referee for many years, were added tributes.

Several congressmen eulogized Roscoe with insertions in the Congressional Record. Congressman George P. Miller of California, chairman of the House Committee on Science and Astronautics, was the most eloquent:

> From very humble beginnings, he rose to worldwide fame through his sheer tenacity and a cooly calculated flamboyance in focusing the attention of the American people, by his exploits in the air, on the tremendous importance of aviation to the military strength and economic vigor we now enjoy.
>
> . . . He was no stranger to the Committee of Science and Astronautics. He served for several sessions of Congress as a consultant to the committee and allowed the members and staff to draw upon his great fund of knowledge in our efforts to expand and enlarge NASA's involvement in aeronautical research.
>
> Roscoe Turner has not passed on to obscurity, because he was a man in the truest sense of heroic dimensions and accomplishments. He lived his last days as a legend which now passes on into history.[12]

Many newspapers and national magazines ran editorials or news columns reviewing Roscoe's life and accomplishments. Madonna received hundreds of letters, telegrams, and phone calls when the world learned of Roscoe's death. Among them were condolence messages from fellow pilots, aircraft manufacturers and aviation associations, Army and Air Force generals, legionnaires, Boy Scout executives and individual scouts, Civil Air Patrol members, and top government leaders. Movie mogul Jack Warner sent a telegram, as did Major General David M. Jones, representing Doolittle's Raiders. Senator Barry Goldwater wrote that Roscoe was "in every sense of the word a man, a gentleman and an American, and I think if a person can be described by any one of these three words, he has had a successful life."[13] President Nixon also expressed his personal sympathy and said, "He was a good friend whose bravery and zest in life won him many admirers and fans. Our close personal association was a source of tremendous satisfaction and joy to me, and I will deeply miss him."[14] J. Edgar Hoover, director of the Federal Bureau of Investigation, also sent a letter to Madonna saying, "I hope you will derive some measure of comfort from knowing that his friends share your grief."[15]

One of the most beautifully expressed letters came from Katherine and Walter Myers of Indianapolis, who wrote:

> Your beloved husband, our valued friend, has taken that journey beyond the evening star which each of us must sometime take, unguided and alone, never to return.
>
> There is comfort in the belief of ages that when our time shall come to take that lonely trip beyond the sunset, the touch of his gentle hand may greet us and the tones of his kindly voice may bid us welcome to a better place. What mortality has lost, eternity has gained."[16]

Madonna was determined that Roscoe's dream of a museum would be realized and that the work would be finished in a manner that would be attractive, interesting, and a credit to his memory. She put additional funds into the Roscoe Turner Foundation and started working to complete the museum with a target date of Roscoe's seventy-fifth birthday—September 29, 1970. Don Young returned from California and agreed to serve as the museum's curator; he was of great assistance since he knew the history of all the racing memorabilia and had the ability to build and repair almost anything. He and Madonna worked from early morning until late at night, seven days a week.

Special display cases were ordered; others were built on the spot. Don Berlin, a native Hoosier and noted aeronautical engineer, volunteered his talents. Roscoe's brother Bill, who had recently retired from the aviation department of Shell Oil and was living in Indianapolis, was also recruited to help out. Madonna's nephews, Steve and Jim Miller, often worked until midnight in their spare time decorating and organizing the displays.

"It was a labor of love for all of us," Madonna said. "I had high hopes for it."

On the day planned, the museum was formally dedicated at a ceremony held under a large tent near the museum with Air Force Lt. Gen. Eugene B. "Ben" LeBailey as the main speaker. Fifty Boy Scouts with American flags formed a backdrop for the speaker's platform, where Roscoe was eulogized by Mayor Lugar and other dignitaries. The guests toured the museum and then attended a reception at the Airport Hilton Hotel.

The doors were opened to the public a month later at a fee of 50 cents per person. A sign in front of the museum noted that it was dedicated to the sons of the American Legion and the Boy Scouts, who "are the best examples of proper youth guidance."

The museum flourished at first but as time passed, the parking space was increasingly limited by airport expansion, which also made it difficult to get to the museum. Access was prohibited at times when new roads were being constructed around the airport.

"Since I am a native Hoosier," Madonna said, "I wanted nothing more than to keep this aviation collection in the state and to make it an interesting display for Indianapolis and Indiana. The entire collection, with the exception of the airplane, had been at our home on 10th Street for over twenty years. After talking to many business and personal friends, I made what truly was the anguished decision to disband the museum."

All personal property pertaining to Roscoe's career as an aviation pioneer, racing pilot, or business executive that might have historic value was left in his will to Madonna as a trustee. With her approval, it was to be placed in one or more museums or left to similar organizations as she might decide within a five-year period. The Smithsonian was designated as the primary recipient. Years before, Madonna and Roscoe had visited the old Smithsonian's aviation collection, which was then housed in a deteriorating building, to discuss the possible disposition of some of his aviation artifacts, but the space was so limited then that they couldn't be accepted. As a result, Roscoe added his voice at the time to the public clamor to obtain Congressional approval for a national museum devoted solely to aviation and space.

In August 1972 Madonna was informed that federal funds had finally been authorized to build the Smithsonian Institution's National Air & Space Museum (NASM) in Washington, D.C. She was contacted by museum curators to discuss the disposition of Roscoe's historic items. An air-racing exhibit was planned for the museum's opening, which would feature Roscoe's Turner Special, his lion Gilmore, and personal memorabilia. NASM is now Washington's chief tourist attraction and is visited by more than a million persons each year.

The decision made, the doors of the Turner Museum were closed on September 20, 1972, when NASM director Michael Collins officially accepted Roscoe's valuable artifacts. The Indianapolis Airport Authority paid the estate $10,000 for the museum building, which was appraised at $35,000. The museum and RTAC hangar were demolished in 1973.

Madonna was invited to a special preview of the National Air & Space Museum before its dedication on July 4, 1976. Roscoe's trophies were displayed in a large glass case in the center of the main entrance. The Boeing 247 he flew in the London-Melbourne race was hanging from the ceiling; the Turner Special was fully restored and on display with Gilmore standing under the wing. Roscoe's uniform, carefully preserved, was exhibited in a glass case. This exhibit remained in place for several years and has since been featured at the Smithsonian's Paul E. Garber Facility in nearby Suitland, Maryland. Gilmore is in cold storage; the Boeing 247 remains suspended in a position of honor in the air transportation section of the museum.

Roscoe's American Legion trophies and awards were donated to the American Legion Headquarters Museum in Indianapolis; his personal papers were sent to the American Heritage Center, University of Wyoming, Laramie, where more than 2,000 pounds of letters, scrapbooks, magazines, and photographs are well preserved and available for research. The memorabilia the Turners had collected pertaining to aviation in Indiana was sent to the Indiana State Museum on Alabama Street in Indianapolis; the 1929 Packard was presented to the Indianapolis Speedway Museum. The balance left in the foundation funds was donated to Depauw University in Greencastle, Indiana, for the Roscoe Turner Science Scholarship Fund.

There is no doubt that Roscoe Turner's personality had many facets. His fellow pilots had a deep respect for his flying ability and persistence. As Harold Neumann, one of the many pilots who raced against him, said, "Roscoe was a gentleman, a showman but also a damn good pilot. Some people didn't like him, but it was envy, jealousy. He was my friend."[17]

Tony LeVier, Lockheed test pilot who had known Roscoe since 1929 and raced against him in 1938 at Oakland and in the 1939 Thompson Trophy Race, gave Roscoe his first flight in a jet aircraft in 1954. He "did a hell of a good job," LeVier said. "He was an aggressive pilot but not wild like some of them and he had a flair for popularizing aviation for the benefit of us all. He put class into the business and was a fine man with high principles and character. His word was his bond. If he said he'd do something, he'd do it. If he couldn't, he'd let you know why. If he owned money and couldn't pay it, he would let people know what the circumstances were and he always paid when he could."[18]

Some ridiculed Roscoe behind his back for his flashy uniforms and showboat personality. Always an individualist, he was sometimes emotional when he talked about aviation and its problems. However, he could be aroused into aggressive action when he perceived government inaction or incompetence that interfered with aerospace progress.

He had a big heart and displayed it without calling attention to what he did. Joe Mackey told of a day in Cleveland when Roscoe gave some of his winnings to a group of broke parachute jumpers he didn't even know so they could get home. It was typical of the many generous, compassionate gestures he made to fellow aviators and friends in need but never mentioned. Roscoe never talked about how he and Don Young had helped Tony LeVier get his aircraft ready to compete in the 1938 Greve Race. If LeVier had not written about it in his own memoirs, no one would ever have known.

On November 22, 1975, Roscoe was enshrined in the National Aviation Hall of Fame at Dayton, Ohio. His presenter was his old friend and fellow racing pilot, Jimmy Doolittle. Madonna accepted the honor for Roscoe, who was recognized "for outstanding contributions to aviation by his participation in early commercial aviation and involvement in air racing leading to important technical advancements in design and performance of high speed aircraft and engines." Because of his many record-setting achievements and contributions to the development of aviation through his racing, he was also inducted into the Motorsports Hall of Fame in June 1991.

On Roscoe's birthday, September 29, 1990, the Roscoe Turner Airport at Corinth, Mississippi, with its runway lengthened to 6,500 feet, was rededicated at special ceremonies. A pictorial display was unveiled in the airport terminal building that represented some highlights of Roscoe's life. The display and the ceremonies were initiated by Jack Tacker, formerly of Corinth, who was interested in perpetuating his memory.

Although known to everyone locally as the Roscoe Turner Airport and so designated by the Federal Aviation Administration, no signs had been erected to indicate its name. In 1993, when Mayor Edward S. Bishop, Sr., learned from the author that there was nothing visible to indicate the airport's location or its proper name, he promptly ordered that several be erected.

Each August, a Roscoe Turner Balloon Festival is held at the airport, which reminds Mississippians that Roscoe was a native Corinthian who never forgot his roots. The three-day affair was first organized in 1986 by Eddie LaFavour, a local balloonist, and his wife, Rebecca. Presented by the Roscoe Turner Balloon Race Association and the Corinth Area Tourism Promotion Council, the festival benefits Kids in Distress and the Northeast Mississippi Abused Children Center. Hot air balloon pilots from fifteen states compete for prizes. Besides various balloon competitions, such as the Key Grab Race and the Hare and Hound Race, the festival includes a multicolored "balloon glow" on the first night, in which the balloons are lighted up by their propane torches and resemble gigantic Japanese lanterns. Other activities and attractions include a carnival, concession stands, arts and crafts booths, helicopter rides, model airplane competitions, and a Civil War living history encampment and battle reenactment.

During the 1990 gala, a wedding highlighted the festivities. The bride and groom were married standing beside a balloon basket; they then boarded it and sailed away into the afternoon sunshine. The 1939 movie *Flight at Midnight,* in which Roscoe appeared, is shown several times each year by the Northeast Mississippi Museum in Corinth. Newsreel films from a number of sources, collected by a local citizen with an interest in Roscoe Turner's life and times, are also shown by the museum.

Since Roscoe started his unique and colorful career in aviation as a balloonist, the picturesque affair is a continuing reminder that the city's most famous former resident made unusual and lasting contributions to aeronautics during aviation's Golden Age.

Over the years, many aviation writers have tried to find the words to summarize what Roscoe Turner had done for aviation, but it may have been said best a quarter-century before his death by Frederick C. Crawford, president of Thompson Products and of the National Air Races. In a foreword to a biographical pamphlet the company produced about Roscoe, he wrote:

> Here is . . . a man, who, in the period when there was little public interest in aviation, when our armed forces had repudiated the sage counsel of Billy Mitchell, zoomed up and down the country, barnstorming, racing, stunt-flying. He was a peerless showman, often bizarre and rococo, and went all out to have the spotlight of public interest turned upon him and through him, to aviation. During those years of public indifference he probably did more than any other man, living or dead, to romanticize and publicize flying in America.[19]

Roscoe Turner was a survivor of the so-called Golden Age of Flight. He began his storied life in aviation as a freewheeling gypsy before the public accepted flying as a safe means of transportation. He helped gain endorsement of it through his flying achievements, which were enhanced by his flamboyance and his genius for self-promotion. When he joined the relentless quest for speed, he succeeded while others had failed and too many had lost their lives. His personal fortune teetered continually between solvency and bankruptcy, but he never lost faith in what the airplane could do to ensure American supremacy in peace and war. He remains one of the most colorful and memorable figures in the history of aviation.

APPENDIX: ROSCOE TURNER'S MAJOR AWARDS AND RECORDS

1929 Set records both ways across the continent carrying passengers in a Lockheed transport: New York to Los Angeles, 20 hours, 20 minutes; Los Angeles to New York, 18 hours, 30 minutes.
Third place in nonstop flight from Los Angeles to Cleveland, National Air Races.
Third place in Thompson Race at Cleveland, Ohio.

1930 Set record, Vancouver, B.C., to Agua Caliente, Mexico: 9 hours, 14 minutes.
Set new transcontinental record from New York to Los Angeles: 18 hours, 27 minutes..

1932 Set record from Mexico City to Los Angeles carrying passengers: 11 hours, 30 minutes.
Won third place in Bendix, Thompson Trophy, and Shell Speed Dash races at Cleveland, Ohio.

Set new transcontinental record from New York to Los Angeles: 12 hours, 35 minutes.

1933   Awarded Harmon Trophy by Ligue International des Aviateurs for being America's premier aviator of 1932.
First place in Bendix Trophy Race and first place in Shell Speed Dash, National Air Races, Los Angeles.
Set new transcontinental record from New York to Los Angeles: 11 hours, 30 minutes. Set new transcontinental record from Los Angeles to New York: 10 hours, 5 minutes.
Awarded Cliff Henderson Trophy as America's No. 1 speed pilot.

1934   Won Thompson Trophy; placed second in Shell Speed Dash.
Set new transcontinental record from Burbank to New York: 10 hours, 2 minutes.
Placed second in handicap division and third in overall speed division of MacRobertson International Air Race from London to Melbourne, Australia. Commanded only American crew to finish.

1935   Placed second in Bendix Race, National Air Races, Cleveland, Ohio.

1937   Placed third in Thompson Trophy Race. Broke American record for 100 kilometers at 293 mph.

1938   Won Thompson Trophy Race. Received Ludlum Trophy for establishing record.
Received Cliff Henderson Trophy as America's No. 1 speed flier for 1938.
Established record for closed course races at 293.119 mph, bringing record back from France.

1939   Awarded Harmon Trophy for being America's Premier Aviator for 1938.
Won Thompson Trophy Race for third time, the only three-time winner.
Set new record for closed course during qualifying race at 299.003 mph.
Awarded Henderson Trophy as America's No. 1 speed flier for 1939.
Received Goddess of Victory Trophy from American Legion as America's ace speed flier.

1952   Received Distinguished Flying Cross from United States Air Force authorized by Act of Congress.

1956 Received Paul Tissandier Diploma from the Fédération Aeronautique Internationale

1969 Received American Legion Distinguished Citizens Award
Received Distinguished National Veterans Award

1975 Inducted into National Aviation Hall of Fame

1991 Inducted into Motorsports Hall of Fame

NOTES

1. THE BOY FROM CORINTH

1. *Time,* October 29, 1934.
2. From undated, handwritten manuscript by Roscoe Turner.
3. Ibid.
4. Interview by Stephanie L. Sandy, Corinth, Miss., March 12, 1993.
5. Interview by the author, Corinth, Miss., November 6, 1992.
6. The Glidden Tour passed through Corinth from Memphis en route to Kentucky in March 1910. The tours, sponsored by Charles Jasper Glidden, a wealthy Boston industrialist, were held from 1904 to 1914 (except 1912). They tested every aspect of automobile performance and reliability except speed. The EMF had a number of epithets given them by unhappy owners: "Every Morning Fixit," "Eternally Mis-Firing," and "Every Mechanical Fault."
7. *Commercial Appeal,* Memphis, February 7, 1910.
8. Ibid., October 4, 1910.
9. *Weekly Corinthian* (Corinth, Miss.), December 8, 1910.
10. From transcript of interview conducted by Wayne Ingles at Indianapolis, October 15, 1969. However, research of Memphis newspapers does not reveal any air show in Memphis that year. It is possible Roscoe meant 1916, when Katherine Stinson performed there.

11. *Weekly Corinthian,* June 30, 1910.

12. From unidentified, undated newspaper clipping in the Turner files, American Heritage Center, University of Wyoming.

2. BALLOONS TO BARNSTORMING

1. Interview, Corinth, Miss., November 6, 1992.

2. *Commercial Appeal,* Memphis, September 14, 1919.

3. Jack R. Lincke, *Jenny Was No Lady: The Story of the JN-4D* (Washington, D.C.: Center of Military History, United States Army, 1988), 230.

4. *Fort Wayne (Ind.) News and Sentinel,* April 23, 1919.

5. *Danville (Ill.) Commercial News,* May 7, 1919.

6. *Lenoir (N.C) News-Topic,* Lenoir, October 3, 1919.

7. *News and Observer* (Raleigh, N.C.), October 22, 1919.

8. Ibid., October 24, 1919.

9. *Air Progress,* August 1976, 61.

10. *Aerial Age Weekly,* June 20, 1921.

11. Ibid., July 4, 1921.

12. *Aero Digest,* May 19, 1936.

13. *Aerial Age Weekly,* June 14, 1920.

14. *Sunday Record* (Columbia, S.C.), October 24, 1920.

15. Letter from M. M. Inabinet, McColl, S.C., *Pee Dee Advocate* (Bennettsville, S.C.), September 23, 1920.

16. Letter from J. C. Piedmont, *Pee Dee Advocate,* September 23, 1920.

17. Ibid.

18. *Staunton (Va.) News Leader,* June 20, 1920.

19. *Winston-Salem (N.C.) Journal,* November 25, 1920.

20. *Fulton Democrat* (McConnellsburg, Pa.), June 24, 1920.

21. *Aerial Age Weekly,*June 27, 1921.

22. Ibid., July 18, 1921.

23. *Hendersonville (N.C.) News,* August 26, 1921.

24. Ibid.

25. Ibid. The type of aircraft they intended to use was never revealed.

26. *Savannah Morning News,* October 14, 1921.

27. *Weekly Corinthian,* October 27, 1921.

28. Ibid.

29. Ibid.

30. *Commercial Appeal,* Memphis, October 28, 1921.

31. *News Scimitar,* Memphis, October 28, 1921.

32. Ibid.

33. Ibid., November 2, 1921.

34. Ibid., November 5, 1921. The item also noted that if the crash were successful, the pair would repeat the performance at Jacksonville, Fla., but gave no further details.

35. *Commercial Appeal,* Memphis, November 7, 1921. During this period Roscoe began to make frequent appeals to the public for support of commercial aviation. It was a message he would expound for the rest of his life.

36. *News Scimitar,* November 7, 1921.

37. *Aerial Age Weekly,* November 14, 21, and 28, 1921. During this period Roscoe worked as a salesman at the Southern Motor Co. in Columbia, S.C., and lived at the Glenwood Hotel. Runser returned to his home in Fort Wayne, Ind.

38. *New York Times,* January 29, 1922.

39. *Savannah (Ga.) Press,* February 22, 1922.

40. Ibid.

41. *Columbia (S.C.) Record,* February 25, 1922.

42. *List of Pardons, Commutations, and Respites Granted by the President During the Fiscal Year Ending June 30, 1925.* Office of the Pardon Attorney, U.S. Department of Justice, Washington, D.C. The pardon was granted one month before Roscoe's marriage to Carline Stovall.

43. Park Field later became the site for the Naval Air Technical Training Command.

44. Interview, Corinth, Miss., November 6, 1992.

45. An article by Grady Peery, *Commercial Appeal,* Memphis, October 24, 1934.

46. Arthur H. Starnes, *Aerial Maniac* (Hammond, Ind.: Delaney Printing, 1938), 73.

47. Ibid., 75.

48. *Weekly Corinthian,* December 11, 1924.

49. From notes of an interview with Mary Emma Hardin conducted by Mary Emma Whitaker, Corinth, Miss., November 16, 1992.

50. Ibid.

51. Starnes, *Aerial Maniac,* 80–81. Curlee loaned Roscoe $5,000 to buy the Brequet. Interest on the loan was considered paid for by the advertising the plane generated for the company.

52. *Sheffield (Ala.) Standard,* September 21, 1923.

53. From undated brochure entitled "Knowledge Is Power—Power Makes Money," published by Muscle Shoals Railroad & City Development Co.

54. *Sheffield Standard,* October 19, 26, and November 2, 1923.

55. Ibid., October 19, 1923.

56. A clipping from an unidentified magazine shows Roscoe hanging from the wingtip without a parachute. It was captioned with the comment that the stunt was "extremely perilous."

57. Starnes later took part in some scientific tests sponsored by Parachute Science Service, a firm he founded. He risked his life to prove that it was possible to survive free falls from a high altitude. On October 24, 1942, he leaped from a Lockheed Lodestar at 31,400 feet, opening his parachute at 1,500 feet, setting a world record for a delayed opening.

58. *Weekly Corinthian,* April 5, 1923.

59. Ibid, October 4, 1923.

60. Advertisement for Roscoe Turner & Co., dealers, *Weekly Corinthian,* December 20, 1923.

61. *Weekly Corinthian,* May 10, 1923. In 1930 the Suratt farm of 157 acres, located

three miles northeast of the city, was selected as Corinth's first official airport.

62. Ibid., May 17, 1923.

63. Ibid., September 28, 1923.

64. Ibid., May 17, 1923.

65. Ibid., October 11, 1923.

66. *Bolivar (Tenn.) Bulletin,* September 26, 1924.

67. *Weekly Corinthian,* October 2, 1924.

68. *Sheffield Standard,* Sheffield, AL, October 3, 1924.

69. Thomas G. Foxworth, *The Speed Seekers* (New York: Doubleday, 1974), 38.

70. *New York Times,* October 12, 1924.

71. *Weekly Corinthian,* October 23, 1924.

72. Undated manuscript from the Turner files.

73. *Florence (Ala.) Times,* May 11, 1925.

74. *Florence Times,* June 20, 1925.

75. *Lexington (Ky.) Herald,* June 5, 1925.

76. Advertisement for Parrish Taxi & Motor Boat Co., *Florence Times,* June 16, 1925.

77. *Sheffield Standard,* July 3, 1925.

78. Ibid., July 10, 1925.

79. *Tuscumbia (Ala.) Times,* July 10, 1925.

80. Starnes, *Aerial Maniac,* 128.

81. Testimony before Civil Aeronautics Board, Washington, D.C., September 14, 1944.

82. Paul O'Neil, *Barnstormers and Sky Kings* (Alexandria, Va.: Time-Life Books, 1981), 30.

83. *Weekly Corinthian,* March 19, 1925.

84. Ibid., May 28, 1925.

3. FLYING THE S-29-A

1. Reply to a reporter's question, September 6, 1967.

2. Letter to Col. Harold E. Hartney, March 31, 1926.

3. Betsy Braden and Paul Hagan, *A Dream Takes Flight* (Athens: University of Georgia Press, 1989), 223.

4. *Constitution* (Atlanta), March 23, 1926.

5. Undated advertisements in Turner files, American Heritage Center, University of Wyoming.

6. *Hartford (Conn.) Courier,* April 18, 1926.

7. *Springfield Union* and *Springfield Republican,* April 18, 1926.

8. Ibid.

9. Ibid.

10. *Press and Banner and Abbeville (S.C.) Medium,* May 27, 1926.

11. Undated telegram to *Atlanta Journal.*

12. *Atlanta Journal,* May 30, 1926.

13. *Anderson (S.C.) Independent,* June 9, 1926.

14. Frank J. Delear, *Igor Sikorsky: His Three Careers in Aviation* (New York: Dodd, Mead, 1969), 115.

15. Letter from W. J. Lyman, treasurer, Southern Surety & Brokerage Co., Jacksonville, Fla., August 17, 1927.

16. Letter from C. W. Hitt, Muscle Shoals Oil Co., Muscle Shoals, Ala., October 5, 1927. Roscoe received many subsequent requests for payment. In one letter, the company treasurer noted that pictures of his plane had been seen in the Birmingham paper and added, "We are glad to know that business is better and feel confident that we can expect a check immediately." Roscoe finally paid off this debt in December 1930, having made infrequent payments in small increments over a long period of time.

17. From unidentified newspaper clipping in Turner files.

18. Ibid.

19. Letter to Adolph S. Ochs, October 27, 1926. Ochs declined the opportunity.

20. Undated press release, Richmond Air Junction. Later, the City of Richmond appropriated $30,000 and purchased 400 acres that included the Sandston Air Junction. When Roscoe returned for the dedication of a new terminal building, aircraft ramp, and parking lot in March 1930, he was introduced to the crowd as "the founder of the Richmond Air Junction, now a part of Byrd International Airport."

21. *Richmond Times-Dispatch,* February 26, 1927.

22. Ibid.

23. Letter to advertising manager, Life Savers, Inc., Port Chester, N.Y., March 24, 1927.

24. Letter to Wm. Randolph Hearst, May 27, 1927.

25. Letter to J. L. Hoffman, December 3, 1927.

26. Letter to engineering dept., Attn: Mr. Rhode, Champion Spark Plug Co., Toledo, Ohio, October 18, 1927.

27. Letter to R. A. Stranahan, president, Champion Spark Plug Co., May 9, 1928.

28. Undated "Confidential" telegram to R. A. Stranahan.

29. Letter to Bob Shank, October 31, 1927. Roscoe began to make payments for the Jenny by the end of 1927, but only a total of $550 had been paid in small increments. It was to be many months before more payments were made.

4. HELL'S ANGELS AND NEVADA AIRLINES

1. *Daily Screen World* (Los Angeles), March 27, 1928.

2. Memorandum to John Fearon, February 22, 1963.

3. Telegram, November 2, 1928.

4. Letter to Lt. Irwin A. Woodring, Rockwell Field, San Diego, February 2, 1929.

5. Undated telegram to Howard Hughes, Caddo Co., Metropolitan Studios, Hollywood.

6. Memo to Howard Hughes, May 12, 1929.

7. Letter to Howard Hughes, May 15, 1929.

8. Letter from Howard Hughes, May 17, 1929.

9. Letter to Howard Hughes, May 22, 1929. This was not the last exchange be-

tween them. In 1939, after Hughes had set a cross-country speed record in his own racer, Roscoe, no longer bitter, sent him a note suggesting "that maybe we can breed our two planes and produce something very interesting to the entire world. Am now in the manufacturing business and would like to consult with you from time to time." Hughes responded cordially and the two met briefly in February 1939, but nothing developed from the meeting.

10. Barton Rogers, "4 Million Dollars and 4 Men's Lives," *Photoplay*, April 1930, 30.

11. Donald L. Bartlett and James R. Steele, *Empire: The Life and Madness of Howard Hughes* (New York: W. W. Norton, 1979), 68.

12. Elinor Smith, *Aviatrix* (New York: Harcourt Brace Jovanovich, 1981), 176–77.

13. Undated letter to Capt. Walter Perkins, Aeronautics Branch, Department of Commerce, Washington, D.C.

14. Letter to H. C. Hoenniger, Richmond, Va., November 12, 1928.

15. Letter to Major Clarence Young, June 1, 1928.

16. Excerpt from interview with Graham McNamee for *Racing Through the Years* radio program, October 1938.

17. Letter to W. H. Dean, from H. R. McClintock, president of Russell Parachute Co., September 13, 1929. In 1994 a company received much publicity for a demonstration of a similar plane-lowering parachute, which was advertised as an aviation "first." There had been other attempts to sell the idea through the years, but none were purchased by light-plane owners.

18. Nevada Airlines advertising brochure.

19. Colonel Roscoe Turner, "The World's Fastest Airline," *Bee-Hive* (United Aircraft Corp.), December 1929, 84.

20. Ibid. 85.

21. Memo from Shell Oil Co., San Francisco, August 13, 1929.

22. *Bee-Hive*, October 1929, 15.

23. Undated plan for "Proposed Transcontinental Air Line," Turner files.

24. *San Francisco Examiner*, January 3, 1930.

25. Telegram from James Rolph, Jr., governor of California, August 26, 1931.

26. In 1961 the governor of Mississippi appointed Roscoe a colonel on his staff.

27. Telegram from Alan Reed to Bill Dean, Bonnie Brier Hotel, Hollywood, September 29, 1929.

28. Letter to Johnson Airplaine & Suplly Co., Dayton, Ohio, April 16, 1929.

29. Ibid., January 25, 1930.

5. FLYING WITH GILMORE

1. Draft of speech given at a meeting of the National Aeronautic Association, St. Louis, in 1934.

2. From interviews conducted by Madonna M. Turner, La Jolla, Calif., during 1975. All subsequent quotes from Don Young are from these interviews.

3. *American Legion Magazine*, November 1973, 38.

4. Roger Huntington, *Thompson Trophy Races* (Osceola, Wis.: Motorbooks International, 1989), 105.

5. Roy Rutherford, *Colonel Roscoe Turner: Knight-Errant of the Air* (Cleveland: Thompson Products, August 1947), 7.

6. *Dallas Morning News,* September 15, 1930.

7. Carl M. Cleveland, *"Upside Down" Pangborn* (Glendale, Calif.: Aviation Book Co., 1978), 180–81.

8. From interview conducted by Stephania L. Sandy, Corinth, Miss., June 10, 1993.

9. Walter S. Ross, *The Last Hero: Charles A. Lindbergh* (New York: Harper & Row, 1964), 182.

10. Letter from F. Hugh Herbert to Los Angeles chief of police, January 6, 1935. Gilmore Stadium was built in 1934 primarily for midget auto racing. Nearly five million fans attended races there until it was torn down in 1951 and the property sold to Columbia Broadcasting Co.

11. Letter to Arthur G. Baraw, secretary, Board of Police Commissioners, Los Angeles, February 4, 1935.

12. Telegram from C. S. Beesemyer to Roscoe at Carter Hotel, Cleveland, March 12, 1935.

13. Letter to S. A. McNeil, Gilmore Oil Co., June 19, 1935.

14. Letter to Louis Goebel, August 10, 1940.

15. *Los Angeles Examiner,* October 1, 1946.

16. This incident occurred in May 1937. Roscoe received press coverage in national newspapers accompanied by a photo showing a doctor dressing his wound. He flew to Chicago and was taken to a suburban hospital where Dr. Charles B. Alexander said for a time he feared Roscoe might lose an arm from the infection. An Associated Press report quoted Roscoe as saying, "Gilmore loves me. When I started to leave [Los Angeles], Gilmore tried to keep me there. He accidentally tore my arm and shoulder with teeth and claw. He was awfully sorry."

17. It has been reported that Roscoe owned two Gilmores. That is not true. When his contract with Gilmore Oil Co. expired, the company purchased two more lions and named them both Gilmore but Roscoe had nothing to do with them and they gained little publicity for the company. Only one Gilmore ever flew with Roscoe and that is the one in the National Air & Space Museum. During the 1930s, trucks with lions in cages and a number of clowns toured the 3,000 independent Gilmore dealers in the three West Coast states.

18. When he began radio programs aimed at the younger generation and realized that he was a hero to the kids who always flocked to see him when he landed, he refused to lend his name further to cigarette and liquor ads.

19. From undated letter from E. L. Eveleth in Turner files.

6. WINNING THE BENDIX AND THOMPSON TROPHIES

1. From undated manuscript in Turner files.

2. Ibid.

3. Letter to George W. Healy, Jr., executive editor, *New Orleans Times-Picayune* and *States-Item,* November 8, 1968.

4. Paul O'Neil, *Barnstormers & Speed Kings* (Alexandria, Va.: Time-Life Books, 1981), 124.

5. Undated manuscript in Turner files.

6. Letter to Governor Franklin D. Roosevelt, Albany, New York, July 2, 1932. When he didn't receive a reply, Roscoe followed the letter with a telegram. In a post-election letter dated November 21, 1932, Roosevelt responded to the latter, saying, "I shall keep in mind the kind offer of service you made in your telegram, and shall look forward to you and all my fellow citizens for support and counsel during the days that are to come."

7. Undated manuscript in Turner files.

8. Ibid.

9. From Frank Kingston Smith, "Call Me Roscoe," *AOPA Pilot,* April 1983, 100.

10. Undated manuscript in Turner files.

11. Letter to W. A. Jones, New York City, January 16, 1934.

12. *Los Angeles Times,* September 25, 1934.

13. *Time,* October 29, 1934.

14. General James H. "Jimmy" Doolittle, *I Could Never Be So Lucky Again,* with Carroll V. Glines (New York: Bantam Books, 1991), 185.

7. THE TURNER-PANGBORN-NICHOLS TEAM

1. Letter from Joseph E. Lowes, Pratt & Whitney Aircraft Co., November 7, 1933.

2. Letter from A. H. O'Connor, editor, Australian Press Bureau, San Francisco, May 15, 1934.

3. *Boeing News,* September 1934, 2.

4. *Letter to Franklin Bell, July 26, 1934.*

5. Note signed at Pittsburgh, September 13, 1934.

6. Telegram from Howard Heinz, September 17, 1934.

7. Letter to Franklin Bell, September 22, 1934. When Roscoe reached England and was again out of funds, he cabled Bell: "Need five hundred dollars additional. Can you do anything?" It was not forthcoming.

8. Cable, June 15, 1934.

9. Telegram to Australian Press Association, New York, July 11, 1934. Sir Thomas Lipton was a British yachting enthusiast noted worldwide for his sportsmanship.

10. Cable, July 12, 1934.

11. Telegram to Australian Press Association, New York, July 12, 1934.

12. Undated letter to Elias Rockmore of Barron, Rice & Rockmore, from T. V. Ranck, Hearst Newspapers, New York.

13. Undated notes prepared by Gladyce E. Lyons, Roscoe's secretary.

14. Ibid.

15. Letter, September 8, 1934.

16. Undated notes by Gladyce E. Lyons.

17. From notes prepared for a radio broadcast, October 1934.

18. Cable to Universal Press, New York, October 12, 1934.

19. Ibid.

20. Ibid.

21. Cable, "Attention Ranck" to Universal Press, New York from Turner-Pangborn, October 18, 1934.

22. Ibid.

23. From notes for a radio program, November 30, 1934.

8. THE RACE TO MELBOURNE

1. Roscoe Turner, "Lost!" *American Boy,* June 1935, 37.

2. *London Morning Post,* October 24, 1934.

3. Richard Rashke, *Stormy Genius: The Life of Aviation's Bill Lear* (Boston: Houghton Mifflin, 1985), 72.

4. Script prepared for a radio program, December 1934.

5. *Time,* October 29, 1934, 49.

6. *American Legion Magazine,* November 1963, 39.

7. Text for news media distributed at Los Angeles, December 1, 1934.

8. Identical letters to C. L. Egtvedt, Boeing; W. A. Patterson, United Air Lines; and Don Brown, Pratt & Whitney, December 12, 1934.

9. Letter to Erik Nelson, December 12, 1934.

10. Telegram to Dean Maddux, Hearst Radio Station KYA, San Francisco, December 18, 1934.

11. *Guideposts,* December 1969, 26.

12. *Weekly Corinthian,* January 24, 1935.

13. Ibid., February 21, 1935.

14. Ibid., February 28, 1935.

9. ROSCOE'S FLYING CORPS AND THE TURNER SPECIAL

1. Telegram from "Quisenberry," February 11, 1935.

2. Advertisement in *Fortune,* February 1935. Never a heavy smoker, Roscoe gave up cigarettes, except on rare occasions, after an accident in which gasoline fumes filled the cockpit. He had frequent nightmares about fires in flight.

3. Interview, Corinth, Miss., November 7, 1992.

4. *Meridian Star,* July 3, 1935.

5. Stephen Owen, *The Flying Key Brothers and Their Flight to Remember* (Meridian, Miss.: Southeastern Printing, 1985), 23 and 25.

6. Paul O'Neil, *Barnstormers & Speed Kings* (Alexandria, Va.: Time-Life Books, 1981), 164.

7. From undated interview notes by Edward Churchill in Turner files.

8. Ibid.

9. Letter to Madonna M. Turner, August 22, 1972.

10. Paul R. Matt, "Roscoe Turner and the Laird Racer," *Historical Aviation Album,* undated, 299.

11. Although some thought the Wedell racer was not much more than junk by this time, Young put it in top racing condition. Today, it is a valuable part of the collection at the Frederick C. Crawford Museum in Cleveland.

12. There has been some confusion about the name of the new racer. When it emerged from the Laird factory, it carried a "Laird Planes" logo on the vertical fin. This remained on the plane through the 1937 Thompson races. The Bureau of Air Commerce issued a license as model no. LTR-14, serial no. 11, type 1 POLM, CAA no. R-263Y. For the 1937 Thompson race, "Roscoe Turner's Ring Free Meteor" was painted under the cockpit, which caused writers to refer to it as the "Turner Meteor." In 1938 the Laird logo was removed and Roscoe thereafter called it the Turner Special. It was also known as the Pesco Special, when the Pump Engineering Service Corp. of Cleveland became a major sponsor. In 1939 when Champion Spark Plugs sponsored Roscoe, it was named Miss Champion.

13. Script for radio program, Turner files.

14. It was later asserted by the French government that the Caudron had been financed entirely by Renault, the parent company, without any government financing. Later, Roscoe advocated that an international trophy be established without any prize money, similar to the Schneider Cup, if foreign pilots were invited to fly at any future National Air Races.

15. Letter to George A. Graham, vice president, Gillette Safety Razor Co., Boston, Mass., August 5, 1936.

16. *Radio News,* October 13, 1936. The program won an award from the National Aeronautic Association "in recognition of the unique contribution to the advancement of American aviation through the medium of public education by radio." Roscoe was also featured on a Gruen Watch Co. program entitled *Racing Back Through the Years,* hosted by Graham McNamee.

17. *The Encyclopedia of American Comics,* edited by Ron Gulart (New York: Facts on File, 1990), 337_38.

18. Letter to E. F. Waits, Corinth, Miss., January 30, 1934.

19. Letter to A. J. McEachern, secretary, Corinth Chamber of Commerce, August 19, 1936.

20. Ibid., October 3, 1936.

21. *Jackson (Miss.) Clarion Ledger,* October 16, 1936.

22. *Weekly Corinthian,* October 22, 1936.

23. Letter to Lt. Joe Mackey, Findlay, Ohio, July 21, 1937.

24. Letter from Rear Admiral E. J. King, chief, Navy Bureau of Aeronautics, April 10, 1936.

25. Telegram from Steve Hannagan, New York, November 2, 1937.

10. WINNING THE THOMPSON TROPHY—AGAIN

1. Tony LeVier, *Pilot,* as told to John Guenther (New York: Harper and Brothers, 1954), 86.

2. Ibid., 89.

3. *Cleveland Press,* August 19, 1938.

4. From undated manuscript in Turner files.

5. Roger Huntington, *Thompson Trophy Racers* (Osceola, Wis.: Motorbooks International, 1989), 128–29.

6. Letter from Jacqueline Cochran, September 21, 1938.

7. Roelf Loveland, column,*Cleveland Plain Dealer,* September 6, 1938.

8. Col. Roscoe Turner, "Air Racing Was Like This," *Pegasus* (Hagerstown, Md.: Fairchild Engine and Airplane Corp., August 1956), 5–7.

9. Telegram, March 27, 1939.

10. Letter from Emil Kropf, Hamburg, Germany, May 13, 1939.

11. Letter to Ralph P. Olmstead, Kellogg Company, July 21, 1939.

12. Letter to Floyd Grumman, Grumman Aircraft Co., May 16, 1938.

13. Later, when a new field was built and the old one abandoned, the name was not transferred. Roscoe also had an airstrip named after him in the 1940s at the American Legion Memorial Shades Park near Indianapolis, marking the first time that an Indiana state park was made accessible by air.

14 *Showmen's Trade Review,* September 2, 1939.

15. *Cleveland Press,* October 17, 1939.

16. *The New York Times Film Reviews,* 1913–1968 (New York: New York Times and Arno Press, 1971), p. 1933.

17. Recorded interview by the author with A. W. "Tony" LeVier, May 12, 1993.

18. Roscoe was given the original Thompson Trophy for winning three times. He loaned it back to Thompson Products to have another made. Weighing more than fifty pounds, Roscoe always joked that they gave it to him because he was the only pilot who could carry it.

19. *Bee-Hive* (United Aircraft Corp.), October 1939.

11. THE ROSCOE TURNER AERONAUTICAL CORPORATION

1. Ernie Pyle, column, "Hoosier Vagabond," *Indianapolis Star,* July 26, 1940.

2. *Pageant,* December 1949, 141.

3. *New York Times,* July 26, 1940.

4. *State Journal* (Lansing, Mich.), January 31, 1941.

5. Joseph A. Kornfeld, "Turner Analyzes Aviation— Stresses Need for Separate Air Force," *Wichita (Kans.) Beacon,* April 25, 1941.

6. Letter from Brigadier General G. C. Grant, US Army Air Corps headquarters, Washington, D.C. April 16, 1941.

7. *NATA Climb* (newsletter), December 1940, 5.

8. Letter to Walter P. Phipps, Hawthorne Flying Service, Columbia, S.C., March 3, 1944. This was written when the CPT program was being disestablished. Roscoe actively supported the CAP during and after the war and served on the staff of the Indiana Wing as a colonel for a number of years.

9. Undated notice "To All Employees."

10. Notice to "All Students and Employees" dated May 27, 1942.

11. Undated notice to "All Employees and Students."

12. Undated memo to students of the institute.

13. Telegram to Major John P. Morris, Civilian Pilot Training, CAA, Washington, D.C., June 24, 1942.

14. *Indianapolis Sunday Star,* June 21, 1942.

15. Editorial in *Times-Herald* (Port Huron, Mich.), December 12, 1943.

16. Letter from Brigadier General C. L. Chennault, China Air Task Force, March 4, 1943.

17. Letter to Group Captain C. McK. Henry, RAAF headquarters, Melbourne, Australia, April 16, 1943.

18. Letter to Lt. Col. James H. Doolittle, U.S. Army Air Corps headquarters, January 31, 1942.

19. Ibid., March 16, 1942.

20. Telegram dated May 19, 1942.

21. General James H. "Jimmy" Doolittle, *I Could Never Be So Lucky Again,* with Carroll V. Glines (New York: Bantam Books, 1991), 292.

22. Telegram from Paul R. Coppock, city desk, *Commercial Appeal,* July 13, 1944.

23. From a statement issued from Indianapolis to answer press queries, Turner files.

24. *Indianapolis News,* April 9, 1945.

25. Interview with Madonna M. Turner, September 23, 1992.

12. THE CRUSADE FOR AIR POWER

1. Associated Press newswire, September 5, 1944.

2. R. E. G. Davies, *Airlines of the United States Since 1914* (London: Putnam, 1972), 390.

3. *Daily Journal* (Rapid City, S. Dak.), May 1, 1947.

4. Roy Rutherford, *Colonel Roscoe Turner: Knight Errant of the Air* (Cleveland: Thompson Products, August 1947), 29.

5. Speech delivered at the national meeting of the Society of Automotive Engineers, Tulsa, Okla., November 4, 1948. The speech created much public interest and was published in "Vital Speeches of the Day," April 1, 1949.

6. Letter to W. Stuart Symington, September 9, 1946.

7. *Washington Star,* November 16, 1963.

8. Letter from A. W. "Tony" LeVier, March 6, 1963.

9. Letter to A. W. "Tony" LeVier, March 25, 1963.

10. *Flight Magazine,* November 1969.

11. Speech given on November 10, 1969, Birmingham, Ala.

12. *Congressional Record—House,* June 24, 1970, p. H5944.

13. Letter to Madonna M. Turner, June 29, 1970.

14. Ibid., June 24, 1970.

15. Ibid.

16. Ibid.

17. Letter to the author, March 24, 1993.

18. From response to written questions posed by the author to A. W. "Tony" LeVier, May 1993.

19. Rutherford, *Colonel Roscoe Turner,* 7.

INDEX

331